RYAN'S HOPE

RYAN'S HOPE

AN ORAL HISTORY OF DAYTIME'S GROUNDBREAKING SOAP

TOM LISANTI

FOREWORD BY
Ilene Kristen

Citadel Press
Kensington Publishing Corp.
www.kensingtonbooks.com

KENSINGTON BOOKS are published by

Kensington Publishing Corp.
119 West 40th Street
New York, NY 10018

All Kensington titles, imprints and distributed lines are available at special quantity discounts for bulk purchases for sales promotion, premiums, fund-raising, educational or institutional use.

Special book excerpts or customized printings can also be created to fit specific needs. For details, write or phone the office of the Kensington Special Sales Manager: Kensington Publishing Corp., 119 West 40th Street, New York, NY, 10018. Attn. Special Sales Department. Phone: 1-800-221-2647.

CITADEL PRESS and the Citadel logo are Reg. U.S. Pat. & TM Off.

Library of Congress Control Number: 2023941505

ISBN: 978-0-8065-4291-1

First Citadel Hardcover Edition: November 2023

ISBN: 978-0-8065-4292-8 (ebook)

10 9 8 7 6 5 4 3 2 1

Printed in the United States of America

For my grandma, Jenny Casamento,
who loved her stories, especially *Ryan's Hope*

Contents

Foreword

by Ilene Kristen

I stood in front of the original *Ryan's Hope* studio at 433 West Fifty-Third Street the other day. It is now a trendy Hell's Kitchen apartment building. My first thoughts were to wonder who was dwelling in the Ryan's Bar area and in my tiny dressing room that I shared with Kate Mulgrew. As generic and mundane as that studio was on the outside, we created magic on the inside. The Ryan family, and those swirling around them, got under the skin of the audience immediately. It was a place of discipline and a monumental amount of concentration and hard work.

As I continued standing there, I was overwhelmed by the fact that the only constant in life is change. My original Delia shoes, that I wore every day for about six months straight, are now mildewed. The fake beige lizard skin is peeled and frayed. Even if they were wearable, my feet no longer fit in them. Life changes, you change and move on, but how wonderful it is to be able to capture this history in this profound way.

Tom Lisanti is giving us the opportunity to share our *Ryan's Hope* adventures with the world—something I was not quite sure would ever happen. The actors' stories are raw and honest because Tom is so easy to talk to. If some of your favorites are not included, please note it was not for a lack of trying on Tom's part. Spliced in between are the myriad of storylines that one was lucky or, in some cases, cursed to partake in. But to write this book, you have to love and respect the genre—the good, the bad, the ugly, and the ridiculous—and I know Tom does. I trust that this book will be enjoyable and enlightening for the show's multitude of fans. I am deeply honored to be a part of it.

Acknowledgments

My deepest gratitude to all the people who contributed to this book, starting with co-creator Paul Avila Mayer's daughters, Daisy Mayer, Rachael Mayer, and Ruth Mayer, who gave their full backing for the book. There's a special nod to Rachael and Ruth, who spoke to me about their dad and the show. I also wish to thank all those who graciously spoke with me or wrote to me about their time on *Ryan's Hope* and their careers before and after *Ryan's Hope*: Jason "Ash" Adams, Rose Alaio, Jose Aleman, Ana Alicia, Seymour Amlen, MacKenzie Allen, Harold Apter, Richard Backus, John Blazo, Roscoe Born, Fred Burstein, Judith Chapman, Michael Corbett, Christopher Durham, Randall Edwards, Helen Gallagher, Duncan Gamble, Ann Gillespie, Tamara Grady, Malcolm Groome, Ron Hale, Joseph Hardy, Catherine Hicks, Daniel Hugh Kelly, Trent Jones, Tom King, Ilene Kristen, Michael Levin, Kelli Maroney, Malachy McCourt, Brian McGovern, Karen Morris-Gowdy, Ariana Muenker, Martha Nochimson, Geoff Pierson, Gerit Quealy, Laura Rakowitz, Lois Robbins, Andrew Robinson, Art Rutter, Louise Shaffer, Jadrien Steele, Walanne Steele, Millee Taggart, Gordon Thomson, Cali Timmins, and James Wlcek.

A special thank-you goes to the wonderful Ilene Kristen for also writing the foreword and for her enthusiasm for this project. She reached out to a few of her former castmates to nudge them to speak with me, which most did. Also thank you to Claire Labine's daughter, Eleanor Labine, and Connie Passalacqua Hayman for their input.

This book would not be so wonderfully illustrated if not for Harold Apter, Fred Burstein, Christopher Durham, Brian McGovern, Jadrien Steele, James Wlcek, and especially Ilene Kristen and Laura Rakowitz who shared their private photos and allowed their use in this book. Thank you so much.

A big thank-you to my literary agent, Lee Sobel, for believing in me and this book. If it wasn't for his cajoling to finish the manuscript and his determination to sell it, I would not be writing this. His surprising good news that Kensington wanted to publish my book came when I needed it most—the day our cat Teddy passed away after twelve years. I still miss my boy, but his sister and my girl, Maxie, keeps us company.

A number of people contributed to this book in various ways, and I am forever grateful for their help—my friend Lis Pearson, who went beyond the call of duty, for taking the time to give my manuscript rounds of editing and for her encouragement; my friend Shaun Chang for his invaluable detective skills (you can run but you cannot hide from him), his prodding of me to be more aggressive in reaching out to potential interviewees, and his continuous support; my Facebook friend Mike Poirier for his leads in finding the soap's cast members and crew, his wonderful suggestions, and for sharing scans of *Ryan's Hope* items from his collection; my friend and web master, Jim McGann; my friend Pete Kaiser for introducing me to Ilene Kristen over twenty years ago and for his help getting me in contact with Roscoe Born and Malachy McCourt; my friend Michael Carroll for his nudging and encouragement about the marketing and selling of my books and myself—something I very much needed help with; my former New York Public Library colleague Greg Cram for his legal advice; and to fellow author Steve Newell for being a good friend and sounding board throughout this entire process. Also, a big thanks to all the wonderfully nice folks at Kensington Books for their help and guidance.

To all my family for their continued support—my mom, Joan Lisanti; siblings Joe Lisanti, Donna Cates, and Lorraine Nicolo; my nieces and nephews, Emily Lisanti, Vinny Nicolo, Christina, and Joey, and Kelly, McKayla, Samantha, and Sean Cates. Also, thanks to Joe and Barbara Casamento, Barbara Reisinger, Michelle and Anthony D'Argenio, Joe Casamento, Michael and Karen Casamento, Paul and Marta Reisinger, Lori and George Youhas, Rosemarie and Larry Festa, Laura and Jimmy Mullins, Tony and Niloo Pellarin, Michael and Diane Pellarin, Paul and Patty Pellarin, and Diane and Vito Vita.

And a special shoutout to Nelson Aspen, Darryl Black, Stephen Bowie, Thom Chavez, Jeanne and Domenic Cirone, John Covelli, Teresa DeTurris, Andrea Felder, Matt Fletcher, Richard Foster, Carl Germann and Fred Nachbaur, Kathleen Germann, Kiowa Hammons, Bill and Diane Hay, Tom and Michelle Homenuk, Clyde Jones, Tom Kazar and Jimmy Fenner, John Kelly, Judy and Rick Kiefer, Jeanne and Tony Koproski, George Laskaris, Phil Lindow, Jeremy Megraw, Alan Pally, Tom and Peggy Quaranta, Jose Reina, Gloria and Dave Russo, Donald Stalknecht, Mark Tolleson,

Peter Vigliarolo and Steven Imperial, Cory and Kevin Wanzor, Paula and Al Whitney, and Kevin Winkler and Richard Schneider, for their continued support.

Thank you to Alan Locher for his support and to my bowling friends: James Campbell and Scott Bolster, Mark Lilakos and Danny Priev, Pete Mercurio and Danny Stewart; and Eric Ryan and Ron Manabat.

The biggest thank-you to Ernie DeLia, who has put up with everything, including my obsessions with Carol Lynley and *The Poseidon Adventure* to sixties' starlets to soap operas to eighties new wave music, and just rolling with the flow over these past twenty-three years.

I couldn't have written this book without using the vast collections of the General Research Division at the New York Public Library and the Billy Rose Theatre Division at the New York Public Library for the Performing Arts. Also extremely helpful were the websites Ryan's Bar Online and Facebook tribute pages Memories of Ryan's Hope, Remembering Ryan's Hope, Remembering Ryan's Hope the Soap Opera, Ryan's Hope, Ryan's Hope (Soap Opera), Ryan's Hope the Soap Opera Fans Love, and Dennis Sisneros (Ryan's Hope) for all the fun facts, articles, fan observations and opinions, behind-the-scenes photos, and trivia they have shared with fans. They were a valuable source of information.

To the late Jon-Michael Reed, who I never met. He was a truly gifted journalist who loved soaps and began writing a weekly syndicated soap opera update column during the eighties that ran in practically all the major newspapers. This was a tremendous help to me in piecing together storylines and their timelines.

Lastly, a thank-you to my late grandma, Jenny Casamento (who this book is dedicated to), for her *Ryan's Hope* updates before our family had a VCR, and to the ladies of Guardian Bank in Hempstead, Long Island (including my aunt, Maria Caldera Casamento, who recommended me for a job there, and *Ryan's Hope* devotees Evelyn Franks and Carol McArdle, who gave me a *Ryan's Hope* button that I still have to this day). They ate lunch while watching ABC soaps in the breakroom adjacent to the mortgage vault where I began working in the summer of 1980. It was their enthusiasm and dedication to the soaps that made me love and become addicted to *Ryan's Hope* even more. It was a habit I never wanted to break.

Preface

I stumbled across *Ryan's Hope* quite by accident in the spring of 1980. I was living at home on Long Island and was a freshman commuting to Nassau Community College. Three days a week, I had a big gap between morning and late-afternoon classes, so I would drive home, stopping to pick up lunch. One day in May, while eating, I was perusing the channels and saw a beautiful blonde who reminded me of my favorite actress, Carol Lynley.

I stopped to watch as the woman fretted to some dude that she was afraid that the mob was going to take away her fabulous restaurant. I learned that the capo, Tiso Novotny, who was her silent partner, had ordered the successful hit on the show's beloved leading lady a few months prior, and in turn was recently killed. I had no idea what I was watching until the end credits. The blonde was Randall Edwards as Delia Reid Ryan Ryan Coleridge, and the show was *Ryan's Hope*. I had not seen a soap since I was a kid and religiously watched *Dark Shadows* for a time and briefly *One Life to Live* when I had walking pneumonia. I was surprised that this soap had a mob plot. As a fan of *The Godfather* movies, I became curious to see more. I was soon hooked and, in the days before VCRs, I would catch the show on and off when my schedule allowed.

A few weeks later, I began a part-time job at Guardian Bank. I filed mortgages in their vault, which was located in the basement adjoining the staff lunchroom. They set me up at a small desk that faced the television where the mostly female staff would venture down on their lunch hours to watch their ABC soaps, beginning with *Ryan's Hope* through *All My Children* and then *One Life to Live*. I became even more addicted to *Ryan's Hope* and the others too. I loved the warmth Maeve and Johnny Ryan extolled with the scenes at their bar or above in their home. It was nice to see such a happily married couple and one so into their faith, even though I was a totally lapsed Catholic.

My favorite character, though, remained Delia. At first I thought she was the show's heroine. She was treated shabbily by her ex-husband, Frank

1

Ryan, and the Coleridge sisters, Jill and Faith, or as I nicknamed them, "the Witches of Coleridge." Slowly some of Delia's machinations began to be revealed (i.e., while married to Roger Coleridge, she slept with her stockbroker to make up losses in her funds; she let Tiso Nivotny secretly back her restaurant, even though everyone suspected him to be a mob kingpin; etc.). Even so, I still adored her.

I had a new favorite character when *Ryan's Hope*, in early 1981, brought back to life the presumed-dead Joe Novak, the nephew of Tiso now played by Roscoe Born. He oozed sex appeal as the conflicted mobster pretending to go straight to win back his ex-wife, Siobhan Ryan, but still had ties with his crime family.

In early 1982, I was saddened when Randall Edwards left the show, but I instantly perked up when actress Ilene Kristen, who originated the role of Delia, returned. She won me over in her first episode. Later that year, my mom (with my prodding) bought a VCR as a birthday present for my dad. It was quite large with a pop-up top loader for the VHS tape. I was now able to see my story daily, but you had to have the television set to the channel you wanted to tape. I had many a frustrating day returning home from school or work to find *Ryan's Hope* was not recorded because my brother or his business partner had changed the channel.

I remained a major fan of *Ryan's Hope* throughout the decade. However, there were years and storylines that had me shaking my head in disbelief. The soap lost me during 1984 with the Ryan family pushed aside for a slew of new characters. This was the only time I ever wrote a letter to the producers of a TV show. I complained about the new format with the invasion of a bunch of teenage twits and the recasting of Delia. I remarked if they could not bring back Ilene Kristen, I would rather not see Delia at all. Shockingly, I received a reply thanking me for being a loyal fan and to please stick with the show. They also wrote that Ilene was unavailable to return. Years later, I would learn that was not true.

The following year was much better, with a new writing team that began to focus the show back onto the Ryan family and sent most of the new characters packing. My favorite storyline was the quadrangle with four of the show's most down-and-dirty characters—Johnny Ryan's bastard son Dakota Smith, troublemaking Delia, manipulative Roger Coleridge, and selfish gold digger Maggie Shelby. It was delicious fun watching these schemers try to outmaneuver each other to get what they wanted.

Like most fans, I was devastated when it was announced in October

1988 that ABC was cancelling the show. I was working as an assistant media buyer for network daytime television at Lever Media, which was headquartered in the iconic Lever House building on Park Avenue. I attended the Daytime Emmy Awards twice (I was the only one at our table who stood up and cheered when Helen Gallagher won for Outstanding Lead Actress in a Drama Series in 1988) and had a friendly working relationship with my contact at ABC. She knew I loved *Ryan's Hope* and called to personally let me know that the network cancelled the show. I was so saddened that to help cheer me up, she sent me a promotional photo of Ilene Kristen, since she knew Delia was my favorite character.

Based on the weak ratings, it was not a surprise that it was cancelled, but there was hope that the network would do something to save it since it was arguably still a much superior show to *Loving*, which stole the *Ryan's Hope* 12:30 p.m. time slot back in 1984.

The last episode aired on January 13, 1989. I watched with tears in my eyes. During the last moments when Maeve sat on the bar to sing "Danny Boy" one last time and then said to all, "Have a good life," I wept like a baby. I thought I would never see *Ryan's Hope* ever again.

Then, beginning in 1996, several cast members (including Kate Mulgrew, Ilene Kristen, and Catherine Hicks) began popping up on *Ryan's Hope* mega-fan Rosie O'Donnell's new daytime talk show, *The Rosie O'Donnell Show*; keeping the memory of the serial alive. Shortly after in 2000, the cable channel SOAPnet launched. It was owned by Disney–ABC Television Group, a division of The Walt Disney Company. The new network sold itself on same-day nighttime repeat airings of the daytime ABC soaps. As an added attraction, the channel also began broadcasting reruns of prime-time serials such as *Falcon Crest* and *Sisters* plus *Ryan's Hope*. SOAPnet began airing daily back-to-back episodes from Monday through Friday and then would rerun all ten in a row, as a marathon, over the weekend. The broadcast began with the show's premiere episode of July 7, 1975. As the channel began increasing in popularity and was being picked up on more cable systems, its audience reach increased tremendously.

When I heard about SOAPnet, I so wanted to get this channel, but my cable service did not offer it right away. It took about a year before it became available in New York City, and I immediately had my DVR set to record *Ryan's Hope*.

Ryan's Hope attracted both former fans like me, who were elated that their long-dead story was revived, and new fans to this original, groundbreaking serial. I was so enthralled when watching the show that when the Twin Towers were attacked on 9/11 during the 9:00 a.m. hour, I was oblivious to what was happening only two miles from my Chelsea apartment. I only learned of the tragedy that was unfolding around me when my mother phoned to see if I was okay.

Ryan's Hope: An Oral History of Daytime's Groundbreaking Soap, is not intended to be a definitive look at the serial. Although the book includes an overview of the soap's history, some brief storyline synopses, and what went on behind the scenes with ABC, its main focus is the recollections of the interviewees. They shared their experiences and backstage anecdotes as well as their opinions about their storylines, cast members, producers, and directors, including how they were hired, why they left the show, and why they think *Ryan's Hope* is so beloved and missed to this day.

Thanks to SOAPnet and YouTube, I have seen a major portion of the series that I missed when it was originally broadcast. With that said, to be clearly transparent, my favorite years of the show were from 1979 to 1983 mostly due to the mob and Crystal Palace storylines. That is not to say that I do not love the early and later years—I do. Just be forewarned—my opinions and observations about certain storylines and characters do rear their head. And I apologize if some of your favorites are given short shrift. Due to page limits, I kept the focus on the interviewees and their story arcs. I reached out to a sizable number of folks associated with *Ryan's Hope* over the course of six years, but some either politely declined to be interviewed or just never replied to my queries. Perhaps I had incorrect contact information? I could not get past their managers or publicists for some and I could not find others at all.

My goal is to make this book interesting not only for *Ryan's Hope* fans but also to lovers of soaps in general in regard to how creative differences, network interference, and outside machinations can affect the quality and life of a program, as it did with *Ryan's Hope*.

The Interviewees
(In order of appearance)

Rachael Mayer (daughter of co-creator Paul Avila Mayer)

Ruth Mayer (daughter of co-creator Paul Avila Mayer)

Helen Gallagher (Maeve Ryan, 1975–89)

Malcolm Groome (Dr. Patrick Ryan, 1975–78; 1983–88, 1989)

Ron Hale (Dr. Roger Coleridge, 1975–89)

Ilene Kristen (Delia Reid Ryan Ryan Coleridge, 1975–79; 1982–83; 1986–89)

Michael Levin (Jack Fenelli, 1975–89)

Jadrien Steele (Little John/Johnno Ryan, 1975–85)

Walanne Steele (mother of Jadrien Steele)

Malachy McCourt (Kevin MacGuinness, 1975–83; 1988–89)

Catherine Hicks (Dr. Faith Coleridge #3, 1976–78)

Andrew Robinson (Frank Ryan #2, 1976–78)

Seymour Amlen (ABC head of East Coast programming/vice president, 1977–89)

Ana Alicia (Alicia Nieves, 1977–78)

Jose Aleman (Angel Nieves, 1977–78)

Louise Shaffer (Rae Woodard, 1977–83; staff writer, 1987–89)

Karen Morris-Gowdy (Dr. Faith Coleridge #4, 1978–83; 1989)

John Blazo (Dr. Patrick Ryan #2, 1978–79)

Gary Donatelli (camera assistant, 1978–83; technical director, 1987–88)

Randall Edwards (Delia Reid Ryan Ryan Coleridge, #3, 1979–82)

Tamara Grady (production secretary/stage manager, 1979–89)

Laura Rakowitz (production assistant/assistant director, 1979–89)

Art Rutter (studio supervisor/coordinator, 1979–81)

Kelli Maroney (Kim Harris, 1979–81; 1982–83)

Michael Corbett (Michael Pavel, 1979–81)

Richard Backus (Barry Ryan, 1980–81)

Trent Jones (Ken George Jones, 1980; staff writer, 1982–83)

Rose Alaio (Rose Pearse Melina, 1980–81)

Ann Gillespie (Siobhan Ryan #2, 1980–81)

Roscoe Born (Joe Novak #2, 1981–83; 1988)

Harold Apter (production assistant/staff writer, 1981–82)

MacKenzie Allen (Sgt. Jim Speed, 1981–82)

Gordon Thomson (Aristotle Benedict-White, 1981–82)

Geoff Pierson (Frank Ryan #4, 1983–85)

Ariana Muenker (Amanda Kirkland #2, 1983)

Joseph Hardy (executive producer, 1983–88)

Judith Chapman (Charlotte Greer, 1983)

Cali Timmins (Maggie Shelby, 1983–88; 1989)

Gerit Quealy (Jacqueline Dubujak, 1983–85; 1987)

Fred Burstein (Laslo Novotny, 1983–85; 1987)

Martha Nochimson (staff writer, 1984–85)

Millee Taggart (co-head writer, 1985–87)

Tom King (co-head writer, 1985–87)

Duncan Gamble (Tiger Bennett, 1985)

Christopher Durham (Dakota Smith, 1985–88)

Jason "Ash" Adams (John Reid Ryan/John Ryan #2, 1986–89)

Lois Robbins (Dr. Concetta D'Angelo, 1987–88; 1989)

James Wlcek (Ben Shelby, 1987–89)

Brian McGovern (Chaz Saybrook, 1987–89)

1

Meet the Ryans, 1975–77

Ryan's Hope was the brainchild of writers Claire Labine and Paul Avila Mayer. Raised in an Irish Catholic family, Claire had attended the University of Kentucky and switched from acting to journalism. With husband R. A. (Clem) Labine, editor of *The Old House Journal*, and her three children (Eleanor, Matthew, and John), she resided in a thirteen-room brownstone that was once an Irish boardinghouse in the Park Slope section of Brooklyn. She met Paul, a Harvard graduate, when he joined her in writing dialogue for the CBS soap opera *Where the Heart Is*. He had come from a show business family (his father, of Jewish descent, was a Hollywood screenwriter, and his mother was Spanish and Irish) and wrote screenplays while adapting foreign classic literature into English. Like Claire, he had three children (Rachael, Ruth, and Daisy) with his wife, actress Sasha von Scherler, but he resided in Manhattan.

> **Rachael Mayer:** My memories of my dad are a very gregarious, optimistic, hardworking, anxious guy who was devoted to his family but also a workaholic.

> **Ruth Mayer:** When we wrote the eulogy for him, the opening line was "Dad must have been born on the sunny side of the street." Rachael wrote that. He was an incredible optimist, and I really feel like that he was brave and he knew it. He took a lot of pride in it. He had gone to Harvard and always said that he went to school with a lot of people who were a lot smarter than he was. And I will just echo what Rachael said, that he was very, very hardworking— always working but up for the party of life [and] a good time.

Rachael Mayer: Our two families spent a lot of time together. We used to joke that they were the tall family and we were the short family.

Where the Heart Is focused on the dysfunctional, sexually obsessed Hathaway family whose patriarch, Julian, was married to his son Michael's former girlfriend. Julian's coldhearted sister Allison had just returned to town with her husband Ray, whom she stole from her sibling, the sexually repressed Kate. Unfamiliar with the world of soap writing, Mayer admitted to writer Cassandra White in *Soap Opera People* magazine that he reached out to Claire, who had been working there for six months, and he asked her, "'How do we do this?' She liked that, and we became friends."

The delight Labine and Mayer had in working together came across in their scripts. After several months, the duo was promoted to co-head writers. Describing how they were revamping the show, Labine told journalist Joseph Thesken of the Copley News Service, "We're trying to move away from soapy subjects, like 14-month pregnancies and strange and exotic diseases. Another thing, we have a policy of playing one day at a time, so the action doesn't run over days at a time. There was a wedding on the show that went on for days and days." Despite the tightening of the serial and the changes made for the better, Claire quipped, "And we wrote the show right off the air." Although the soap became popular with younger viewers (something not so desirable by soap advertisers in the early seventies), it languished in the bottom of the ratings pack (sixteenth place out of seventeen soaps). With CBS losing ground to NBC's popular block of TV game shows, it was cancelled, along with *Love Is a Many Splendored Thing*, in early 1973, but not before Labine and Mayer received their first of many nominations from the Writers Guild of America for Best Television Writing in Daytime Serials.

After *Where the Heart Is* ended, the pair began to collaborate on an original show. Soon after, ABC approached the duo about creating a brand-new soap to be called *City Hospital*. Claire and Paul declined but countered with their soap about an Irish family living across the street from a hospital. Per Claire Labine in Louisville's *Courier-Journal*, "They gave us what they call a development fee to sit down and work with an idea and to come up with a thing called the canvas, the basic characters, and the situations in which they find themselves when the story begins. Plus, you write a projected long story six months to a year. So, you have the beginning of a show right there. In serials, you don't do pilots."

Rachael Mayer: They just clicked intellectually as writers. They were both very well-read, and I would argue that neither one of them watched much television, so *Ryan's Hope* in their minds was going to be Bergman and *Masterpiece Theatre*. They were bringing the theatre to soap opera. They started conceiving *Ryan's Hope* as a fantasy as if they had their own show.

In August 1973, the pair agreed to ABC's offer. However, the next day CBS came with a proposal to head write their struggling long-running soap *Love of Life*. The show barely escaped the axe that year, and the network was hopeful they could rejuvenate it, as they did with *Where the Heart Is*. The writers took the job but included an out in the contract in case their new serial was picked up by ABC.

Reaching into the show's rich history, Labine and Mayer brought back to the canvas heroine Vanessa Dale's conniving sister Meg (now played by Tudi Wiggins) and her now-grown, lothario of a son Ben (played by future *Superman* Christopher Reeve in his first TV or movie role). It was just what the serial needed, and it jumped from the ratings cellar (fifteenth out of sixteen soaps, with an average 6.0 rating) to the middle of the pack (ninth place out of fifteen soaps, with a 7.3 rating). Their peers took notice and the duo received Writers Guild of America nominations for Best Television Writing in Daytime Serials in 1974 and 1975.

Rachael Mayer: Christopher Reeve was young and just out of college. They loved Chris. I think Claire and my dad really honed their skills on *Love of Life* and *Where the Heart Is*.

Labine and Mayer left *Love of Life* in March 1975 after, to their astonishment, ABC picked up their new soap based on a submitted bible detailing the lives of thirteen major characters from birth to the present. Michael Brockman, then thirty-four years old, was ABC's vice president for daytime programming. He told writer Tom Sullivan, "We worked on it a year before the first show was taped. We retained the traditional elements, the interwoven family affairs." He added, "In my years in daytime programming, I have been in on the incubation of some of our shows, but on a day-to-day basis, no. You hire pros and you let them work, though there does come a point sometimes where we do make a decision." Brockman transferred shortly after to a new position at ABC on the West Coast, and his replacement took a totally different approach.

Commenting on the characters in their bible, Paul Mayer remarked in *The Philadelphia Inquirer*, "We figured out who their parents were and who their grandparents were and how they'd been raised and where they'd gone to school." Labine added, "We'd get a sense of who the characters were and then set reasons in terms of their family and their background for them being the way they were. We ended up with very fully blown characters by the time we hit the air. We try very hard not to violate those original concepts."

> **Rachael Mayer:** The bible went back to the 1800s and had back-stories for all the characters. They had Johnny Ryan's grandfather and the famine. It was incredible, so by the time they were writing *Ryan's Hope*, they knew those characters like their own ancestors. I thought it was amazing. I wish that we still had it.
>
> I think a slot unexpectedly opened up, and the show got shoehorned in as a replacement. I remember my dad was just elated because he didn't have any expectations for the show getting picked up. He thought it was a miracle that it did because it was so different from everything that was on the air. They had the show developed . . . to counter the suburban WASPy soap operas that existed. They wanted it to be set in New York.

The network wanted to name the new show *A Rage to Love*. The absurd title *In Sunshine and In Shadow* was also suggested, but the writers' catchier choice of *Ryan's Hope* was used despite the network's trepidation that the Irish Catholic theme would scare off potential viewers. Claire Labine revealed in Louisville's *Courier-Journal*, "We had the idea of the Ryans; the Ryan family just sort of happened. It seemed that they had always been there. We knew about Johnny, and we knew about Maeve. And we knew about their daughter, Mary, who really is the heroine."

"*Ryan's Hope* started out with three long stories," continued Labine. "In the physical writing of them, Paul committed two of them, and I did one. Mine was longer than the other two. We don't write together. We edit what the other one does."

From there, breakdowns were done for a week at a time. Then, each day's episode was written in sequence, and a two-page outline produced. Paul and Claire wrote two, and a scriptwriter named Nancy Ford, replaced by Mary Ryan Munisteri, was hired to write two as well. There was no writers' room because all three worked from home, though Claire's Park Slope townhouse became a de facto office.

Paul Mayer told the Gannett News Service, "We use the same technique as the old Saturday morning serials. We like to open with a dramatic point and close at a dramatic point with a cliffhanger." He also revealed that they tried to focus on the major storylines on the Monday, Wednesday, and Friday episodes and the lesser stories on the other two days.

Rachael Mayer: We lived in an eight-hundred-square-foot apartment in New York City—three kids, two dogs, two cats, a lot of bicycles. When we were little, my dad was able to manage being in his 9-by-10-foot office, but as we got older, it was just chaos. I think at that point, Claire and Clem had finally renovated the brownstone. It was a gut renovation, and there was a space where Claire and Paul could work. I think it was in the basement. For my dad it became like a nine-to-five job. He would drive to Brooklyn in the morning and then drive back. He was always home for dinner.

Ruth Mayer: He wrote every single night. He went back to work right after we ate.

Rachael Mayer: We fell asleep to the sound of his typewriter pretty much every night of our lives until he got a computer.

There was a third writer that worked with them named Mary Munisteri. Claire and my dad would write the story and the plot together. They would each have to write a couple of scripts per week to keep up with the pace and it was divided between the three of them. They really worked all day and all night. Eventually, other script writers were hired.

Ruth Mayer: None of them had individual story threads. However, Claire wrote the heartfelt scenes—the mother-daughter moments that would make you cry.

Not only were Claire and Paul the head writers of their new soap, but they were also the executive producers and formed their own company, Labine-Mayer Productions, Inc. This was quite rare for the time and gave them almost complete creative control.

Rachael Mayer: They had a great lawyer and were very brilliant in those contract negotiations. My dad's father was in film and theatre, and because he pretty much died penniless, without any residuals, my dad was not going to make that mistake. They were smart. In fact, they were the first to tape the show and then keep the masters in a warehouse in New Jersey. ABC would not pay for it. They paid a fortune to store them. The other soaps just erased the tapes and kept going. They were proud of saving the tapes despite the crazy expense. They were protective of that work and knew it might have another life in some way, but they couldn't have envisioned SOAPnet.

Paul Mayer contributed a chapter about making *Ryan's Hope* for *TV Book: The Ultimate Television Book* that was published in 1977. He shared his (and Claire's) experience as the show was coming together. He wrote, "Since we were fortunate enough to be invited to produce as well as write the show, we had the opportunity to oversee casting, scenic and costume design, makeup, hairstyles, and all the other elements of physical production. We wanted to create a world that was entirely new to the audience, so we looked for performers who had not had heavy daytime exposure ... Then our designer set out to create rooms that would truly reflect the lives of the people they contained ... When we first saw *Ryan's* kitchen, with its huge old-fashioned iron stove, great ancient refrigerator, and terrible/wonderful rose-patterned linoleum, we felt we had the kind of reality in which our stories could grow."

The writers had about six weeks of outlines and four weeks of scripts in the can before taping began. Since Paul and Claire were also the executive producers, they were heavily involved with choosing the actors to make their characters come alive on the small screen. Shirley Rich was hired as the casting director. She had worked for almost twenty years in musical theatre, mostly casting for producer/director Hal Prince's shows, and broke into films with *Serpico* in 1973. *Ryan's Hope* would be the first TV show that she would work on. Rich pushed actors who had a theatrical background, prior soap opera experience, or a combination of both for major roles.

Writing in her book *Born with Teeth: A Memoir*, Kate Mulgrew shared Claire Labine's description of the show when she met her at Shirley Rich's office. "Da and Ma had come over from the old country and begun their life afresh, producing four children, all of whom contributed to the drama, dreams, and high jinks of life in an Irish bar, but none more so than Mary Ryan herself, who, Claire assured me, would bear all the trademarks of a heroine. She would be smart, brave, funny, strong, and fiercely loyal. The serial would be unlike anything ever before done on daytime television."

Helen Gallagher (Maeve Ryan): What made me do a soap opera was that I had played a lot of parts, and I was out of work. It sounded like an interesting role. I always wanted to play a mother with a lot of children, so that is why I did.

I read a couple of times, as a matter of fact. I just loved the character—the fact that she had children and was Catholic. It just fit me.

Ilene Kristen (Delia Reid Ryan Ryan Coleridge): My agent told me *Ryan's Hope* would only last six months. I don't know what made him say that, and then he said I could go back to making people laugh. When I read the description for Delia, this ragamuffin, I knew that I could do it, and I knew it was calling out to me. The role had a lot of texture to it. Also, I was always looking for something different.

Shirley Rich was casting the show. She was brilliant and was the Rosalind Russell of casting directors. She was a no-nonsense, no-bullshit person. If I had said to her that I had no interest in doing it, she would have been very pissed with me because she was a big champion of mine. I had just read for the Burt Reynolds movie *W. W. and the Dixie Dance Kings*. It was directed by John Avildsen. She had me go in for that, and I gave a great audition, but they decided to go with a Southerner (Conny Van Dyke). You didn't refuse Shirley. When Shirley called, you didn't say "No, Ilene is not interested." If I was working, that is one thing, but not if I wasn't.

I had just left *Grease*, and I was doing a show where I played a Janis Joplin–type character. I was wearing bell-bottoms and a peasant blouse with a wild mane of hair when I went to meet with Shirley. She said, "Darling, you really are right for this part, and I am going to have you come back, but you must not wear that! This character is not a hippie. She is a very fragile girl. And you can do this part." Sure enough, I came back wearing a white lacey blouse and black velvet pants. Shirley was one of those casting people that would talk about you, so when you walked into the room, you weren't walking into a refrigerator. I entered and remembered the looks on the faces of Claire Labine and Paul Mayer. I knew then that I had the look that was right and a certain sophistication as a human being. I think they knew I had been an actress since age fourteen and that I knew the difference between reality and how you had to act. My audition went great. I read with Shirley, who would lead you in all the right directions. She took responsibility for stuff, where most casting directors just throw you into the lion's den.

I got a callback and wore the same outfit, even though you didn't wear white on camera back then because it can flare. But it was good I did that. I had rehearsed with a guy that I was working with, and he was a bit arrogant and cocky. Though I had done a Broadway show for two years, this was a new milieu for me, so we rehearsed a lot. I went in really prepared. My button flew off in the middle of the audition, and I just kept on going. I heard them say, "That's Delia." I got it and thought, "Oh God, now what?"

Malcolm Groome (Dr. Patrick Ryan): I was mainly a theatre actor. Shirley Rich must have known my stage work and brought me in for the role of Bucky. When I read for him, they decided I would be good for Pat. I think at that same audition they gave me Pat's lines, and it clicked. There you go.

I did not read with any of the other actors. They did not do that at the time. They just put it all on tape and made their decisions. Later, when I was already playing the role of Pat, I read with several people. For instance, when Julia Barr was auditioning for Reenie Szabo, I read opposite her, even though I was not going to have a storyline with her.

Ron Hale (Dr. Roger Coleridge): While I was working on the film *All the President's Men*, my agent gets a call from one of the sweetest ladies and greatest casting directors of all time, Shirley Rich. There was a new soap opera being cast for ABC, and she thought there was a role I might be right for. We found a day off from the film. I took my little beat-up car and drove to New York for the audition in front of Claire Labine, Paul Mayer, George Lefferts, and some others I cannot remember. I did a reading, and Claire, being Claire, had no self-control, stood up, and said, "Wow, that was terrific." I went back to DC, and a couple of weeks later, my agent called for me to come back for another audition for the same show. I did, and they gave me a two-page scene, and I had about an hour to look it over. It was with the character of Jillian. I went in and read with this young lady. It went okay and I was about to leave, but they wanted me to read with some other people. I read with about three other gals, and one of them happened to be Nancy Addison. Then that was it. They said thank you, and Claire came over and gave me a hug, and Paul shook my hand.

I had done bit parts on some other soaps prior to this because my agent insisted that I get some work just to know what it was about. Also, it was a paycheck, and I was still tending bar on the side. I think right after I wrapped on *All the President's Men*, I got a call from my agent to meet with him. I was living on Staten Island, so I came into Manhattan, and he told me that the new show *Ryan's Hope* wants me. The deal was a three-year contract. I was so naïve that I did not know it is only a thirteen-week contract and they could drop your ass anytime. I might be incorrect, but if memory serves, I think I was offered somewhere between $175 and $225 an episode with a guarantee of one a week. They didn't know if this show was going to fly. They had no damn clue. I didn't have anything else paying the bills, so I signed on. I always tell people what started off as a thirteen-week contract turned into thirteen years.

Michael Levin (Jack Fenelli): They were in a desperate need for someone to play Fenelli. It was very close to the start of production, and they still didn't have an actor to play him. I was recommended by a friend who was hired to be on the show. I read for it the day before filming began, and that was it. Claire and Paul were there, but I really did not have an opinion of them because it went so fast and quick.

Walanne Steele (mother of Jadrien Steele): Jadrien was five months old, and we had been at the beach for the day. When we came back, Claire Labine, a neighbor of ours that we did not know very well, called. She had seen Jadrien when he came home from the hospital, and he was a big baby. She needed a big baby in Central Park later that afternoon and thought of Jadrien. We agreed and went to the park where they were taking the show's opening title photos. They took some of Helen Gallagher and Bernie Barrow holding the baby in the air. That was the beginning, and Claire said they may need Jadrien for a few episodes after this. It went on for nine years. Jadrien never had a contract. He was always a day player, and they would call us when he was needed.

Ilene Kristen: The show was impeccably cast. I had not been a watcher of soap operas, but I was a huge fan of Bernie Barrow on *Secret Storm* and now he was playing my father-in-law. I was sure they were going to go with an actor named Roy Poole, who was very Irish-looking. I had just done a television show with Roy where we played Quakers.

Helen Gallagher: I never read with Bernie. They just put us together. I do not know why we clicked. To be honest, at first, I really did not like him much. Then he grew on me. Sometimes you take to people, and sometimes you don't. I didn't take to him right away.

When the soap began, George Lefferts was signed as producer. As executive producers, Labine and Mayer had control over a lot of things that other head writers only wished they had. Francis Clines, writing in the *New York Times*, expounded on this and wrote that besides casting, the pair, "control the lighting, bringing in an artist who can create the urban shadows and dinginess they visualize. They even control the color schemes, taking Ingmar Bergman–type liberties in limiting the number of tones and having certain actors and roles linked in color harmonies." Despite being in charge, the duo also revealed in the *New York Times* that they only went to the studio once a week "just to keep in touch with everybody," preferring to concentrate on writing the stories from Labine's home in Park Slope.

The show was filmed at the ABC Television Center on Studio 15 and could have close to one hundred people working per day. Per writer S. Ezra Goldstein, who wrote in *Dramatics*, "*Ryan's Hope* has its own studios, offices, dressing rooms, hair and makeup salons, and costume shop. There are carpentry and painting crews, costume designers and seamstresses, two full-time hairdressers, a makeup artist, office staff, and state-of-the-art technical equipment in fully equipped control rooms."

On July 6, 1975, ABC gave *Ryan's Hope* a prime-time promotional boost with a ten-minute preview hosted by actress Mary Fickett (Ruth Martin on *All My Children*). It followed *Lady Liberty* starring Sophia Loren, which aired on *The ABC Sunday Night Movie*. *Ryan's Hope* then debuted on July 7. It was given *All My Children*'s 1:00 p.m. time slot, with that soap moving to 12:30 p.m. as its lead-in. Claire Labine remarked to

writer Tom Dorsey that it "was a wonderful, nurturing place" for the soap
to gain an audience and thrive. Rare for a daytime serial, it was set in a
real city and had its core family's religious faith play a major part in the
drama. Claire Labine felt this is what, at first, brought the show much
attention. She remarked in the *Los Angeles Times* in 1980, "I drew upon
my own roots—the Catholic experience in America. At the beginning,
we did things that seemed new. At first, it startled audiences to see Maeve
with her rosary, going to confession. We are not making religious points,
but we do keep up with the Vatican actions."

Devout Catholic Maeve Colleary Ryan (Helen Gallagher) and her hard
working husband Johnny Ryan (Bernie Barrow), a former boxer, owned
a bar across the street from Riverside Hospital in northern Manhattan
(most likely around 168th Street, where New York-Presbyterian Hospi-
tal/Columbia University Irving Medical Center is located). Three of their
five adult children were seen when the show premiered—arrogant attorney
and would-be politician Frank Ryan (Michael Hawkins), who was having
an affair with fiercely independent lawyer Jillian Coleridge (Nancy Addison), despite his marriage to the immature, grasping Delia Reid (Ilene
Kristen), the mother of his infant son John (Jadrien Steele); the nice but
commitment-shy Dr. Patrick Ryan (Malcolm Groome), an intern at Riverside Hospital; and feisty Mary Ryan (Kate Mulgrew), a new graduate from
journalism school who falls for the hotheaded newspaper reporter Jack
Fenelli (Michael Levin). Other major characters at the time included:

- Delia's affable brother and Frank's best friend, Bob Reid (Earl
  Hindman), a police officer
- Dr. Ed Coleridge (Frank Latimore), acting chief of neurology at
  Riverside Hospital and father of adoptive Jill and his biological
  children
- Dr. Faith Coleridge (Faith Catlin), an intern with daddy issues
- The roguish Dr. Roger Coleridge (Ron Hale), a resident surgeon
  who butted heads with his father constantly
- Dr. Seneca Beulac (John Gabriel), a rival of Ed Coleridge at the
  hospital and his estranged, abrasive wife, Dr. Nell Beulac (Diana
  van der Vlis), who rubs most of the hospital staff and her patients
  the wrong way

- Nell's charming nephew and intern, Dr. Bucky Carter (Justin Deas), heir to a shoe fortune and Pat Ryan's best friend
- Neurosurgeon and Ed Coleridge's protégé, Dr. Clem Moultrie (Hannibal Penney, Jr.), who was in charge of Riverside Hospital's interns
- Stern head nurse Ramona Gonzalez (Rosalind Guerra)
- Nick Szabo (Michael Fairman), a shady local landlord and loan shark who Roger Coleridge was indebted to due to his gambling addiction

Other important, early recurring characters included the Ryan family's parish pastor, Father McShane (John Perkins); Sister Mary Joel (Sylvia Sidney, followed by Nancy Coleman, then Natalie Priest), who taught at the Catholic orphanage where Jack Fenelli resided as a child; Seneca's mother, Marguerite Beulac (Gale Sondergaard, followed by Anne Revere); Jack's older friend Jumbo Marino (Fat Thomas), whom he knew from his days working on the docks; eldest daughter Kathleen Ryan (Nancy Reardon), who was married to chemical engineer Art Thompson (Gregory Abels) and lived in Philadelphia with their two daughters, Maura and Deidra; and bartender JP (John Scanlon). Scanlon left about two months into the run, and his replacement was Malachy McCourt as Kevin MacGuinness, an old friend of Johnny's from Ireland.

> **Malachy McCourt (Kevin MacGuinness):** I was acquainted with John Scanlon, who was also doing public relations work. He was a friend of either Claire Labine or Paul Mayer or both—I can't recall. We bore a certain resemblance to each other because we were both bearded at the time. John got very busy with his PR business and asked if I could take his place. He introduced me to Claire and Paul. They said fine, and that is how I was cast as Kevin.
>
> At the beginning, I did not even have enough lines to qualify for full salary. I was an under-five player. It took quite a while before they began to write me into the story more.

When asked if any of these characters were based on real people, Claire Labine responded to Joanna Coons of *Rona Barrett's Daytimers*, saying, "Partly. Maeve is part my mother, part my grandmother ... Mary was named after my best friend in the whole wide world, Mary Ryan Munisteri, who is one of our dialogue writers . . . Delia is based on one of the most stunning neurotics I've ever known in my life, who must remain nameless."

When *Ryan's Hope* began taping, it was baptism by fire for some of the cast new to the medium. During these early years, most soaps were shot like a live TV show or a play. It is no wonder that many actors who had stage experience and who could handle the pressure were hired.

Ron Hale: A lot of the actors on the show were very serious about the craft, as I am. The work situation, especially the pressure we were under when we first started that half-hour show, was intense since we had only forty-five minutes of tape per day. We shot literally as a live show. For a thirty-minute show, we had maybe twenty-two or twenty-three minutes to fill the slot. When we were called to shoot, everybody had to be in place on their set. Dickie Briggs was such a great stage manager. When he would say, "Cut!" the crew had to break down the booms and cameras and set up for the next scene in a minute or two during the commercial break. The next thing you know, Dickie is back to counting down from five to start the next scene. If you were in scene one and you were in scene three, you had to tiptoe around the first set—and maybe make a costume change—to be ready for the third scene while they rolled the cameras down and set up on your set. You had to be in place before the countdown.

Ilene Kristen: We would do blocking all morning long. Then we would do a run-through after lunch with full notes. Then came a full-dress rehearsal with notes. A wall had to come down, basically. If there was a disaster, we would do a retake. I had real difficult stuff. One time I had a confessional scene where I had twelve pages of dialogue. At some point I just lost my train of thought, and we had to stop. We had the monitors (they were on paper and made a sound), but I was in the confessional and couldn't see. We all used the monitors for phone conversations because you had to be looking at the camera anyway.

Ron Hale: If you were an actor who stopped a scene because you went up on your lines—*oh my God*. Over the PA system you would hear the irate producer. They would not allow that. Actors do not stop for anything. It was up to the control room. You only had forty-five minutes of tape time, so if you screwed up and wasted five minutes doing something and then resetting, it hurt. In the last scene of the day, what would happen all the time is that Dickie would come over and say, "You got to pick up thirty seconds." It happened practically every day that we worked—sometimes it was more. You could have a two-minute scene, and you were told you had to pick up a minute. You are then looking at your fellow actors and asking, "How are we going to do this and cut a minute?" We would have to work it out as the countdown to shoot began. You'd be amazed about the percentage of the time we successfully made it work. This is absolutely why practically every actor cast early on had stage experience. That is one of the things that just made me so proud when we started and we got to know each other and our backgrounds. Ilene had never done a soap. Nancy Addison had. I did a few minor parts on soaps. But there were like three or four people who had never been in front of a camera. But again—theatre, theatre, theatre background. It is where you learned discipline. It is a thing that does not exist today in the world—except in theatre, of course.

Walanne Steele: When he was a baby, Jadrien was not there all day. They would figure out when they would actually need him. I know the rules for children working in New York were not the same as they were in California at that time. Maybe they have changed since then.

Jadrien did go through a period of crying and fussing. Another thing that happened was when children leave their parents, they can get separation anxiety. The way that was worked out ultimately was that you did have to have a nurse on set with a baby. She would take him down to the set, and I would wait upstairs. By the time he got down there, he would be over his anxiety and engage with the people there. It was not a problem anymore.

With an Irish Catholic immigrant family, the main focus; and a setting in a real, bustling urban center (and not a small fictitious town in Middle America) without a homemaker in sight, the groundbreaking *Ryan's Hope* debuted. This was not going to be your grandmother's stereotypical soap. All the female characters had careers except clingy Delia, who was as far from being a homemaker as could be. The serial's opening shot was of perky Mary Ryan strolling down the street in the Riverside neighborhood of New

York City. She then enters Ryan's Bar (her family's establishment), with new posters touting her older brother, ex-police officer Frank, for local city councilman. Mary and her parents are elated and eagerly waiting to share with Frank, who so far is a no-show.

At this point, repeated slow-motion scenes of Frank tumbling down a flight of stairs, accompanied by eerie music (composed by Carey Gold who worked on *Love of Life* prior) reminiscent of *Dark Shadows*, was intercut into the episode. Lingering in the bar is reporter Jack Fenelli, who has made himself foul to the family with an unflattering column on the police department. He wants to do a piece on Frank. Johnny reluctantly lets Mary be interviewed since she knows the most about Frank's political aspirations and his platform.

At Riverside Hospital, across the street from the bar, new residents Pat Ryan and Bucky Carter get a stern reprimand from head nurse Ramona Gonzalez for not following her protocol with patients. Dr. Faith Coleridge comforts Bucky and tells him even her father, who is the chief of staff, is afraid of Ramona. At the end of the episode, a frazzled blonde comes bursting into the bar, very upset. It is Frank's wife, Delia, who claims she was almost run over by a taxi but seems to be hiding a secret. The following day, it is revealed that Roger Coleridge found Frank unconscious at the bottom of a stairwell in Riverside Hospital with $6,500 on his person. While in the emergency room, the money is logged in with Frank's other personal possessions, but it disappears shortly after.

Within its first two weeks on the air, reviews from the mainstream press were mixed. This was not surprising since TV critics seemed to have a bias against daytime serials in general—not that soap opera fans took their opinions seriously. On the positive side, Tom Donnelly of *The Washington Post* liked that the show took a risk and introduced its leading man in the hospital fighting for his life with flashes of him taking a tumble down a flight of stairs. Normally, he would first be seen in robust health, pursuing a romantic partner with a leisurely buildup to a climax that involves hospitalization. Regarding *Ryan's Hope*'s novel approach, Donnelly commented, "The effect was positively surrealistic, especially in a soap opera context." He added, "All in all, *Ryan's Hope* has started out like a bucket of suds afire." The review in *Variety* began with, "To the occasional viewer of soap operas, *Ryan's Hope* seemed particularly lively. No doubt that was because the show moved its characters into focus quickly to introduce them to the audience. But the effect . . . was to give the show a fairly rich texture."

On the other end of the spectrum, Gregg Kilday, writing in the *Los Angeles Times*, thought the soap "lacked substance." He said, "Its little fillips of relevance aside, *Ryan's Hope* devotes most of its time to dilemmas more familiar to the soaps. Its women, however independent they might look at first glance, apparently exist only so they can be pursued by all the doctors, lawyers, and journalists who crowd the premises . . . And when it comes to extended families, you don't find them any more complicated than the Coleridge and Ryan clans."

John J. O'Connor of *The New York Times* commented, "As usual, plotlines are stretched to the point of minimum mobility. The smallest dung of inspiration is milked thoroughly." He added, "For all its avowed dedication to the contemporary and the urban-centered, *Ryan's Hope* might just be as well set in anonymous suburbia."

At the beginning of the show, New York City was a character in itself. As Francis Clines wrote in the *New York Times*, scenes were set "on the Long Island Expressway, in Central Park, the local Chinese restaurant, a Hamptons beach house, and . . . a shadowy, plant-infested brownstone." Plus, of course, scenes in the Ryan Family's Irish pub, their home above the bar, and the local hospital. Patriarch Johnny Ryan was a big baseball fan and loved the New York Mets. His favorite player was pitcher Nolan Ryan, whose photo hung in the bar. The show was able to get Ryan to make a guest appearance as himself during the first year.

Rachael Mayer: Little known fact: Ruthie was on that show with Nolan Ryan, and she was maybe ten years old. There is a scene [in the hospital emergency room] where Ruthie and Claire's son meet him.

Ruth Mayer: Don't Google it—it is horrible.

Rachael Mayer: I was in a scene with Malcolm Groome and wish I could see that again because it was my only celluloid appearance. He was so cute. I was about sixteen, and he was in his twenties.

Ruth Mayer: We had such a crush on Malcolm, and I loved Justin Deas, who played Bucky.

As the weeks progressed, Frank Ryan was originally slated to die. Not surprisingly, giving the continued guilty look on her face and her overreaction to any news of Frank's recovery, it was revealed that Delia gave him that almost-fatal shove when he demanded a divorce to marry his paramour, Jill

Coleridge. Though it was an accident, Delia fled in a panic and abandoned the two-timer. She shamefully kept her mouth shut because she was terrified of the consequences. As he lay in his hospital bed with Maeve and his family praying for his recovery, flashbacks were used to fill in storyline details. These were so successful in humanizing Frank that ABC interceded and convinced Labine and Mayer not to kill the character off, causing a necessary rewrite of their story bible. It seemed around week six that Frank Ryan was due to expire, but instead he makes a miraculous, but slow, recovery when his temperature broke and his breathing improved. The lesson learned from this story is that when a cheating husband wants to ask his wife for a divorce to marry his mistress, do not do it at the top of a stairwell.

Allowing Frank to live was the correct decision for the show, as Frank and Jill's on-again, off-again romance lasted for years and caused all sorts of entertaining drama. Commenting on this major change, Claire Labine remarked in *On Writing* magazine, "It was a power play on their [ABC's] part, but the fact of the matter was, they were right. Part of the reason they fell in love with him was because we fell in love with him. We were writing all these flashbacks—they were backstory incidents that explained why the family was so upset and what their hopes had been for this person who was lying in a coma in the hospital. And by the time we had done three or four weeks of that, we thought, 'Oh my God, he's too wonderful to kill.' That was the point at which they said to us, 'You can't kill him; the audience loves him.' So consequently, we really were without story practically from the beginning of *Ryan's Hope*, and it was wonderful, because the characters told the story."

> **Rachael Mayer:** I am sorry to say that I do not know [what was to happen in the original bible]. I certainly remember anxious conversations that went, "What are we going to do? The network wants us to keep Frank alive." The actor, Michael Hawkins . . . was hired because the character was going to be short-lived. Again, they could not see anybody else in the part. They loved Michael. I think they scrambled to reassess, but I do not know what the plot line was.

Though the viewers were delighted that Frank was going to live, the story shift may have caused the writers to rethink the character of Pat Ryan. It looked like he was headed for a renewed romance with his high school sweetheart and sister-in-law, Delia, but that was temporarily shelved, and instead he wound up as emotionally disturbed Faith Coleridge's obsession while she knowingly strung along the adorable Bucky Carter, who was in love with her.

Meanwhile, Frank recovers and promises Delia that he will keep what happened between them a secret if she does not reveal his affair with Jill. With no other alternative, she agrees. He also makes her stop looking into the missing $6,500, knowing Roger took it to pay off his debts. Meanwhile, Frank's indifference toward Delia exasperates her disturbed desperation to remain part of the Ryan fold. As the wheelchair-bound politician regains his strength, he decides to bow out of the city council race after his disappointed parents learn of his long-term affair with Jill, as does Nick Szabo, who is going to expose him. Delia, terrified of a divorce and losing her ties to the Ryan family, goes to Frank's political backers' meeting and lies that she and her husband have reconciled. She wins over the room. A conflicted Frank does not interject and sits there silently. He remains on the ballot, opting for a loveless marriage and a political career over Jill.

> **Malcolm Groome:** They wrote Pat originally as a ladies' man who played the field. He was very hip and truly kind of New York. I started playing it that way. He would flirt with Faith and sort of toy with her. He was also seeing other women at the time. I do not know why, but they ended up writing the character more for me than the character they had started out with. I wish they had kept Pat in that ladies' man direction. It was more interesting than what they ended up writing him, which I felt was a little more boring. He became the good son, and he was not as much fun to play as it was the first year of the show.
>
> Perhaps, [keeping Frank alive] was the reason. They had to have some contrast between Pat and Frank. Pat was the middle son between Frank and Mary. Then they introduced Kathleen, the oldest daughter and then later Siobhan, the youngest. Pat became the peacemaker.

During this early period, another major story centered around Mary Ryan. Although she loves and respects her parents, that did not stop her from seeing an older, seasoned reporter, Jack Fenelli. The Ryan family still has a grudge against him due to his past negative columns about the police force. After assuring the Ryan family that his new piece on Frank would be fair, Mary begins spending a lot of time with him. However, Jack's column is damaging to Frank's political career when he reports about the missing $6,500 and implies Frank has ties to Nick Szabo. To the Ryans' relief, an infuriated Mary breaks it off with Jack and is briefly distracted by the romantic interests of Bob Reid and Roger Coleridge. When Maeve and Johnny discover that Mary is back with Jack and is in a sexual relationship with him to boot, they are outraged, and he is barred from their home. Rebelling against her parents for foisting their strict Catholic beliefs onto her, Mary moves in with Jack and settles in his small downtown apartment on Weehawken Street.

Kate Mulgrew as Mary and Michael Levin as Jack quickly became the soap's most popular couple due to their wonderful chemistry. However, sometimes they could be hard to like, and that was due to the expert writing of Claire Labine and Paul Mayer, who created their characters in shades of gray. Mary was bright, caring, and independent but could be condescending, strong-willed, and self-righteous. Jack was stubborn, arrogant, and quick-tempered. Growing up without parents, he abhorred family closeness but because of Mary came around to being a part of the Ryan family. The volatile couple fought hard but loved even harder. They were never boring. This well-written love story was obviously penned by Claire Labine and, arguably, was the one she favored above all others.

> **Malcolm Groome:** Although Paul and Claire were partners, it felt like Claire had the stronger say in things. It was obvious that the characters of Mary and Maeve were favorites of Claire. Mary seemed to me to be an alter ego for Claire, and Maeve was a stand-in for all of Claire's more Catholic values. To me, this matriarchal aspect of the story [was] the heart and soul of the show for Claire. Those storylines got all the press. Helen Gallagher was wonderful. She and Kate Mulgrew received a lot of the attention. We all felt that this was the thrust of the show. It is great we are here, but that is where Claire's heart lies, in the characters of Maeve and Mary.

> **Helen Gallagher:** I loved both Claire and Paul. Claire was an unusual woman, and I liked her on sight. She was not just cut from the cloth. She was a writer and just had interesting ideas. She also had a knack in casting people who were human. Most were not typical 'soap pretty' actors.

> **Malcolm Groome:** All of us were constantly lobbying for, or at least wishing for, juicy stories to play. There was only so much input we were able to give to Claire and Paul. They were listening to their own muses.

We were all like a family—the cast and Claire and Paul. They loved the show. They loved their actors. They loved the characters. We all became close. We ended up socializing together. Claire would have people over to her house. They were like our mother and father, and I guess at some level they took that seriously.

Ron Hale: This was the most incredible relationship I ever had. I had never worked with people who were head writers and producers. They gave us all like a thirty-page bible about our characters. I knew everything about Roger Coleridge from the first day I pooped my pants and momma had to change my diaper. That's how incredible they were. So, when you first started and didn't know the background of where your character came from and why they were what they were, then go find another job. They were phenomenal in that regard. Plus, they let all of us know if there was one problem with a line or something in the scene that we didn't feel was right, we should come to the office immediately or call them the day before. If you were studying your script and felt you couldn't see something a certain way or it didn't make sense, we could let them know. And they would make some changes.

Ilene Kristen: Claire and Paul were incredibly collaborative to work with. I had ideas for Delia that did not freak them out so much but did one of the directors. I wanted the makeup people to make sure if Delia was crying that it looked real with makeup running down. They were always trying to set my hair. I remember going to Steve Schenkel, the creative consultant, and asking to have my hair disheveled for at least a week. I said to him, "Delia is stuck in a revolving door she cannot get out of. If you have problems with it after that, I will neaten it up." It worked. Delia was tortured and in over her head—as was Ilene. I felt I could only do this character for *real*. She was in a dilemma.

Malachy McCourt: I got along very well with Claire and Paul. I liked being with them both. Neither of them ever said anything to me about expanding my role. At first, I don't think they knew if I was capable of doing anything more than being an under-five, saying one line or two. When they realized that I could—I was not an accomplished actor but I could act—they gave me more.

Other than the major change in allowing Frank Ryan to live, the show remained on a steady course through the end of 1975. Jack (knowing how Mary is hurting in regard to her family) reaches out to Johnny. They form a truce, allowing Mary to return home but still being able to see Jack. Roger's gambling addiction comes to light, as does his blackmailing Frank to keep quiet about his affair with Jill. Roger's father is furious with his son, and Jill is angry with him as well. Faith admits her love for Pat to Bucky, who then spills the beans. This infuriates Faith, who resorts to trickery to nab the uninterested Pat. Faith then has a bigger problem when she discovers that she has a secret admirer at the hospital: neurology technician Kenneth Castle (Ty McConnell). Seneca learns of Nell's irreversible brain damage, but she refuses his support.

The first portion of 1976 saw the wrapping up of some of the lesser storylines and the start of the serial's recasting woes. An understanding Jill bows out of Frank's life, although she is still deeply in love with him. She is distracted by Seneca, and she begins defending him when he is charged with murder for the mercy killing of Nell (carrying out her wishes not to be kept alive by artificial means). After a long trial, Seneca is found guilty of assault in the second degree. On a happier note, he and Jill admit they have developed feelings for each other and begin a romance. Headstrong Seneca then refuses to appeal his conviction, despite Jill's prodding, and is sentenced to a week in jail and two years of probation. Luckily, the hospital allows him to keep his job.

Kenneth Castle, meanwhile, becomes obsessed with Faith and begins stalking her. This story seemed to be lifted straight out of *Dark Shadows*, as Kenneth kidnaps Faith and keeps her captive in the creepy subcellar of Riverside Hospital for weeks. The trauma of her situation causes Faith to suffer from hysterical blindness. After being freed, she regains her sight. Kenneth tries to get to her in the Coleridge townhouse and is chased to the roof by Ed Coleridge, who tragically plunges to his death. Kenneth is later apprehended, and Faith suffers a breakdown.

Ron Hale: Frank Latimore [who played Ed] was a very sweet man—very gentle and nice. However, I think his nerves were shot. He was in movies during the forties and fifties and had never done anything like this. Even though he had time to prepare, every time we had a scene, his pores would open, and I could just see the fear in his eyes. I mean that in the kindest sense because I am an actor too and have been scared so many times. There is just no getting around it. He couldn't hold on to it.

When he did have some control, he did very well. He gave me a lot. I am certainly not a great actor. I am passable and damn good sometimes, but I always come prepared and am never late. When I knew I had a scene coming up with Frank, I would double down and learn his lines, which on a soap that sometimes automatically happens. If I knew camera two was on him, and I saw him going up on his lines, I would mouth the words for him. That's what you do on stage if that happens. I think—and again, I am certainly not sure—that Frank did not come up to their expectations.

After only eight months on the air, *Ryan's Hope* received its first bout of Emmy Award love. Helen Gallagher was nominated for Outstanding Actress in a Daytime Drama Series. She deservedly would go on to win the award (her scenes grieving for the comatose Frank while she sat at his bedside were riveting). This began the show's winning streak of going home with at least one Emmy every year until 1982. The year prior began the show's winning streak of Writers Guild of America Awards for Best Television Writing in Daytime Serials, with the soap taking home the prize each year from 1975 to 1978. After losing in 1979 to *Guiding Light*, its winning streak would begin again in 1980 through 1983 and then pick up again in 1986 through 1989. For many, it was the best-written soap of the time and perhaps of all time.

Although *Ryan's Hope* quickly became popular with Emmy nominators, the soap press, and viewers, it would become hampered by the almost constant recasting of many of its lead characters, causing audience frustration. Faith Catlin was the first original cast member to be let go and replaced. With the rewriting of the original bible, Claire and Paul may have decided to go in a different direction with the character. Faith was off the screen for a few months, and when she reemerged during the summer of 1976, she was played, very briefly, by *Dark Shadows* alumni Nancy Barrett (ex-Carolyn Stoddard). Barrett claimed she asked to be set free after only nine episodes because she was unhappy with the character. Newcomer Catherine Hicks took her place as a more mature and refined Faith.

Malcolm Groome: I knew Faith Catlin before the show. We had been in the same repertory company a couple of years before that was based in Chapel Hill, North Carolina. She did not last long. They apparently did not think she was working out in the part.

Ron Hale: I remember Faith Catlin being very energetic. That's all I want to say there.

Ilene Kristen: Faith Catlin was not glamorous enough for them, but she was such an interesting choice for the part.

Malcolm Groome: I didn't get to work with Nancy Barrett long, so I didn't get to know her at all. I didn't think she resembled Faith Catlin, except she was blond—with long, beautiful, straight hair! I remember her as being rather quiet and to herself, and perhaps a little nervous. Who wouldn't be on a new job, plus having to replace someone? I'm not sure why she left . . . I don't think it was working out for some reason, so it could have been her choice or the producers'.

Catherine Hicks (Dr. Faith Coleridge #3): I received a scholarship to Cornell in their two-year Master of Fine Arts program. It was rigorous, and I really became an actress. When I graduated, while my classmates went on vacation, I got on a bus and went straight to New York City. It was August, and not many people were there, so I cleaned up. I got a couple of national commercials, and within two weeks I had my audition, then screen test for *Ryan's Hope*. I think I got it because I just had great training and was at my best, in terms of being truthful. I was blond, and sometimes it is visual as well. I read with Malcolm Groome. I had no idea that there were two previous actresses as Faith, and nobody told me. I did not know anything about the soap world.

I was a very dedicated theatre actress, and I did not want to do a soap, but I thought, "It's not Broadway, but it has a good group of New York actors." It felt good at the audition. I was able to get a short contract for a year and a half. I think they needed someone and really liked me, so my agent made that happen. The truth was, and I always say, that *Ryan's Hope* was not a polyester soap opera. It was a nice, herringbone tweed. It had good actors and just not beautiful people.

Malcolm Groome: Catherine Hicks and I worked great together.

Ron Hale: I do not remember much about Nancy Barrett, but I loved Catherine Hicks. She was so much fun to work with.

Catherine Hicks: Ron Hale was a dear. He was fun with a twinkle in his eye. Malcolm Groome was always nice. He has a very gentle soul. Justin Deas and John Gabriel were nice guys—so was Earl Hindman.

   Nancy Addison was lovely. She taught me how to spend money, like having lunch at the Algonquin. She had been on the show for a bit and was a woman of wealth. I was just starting to earn my first paycheck.

The digressions from Claire and Paul's original bible kept the duo on their toes. As for their process in writing the show and delivering five scripts a week, Paul Mayer revealed in *TV Book*, "We try to write scenes we would want to see and desperately try to avoid scenes that would bore us. Whenever we feel that some proposed incident or confrontation is dull, we look for another, better way to advance the story. If we were able to write *Ryan's Hope* as we'd like, each daily episode would have the emotional intensity of *Wuthering Heights* ... We can't do that, of course, but we do take the challenge seriously and do the very best we can." He went on to add that what made writing the show so much fun was because "Claire Labine and I share a common fantasy life. We both enjoy the same kinds of sentimental, upbeat, love stories. The title of the show reflects our attitude—we are hopeful and so are the Ryans ... The whole experience of the show—while exhausting—is a labor of love for us."

Ratings-wise, the curious began to tune in to *Ryan's Hope*, and most kept coming back—especially women under age fifty-five. Within one year, *Ryan's Hope* was ABC's second-highest-rated serial after *All My Children*. Although the show rarely placed in the top five in household ratings, it drew the younger audience advertisers began to covet in the late seventies and eighties and almost always made the top five in the Women 18–49 Demo.

There were two standout storylines from this period, from 1976 through the end of 1977. Mary and Jack continued as the soap's unofficial "super couple" with their on-again, off-again relationship. They are happy, but she becomes distracted by handsome Sam Crowell (Dennis Jay Higgins), a producer from local TV Channel R. He comes to interview Frank and Delia and is charmed by Mary, who helps with the shoot. He then offers her a job as a production assistant at the station. She accepts, making Jack jealous.

Sam later hires Nick Szabo's spoiled daughter Reenie (Julia Barr) to take Mary's place when he promotes Mary to on-air journalist.

During this time, Mary and Jack break up (due to his jealousy of Sam and her rightful resentment of Jack's flirtatious colleague, Martha McKee played by Tovah Feldshuh), get together, and then break up when the hatred between Johnny and Jack finally leads to fisticuffs. The couple then reconciles once more and Jack proposes. Then, realizing what he is getting himself into, Jack tries to back out because he is uncomfortable with her close-knit family but cannot do so. Despite having to be dragged to his wedding to Mary by her father, the couple is happy until Jack is injured in an accident. Paralyzed from the waist down and not able to be a complete husband to Mary, he begins annulment proceedings, even after learning that she's pregnant.

The story took this turn due to the real-life pregnancy of the single Kate Mulgrew. She revealed in her memoir that when she told Claire Labine the news, she offered to quit. Claire instead responded, "We'll write the pregnancy into Mary's story. She and Jack are madly in love, she gets pregnant, he isn't ready for a baby, they break up, she decides to go it alone, lots of turbulence with Jack until, ultimately, she has the baby and names her (it has to be a girl) . . . Ryan Fenelli." This is exactly the storyline Claire gave the viewers, and it kept Mulgrew working right up to her due date.

Jack then became the show's de facto villain—for some even more so than Delia. His actions (including filing for an annulment, abandoning his wife and newborn child, and rekindling his relationship with Martha McKee, now played by Dorrie Kavanaugh) causes Mary to fall into the arms of Irish boxer-turned-hospital-administrator Tom Desmond (Tom McGreevy), to the delight of Johnny Ryan. For a time, most of the audience disliked Jack for mistreating Mary. Michael Levin told syndicated columnist Jon-Michael Reed, "I've walked into fan gatherings for the show and heard women moaning and groaning. Their reaction, of course, is to the persona of Jack, not me."

Michael Levin: I remember those appearances. I tried to protect Jack as much as I could. He was well-meaning, but you have to remember that soap operas are female-driven and written with them in mind.

Rachael Mayer: I think Kate was like a daughter to Claire. They were so close and remained so right up to when Claire died.

Ruth Mayer: They shared a faith—Catholicism—that was particularly important to them. I think they were like mother and daughter. I know my dad and Claire were just wowed by Kate. You can see by the career she had that she had something special.

Helen Gallagher: I remember Kate very well and was crazy about her. She played my daughter, and I always wanted a daughter. She was wonderful to work with, and she was a good actress. She did her job. The show was really written for her.

Michael Levin: Kate was a very talented young lady on her way up. She was fun to work with because she could act and we had a relationship where you play off each other. That is very exciting and the best acting situation you can have, so that was quite good.

Ilene Kristen: I remember I was on the floor tying my Keds sneakers the first day I met Kate. She leans down and said, "Hi, I am Kate Mulgrew. And who are you?" I told her my name and she replied, "And how old are you, Ilene?" I told her I was twenty-two, and she said she was twenty. I was like, okay. It was most interesting.

Catherine Hicks: Kate Mulgrew and the character of Mary Ryan were totally considered the center of the show. Claire and Paul were obsessed with her. She was the favored child. Kate had this persona, and I preferred actors who you could have a giggle with. She wasn't a gal pal. She didn't have to be, but I am an only child, so I was always looking for a friend.

Ilene Kristen: Kate was the translation of Claire. However, I think if Claire were alive today, she would say I shared the attention. I didn't feel a lack of consideration from Claire and Paul, believe me. I just knew my job was extremely hard because of what I had to play. I just didn't want to play someone the audience would groan, "I hate her!"

Ron Hale: Kate Mulgrew was difficult. We were like fire and water.

Malachy McCourt: I was very fond of Kate. She was new to the whole thing of soaps. When I started, she was working on *Ryan's Hope* during the day and then would get on a train to do Shakespeare in Connecticut at night. She was amazing that way.

Oddly enough, although she is much younger than me, she was very helpful when I needed to do a scene that required *acting*. Kate would suggest how to do it. I had no hesitancy in asking her. I'd say, "How should I do that?" and she would reply, "Try this or try that." And she laughed at all my humor as well. She is a very sweet, decent, lovely woman. I am still very friendly with her.

Rachael Mayer: I also know my dad loved Michael Levin in the role.

Ron Hale: Michael was a very private man. None of us knew actually how old he was when we started. He was in his early forties and playing a character who was supposed to be about thirty years old. He took it on physically and vocally—he kind of had his voice a little higher. Plus, he was quite an energetic man. Not only did he pass as being much younger, but how about his toupee—it was incredible. None of us knew that he was about 90 percent bald until about six or seven years into the show.

Michael Levin: I am flattered that they did not notice and hope it's true. I was careful in protecting that image and never appeared without my hairpiece if it had anything to do with *Ryan's Hope*. That's terrific to know that I fooled some of them for so long.

Malachy McCourt: Michael was great fun with a good sense of humor. I would say he was sort of the quintessential New Yorker.

Malcom Groome: Michael and Kate had the most major storylines, so that was no doubt stressful. And if there was tension between them, it certainly fed their volatile romantic storyline. Both were pretty fiery! Besides Michael, everyone admired Kate's talent.

Ilene Kristen: I loved working with Ron Hale and Michael Levin. What great actors. We really loved each other. Michael, though, could be wild, and certain people felt his wrath. Lela Swift would drive Michael fucking crazy.

Michael Levin: We didn't work together very much, but Ilene Kristen was terrific.

In one of the show's most memorable moments, a bit of Delia rubbed off on Maeve. With the aid of Tom Desmond, who had feelings for Mary but put them aside, she purposely locks estranged, obstinate lovers, Mary and Jack, in the bar's basement so they can hash out their problems. It works, and the pair emerges reconciled. Kate Mulgrew, writing in her memoir, said, "The outcome was determination to try a little harder to understand each other, to quit trying to change each other, and to make an earnest effort to make the marriage work."

The other two main characters that stories sprung off were Frank and Delia. The estranged couple reconciles for the sake of Frank's political career, but a marriage of convenience without sex is not what Delia has in mind, and she begins spending time with Roger Coleridge. Soon, Delia is going to "Chinese cooking school" with her imaginary friend Sheila so she can be a better homemaker to Frank. The platonic relationship with Roger then turns into a full-blown affair. Jill accidentally stumbles upon the two lovers, and although disturbed by their deceit, decides to stay mum. Frank has a change of heart about Delia, and after they become intimate again, she tries to break it off with Roger, who threatens to tell Frank everything if she doesn't remain his lover. Frank, knowing a thing or two about two-timing, suspects something is afoot and follows Delia to "class" one day. Instead of finding her in front of a stove with a chef, he finds her in the arms of a doctor.

In a series of riveting episodes, a teary-eyed Delia at first tries to lie her way out of it by accusing Roger of forcing himself on her (not true) and blackmailing her to keep the affair going or he would use it to ruin Frank's political career (true). The indignant Frank plays the wounded husband, gaining the family sympathy (except from Pat), which was sorely lacking for Delia when Frank's three-year affair with Jill was revealed. When Delia calls him and his family out on their hypocrisy, Frank condescendingly retorts, "What Jill and I had can't be compared to your situation." Delia shoots back, "The only difference is you enjoyed yourself, at least." This enrages Frank, who says that his biggest mistake was marrying her and that he wants Delia out of the house immediately, but Maeve and Johnny intercede, thinking of their grandson.

Frank's threat of divorce sends a distraught, but calculating, Delia (with her baby son in tow) to a hotel ledge high above the streets, where she pretends to threaten to jump. Frank promises to stay married to her, but when she is safe, he initiates the divorce proceedings.

Walanne Steele: Michael Hawkins and Ilene Kristen were nice. I do not remember Michael being on for that long. Kate Mulgrew was okay. We never had a lot of interaction with her. Helen Gallagher and Bernie Barrow were nice to Jadrien as well, but I think his best relationships were with Malcolm Groome and later Daniel Hugh Kelly. They went more out of their way—Randall Edwards also later on. Malcolm would spend time talking with Jadrien if he were hanging around or sitting on the bar waiting to shoot. A few others, too, made an extra effort to deal with a child.

Malcolm Groome: I got to spend a lot of time with Jadrien on the set. When he was first starting as an infant, then toddler, he cried a lot. They saw he did well with me, so they wrote a lot of scenes with Little John and his Uncle Pat. I was really fond of him.

Helen Gallagher: My favorite memory of Jadrien was when he was a little child. He wanted to get out. He was crying and making a fuss. I carried him out of the building to get him off the set, and he was all smiles because he got his way. I will always remember him like that.

Ilene Kristen: I watched Jadrien grow up. I love him, and as an adult he came to see me in a play in LA once. He walks in and says, "Guess who I am?" I looked him up and down and said, "Jadrien?!" He was great on the set, and his parents were always with him. He was a good kid and has become a very responsible man.

In the middle of the custody case during the fall of 1976, Michael Hawkins was replaced by Andrew Robinson. In a surprise to both Frank and Delia, the judge wisely deemed them both unfit parents (Delia was too unstable and a busy Frank, newly elected to the city council, was reinvolved with pregnant Jill, which the judge felt would affect Little John). He then awarded custody of their son to grandparents Maeve and Johnny, who magnanimously allow Delia to reside in their home to be closer to her son.

Although Hawkins proved to be extremely popular with the audience, he had only signed on for a short-term role. When they decided to allow Frank to live, things became problematic on set, and he was not very popular with his castmates. In an interview Hawkins gave at the time, he told Jon-Michael Reed, "Some people pick up soap acting just like that, but not me. It's taken me six and a half years and many soaps to really get a handle on what I am doing. And I've been ignominiously fired from many, no, practically all of them." The actor blamed the fact that he was appearing on Broadway as Dr. Watson in *Sherlock Holmes* for the reason he was having trouble with the scripts on the soap.

Ilene Kristen: We shot the flashbacks with Michael Hawkins. Those [scenes] they would mold and really rehearse because it told so much of the story. Michael became dependent on reading the monitor because something was not right with him. I could never read the monitor, and I will never forget one time I was doing a dress rehearsal with him. He was constantly looking at the monitor, so he knew exactly what came next. I was floundering for a line, and he knew what the line was but didn't even give me a hint. I just couldn't find it.

Helen Gallagher: The character of Frank was my oldest child, so I did not want him to die. Michael perhaps was not well mentally, though. You'd look at his script, and it was all blacked out. He was not well enough to continue.

Malcolm Groome: Michael Hawkins did not last long and was having problems with his lines. I remember they had him in a wheelchair. They had a cue card opposite him, and he was not too present. He would just read the lines without too much invested in it. I think he was having some emotional or psychological problems at the time.

Rachael Mayer: I think Michael was a stressed, vulnerable actor, and he did not want to do it long-term. I do remember the problems with him, and this all rings true.

Andrew Robinson (Frank Ryan #2): I was living in California at the time and in New York doing a workshop production at the Public Theatre. I think it was the last performance when Paul Mayer and Claire Labine came to see the play. When I walked out onto the street, they were waiting for me, and they essentially offered me the role of Frank Ryan. It was stunning—that certainly never happened to me before nor has it happened since. They made their pitch. They told me about the series and how it was just on for a few months. Frank was a lead, and they were making a cast change. I said, "No, thanks. I live in California." I was still angling to do films and television. They were very sweet people, and I loved them both, but that was it.

I went back to LA, and about a week later they called me again and said, "Listen, we are going to be in California on business and we'd like to take you to lunch." I hate business luncheons, so I invited them to my house instead. They came over and made their pitch again—it was quite extraordinary. When they left, my wife said, "What could be terrible? These are very nice people. Obviously, they want you." I agreed, and that is how I got the job.

However, the moment that they hired me, there was a guy in daytime programming at ABC who said, "Wait a second. Isn't that the guy who played the killer in *Dirty Harry?* We cannot have him as a leading man in a soap opera." Claire and Paul said, "No, he is absolutely right for the role." They insisted. Claire and Paul owned the show at that time and had that kind of clout.

Rachel Mayer: Michael Hawkins . . . was hired because the character was going to be short-lived. Paul and Claire could not see anybody else in the part. They loved Michael.

Ilene Kristen: If Michael Hawkins had his mental act together, he would have been brilliant.

Andrew Robinson: I knew Michael Hawkins and had done a play with him a few years before in New York. The thing was that Frank was supposed to be a family tragedy. After getting fan mail pleading for him to live, they did. But for whatever reasons—Michael was a difficult kind of guy—they decided to recast the role.

Ilene Kristen: Andy Robinson was a fabulous actor, and I loved him. However, ABC only saw him as the psycho he played in *Dirty Harry.*

Andrew Robinson: Ilene Kristen has a wonderful sense of humor and so relished playing that role. She was delicious as Delia. I had the most fun working on the show at the beginning because I got to work with Ilene acting out these absurd, outrageous arguments and fights.

Malcolm Groome: Andy Robinson, his wife, and I became close friends. I still see them out here in California. I loved working with Andy. For me, that was the best brother relationship due to our real friendship, and we worked well together. I felt we really clicked, and it worked well for both of us.

Andrew Robinson: Malcolm and I just had chemistry. We became close friends from the moment we met. I found him incredibly empathetic and open as a human being. We also had a lot in common in terms of our politics and spiritual side. It was just one of those things, but I also hit it off pretty much with the entire cast. It was a great company of actors.

Ron Hale: Andy Robinson was a hell of an actor and a good guy. I came to New York at age nineteen and considered myself an East Coast actor. Andy came out from the West Coast. I knew who he was but did not know what to expect but thought he might have that Hollywood attitude. He came in and kicked butt. He was quite good as Frank.

Andrew Robinson: I really was not a Hollywood actor. By that point, I think I had done two films, but because one of them was enormously popular, people thought I was a movie star—I wasn't. As a matter of fact, after *Dirty Harry*, I couldn't get arrested because the character was such a bad ass. I was glad to come back to New York to do the soap and the play that Paul and Claire saw me in. It was chosen to open the Joe Papp Shakespeare Festival. I had to juggle both, and they worked around my schedule.

Catherine Hicks: Nothing is as fast as doing a soap opera. It was daunting—the number of pages and dialogue, but of course, you are young and smart. I learned quickly that the brain is a muscle, and it develops sense memory. You almost become a sight-reading memorizer. After a couple of months, it was fast to learn.

Andrew Robinson: *Ryan's Hope* was like doing a one-act play every day. It is not stage and not the single-camera format, so it was not fish nor fowl. It was a very challenging format for me. When you are young enough, you can learn all that dialogue. But the thing is, when I first started working, I was very heavy on the show. I was doing three or four or even five episodes a week because they were catching up with Frank's story and establishing his character. Every night there were enormous amounts of text to memorize. I was primarily a stage actor and played a lot of big roles, so I knew how to learn lines. The next day you show up and you do it. Then you'd get the next script for the following day. It was exhausting work. Doing a soap opera and playing a major character on it is not for the faint of heart.

To Claire's utter surprise, many viewers felt more sympathy for the desperate, conniving Delia than she anticipated. Mayer was less surprised. Invited to Claire's townhouse where she and Paul worked, Cassandra White witnessed and reported this exchange in *Soap Opera People* magazine: "'I simply don't see how you can be so blindly unsympathetic to Delia,' Paul says . . . 'I am not unsympathetic,' Claire cuts in . . . 'I agree she's had a lousy time, but she is still a scheming, vicious bitch!' Now Paul's voice rises. 'She also happens to be my favorite person in the whole blasted show . . .' And Claire: 'I know that . . . You always take her side.'"

Claire also admitted to Judith Klemesrud of the *New York Times* that she and Paul fought "loudly." Labine added, "But it's never personal. It's always about story differences or what the characters should do. Sometimes I burst into tears of rage, and Paul leaves for the day."

> **Rachael Mayer:** Delia was my dad's favorite character, and she is based a lot on my mother—meaning the vulnerability, the naughtiness, the sexiness.

> **Ruth Mayer:** Quietly brilliant but hiding it—not always looking like a ditz but smart as a tack underneath. Although we should never confuse the two. My mother intellectually was off the charts, where Delia was not.

A lot of the audience agreed with Paul and rooted for Delia over Frank, Jill, and Mary. Those characters were written with flaws as well. Frank was sanctimonious and conceited. He used Delia's immaturity and neediness as an excuse for his philandering. Although Mary and Jill were lauded by many for being atypical soap heroines at the time, depicted as being fiercely independent women who stood up for themselves in their personal lives and professional careers, they were not always likable. Mary was obstinate and could be a smug bully toward Delia—even slapping her during a bedside vigil when Frank was comatose. She always turned a blind eye to the misdeeds of her older brother, whom she worships, and puts all the blame on her sister-in-law. Jill is self-righteous and took no responsibility when accused of her part in wrecking a marriage. And even though the creators thought Delia's destructive actions would diminish her in the eyes of the audience, it did not do so for many. Delia was an underdog and had to resort to underhanded tactics to fight back because she felt inferior to this trio, both in intellect and upbringing. The brilliant Ilene Kristen was able to gain empathy with many viewers, even if she did resort to high crimes and manipulations.

Ilene Kristen: Yes, Paul and Claire were shocked with the fan support for Delia. I think they saw that there was a vulnerability about Delia, who was a character everybody was supposed to love to hate, but everybody loved her. I really assumed the position of being the underdog, or as I called her, Pitiful Pearl, which was a doll I had as a kid. If you turned her over, she turned into a princess, but I kept Delia at a Pitiful Pearl level. I felt that there had never been a character like this on soaps who was so vulnerable. I was really guided on this, and the more nervous I was about doing this part—I was intimidated by these actors who had experience in television before—the more I would train myself to listen in between my own lines.

Ron Hale: That first year I felt they did not quite know what to do with Roger until his affair with Delia. It is all her credit. If it weren't for Ilene Kristen, I would have been back pouring drinks somewhere. In the beginning, a lot of the things we did—even though her character was already the crazy wacko—had to do with her so desperately wanting to be part of the Ryan family. She worshipped them. There was a point during some scene that was kind of written in a light manner that we took hold of it.

We knew by the amount of time we had spent working together that we had great chemistry, and we just went for it. It ended up making the people in the control room laugh with tears in their eyes. We knew that we could do the lighthearted stuff, and the characters would be expanded. She was not just poor, little Delia and I was not just Roger the cad—I think Claire used to call me "the rogue."

Roger Coleridge was a son of a bitch but was a great surgeon. That is what always brought me back from the brink. They would take Roger into a corner where there was just no escaping, and they would come up with something to get me back in the good graces of the rest of the characters.

Malcolm Groome: Frank, Jill, and especially Mary come off arrogantly. Mary comes off as the most arrogant person in the world. And Kate knew how to play that very well. She was not soft.

Helen Gallagher: The audience's sympathy toward Delia was because of Ilene. That was her. When you go on television, you become yourself. Ilene had a good heart, and that is what showed. I loved Ilene, and she was a lovely girl.

Ilene Kristen: I think what people really loved about this character was Delia just listening to Maeve or the abuse Delia had to take from Mary, who thought she always knew better. In fact, it was through the Mary character that I really learned about the vulnerability of Delia and that was everything. She'd call Mary "Miss Know-It-All" or "Miss Mary Perfect." Or she'd say, "Mary knows everything." I had to be vulnerable to make Delia just not be another villain. She felt beneath certain people and knew some were smarter than her and more successful than her. There was this added vulnerability when Delia would have a conversation with Mary, who would be mentally smacking me around. It would make me look into Kate's eyes and find that vulnerability of Delia. It was very helpful that Kate was so strong in that role.

Some women, when they watched it, needed to be empowered insofar as having an occupation. Other women felt for Delia because they may have been trapped in a relationship. Delia was jealous and desperate, and I didn't shy away from those emotions.

Rachael Mayer: I think they understood that that was the brilliance of Ilene Kristen because she could be naughty, but you were still rooting for her. You understood that Ilene had tremendous vulnerability as an actress, and you felt for Delia. You gave her a pass. So, I do not know if they were surprised. They loved Nancy Addison, but she was more of a straight woman—she was pretty consistent. I think that Ilene went to different places as an actress. She was just astonishing.

Ilene Kristen: Ron Hale was incredible and like my anchor because he knew they threw so much stuff at me. He was always there for me. He was always there to run lines with me—always, always, always!

Ron Hale: I was not surprised with the audience's reaction. The Ryans were presented as the goody-two-shoes family. Roger and Delia in so many ways were a little more believable in what real people are. The Ryan family were sanctified. That was one of the things that I used as a character that totally made it honestly real for me. I knew that Roger came from a rich family and had it made financially all of his life. Roger knew that but also had a tough time with the Ryan clan. Mary should have been a nun and the boys the pope. It just made sense to me that my character would dislike those guys—well, Frank. Pat was a good guy just like Malcolm Groome is. There couldn't be a nicer person in the world than Malcolm.

Ilene Kristen: Delia was this bedraggled person, but you don't want people to treat you like that off the set. I had the same problem when I did *Grease*. I was not a goody-two-shoes. I did not like girls like Patty Simcox. I had to like them so I could play them convincingly. But I did not want to be not included in things. It was tough playing those characters because they are always going against the grain.

Malachy McCourt: I think Paul and Claire rather liked the idea that Kevin was sardonic with Delia and not respectful of her. Kevin was a tease and put her down.

There was one case where Kevin had to go upstairs to fetch Delia or tell her something. I was standing off camera, talking to somebody—I forget who it was—and the stage manager said, "You are on." I entered the scene, and Delia is on top of a ladder, changing curtain rods or something. I started to speak, and I said, "Will you blah blah blah." I didn't realize I was not speaking the lines. I was so flustered. Then I turned and said, "Who the fuck said that?" I realized it was me. Somebody from production sent that into a show about bloopers where unintentional things are said. I got [paid] $300 for saying *fuck*.

Despite the replacement of its top leading man, the show's popularity continued, and that translated into lots of press in the soap opera magazines of the day. For instance, in a February 1977 poll in *Soap Opera Serials*, *Ryan's Hope* was voted the second favorite show on the air, placing behind *One Life to Live* and before *The Edge of Night*, *The Young and the Restless*, and *Days of Our Lives*. Michael Levin and Kate Mulgrew were voted favorite actor and actress, with Nancy Addison placing ninth. In the June poll of that same magazine, *Ryan's Hope* was voted favorite soap, with Levin and Mulgrew maintaining their number one positions. Addison dropped off the list, but

Ilene Kristen came in seventh and Malcolm Groome came in tenth in the Favorite Actor category.

Ryan's Hope's early success was most likely because it was about a close, traditional family with immigrant parents from Ireland that the audience could identify with, even if they were not Irish Catholic. Simple, beautifully written scenes of Maeve lending a sympathetic ear or administering advice over tea in her homey living room or kitchen to her children, Delia, or the Coleridge sisters resonated with audiences maybe because they wanted a Maeve in their life too. Claire Labine remarked to Joanna Coons in *Rona Barrett's Daytimers*, "I do try to touch my audience. All those things about families—parents and children—those are the parts of the show that I love the best; things about compassion and love and what it can do to you in good ways and bad ways." The actors also gelled quite nicely, and their closeness off camera came through on camera.

Malcolm Groome: During the first three years, there was a strong family vibe, although I may have felt it more than some of the other actors. But I felt it was like a pseudo-family. Bernie Barrow was like a second father to me. He and his wife, Joanie, would have me out to their country house in Bucks County, Pennsylvania, quite often. Similarly, Helen Gallagher was like a second mother to me. I went to her country place, too, as well as Nancy Addison's. We were all great friends and got together often in the city as well.

I was particularly good friends with Nancy. We could never keep a straight face together in the scenes. There was one time where Faith Catlin was in the closet having a breakdown [during the Kenneth Castle kidnapping storyline]. I had to pull her out of there and put her in a straitjacket. Nancy's Jill says, with a very straight face, to Pat, "Was that really necessary to put her in a straitjacket?" And with just as straight a face, I reply, "Jill, we found her in the closet." We could not get through that without cracking up. First in dress rehearsal and then we have about five different takes. Some of my favorite times was when the cast would break up laughing at the seriousness of something very ridiculous.

Ilene Kristen: Nancy Addison's brother lived in my parents' building. We were friends since I was seventeen years old. Nancy was about twenty-two, and she was playing Kit Vested on *Guiding Light*. I thought she was the most beautiful girl that I had ever seen. She thought I was the most beautiful girl she had ever seen. We were huge fans of each other. But I didn't know she was doing *Ryan's Hope*.

Nancy and I became like sisters. She considered Kate Mulgrew her best friend, but I was family. Nancy and I had a similar upbringing. We were Jewish girls from nice homes, but she was probably more upper class than I was. Her father was a furrier, and my father was a hairdresser. It was tough doing those types of [confrontational] scenes. I would throw myself into it.

Helen Gallagher: Nancy Addison was wonderful and such a doll. I would throw parties, and Nancy came to one. She said, "I would love to live in this building." She then bought an apartment two floors above me. The whole cast became my family. I was with some of them for fourteen years. It is a long time to be with a group of people.

Ron Hale: Nancy Addison was an excellent actress. I loved her, and she was like a sister to me in real life. When I look back and think of everybody in the company, there are only three people there that really knew Ron Hale—really knew the inside of me deeply. Ilene Kristen, of course, Nancy, and my dear, dear friend to this day, Geoff Pierson.

Ilene Kristen: I also loved working with Helen. She really assumed the matriarch position. I loved working with Bernie Barrow too.

Ron Hale: Just to be around and work with a caliber of actors like Helen Gallagher and Bernie Barrow was wonderful. I didn't work with Helen as much as I would have liked to. Not being liked by Madame Ryan kept most of our scenes on the brief side. Most of the time she would say "Hello, Roger" and walk away. Just to be on the same stage of a Broadway icon and acting teacher of her quality—she's a legend.

I loved Bernie with all my heart. His Johnny Ryan was just so wonderfully over the top. It should have been and it was perfect. The original cast was all just wonderful.

Michael Levin: I liked Helen Gallagher very much, and she was just terrific. Bernie was a very good actor who was wonderful to play off of. He was a solid force on the show, bringing a lot of positive or negative energy (depending on what was needed) to the scene.

Malachy McCourt: Helen Gallagher and Bernie Barrow were very fine actors. They knew their business. I did not have the experience that they had, and they were extremely helpful to me—telling me how to move or remember lines. They would make suggestions and say, "Why don't you try this or that." I would, and it would work.

Andrew Robinson: Bernie was a real theatre person, so we got along great. He was a professor at Brooklyn College and ran the theatre department there for a while. Helen was the classic trouper. The woman was a singer, a dancer, an actor—no nonsense. She showed up to work—her lines were ironclad learned. She wasted no time. I loved her, and she reminded me of my mother—Irish and a straight shooter.

Catherine Hicks: I remember Maeve Ryan being a tough nut and so was Helen Gallagher. She was intimidating. Bernie was nice. We just acted with each other—nothing more.

Malachy McCourt: I was especially very fond of Bernie. Sometimes I would say things that were totally inappropriate. Helen would be shocked, and Bernie would laugh.

Ruth Mayer: I remember parties on set at Ryan's Bar. They would throw Christmas parties and big parties for things like that. It was very festive. There were no parties at our home or at Claire's.

Rachael Mayer: My father did not hang out with the cast because he was trying to keep that boundary. And he was too busy—three kids and working all the time. I think the cast was really close.

Malachy McCourt: Claire and Paul were not on set much, but I did become friendly with Paul. I would be a guest at his house frequently, and many times Claire would be there. We developed a personal relationship that continued for many years after the show went off the air. I was even friends with their children. I remember Paul's daughters who, when I first met them, were young kids. It was very nice to stay friendly with them all that time.

Most agree that the strong Catholic beliefs of Maeve and Johnny and their tight, loving bond with their offspring helped *Ryan's Hope* stand out from the other daytime dramas at the time. Maeve and Johnny were the glue that held the show together. Audiences watched the Ryan children and their friends run the gamut of soap staples, such as adultery, divorce, premarital sex, living in sin, out of wedlock pregnancies, and threats of abortion, but now it was through the prism of devout Catholics. Maeve and Johnny had to balance their faith with the love they had for their errant family members. This made the show real and gave it a totally new, fresh approach in daytime.

Malcolm Groome: Religion was such a strong part of the show—the modern children being juxtaposed with the strong traditional faith of the parents. I loved the scenes with Helen and Bernie when their characters' Irish Catholic values came up against the more secular lives that their children were leading. Pat was always torn between the two polarities. That was a wonderful push-pull ingredient to juggle.

The show's early success was credited to the sharp writing of Claire Labine and Paul Mayer. Religion played a key part of this working-class, Irish Catholic family's lives, and local politics affected them, as it did for many from that community. This mixture came through via the wonderfully realistic scripts delivered by the writers.

Malachy McCourt: There was a certain earthiness about *Ryan's Hope*. Here you had an ordinary, big Irish family running a saloon in New York and what they had to go through with big-city living. It had regular local New York politics and the stuff that went on with it that made the show so real and truthful. The hold the Irish had on the city wasn't explicit, but it was there. People understood the political power of the Irish, and it was brought out so clearly by Claire particularly. She understood the history of Tammany Hall, and it was all here.

Helen Gallagher: The show was about a family. The writing was absolutely down that hole. *Ryan's Hope*, though, is the children. I thought it was about me, but it was not; it was the kids. And that is how the audience took it.

Michael Levin: *Ryan's Hope* was very different from the other soaps at the start. To have an Irish Catholic family in New York

City that owns a bar as your main family was quite radical. I think it was an achievement of sorts.

Walanne Steele: I think the premise of the show makes it accessible to audiences in a way that some of the sprawling soap operas are not. It was relatable and not escapist. I think people felt they could connect to the characters. On the other soaps, they were usually upper-middle-class people living in the suburbs. They were not down-to-earth the way the Ryans were.

Malcolm Groome: We all felt terribly lucky in those first few years to be working with the superior storytelling capabilities of our writing team. The writing felt elevated, not typical of soaps up until that time. There were several straight years of Writers' Guild Awards [and Emmy Awards] at the beginning of the show, which gave us all such pride.

Catherine Hicks: Claire and Paul's writing was not of a typical soap opera or melodramatic. It was more intelligent, more aware, and more creative. They wrote Faith strong at first. I remember always being frustrated with the role—if you want to become a star, you have to have that ego—because Faith was always second fiddle to Mary. You get tired of it. I was always wanting more of a storyline. It was like trying to convince parents that you are just as good as their favorite.

Ilene Kristen: Scenes were beautifully written. They were *scenes*. We don't have those anymore. Claire and Paul created exquisitely detailed characters, especially with Maeve and Johnny. They were real and a family that was trying to move up the ladder to some degree. But they kept particularly good values.

However, to a few cast members, Paul Mayer seemed to have taken a backseat to Claire Labine regarding the soap's early writing success. This may have been due to Paul taking more of a producer role in the show and the difference in their personalities when interacting with the cast.

Malcolm Groome: Although Paul and Claire were partners, I felt that Claire had the stronger say in things. All the actors were excited whenever we got a script written by her. She always dove into the heart of the show, and sometimes her writing was like poetry. The other writers paled in comparison. The one that came closest to Claire's excellence was Mary Ryan Munisteri. She got what Claire was trying to do.

Andrew Robinson: It is kind of sad to hear that about Paul Mayer because I thought he and Claire were incredibly complementary. The show would not have existed without either one of them, I think. Yes, Paul was a quieter man and less effusive, but he was incredibly warm and friendly—a very decent man.

Malcolm Groome: I would say that Claire was the more gifted script writer of the two. Her scripts were always deeper than Paul's, whose scripts were more prosaic and formulaic. I felt more simpatico with Claire. Paul was a nice guy, but he seemed auxiliary to Claire, who was the main creative force of the show, at least in my perception. I think Paul's role was to be more of a sounding board to Claire's inspiration. I think most of us felt it was Claire's show, and Paul was along for a good ride. Together, though, they were a good team and well respected.

Andrew Robinson: Paul's scripts were good. Sometimes Claire would pop a brilliant script, while other times they were not so brilliant. But who was the better writer? I really cannot say simply because, as I said, they complemented each other. Each of them brought a quality to their work that added to this stew called *Ryan's Hope*. Mary Munisteri was also a wonderful writer. Her scripts were really good as well.

Ron Hale: Paul was just more of a quiet man and more private. We rarely saw his family. But he was just lovely and always wonderful with me. And he was a hell of a writer. But again, Claire was the bubbly Irish lady. She was more outgoing than Paul.

Michael Levin: Claire was the more creative of the partnership, and Paul was the overall organizer. Also, I think it is probably true to say that Claire was the better script writer.

Malachy McCourt: Paul was very intense. I would have to tell him to just relax. I'd say, "You don't have to write classic novels every time you do a script. You could put in some shit. This is not a soap opera anyway. It is a story. Just tell the story, that's all."

There were some people who didn't like Paul. He was more professional than Claire was. He had to act—how do I say this?—less human because she was very softhearted. That was a problem with her and with them as a team.

Rachael Mayer: It was definitely both their show. My father would say that Claire was the heart of the show. She was the liaison with the actors and mothered them. My dad loved her as a writer. She was a poet—her prose was lyrical. He counted on her for that part of the writing. My dad was a playwright, so I would say that he brought structure and plot. He would say, "The course of true love runs dull." He was known to keep it moving. They were a wonderful team.

Ruth Mayer: Claire Labine was the type of person who would make you feel like you were the most important person in the room. She was incredibly charismatic. For the actors to have that kind of mother figure who envelops you with that kind of warmth is very comforting. But the show was 100 percent the two of them. They were equal partners and equally hardworking.

Rachael Mayer: I also would say that my father being married to an actress made him probably more reticent to get personally involved with the actors because he really understood their vulnerability and needed to keep some boundaries. My dad was always the one who had to be bad cop. They were on a thirteen-week cycle, and my dad would have to do the firing. He hated it.

Ruth Mayer: He would have to be tougher because Claire was so sweet.

Ron Hale: Rachael and Ruth's comments are so true. That was absolutely the way it went down.

Although the cast and the crew felt like family in the early years, it was not all moonlight and roses. George Lefferts vacated his role of producer in September 1975 after only three months to return to his production company, George Lefferts Productions. Bob Costello, who worked as a producer on the gothic soap *Dark Shadows* from 1966 to 1969, revealed that he was recommended to the show and took over as producer. Coincidentally, *Ryan's Hope* was filmed in the old *Dark Shadows* studio, and Costello remarked in

1998 to Henry Colman of the *Archive of American Television*, "We had some of the same crew—it was old home week."

Costello revealed to Colman that he did not have input into the stories; that was all Labine and Mayer: "They had to set the tone. There are advantages and disadvantages. Sometimes they have no production experience. They know what they'd like, but you know it's not going to work. Sometimes there was conflict." Per Costello, sometimes production could not deliver the way the writers envisioned and compromises had to be made. Working for Costello was Ellen Barrett as associate producer.

> **Malcolm Groome:** Robert Costello was sort of stern and in conflict with Paul and Claire. He was a good producer, though, and got it done. Robert was on the set, and he had an office in the studio. He was more hands-on. As executive producers, Claire and Paul would make the decisions about the story, laying out the plot and the direction of the show. Robert would execute their vision.

> **Helen Gallagher:** I recall much strife between Robert and Claire and Paul. He was very dogmatic, and they were very loose. They did not get along. Claire was extremely imaginative and would go with the flow. Robert was by the book.

> **Rachael Mayer:** Bob was beloved by both Claire and my dad. I remember being at Bob's house on Long Island. However, I do not think it was smooth and easy all the time. Although they loved him, I am sure they would argue over things, too, but like a family. I have no memories of my dad disliking him or getting into terrible things, just the usual creative stuff.

> **Ilene Kristen:** At first, I found Ellen Barrett to be difficult to deal with, and she could be demeaning and condescending, but I developed a good relationship with her. She was in over her head. You know when sometimes people are underqualified, they act like they are visiting royalty? Everything they do is right and everything you do is wrong. That was Ellen, but I ended up liking her a lot.

> **Andrew Robinson:** I liked Ellen a lot. She was always very kind to me and was very sympathetic when I left.

On the directing front, Lela Swift was a pioneer among female directors, having begun directing live television programs for CBS-TV in the fifties.

In the sixties, she worked on the failed serial *The Young Marrieds* and then had a nice run directing *Dark Shadows*, where she worked for Bob Costello. Another early director was Robert Myhrum, who did not last long despite being a veteran, having worked on *The Doctors*, *The Secret Storm*, and *Love of Life*. He was followed by soap director Jerry Evans. In an interview with Clifford Terry of the *Chicago Tribune*, Evans gave praise to the crew: "The cameramen on this show are saving my ass all the time. They compensate for the actors missing their marks or leaning back too far or whatever. On *any* soap, the cameramen are the best there are."

Ilene Kristen: Robert Myhrum was an old-timer and could be crazy at times. He thought he was Orson Welles and would drive you fucking nuts. We lived near each other, and sometimes I would purposely walk home with him so I could try to get him off my back. The day Jerry Evans replaced him was like heaven.

Helen Gallagher: Lela Swift was lovely, but she drove you crazy. She was very dictatorial. But I got along with all the directors.

Malcolm Groome: I was very fond of Lela Swift and Jerry Evans and enjoyed working with them both. I thought Lela went more for the heart of the show. She delved a little deeper. She was extremely specific in what she wanted you to do, but I also felt that she had more of an emotional connection to the material. She was tuned into it but was a bit ponderous with her directing—her notes would often ask us to play results, that is to be overly demonstrative of what the story was. I think all of us had to have a bit of a buffer to her direction so that we wouldn't overact.

Jerry had a little more facility and was more freewheeling. [He] seemed to trust the creative organic process of the actors. It just moved along a little quicker with him. It did not feel like he plumbed the depths as much as Lela. Don't get me wrong, I loved working with Jerry. I ran into him a couple of years ago in California, and it was great.

Michael Levin: Lela and Jerry very much so had a different style of directing. Lela was very hands-on and very serious. Jerry was much easier, but I did not necessarily prefer working with him over Lela. Because she was much stricter and he was more relaxed, it really depended on how it was going and what we were shooting that day where one could be better than the other.

Andrew Robinson: Lela and Jerry were both terrific people—collegial, helpful, efficient. We would be in and out of the studio—it was great. Lela was more demanding, which I am grateful for. I probably did my best work for her because she was tough in a good way. She did not let you off the hook until you came close to fulfilling the potential that she saw in you. I liked both of them very much.

Malachy McCourt: Jerry Evans, personally, was more tolerant of me because I was not a very experienced actor. He understood that and put up with my shenanigans. Lela was less tolerant, but she got me in shape and made me toe the line.

Ilene Kristen: The first week was frightening for me. I had more dialogue than I ever had in my entire life, and I had not really done any camerawork before. Also, Lela Swift tended to push. I had done a film, but that was quieter than this and not so obvious. Lela pushed and pushed me. I did not do exactly what I wanted to do with Delia, but visually I looked the way I should.

Catherine Hicks: Lela was intimidating but good to me. Jerry was a very nice guy. I have no memories of ever being cramped by either director or one being more or less helpful. It was scary because it is not like film where you can stop—you can't. It was like boot camp.

Ilene Kristen: I preferred working with Jerry Evans, truth be told. I liked Lela but found her to be a manipulating director. Everything with her was choreographed. She'd say, "Count to five. Turn your head." There was a lot to remember with Lela. I used to take copious notes. I'd think, "How am I going to do this and put this together?" There was just so much. Believe me, if you didn't perform the way she wanted you to, she'd be a little cold toward you afterward. Jerry was laid-back and would always thank us. I loved working with Jerry and adored him.

Ron Hale: Jerry Evans did more than Lela did about scenes. Jerry could be very opinionated about what he saw or what he wanted. There again, you could have some sparks between the actors and Jerry, but Jerry's ideas were not stupid. He had a vision about how a scene should go—that's how he read it and that's how he saw it. The actor, on the other hand, might agree to a certain extent, so you would have a discussion to talk out your differences. Lela had been doing this a long time. She was set in her ways. She was a sweet lady and her work there, on the whole, was excellent.

Ryan's Hope was doing quite well ratings-wise in its comfy 1:00 p.m. time slot, sandwiched between *All My Children* and the game show *Family Feud*. Its competition on the other networks was local news or something similar. The show had jumped from the lowest-rated soap at fourteenth place in 1975 to eighth place—ahead of *One Life to Live* and *General Hospital*. It was a surprise, then, when ABC, in January 1977, moved *Ryan's Hope* to the 12:30 p.m. time slot in anticipation of the new hour-long *All My Children* that began in April. The show was now competing for viewers with two other soaps—the very popular *Search for Tomorrow* on CBS and the new *Friends and Lovers* on NBC. Even so, *Ryan's Hope* held steady in the ratings.

Ryan's Hope's problem with the audience was that while it was strong in the Women 18–49 Demo, it always had trouble attracting the traditional older female soap viewer. It was never able to woo away those fans from their long-running serials on CBS and NBC. Although the show focused on a close-knit, loving family, they were Irish Catholic immigrants who owned a bar in New York City. The older audience was not going to abandon the Waspish families of the fictional towns of Henderson or Genoa City or Oakdale for the Ryans in gritty New York. In a 2022 tribute piece to deceased writer Mary Munisteri in the *New York Times*, Gina Bellafante shared a story about her grandmother that exemplified this. She wrote, "One summer in the late seventies, I discovered . . . *Ryan's Hope* . . . but I couldn't get her on board. It dealt with the generational tension between Old World cultural and religious values and the new freedoms embraced by the young; the modernity did not appeal to her." This probably held true to many older female viewers. Hence, the show's household ratings always kept it in the middle of the pack, and it seldom cracked the top five.

Another network change that would have a profound effect on the show was the replacement of Michael Brockman with Jacqueline "Jackie" Smith as vice president for daytime programming. She had worked before at WPIX-TV as director of on-air promotions and at CBS as executive producer for daytime programs. Her approach to the network's soap operas was much more hands-on than Brockman's—much to Labine and Mayer's

dismay, one would imagine. Seymour Amlen was working at ABC as head
of strategy in the network's program department at this time. Shortly after,
he was promoted to head up East Coast programming, which consisted of
Good Morning America, the daytime shows, and children's programming.
Jackie Smith then began reporting to him.

> **Seymour Amlen:** The daytime shows were run by Jackie Smith. I
> had little input into that operation. I thought she did an excellent
> job. She knew all the producers and the head writers of the soaps
> and had a good relationship with them. There was no reason for
> me to intervene.

Time slot and network executive changes aside, the show had to go on. After
the custody hearing, Frank and Delia remain separated and veer off into their
own popular and well-written storylines. Frank is now happy with Jill
Coleridge. Delia realizes it is a lost cause with Frank and, to get back into
the good graces of the Ryan family, agrees to a divorce so Frank can marry the
pregnant Jill. However, she has an ulterior motive. Beginning in the fall of
1976, one of the show's most popular plots began. Desperate to keep her ties
to the Ryan family, an unhinged Delia uses Roger with promises to run away
with him to make protective Pat jealous. They were high school lovers; Pat
broke up with Delia to go to college, and she turned to his brother Frank,
whom she eventually married. Even so, Pat always had a soft spot for
Delia, who took advantage of his feelings toward her a few times earlier
(including engineering him to take her to the Coleridge beach house, where
she knew she would catch Frank and Jill together for her divorce case).

Delia planned to get Pat into the sack, even though he was now engaged
to a more psychologically stable Faith. Delia was so intent on making this
happen that she invokes the wrath of the Ryan family again when she loses
Little John at the playground in Central Park. Distracted by Roger profess-
ing his love and a contest she is trying to enter, she does not notice that her
son has wandered off. Luckily, he is later found safe and sound. Delia then
makes sure Pat knows exactly where she is staying in Boston before her
worldwide trip with Roger begins.

Pat comes to her "rescue," and Delia seduces him just about the time
she is ovulating, as planned. She returns to Riverside with him and bides
her time until she can confirm that she is pregnant. When she does, she
demands that he break it off with his stunned and hurt fiancée, Faith, and
marry her. Delia stubbornly refuses anything less. To prove her point, she

goes to an abortion clinic with no intention of going ahead with the procedure, and makes sure Maeve knows where she has gone. Trapped and now coerced by his parents to do right by Delia, Pat reluctantly concedes to marry her and breaks it off with Faith.

> **Jadrien Steele:** My first memory is shooting this scene and then I hide in some building in the park during a storm. I do not recall how old I was.

> **Walanne Steele:** You were two years old. When you heard the lightning, you said, "What's that?" I think that was the moment you became a real acting character on the show. Before that, you more or less were somebody who sat on the bar or was carried around.

In one of the show's many standout scenes, a fed up Mary rightfully confronts Delia after finding out about the upcoming nuptials. She berates her for using her family for all those years, for her lies and manipulations and failing to take responsibility for herself. Delia turns the tables and shoots back, "You've always hated me. You know why? Because you can't stand your brothers being in love with somebody other than you. And what's really a pity is that you couldn't have married Frank because the two of you are the only people perfect enough for each other!"

Shortly after, Delia miscarries but keeps it a secret by going to a clinic and giving a false name. However, it does not stop her from going ahead with the sham of a wedding. She then stages a phony miscarriage and keeps Pat tied to her out of sympathy for losing the baby.

It was during this point that *Ryan's Hope* introduced its second Hispanic character and, once again, she was a nurse. When the show premiered, Rosalind Guerra appeared as RN Ramona Gonzalez, a character that was gone within a year. As with African American Dr. Clem Moultrie, Ramona was never given prominence in any story arc. Now, Ana Alicia (the creators asked her to use her full name, Ana Alicia Ortiz, to highlight her ethnicity) was hired as the soft-spoken, caring Puerto Rican nurse Alicia Nieves, who was the guardian to her twelve-year-old brother, Angel (Jose Aleman). She fared better than Guerra and became important to the Pat/Delia story because she was the nurse on duty when Delia miscarried. Other new faces were Bill Woodard (Wesley Addy), a wealthy business industrialist, who is a patient at the hospital after surviving a private plane crash, and his younger, sophisticated wife, Rae (Louise Shaffer).

Ana Alicia (Alicia Nieves): I am originally from El Paso, Texas, but was living in LA. I had just signed with an agent named Carlos Alvarado. A few weeks later, he wanted me to meet a casting director named Joel Thurm, who was one of the heads of casting at ABC. Joel said I was a few pounds overweight and did not have any good photos, but he found something interesting about me. He had a screen test coming up for a part that was not for me on this show, but he wanted to see how I would come across on camera. I showed up at the ABC Studios, and I had never seen a camera because I had only worked in theatre. He instructed me to hit the marks, like we do on stage, because it was a three-camera show. He also lent me his sweater to wear because I came only in a T-shirt and jeans. I did the scene, hitting my marks and trying to connect to the material. He then asked me to state what I had done. Because I had no credits, I just said that I loved acting. When we finished, he said he would watch it and get back to me. I was the ninth and last girl tested.

I never expected to be considered for the show. There were girls in the waiting room who had a lot of credits. Right before I came in, I heard one say that she just finished a movie with Paul Newman. I forgot about it because I had a lot on my plate between my waitress job and doing theatre. Then Carlos called me on a Friday and said, "I thought you said that you were a decent actress?" I replied, "I thought so." He then told me to sit down and said, "You have to be in New York by Monday." I was elated and could not believe it. Joel wound up sending my tape along with the others to *Ryan's Hope*. The producers and directors in New York picked me, and I had to be at the studio in three days to start shooting.

Jose Aleman (Angel Nieves): I had an agent named Betty Birnbaum of Associated Talent who sent me out to read for Angel Nieves at ABC. I had done a number of children's shows on PBS. I went through the audition process and got cast. I was thirteen years old. I am not certain, but I think Claire Labine and Paul Mayer were there, but I know I met the director. From what I remember, Ana Alicia was already cast as Alicia, but I did not audition with her.

I was signed to a contract because that came into play when I was cast as Lopez shortly after in *Saturday Night Fever*. It was a small role with two scenes with John Travolta. ABC gave me permission to go shoot the movie. My first day on the set in Bensonhurst was to film the opening with John Travolta walking down the street. But it was crazy. There were hundreds of people all over the place. It was a mob scene. Every time John Travolta came out of the trailer, there was yelling and screaming. The girls were going bananas. People were even climbing on top of the elevated subway tracks to look down at the set. The police were called, and they eventually cancelled the day's shoot. I was called back about a week later to shoot the scene, but then John Travolta's girlfriend Diana Hyland died, and it was postponed again. When they called me back a third time, ABC would not allow me to go. The director, John Badham, decided to pay me anyway, per my contract, and to this day I still receive residuals.

Louise Shaffer (Rae Woodard): Claire and Paul were the writers when I was on the soap *Where the Heart Is.* They called me and asked if I wanted to play Rae Woodard. I was residing in LA at the time because I had just done a show [*All That Glitters*] for Norman Lear. I came back to New York to do this.

They never shared Rae's storyline with me. Claire and I had one conversation. It is sort of funny if you are an actor, but I kind of had a type that I think I played, which was the aristocratic, rich bitch who is very emotional under exterior ice. That is sort of what I did, and that is what they wanted.

I told Claire that I wanted to play somebody who wasn't gloating or pleased with their bad deeds. So many of those characters were sort of one-dimensional, and they knew it. We wanted to create somebody who really justified everything she did. She didn't have a lot of guilt. She didn't have a lot of self-doubt. She knew what she wanted. She knew the way life is set up; you go after whatever you want.

Ana Alicia: I met the producers and the director my first morning at the studio. My contract was for just one year because I was not a principal character. I think they wanted to bring some diversity into the show and they wanted to try out this new character to see if she would work out or not. What is interesting is that in the audition, I did not use an accent at all. Joel did not tell me to use one. I was born in Mexico, but I have no accent.

That Monday morning, I had all my lines memorized because the way it was shot was pretty much like live TV. After the first run-through, Lela Swift says to me, "We were thinking that it would be interesting to give Alicia an accent. Can you please do an accent?" I had never done one in my life. I asked, "Like now?" And she replied, "We are going to film in about thirty minutes." I had the presence of mind to give them what they asked for because I did not want to make anyone upset or anything. However, I said to her. "Listen, I'll do the best I can in thirty minutes, but all I ask is that by the time the contract is done that I no longer have an accent." I was thinking of the future and did not want to get typecast.

Lela then talked to the writers, and they agreed to slowly let me lose the accent. This was a crazy thing to agree to. Sure enough, I threw together the craziest, inconsistent Puerto Rican accent I could come up with considering I had never heard a Puerto Rican accent in my life. It came out like a combination of Mexican and Puerto Rican.

Malcolm Groome: Ana Alicia had no accent at all, but they made her adopt a very exaggerated Puerto Rican accent for the role. She made it work and kept it from being a stereotype because of her good acting and genuine humanity.

Jose Aleman: They did the same thing to me. They wanted some sort of Mexican or Spanish accent. I look very Latin with the high cheekbones and straight black hair—kind of Mexican-looking. I tried my best. I don't know if the accent came across though. I watched some of the episodes, and I think I can hear it a little bit. For a kid, I thought I wasn't that bad in the part.

Ana Alicia: The entire cast was friendly and inclusive, but there was already a community there. I felt more like a guest star. The one person who was wonderful to me from the start was Malcolm Groome. He was a talented actor and just really a warm, caring human being. He reached out to me and would take me to publicity functions, making sure I was photographed with him. He was absolutely delightful, as was Ilene Kristen. She was accessible and incredibly generous. I became close friends with Catherine Hicks. We were both Catholics, and I remember going to her brownstone.

When I got to know Earl Hindman later on, I discovered what a truly kind person he was.

They were all kind, but what was exceptional was the level of talent. These were trained, serious actors. From the directors to the producers, it was a very well-run show. I certainly did not have the acting background like some of them. I had natural talent but no craft, and it was shocking that I could even manage the waters with these actors. I was really like a fish out of water a little bit.

Catherine Hicks: I liked Ana Alicia a lot. She was so sweet, and we had similar personalities. We were more softhearted, and we eventually shared a dressing room.

Jose Aleman: It is funny because it is hard to tell if I was not accepted being a newcomer because as a Latino, you sort of feel that anyway if it is true or not. I did not sense anything like that, though; I was a kid and did not have my antenna up for these kinds of things.

Ana Alicia: Jose was lovely to work with, and I became very friendly with his mother. They didn't give him a lot to do. I would do most of the stuff in our scenes. His character was there to show off Alicia's love and depth as a human being caring for a little brother. It also gave me motivation. They rarely gave Jose anything to do that was really going to be exciting for him, which was unfortunate.

Jose Aleman: I would show up at the studio about seven or seven-thirty in the morning. There would be breakfast out, and we would go over the lines. There was a big rehearsal hall, and we would sit around this large table for a read-through. I was a Hispanic little boy (the first Hispanic actor on the show, actually) among all these white people and was intimidated a bit, but once I got on the set, I was fine. They all were genuinely nice. Next, it would be broken down by scene, and we would do a walk-through. I learned so much doing this show.

Ana Alicia was the nicest and most down-to-earth person you could ever meet. I do not think she had a lot of acting experience then, and that was perhaps her first TV role. She became friendly with my mom at some point. The hair and makeup guys were great. The one crew member who stands out because he was extremely nice to me was the stage manager, Dick Briggs. He was always making sure I was okay or joking with me. A few of the actors did too, but there were also some who were profoundly serious and did not want to be bothered with a kid. Ellen Barrett, the producer, was nice to me too and occasionally would walk into my dressing room to check up on me to see if I was doing okay.

The Emmy Award nominations were announced in spring 1977, and *Ryan's Hope* was up for Outstanding Drama Series and Outstanding Writing for a Daytime Drama Series. Lela Swift was nominated for Outstanding Individual Director for a Daytime Drama Series. In the acting categories, Helen Gallagher and Nancy Addison were nominated for Outstanding Actress in a Daytime Drama Series. When the Emmys were bestowed a few months later, *Ryan's Hope* nearly swept the awards and won every category where it was nominated. Helen Gallagher picked up the Outstanding Actress award for the second consecutive year.

The end of 1977 began on a happy note with the second trip down the aisle for Mary and Jack, followed by a honeymoon in Ireland shot on location in the picturesque country. Filming in Europe was a first for a daytime soap. Labine and Mayer packed their bags, along with their two actors, and headed to Ireland, where they met with a crew hired from London. Per writer Tom Sullivan, the viewers got to see Mary and Jack "pub crawl around Dublin; visit Blarney Castle and take a stab at kissing the stone; spend a few minutes at Queen Maeve's Cairn, St. Columba's tower, and the racetrack at Curragh, where the horses go the wrong way."

The show then suffered a major blow when Catherine Hicks and Kate Mulgrew vacated their roles as Faith and Mary respectively, and Andrew Robinson was let go as Frank.

Catherine Hicks: This was when I got my so-called own storyline [Faith's romance with Mary's jilted ex-boyfriend, Tom Desmond]. It was fine, but I do not recall any wonderfully, challenging monologues about Faith's childhood where we could get a window into her soul. I did not have much interaction with Claire or Paul—I was also too polite and not demanding.

I landed a Broadway show and was very proud. I won the part opposite Jack Lemmon in *Tribute* over Kathleen Turner and Kate Mulgrew. There weren't many ingenue roles on Broadway at that time. At the holiday party, Kate announced it to the cast and crew, which was nice. Claire and Paul wanted me to stay and were going to work it out with the play's schedule. You get a role in a big Broadway show with Jack Lemmon and all of a sudden, it's like, "Wow! What have we got here? Let's try to make this work." Ultimately, I decided it would be too hard to do both, plus we had two months on the road. It was just not realistic. They threw me a wrap party, but Kate did not come.

Ron Hale: When Catherine left us to do *Tribute*, I went to see it and came backstage afterward. She was talking to somebody on stage. She saw me, screamed, ran across the stage, jumped up, and straddled me, wrapping her legs around my waist. She was so good in the show.

Catherine Hicks: After the play closed, I went to Hollywood and played Marilyn Monroe [in the 1980 TV-movie *Marilyn: The Untold Story*]. It was a national hit, and I received an Emmy nomination. I remember getting a long, gushy letter from Claire Labine after this. I felt vindicated. I went on to do films with Francis Ford Coppola, Sidney Lumet, *Star Trek IV: The Voyage Home*, and lots more. I was treated second class at *Ryan's Hope*—everyone was to Kate Mulgrew. It made me very happy to become first class in a bigger world.

Malcolm Groome: Nobody was surprised when Kate quit. She clearly had a lot going for her and was an extremely talented actress. I think they let her out early because she went on to work on prime time at ABC. She already had projects lined up. I did not work much with her. Occasionally, we had scenes when there was family stuff. Kate put such an imprint as Mary on the show.

Andrew Robinson: I got along with Kate wonderfully. What was she, nineteen years old? As far as I was concerned, she was a kid. She made me laugh because she was so sassy and full of herself. She was young and just learning how to act—but obviously a great talent. She has gone on to do what she has done. But at the time, she was like a kid sister to me, and I treated her like a kid sister. We still have a relationship until this day. We see each other occasionally at *Star Trek* conventions [Andrew recurred as Garak on *Star Trek: Deep Space Nine*, 1993–1999].

Michael Levin: The romance between Kate as Mary Ryan and Jack was probably my favorite storyline from the show. It was quite popular. That was because Kate was a good actress, and it was fun to work with her. With soap operas, if you get two actors who work well together and have talent, you can have very powerful scenes because the actors are working together creatively.

Andrew Robinson: I got fired because of ABC. There was one executive who really had a hard-on about me. From the start, he was out to get rid of me. I was fired on Christmas Day. Claire phoned me that night, and she was very upset. She apologized for calling on a holiday, but she wanted to warn me. She revealed that they had been fighting off this guy all year. The sad thing was that I was getting really comfortable in the role. They were writing well for me, and then the axe came down.

ABC used the female audience not accepting me in the part due to *Dirty Harry* as the excuse. I think that was bullshit and how they justified their actions. The response that I got was that people became very interested in having me as Frank and accepted it simply because the character was who he was. He was a complicated guy. My feeling is that maybe ABC wanted Frank to be more of the straight arrow kind of leading man—but I am not sure. But this is water under the bridge—an actor's life. Any actor worth his or her soul gets fired at least once in their lives.

By the time I was let go, I was crushed. Not just because of the humiliation of being fired, but because I felt part of that family. Having said that, getting fired, in the long arc of my life, was a great thing. I was seeing myself buying a brownstone, etc., but there are things in my life I know I would not have gotten to (that were really important to me) if I had stayed in New York doing a soap. It is a very comfortable existence.

2

A Change Is A-Coming, 1978–80

The year 1978 was tumultuous for *Ryan's Hope*. It had already begun with three actors departing as Frank, Faith, and Mary. This was just the start of many more changes that would occur during the next three years—from a roundelay of recasting of more characters, to some misguided storylines, to the eventual sale of the show to the network. All would have a profound effect on the soap.

Having an even bigger, long-term effect on the show was the decision by Claire Labine and Paul Mayer not to accept ABC's offer to expand to an hour. The network, which was thrilled with the show's critical and ratings success, offered them that chance. The creators, however, surprisingly passed on the opportunity, which may have been one of their biggest mistakes.

> **Rachael Mayer:** My dad never wanted it to go to an hour because he did not think they could work any harder. They were working—I don't know—like eighty-hour weeks night and day. He felt that they did not have the manpower to do it. I think he also thought that there would not be any benefit and that another half hour was filler. He may have been a little outdated at that point as a lot of soaps were going to an hour. I think he was just holding on to what he knew and that it was going to be too much work for them.

This decision most likely helped save the lower-rated *General Hospital*, which expanded from forty-five minutes to an hour instead, along with *One Life to Live* in January 1978. Shortly after, its ratings skyrocketed with the introduction of Tony Geary as low-level mobster Luke Spencer, who began an extremely popular (though controversial) love affair with his rape victim, teenager Laura Webber Baldwin, played by Genie

Francis. Their romance and adventures would change the face of daytime soaps forever. Credit goes to new executive producer Gloria Monty, who reshaped the face of daytime soap operas.

However, for Claire Labine, this was not for the better, as she and Paul Mayer would later clash with ABC about the direction the network wanted to take the show. Labine commented in *On Writing* magazine, saying, "Well, when Gloria Monty came on *General Hospital* . . . she essentially took what everybody had been doing, which were longer scenes, and broke them up into a much more cinematic form. When everyone copied it, it became so goddamned destructive. I think serial is a lot closer to theater than it is to film. You start a scene, you build a scene, you pay off the scene."

At the moment, *Ryan's Hope* had to contend with three new cast replacements coming aboard. Twenty-five-year-old Daniel Hugh Kelly became Frank Ryan #3, debuting in January 1978. Former Miss Teen USA, Karen Morris, later Karen Morris-Gowdy, would assume the role of Faith shortly thereafter.

Karen Morris-Gowdy (Dr. Faith Coleridge #4): I had just transferred from Wyoming to NYU. I was doing a lot of commercials here and there. I got a call that *Ryan's Hope* needed an immediate replacement for Catherine Hicks. I thought, "Oh my gosh!" I was a freshman in college and had stumbled upon *Ryan's Hope* at lunchtime and we were all obsessed with it—Jillian and Frank and Delia, all of them. It had incredible characters and the grittiness of New York. It was not set in some fake place but New York. When I got the call, I could not even imagine filling in for Catherine Hicks. I went to the audition and I read. I was very green, and I had very little experience in terms of soaps and theatre. The casting agents really thought that I was right for the part, so I read a couple of times. Then I auditioned with Tom McGreevy. I remember leaving the studio after that thinking, "I got this." It was that kind of feeling that was wishful but not wanting to jinx it. I walked straight from the studio to St. Patrick's and thought, "If it's meant to be, it is meant to be." They called me that night and offered me the part. It was quite a thrill.

With Kate Mulgrew out as Mary, Labine and Mayer wanted to kill off the character because they felt no one could come close to playing the part as well as Mulgrew. ABC interceded and pushed for a recast. Mary Carney became Mary Ryan Fenelli #2, making her first appearance when she and Jack returned from their honeymoon. She did not have time to make an impression because, after only a few months, she was released from her contract. Carney was replaced by stage actress Kathleen Tolan.

Rachael Mayer: Killing off Mary was true, and I even remember the kind of cancer they were going to give Mary Ryan. I was in the car with my dad, and he said, "There's this cancer where you get a mole and you're dead within six weeks." I thought that was so awful. They could not see another actress in the role and felt no one could replace her. If Kate was leaving, they were going to end the character. However, ABC did not give them a choice.

Michael Levin: I did not know they were thinking of doing that at the time and the decision that was made. In retrospect, I think very much so they should have killed Mary off then, but I do not know what would have happened story-wise.

Malcolm Groome: I knew Mary Carney before she was cast as Mary. We had done a commercial together where we were on a roller coaster. It was refreshing to then meet Mary again in a different setting. I do not recall the circumstances of her departure. We had minimal scenes together and got along well.

Ilene Kristen: Mary Carney was not the right choice at all to play Mary.

Malcolm Groome: I also knew Kathy Tolan. I had seen her perform in three plays, the last being with Helen Gallagher, where they played mother and daughter. I finagled an introduction to her, and we ended up dating for a while. As I recall, Helen recommended Kathy for the role of Siobhan Ryan when it was open for casting. That didn't happen for some reason, but they did audition Kathy and later decided to cast her in the role of Mary Ryan. For some reason, she did not quite click, either for the audience or the producers. I knew her theatre work and thought she was a compelling, charismatic actress. I have the utmost respect for her as a human being.

Ilene Kristen: I thought Kathleen Tolan was very good, and I didn't think she was a bad replacement for Kate.

The Pat/Delia story continued to roll on as well, with the newlyweds making each other miserable. Pat becomes addicted to uppers to keep his energy level up to deal with his challenging job and his demanding, neurotic wife. In the what-goes-around-comes-around department, Delia is accidentally pushed down a flight of stairs by a zonked-out Pat. However, unlike when she shoved Frank, Pat does not run away but gets her immediate medical attention. As she recuperates, Roger threatens to reveal the truth about when Delia miscarried, which he has pieced together from talking with the evasive Alicia and listening to a sedated Delia's mumblings. Terrified of the repercussions, Delia suffers hysterical blindness, which she milks even after she regains her eyesight to hold on to Pat. This all comes to a head on an ocean cruise that Delia guilts her in-laws to let her and Pat take in their place. Delia's ruse is quickly unearthed by a married letch who wants to have sex with her, and his wife makes Pat question that Delia may be lying to him. In what is considered one of the soap's most popular scenes, while they are in their cabin, a suspicious Pat tosses a hairbrush to Delia, who instinctively reaches out to grab it, revealing that she is no longer blind.

Once Pat and Delia return home from their disastrous trip, Pat finally learns from Faith and then Roger the whole miscarriage saga in the Coleridge kitchen, minutes after Faith (despite reservations from Maeve and Roger) ties the knot with Tom Desmond to stop him from being deported. This was a powerfully enacted episode with writing that cut Delia to the core. First, she gets an earful from an angry Faith, which Pat overhears. Then the weepy blonde desperately tries to defend her indefensible actions, but all the tears in the world cannot stop an irate Pat from heading straight to Annulment Central after Roger fills in the missing details. To say the Ryan family is disgusted with Delia is an understatement.

Karen Morris-Gowdy: I was thrown in, and it was a lot. It was the height of the storyline with Pat not marrying Faith and all of that with Delia. It was five days, six shows a week. It was a lot of memorizing and learning how to be on a set and how to be a professional. I was working with all these people that I was absolutely in love with from watching the show. I was like, "There's Roger! There's Delia!" I was starstruck. All of them were very respectful and somewhat welcoming, but they had worked with Catherine and had all started out together. I was the newbie on the block, and they knew I did not have a lot of experience, which was obvious. They really made me pay my dues, and I am very grateful for that. In the end, they became family to me.

Claire Labine and Paul Mayer nurtured me a lot. I was not coming off another soap or from the theatre, like a lot of other people. They really believed that I fit the character that they had always pictured. They said, "You are how we always envisioned Faith—physically, your manner, your humor, your vulnerability. We will guide you and help you through this." And they did.

Malcolm Groome: In Claire and Paul's bible, Pat and Delia had been lovers originally when they were in high school. They had a history, and Delia always had, in her heart, a soft spot for Pat. She was desperate to be a Ryan, as was evident in the storyline. Whichever brother she could attach herself to she did, so she could be part of the family and be loved and accepted by Maeve. That is the way she went.

Pat had a deep connection to Delia. He was always attracted to her sexually, which he sublimated into taking care of her even when they were acting on that. He was her protector and used his influence in the family to even protect her from Maeve and Johnny.

Ron Hale: Delia went too far here. Roger hated the fact that Delia was so dependent on the Ryan relationship. She would do anything to be a Ryan and be a part of that family. It would drive Roger crazy because he would try to get through to her that she did not need them. Roger would tell her that she was strong and had so much to offer. He could not understand why she felt so unfulfilled because she was not a damn Ryan. A lot of his actions were coming out of his love and care for her.

Ilene Kristen: During this storyline, Malcolm and I went very deep into our characters. We had been on stage together in *Grease*. He was an understudy, and I was one of a few people that treated him well. Understudies in *Grease*, including Richard Gere and Treat Williams, were treated like shit. I maintained great relationships with all these guys. Malcolm was amazing, and we had such intense scenes. I absolutely loved, loved, loved working with him.

Malcom Groome: I just loved working with Ilene Kristen. The character was delicious, and so was Ilene! Anything with Ilene was a pleasure, especially the hysterical blindness story. Tossing her the hairbrush and seeing the "blind" Delia catching it was a favorite moment for both of us. I loved that storyline, but I think there was more sympathy for Pat than Delia because she started playing him and cheating about the pregnancy. I thought Pat and Delia had a wonderful love story going, even with all the machinations.

Ilene Kristen: The scenes on the boat were some of my favorites. First, Joe Bova, the actor who played the guy flirting with Delia, had a kids' TV show I used to watch, and I was completely starstruck to be working with him. I couldn't believe it. Those scenes were hysterical. The great Alice Drummond played his wife.

Malcolm Groome: Pat was really shamed by his parents after he got Delia pregnant. That is probably when Pat got told off the most and when his parents were most disappointed with him. Pat was too mild-mannered to stand up to them and not marry Delia. That is why I felt he sometimes was not as fun to play compared to how he was written originally.

Ilene Kristen: Even during that storyline, I received nothing but love just walking down the street. I think people saw an actress underneath that character. Although, I would get people sternly say, "Oh, Delia!"

Malcolm Groome: Pat had to take care of Delia and with his work schedule he had to take speed. I think when it was revealed, they said it was a caffeine dependency. Now they would probably have it be cocaine. Then when she became blind—that whole arc with Ilene was the best storyline I ever had. It came full circle when Pat let go and Delia fell down the stairs at the hospital, where, years earlier, she had pushed Frank. In the eighties, I do not think I had a storyline that compared to that. They never wrote me as interesting a story to play.

Malachy McCourt: Ilene Kristen was just lovely. It was great fun working with her. We had a great understanding of our characters. I was going to be sarcastic and she was going to be hurt, so we had fun with that.

Ana Alicia: Kate Mulgrew was treated like she was the core of the show. However, for me, it was always Ilene Kristen. The creators were crazy about Kate. It was like a love affair between her and them. She was a marvel to watch. Ilene, however, taught me how to play different sides of a character. I just think she made *Ryan's Hope* flow. Kate grounded the show with her intelligence—she is a very intellectual actor, and I had never met anyone like her in my life. The way she would approach things was so interesting to me, and I was in awe. Ilene gave Kate that foil to be able to do what she did.

It was just glorious working with Ilene. I deeply appreciated her as an actor and as a human being. She was incredibly generous, incredibly present, and incredibly gracious. She was so talented and always looking for the real connection to the material she was given. She would put herself emotionally through so much to get where she needed to get. I was a huge fan of hers and just loved working with her. I really liked her personally. She and I became friends.

Catherine Hicks: That is really true what Ana Alicia said about Ilene. She had a better instrument and wasn't in her head. She had a lot of emotional scenes. I liked Ilene because she wasn't mannered. For example, Kate Mulgrew does Katharine Hepburn. Ilene is just Ilene doing Delia and played the role more moment to moment. Ilene had a good instrument, and she used it well in ways no one else was doing on the show. She had such a challenging role, and she pulled it off. She deserved an Emmy nomination. It wasn't fair that she did not get one.

Ilene Kristen: Both Ana Alicia and Catherine Hicks were very talented actresses, and I liked working with them. I was very lucky because I had a role with Delia that could go in many, many different places. They were extremely lucky in finding themselves in roles with far more freedom after they left. Ana Alicia, because it was her first job, felt very restricted as Alicia. And it was also probably confusing for her because the role was a bit undefined, and they had her do an accent and then they didn't. But she was the right person for the role, for sure. As soon as she was out of the clutches of *Ryan's Hope*, she really looked like she was having fun and happy to be playing a wild and crazy character like Melissa on *Falcon Crest*. From an inexperienced actress, she became a total pro and very exciting to watch.

I want to say the same thing about Catherine Hicks as Faith, which was another restricted role. Catherine, though, was a bit surer of herself and did not lack for confidence. Her portrayal of Marilyn Monroe was luminescent—it was exquisite. She did a beautiful job and was able to do things that she would have never been able to do with the refined role of Faith. I ran into Catherine in LA while she was shooting *Marilyn: The Untold Story* because we had the same hairdresser. I am not saying that she lived the role, but I could tell that she was so immersed in it that seeing her was part Catherine but more Marilyn. She was so deeply into that character, and you can see it in her portrayal. She is magnificent. Sometimes on the show, you never got to see the full capacity of what someone really has as an actor. You learn a lot doing a soap, and it almost makes every other job easier. Both Ana Alicia and Catherine took what they learned and ran with it.

Jose Aleman: Malcolm Groome and Earl Hindman were extremely kind. Malcolm would go out of his way to talk with me. Justin Deas was just as friendly. All of them were so professional. It was one of the best acting experiences in my life. Behind the scenes, between takes, we would joke around. When Angel was in the hospital with convulsions, I used to make them laugh. While we were waiting, I would act out a convulsion and drop to the floor. It was funny.

Ana Alicia: Helen Gallagher and Bernie Barrow were nice to me, but I hardly had any scenes with them. Both were lovely and I admired them—talk about *actors*! To me, they were such grounded, theatre actors—intelligent and very connected to their characters. I would sit there and watch them work sometimes because they were so smart in their choices. I felt so lucky to be there working with them.

Jose Aleman: I had a couple of scenes with the Ryan family— Maeve and Johnny. Helen Gallagher was not very approachable, but then again, I did not have a lot of scenes with her. Bernie Barrow was nicer. The few scenes we had together centered around baseball or sports.

The Emmy Award nominations covering the March 1977 to March 1978 period were announced. Most felt that Kate Mulgrew (for her final year on the show) would be honored with a nomination, but she was snubbed. Writing for *Afternoon TV* magazine, critic Merrill Cherwin remarked, "Andrew

Robinson was nominated for his role on *Ryan's Hope* . . . while the luminous Kate Mulgrew, who turned in one magnificent performance after another, was not. Also at *Ryan's Hope*, the bewitching Ilene Kristen, whose work in a consistently demanding role continues to amaze us, was ignored—again." *Afternoon TV* remedied that and awarded Kristen its award for Best Supporting Actress. Michael Levin was nominated for Outstanding Actor in a Daytime Drama Series, and Lela Swift was nominated for Outstanding Individual Director for a Daytime Drama Series. The show picked up additional Emmy nominations for Outstanding Drama Series and Outstanding Writing for a Drama Series. It won for the latter category only.

> **Ilene Kristen:** I thought I should have been nominated for the Emmy. I did not think about politicking for it—my mental energy was focused on doing a good job in that role—but knowing what I know now, that was very stupid. The producers were always pushing Helen Gallagher for the prize. I did win an acting award from one of the magazines of the time.

> **Michael Levin:** I only went to the Emmys the first time I was nominated. I was surprised because I did not think I had any scenes that were worthy. I don't know why I was nominated and don't understand the selection process. I suppose people liked my work, but then you have to submit a scene. I thought I didn't have any good ones.

> **Andrew Robinson:** I was back in California when I found out I was nominated for the Emmy. They flew me to New York to attend the ceremony. I *so* wanted to win for no other reason than to stick it in that guy from ABC's face. I even remember the episode I submitted. It was based on one scene—Frank discovers Jill's infidelity, and I just break down. I was very proud with the work I did on that episode because Frank was crying, screaming—it was an emotional episode.

Frank, meanwhile, has become immersed with the Woodards after meeting them at the hospital. Impressed with Frank's good looks, charisma, and political savvy (sort of a young John F. Kennedy), Bill offers to back him for state senator. Of course, things take the typical soap opera twists and turns. Bill learns that Rae is carrying on with his doctor, Roger Coleridge, but before he can cut her out of his will, he suffers a fatal heart attack, leaving his wife an extraordinarily rich widow. She then turns her attention to candidate Frank and is there for him with financial and emotional support, as he is still reeling from his problems with Jill, caused by a lie. After learning how far along she is with her pregnancy, Jill realizes Seneca, and not Frank, is the baby's father. She remains mum for a period of time but finally confesses. Prideful Frank is unwilling to raise another man's child, although the hypocrite expected Jill to play mother to his and Delia's son. And, once again, Frank and Jill break up.

> **Louise Shaffer:** In a strange way, I was not one of the core characters. I wasn't there when the show was really finding its feet. By the time I came on, I think the show had its balance and a special thing [in the Ryans] that audiences responded to. I wasn't really a part of that, and my character wasn't a part of that.
>
> I really don't know what the relationship between Rae and Roger was about. We were friends with benefits. I always saw that relationship the way Rae kept her relationship with a much older man. I assumed Roger was certainly not the first attractive young guy she had sex with because she had an older sick husband that she adored. That is how she kept her marriage together. But that was my backstory that I created. The writer in me says why load that relationship with anything more? It was something a little bit unique and special. You had the more fraught relationships for both Roger and Rae—he with Delia and her with Frank. There weren't those kinds of friendships back in those days with people just doing it for the fun of it with no strings attached.
>
> **Ron Hale:** I totally agree with Louise about the Roger and Rae relationship. We had tons of good scenes together. We were connivers. These two characters were very similar, and it made sense that they were comrades.

While Frank is dealing with his complicated personal life, Delia, realizing that she has truly lost the love of the Ryan family, has a real mental breakdown and disappears. Because she has cried wolf so many times, Delia's brother and the Ryans think it is just another stunt. They opt not to look for her. A few days pass, then Angel Nieves stumbles upon a disoriented Delia on a bench in Central Park. He tries to coax her to come with him, but she declines. Sensing something is not right, he informs Alicia—who is now working as Rae Woodard's assistant. The wealthy widow liked how Alicia cared for her husband and made the financially struggling nurse an offer she could not refuse. After hearing about Delia, Alicia shares her brother's story with Bob, who finds his sister.

> **Ana Alicia:** Louise Shaffer was a lovely, incredibly talented woman. When Alicia went from nurse to working for Rae Woodard, though, I do not remember having any discussions with the writers about this change for my character. I really feel that they focused—and rightfully so—on their main characters. I think the rest of us just winged it. I would get a script, not fully understand it, and being the good girl that I was, I did not question anything and just did the best that I could. We did have readings in the morning, and sometimes during that they would give me a note or two, but there was not much attention given to me, and there was not much attention that I asked for.

> **Jose Aleman:** My storyline ended, and they dropped me. A few months later, my agent called and said that *Ryan's Hope* wanted me back if I was interested. Of course, I said yes. It was for two or three episodes. We were hoping that would turn into more work, but I guess it did not pan out. I had a wonderful scene with Ilene Kristen that I will never forget. Angel comes upon a confused Delia in the park and tries to help her. Ilene is so professional. I came in and we did it.

Once Delia is located, and with nowhere else to turn, Roger of all people takes her in, hoping this will force her to finally grow up, get some real psychiatric help, and gain her independence from the Ryan family.

Around this time, in mid-1978, Malcolm Groome followed Kate Mulgrew out the door and decided not to renew his contract. The popular actor was replaced by John Blazo. The character going forward was written more sensitively and soft-spoken, perhaps to match Blazo's personality and to highlight the contrast between Pat and his rival, burly Tom Desmond.

> **Malcolm Groome:** Pat was the nice guy. I had a lot of fans because of that, but as an actor it did not give me the texture or full spectrum to play. I had ambitions to do more. As wonderful as it was to be on a soap, it is a limiting medium in terms of character development. They can write your character to further the plot, but it may

not be true to the character or evolve them or make them stronger. I thought Pat was weakened at that time in terms of being a strong character. I decided to give it a whirl out in California.

It was sad to leave all my friends on the show, but I also knew we would all stay in touch, which we did. Most of us had started with a three-year contract. In retrospect, I wish I had stayed on the show longer.

John Blazo (Dr. Patrick Ryan #2): I had only been in New York for three months when I was cast as Cassio in a repertory company doing *Othello*. The cast included Ron O'Neal of *Superfly* fame and Kate Mulgrew as Desdemona. Kate and I had the same agent, who was the best in New York. Kate had just left *Ryan's Hope*, and the creators, Claire Labine and Paul Mayer, saw me in the play. They knew Malcolm Groome was going to leave, so in the spring, after the run of the play, they asked me to read for the part of Pat Ryan.

I had several auditions, and the most important one was the screen test on the soundstage. They brought me in, and I have a scene with Karen Morris, who played Faith. By this time, it is June of 1978, and I had showed up in Ne w York in September of 1977 just to see if I could get work. I had no formal training. So now I am sitting opposite Karen, almost having a complete nervous break-down. I knew enough to go with what I had—that was my forte. I came with a sense of vulnerability that I made no attempt to hide. The scene that I read for had Pat confessing to Faith how much he loved her and how he always loved her from afar. He then had to kiss her. I am sitting on the sofa beside her and I say the lines, but she is barely giving me any response as an actor. I get to the moment when I am supposed to kiss her, and I cannot. I will never forget that moment. She looked into my eyes—it was a Montgomery Clift moment—and I could not even hardly look at her. She saw that and kissed me. The producers and director all rushed down from the control room because it worked, even though it was not in the script. It just happened spontaneously. I brought something different to the part. I then had a second test with Tom McGreevy, who played Tom Desmond. The network was not sold on me and thought I looked nice but could I stand up to my rival, the Irish boxer? I knew what they wanted, so that, too, went well because I channeled my dad. I had to face Tom down without doing anything physical. I guess they felt I was man enough and that sealed the deal.

After I got the part, I did not have much interaction with Paul Mayer. When I auditioned in the studio . . . it was Claire who came down from the control booth to offer me encouragement and tell me what I did worked. Sometime after, she invited me to dinner with her husband at her home, which was an unbelievable Victorian brownstone in Park Slope. In 1978, it was transitioning, but it certainly was not the Brooklyn we have today. I went there on several occasions. I am thinking this is good, the creator and head writer of the show likes me. I then decided I wanted to buy a home and Claire helped me find one, which I bought. I considered Claire my friend.

Karen Morris-Gowdy: John Blazo was such a sweet guy. It was hard to fill the shoes of someone like Malcolm Groome or a Catherine Hicks. Those soap relationships make you become the character—you just do, when you do it five days a week every day. It is difficult to come in—not impossible—but we all had to stick up for each other. Andrew Robinson left as Frank and Daniel Hugh Kelly took his place. We were all kind of the newbie group.

Also departing (either of their own volition or contracts not being renewed) were Justin Deas as Dr. Bucky Carter and Hannibal Penney, Jr. as Dr. Clem Moultrie. Neither Bucky nor Clem were recast. Deas was charming and quirky as Bucky but was never given a major lead storyline. He seemed to be there just to lend an understanding ear to his buddy Pat or his uncle by marriage, Seneca. And despite having such a handsome and talented African American actor as Penney on a show that was set in New York City, which had a sizable Black population, the writers never brought his character to the front burner either. He had a lot of screen time but only in support of the young white residents who reported to him at the hospital.

Malcolm Groome: I thought Hannibal was a particularly good actor and very charismatic. In my opinion, he was given short shrift on the show and never got a well-deserved storyline. I knew he wasn't happy about it, but he didn't complain too vocally for all to hear. Despite his disappointment, he always showed up and did a good job. I very much enjoyed working with him.

Ana Alicia: Hannibal Penney was a tall, dark, and handsome kind of guy. He was also a good actor, and he had a good role. They could have done something more with him.

The same goes for my character. They were playing with a character that was not connected to the Irish family and not in the grain of the story bible they had created initially. With Delia, although she was from the other side of the tracks, she still fit to the overall story. They wanted to bring in diversity, but they were not sure what to do with Alicia. Because she came in so sweet and almost pale in character, there was no oomph about her. There was nothing they could do. I would be playing her with the accent and that sugar-sweet kind of stuff, but it doesn't go anywhere. It was a mixture of they didn't know what to do with her and I didn't know what to do with her. I did not have enough hutzpah or experience to go up to them and say, "This is what I see. This is what I think would be interesting." I do not think there was ever a chance for that character.

Ruth Mayer: You write best what you know. Claire and Paul each had Irish ancestry, and they are writing from the heart. My dad sent us to the only truly integrated private elementary school in New York City. My dad was the classic liberal and started a group to try to get private schools to take kids of color. But I think in terms of diversity on a show, Lena Dunham had *Girls* on just a few years ago, and she is apologizing now for having no Black storylines, but she said, "I wrote about the kids I knew at Oberlin." So, I think Paul and Claire wanted—in their heart of hearts—to be more diverse but . . . probably connected with their own stories most of all.

Rachael Mayer: That is the classic soap opera conundrum. You have the family, and if you are bringing new characters on, do they light up with the audience and can they get a following if they are not connected to the family in a deeper way? They have to marry someone, and it is tricky.

Ruth Mayer: Claire and Paul were being radical just by setting the show in a hospital in New York City. The soaps were Pine Valley and the land of tea parties. When we were growing up in New York City in the seventies we would always get, "Your parents are raising you here?!" It was dirty. The subways were full of graffiti. It was gritty. Forty-Second Street was not Disney-fied.

Ana Alicia's contract was also not renewed. After being part of Delia's lies and manipulations and now Rae Woodard's, the good-hearted nurse had had enough. She quits her job working for Rae and then bids farewell to Bob Reid at Ryan's Bar.

Cast members were not the only ones leaving. Executive producer Robert Costello also left. He revealed that Labine and Mayer fired him. When asked why, he quipped, "Because I was saving them from themselves." Getting serious, he replied, "There was frustration on both our parts." There were no hard feelings, and they remained good friends. Costello was even at the Emmy Awards ceremony the following year to pick up his second Emmy when the show was voted Outstanding Daytime Drama Series for the 1978–79 season. Labine and Mayer replaced him with Ellen Barrett, who was promoted from associate producer. Nancy Horwich took Barrett's old job.

Ana Alicia: I wasn't stupid. Honestly, I knew by the lack of interest from the producers and writers from the very beginning that Alicia was a character that they were going to try out for whatever reasons—maybe ABC asked them to—and I knew I was never going to be important to the show. They never gave me any encouragement or indication that they wanted this character to stand out. I knew it was a one-year contract and fulfilled my obligations the best I knew how. The fact that on my first day they threw an accent at me proved that they did not care about the longevity of me.

Ryan's Hope taught me that good, sweet little girls don't have interesting things to do and often get written off. They kept my character so consistent with her moral convictions that there was no interest there. As I look back now—not that I was in any way a consummate actress like Kate Mulgrew was—but her Mary was the wholesomeness in that show, but she was intelligent, vibrant, and stood up for herself. If they had given any of those traits to Alicia, I think it would have been a conflict with the heroines on the show. Alicia had to be kept a certain way; therefore, there were never any meaty scenes to play or growth in that character.

Three months before my contract ended, my agent had already set me up to work at Universal Studios under contract. I was offered a virginal role on *Flamingo Road* and told the casting director I did not want to play those parts anymore. She said, "I will find you something else," and six months later, I got Melissa on *Falcon Crest*. It is so interesting, but then I never thought to compare Melissa with Delia or put them side by side. Now that I think about it, Ilene Kristen must have influenced my creativity because I did admire her work. I never consciously made choices based on anyone but every time you work and are exposed to that kind of talent, it has to impress you.

Karen Morris-Gowdy: Bob Costello was a sweet but tough character. I remember ad-libbing lines one time. He came out of the control room and said, "I know you are new at this, but we pay the writers a lot of money to write this dialogue, and we don't pay you to write. We pay you to act." I said, "Okay." He ran the ship how it was supposed to be run—his way. And that was that. Ellen Barrett was a little more forgiving. I loved working with her. She was very good to me.

Amid all these departures, two new characters appeared on the canvas. Nancy Feldman was a dancer and the daughter of Dave Feldman (Joseph Leon), a political bigwig backing Frank's campaign for senator. She is injured in a car wreck and winds up in Riverside Hospital being cared for by Pat Ryan. Continuing with the show's recent bad luck with casting, the original actress hired, Lisa Sutton, was quickly replaced by Megan McCracken and then Nana Visitor (billed as Nana Tucker then), who played the part the longest.

Nancy becomes romantically involved with Pat after he finally accepts losing Faith to Tom Desmond and his guilt for inviting a pregnant Faith (who was not thrilled to be with child) onto Bucky's houseboat where she was accidentally stabbed in her gut. She later miscarried and is truly saddened with the loss of her child, which psychologically scars Tom, who becomes violent. After Nancy recovers, and with her dance career over, she begins working for Frank's campaign. At first, Nancy wants to keep it platonic with Pat due to her being devoutly Jewish and he a Catholic, but mostly because she knows that deep down, he still pines for Faith.

John Blazo: I do not recall Lisa Sutton but do remember Megan McCracken. You never know as an actor, but I think they let her go because of me. They did not like the way we looked together or how our scenes went. When they cast Nana Tucker, she and about forty actresses auditioned opposite me. They were trying to pick somebody they thought worked better with me than Megan, though there was nothing wrong with her.

Nana was great. She is one of those actresses who is just simply present. She was a professional dancer and had a small part in a horror movie [*The Sentinel*]. She always gave a simple, clear, compelling performance. She made me want to be her—to get to that place as an actor. I do not think I ever made it. Whatever chemistry I had with Megan, it was a little better with Nana.

During my first few weeks, Helen Gallagher looked at me and said, "You're my son that I thought would be a priest. I thought you would be the one, but you became a doctor." I just grinned. I am attracted to powerful women like that. She conducted a singing instruction class for actors at her home on the Upper West Side weekly. I made it my business to go. She was not the most open personality in the world, but I knew she liked me and vice versa.

Bernie Barrow was easy to like. Early on, he came over to me—they were all trying to bring me under their wing—and stood beside me. Without looking at me, he said, "So, you came to New York and got yourself a job." Then, I did not know exactly who he was but learned he was a character actor and taught at Brooklyn College. Bernie had a standing poker game with Earl Hindman and a few others. I never became part of that because I am not that kind of guy. I really did not become friendly with any of the cast outside of work. That was probably my downfall if I wanted to be a professional actor. You have to hang out. You have to get yourself into an acting class or be around a group of people who write or sing for inspiration. I was a loner.

The other new cast member was Sarah Felder (a redhead with a long, wild mane of hair) in the role of Siobhan, the youngest Ryan offspring, newly returned to the family fold along with her wolfhound, Finn McCool, who always seems to be in the way of Johnny and Maeve. Siobhan's presence immediately brings back childhood rivalries with her older sister, Mary, rivalries made worse when Siobhan bonds with her brother-in-law, Jack. Felder was the breath of fresh air that the soap needed at this time because it was going through a period of dead seriousness. The youngest Ryan is quirky, free-spirited, funny, and calls out some of her family members for their hypocrisy. She is a loyal friend of Delia's and sticks up for her. She has no qualms reminding her parents that "Saint Francis" cheated on Delia with Jill first. Siobhan also earns her parents' displeasure when she later accepts a job at Planned Parenthood, which is the Catholic church's archenemy due to their abortion services. Siobhan is pro-choice, and that does not sit well with Maeve. She also sides with Jack when he complains that Mary's new job at the TV station is keeping her away from him and their child too much.

Michael Levin: I thought Sarah Felder was a very good actress, and I enjoyed working with her. She was talented. Beyond that, I felt it would have been better to go in the direction of a romance between Siobhan and Jack. I often thought it would have been nice to work with her more. However, it was a decision by Claire and Paul not to, so there is nothing more to say about it.

John Blazo: I loved Sarah. She was a lot like my mom. I do not know what it is with women like that. I was hardly acting with her. When they bring you on and know you have never been in front of the camera, they know how hard it is for you. You've never seen marks on the floor. You've never had a rehearsal for the cameras. And you would shoot it live top to bottom with no stopping the way it was later. Sarah was cast after I got there. Six months into my time, Lela Swift called down from the control booth and said to me, "Okay, John, listen. You're happy now, okay. Things are better, so let's go with that, okay. Let's have some fun." That was exceedingly difficult for me still at that time as an actor. That is why my scenes with Sarah were so great because I could relax. She'd been to Juilliard and was well trained. She said, "Just pretend there is something in your shoe." She was just giving me an idea for a moment in the scene. I appreciated that. We were together in the good times. It was after I left that Sarah had a tough time with the network.

Ilene Kristen: I loved working with Sarah Felder. She was not glamorous but earthy in a beautiful way. She was very well trained. She was extremely unique—extremely real. She was a very skilled actress with a lot of oomph—she was very right for the character. But she had her own ideas about doing things and did not understand about authority at all. She butted heads in a way that, at times, was not appropriate.

You have to understand that you did not write this series and that you are part of an ensemble. When someone does become a squeaky wheel, it is unfortunate because it makes them look like it will be too labor-intensive to work with them. I did not personally find this, but I used to talk to her and say, "You need to calm down and not get so angry." She trusted me, but she had her own issues—and I am not even sure what they were—that made it impossible for her to just say, "Okay. I'll do this."

I understood that because at the very beginning of the show, I had eye makeup rolling down my face and my hair was a mess. They were trying to clean me up, and I said, "Look, my character has just been through the mill. Can we just let it go on the air for a week or two and see how it plays? If it doesn't work, I'll do what you need me to do." But it worked. I was lucky and pretty much got to things the way I wanted to do them. Artistically, people trusted me. I didn't have those same issues and also, I was a good egg. I was a hard worker, and I was kind to people.

I think Sarah could get very brusque with people, and she had an angry streak. Sarah respected me to the point where she would share with me what her grievances were, and I would calm her down.

The introduction of Siobhan greatly affected Mary's character, especially in the eyes of viewers. She was still written as being opinionated and strong-willed to some degree. However, while Kate Mulgrew was able to walk that fine line, keeping Mary a fan favorite with most of the audience, current replacement Kathleen Tolan arguably could not keep that balance. She also was hindered by her storyline.

Whereas Mulgrew's main adversaries were her stubborn paramour Jack and deceitful Delia, Tolan's Mary battled the likable Siobhan with whom a condescending Mary seemed to always find fault. The hostility between the sisters reaches a boiling point after Siobhan accidentally lets it slip to a reporter that Maeve has two grandsons, almost exposing that Frank is Edmund's father (Rae had convinced him to keep this a secret from the public) during the height of his senatorial campaign.

Siobhan then becomes involved in a story about tenants' rights after meeting Ethel Green (Nell Carter in an early TV role), an influential member of the local community. She, Jack, and rival Wes Leonard (David

Rasche), aid Ethel and her neighbors in their battle with their landlord. It gets so intense that the company tries to knock off Siobhan, but Jack saves her, getting injured in the process. This and the attraction they have for each other causes an even more serious rift with her sister, Mary. The writers also flirted with a romance between Siobhan and the brash, outspoken Wes.

John Blazo: I was astounded by David Rasche. He was *amazing!* I had not worked with him before or knew who his character was. I had a scene with him, and I show up on set. He is in a bed with an eyeshade on. He pulled it up to his forehead and said to me, "I am just working with this." He was remarkable.

It is so personal, so you are always going to have favorite directors. Mine was Jerry Evans. He and I liked working with each other. He admired the fact how I came to New York, my background, and who I was. He supported me. It was different with Lela Swift probably because of how she came up in the business. She was a tough woman. I was afraid of her. She was always a hit-your-marks type of director. I remember she embarrassed me in a bed scene once. I was lying under the covers in my underwear or something—I cannot remember with who—and I hear her voice booming down from the control booth saying, "Don't touch yourself, John." I could not believe it. I never had any disagreements with her. I got along with everybody.

During this period, other major storylines included the Faith/Tom Desmond fantasy story, complete with the spirit of his deceased love, Teresa Donohue (Alexandra Neil), taunting him with vicious thoughts about Faith lying about not loving Pat. This plot was another one reminiscent of *Dark Shadows*, which is subtly referenced in the dialogue when Terry responds to Tom about his and Faith's planned trip to an upstate lake house. She says, "The lake—so cold and clear and quiet. And the mountains rising straight up out of it—all dark and shadows." Teresa goes on to cajole a confused Tom that it is the perfect place to off his wife, and he almost succeeds, but he comes to his senses just before she goes over a waterfall in a rowboat. She is later locked in a basement where she becomes ill. Delirious with fever and reliving her time trapped in the cellar at Riverside Hospital by Kenneth Castle, Faith still has some fight in her and stabs the deranged Tom in the chest while screaming for her daddy. She passes out, and he carries her out to the road, where he collapses. They are found and are transported to

Riverside Hospital due to the lack of equipment at the local clinic. When Faith recovers, she reveals that Tom tried to kill her just as he suffers a heart attack.

Karen Morris-Gowdy: I knew where my storyline was coming from. Claire and Paul loved it because they had been over in Ireland filming with Kate Mulgrew. They fell in love with Ireland and all the mystic and ghostly kind of stuff. I knew as writers and creators how they developed this story. It was a fantasy for them. They invested a lot into it. Economically, it was a big shoot on location in, if I remember correctly, Mohonk Lake. It was very cold and a tough shoot. But it was fun to do. And I loved working with Tom McGreevy.

For me, I was so new at this and so thrilled to be working with this group. The story was what it was. I didn't second-guess it. You are going to pay me to show up and work with these wonderful people every day—I will do whatever. I was not in a place to say this storyline is ridiculous. It might have been. I just don't think the audience grabbed on to it.

The triangle with Frank, Jill, and Seneca still remained extremely popular and was enhanced once Rae Woodard sets her designs on Frank. After Jill and Seneca's son, named Edmund, is born, he needs a transfusion and Seneca learns that, based on his blood type, he cannot be the father and stays quiet because he is afraid he will lose Jill. Roger becomes aware of his nephew's true parentage and blackmails Seneca to reinstate him to his former position at Riverside Hospital in exchange for his silence. Once the truth is finally revealed, Jill leaves Seneca and tries to reconcile with Frank, but his senatorial aspirations come between them when his political backers urge him not to claim Edmund as his son until after the election. Tired of waiting for a torn Frank to decide if he can reconcile with Jill and raise their son, conniving Rae, who desperately wants to become Mrs. Frank Ryan, arranges for her rival to find Frank in her romantic clutches in Frank's hotel room. Her scheme succeeds, and Jill rushes back to the dishonest Seneca, who truly loves Edmund despite not being his biological father. Soon after, they are wed.

This was considered one of the show's best storylines. Geri Jefferson, writing for *Soap Opera Digest*, described Frank and Jill to a T and beautifully summed up why these characters had their detractors in the viewing audience. She opined, "When two strong-willed people try to be lovers, there is invariably a conflict. Both seem able to do whatever moral or immoral thing they please while still managing to be terribly righteous." She then added that with Frank, his religion and his relationship with his deeply Catholic mother should have affected his behavior. It did not. After listing all the transgressions that went against Maeve's religious convictions, Jefferson wrote that he was able to "still find favor in his mother's eye. Somewhere along the line, it has been decreed that Frank can do no wrong, and when he does, it's always for a reason."

It was during this time that Daniel Hugh Kelly really came into his own as Frank and owned the role. He still brought out Frank's unlikable traits (i.e., acting the jerk about Edmund, putting his political career over all else, etc.), but his boyish charm had more than half the audience on his side, while a lot of viewers decried Roger for putting himself above doing the right thing and not telling Jill the truth.

Daniel Hugh Kelly (Frank Ryan #3): I have only fond memories of all the great writers, directors, producers, crew and, especially, the wonderful, patient and unbelievably talented actors who all contributed to make *Ryan's Hope* one of the best daytime serials to ever air.

That show, and everyone involved in its creation and production, certainly deserves it. Sadly, many of the most talented are no longer with us. But I can attest that everyone was deeply committed, gracious, and beyond generous—who desired only to do their best work, for the sake of each other as much as for an extremely loyal audience. I miss them all and have since the day I left.

Helen Gallagher: I liked Andy Robinson, but I think Daniel Hugh Kelly was my favorite. We just hit it off, and I liked the way he acted and conducted his behavior.

Jadrien Steele: My parents kept changing, but I was not confused by it. As an actor you just accept it and play off it. As my mother said, sometimes you have better or special rapport with some over others. For me, I got along super well with Danny Kelly. He took more of an interest in me than the other actors. For example, if we were doing a scene, he would give me some acting tips in a nice way, which I appreciated.

Walanne Steele: I remember Danny once telling Jadrien not to act like R2-D2. He was always trying to get Jadrien comfortable. He was particularly good interacting with a child.

Ilene Kristen: Daniel Hugh Kelly is a great actor and had a real sex appeal.

Ron Hale: Danny could be very volatile, but I do not mean that in a bad way. He was a younger actor, and with many younger people when they are starting off, they have ideas about what they want to do and want to be. I think it took Danny a while to adjust to some of the mediocrity that you have to deal with in our business and especially in daytime. You have to take the bad with the good. Every day can't be *A Streetcar Named Desire*. You have to fight, as we all did, to keep our characters in line.

John Blazo: Danny Kelly and I shared a dressing room. He never offered any advice to me, but I think if I asked—but I was afraid to—he would have, but I did not want to mess with what had been working for me—if it ain't broke, don't fix it. Danny was a son of an Irish cop and was great.

Rachael Mayer: Daniel Hugh Kelly . . . fit nicely into the role. Danny was great and . . . beloved.

As the year wound down, Faith is released from the hospital and returns home with Pat by her side. Thinking they now have a chance at happiness, Faith learns from Seneca that Tom has opted for risky brain surgery to remove a chemical imbalance that may be the cause of his hallucinations and irrational behavior. The Ryans remain loyal to Tom and are at his side. Despite that he unconsciously tried to kill her a second time in the hospital, Faith concludes she should be at his side as well since he is taking the risk to be with her.

The show then took a big hit when powerhouse original cast member Ilene Kristen called it quits and decided not to continue as Delia. Since the breakup with Pat, Delia had ensconced herself in Roger's apartment. He guided her on how to fend for herself and to break ties to the Ryan family. The pair then decided to take their relationship to the next level and elope to Las Vegas.

She takes the money she got from Frank in their divorce settlement and invests in the commodities market and makes a killing by secretly investing in whatever commodity Maeve mentions in her kitchen that day. Obviously, the devious side of her remained, even though she was maturing, and she continued being a thorn in the side of Tom and Faith, who live above her in the Coleridge brownstone. She even schemed to take over Faith's portion of the home while Faith was recuperating in the hospital after her harrowing trip with a demented Tom by using custody of Little John as the reason she and Roger need more living space. However, a clever Maeve calls Delia's bluff and lets her take Little John over Christmas night and then extends the stay by pretending that she hurt her back. After a few days with a demanding toddler, Delia is happy to give him back and drops any ideas of obtaining her son full time. Although Delia had some amusing moments during this period (including flaunting her newfound wealth by parading around Ryan's Bar in a garish fur coat with matching hat), it seemed it was not enough for Kristen to stick around.

Robyn Millan (ex-Vicki Lucas Hathaway, *Where the Heart Is*) stepped in as Delia for a handful of episodes before newcomer Randall Edwards became the permanent replacement beginning in March 1979. A graduate of the California Institute of the Arts, she was a well-trained stage actress living in Los Angeles when she tested and got the role. Her Delia was less calculating and more scatterbrained than Ilene's interpretation.

> **Ilene Kristen:** I have to say that at the beginning of the show it was so hard—although that original cast was so powerful and great to work with—and such a burden at times. I had to cry so much. That is tough to do all the time. I wanted to do comedy. I didn't want to work with Lela Swift for a while. I was not unhappy there, but I wanted to go to LA before I turned thirty. Paul and Claire were very upset with me for wanting to leave. They persuaded me to stay for an extra six months.

> **Randall Edwards (Delia Reid Ryan Ryan Coleridge #3):** I was living in Los Angeles and had done a screen test for *General Hospital*. They were looking to recast Delia because Ilene Kristen left to do other things. I didn't get that part on *General Hospital*, but they sent the tape over to casting at *Ryan's Hope*. They flew me to New York to screen-test, and I believe I did a scene with Ron Hale. There were several actresses testing that day. They had scheduled me last. At the end, Ellen Barrett came over the speaker and made sure it got on the recording when she said,

"Delicious." She put her two cents in, and it was lovely. She was always very supportive.

I had never watched a soap opera and was not familiar with *Ryan's Hope*. I found out that it was the only soap opera set in a real place, which I found really interesting. The whole theme of the show [was] about an Irish immigrant family working hard and running a business and being very strong on family values. As Helen Gallagher used to say, "the hope." The hope was passing it on to the next generation—the children. That is why she and Bernie are holding up Little John at the end of the opening titles. That's the hope—the hope that we build a better world for our children.

John Blazo: This was a time of transition, even though it was only three years into the life of the show. What was interesting is that when I showed up, Kate Mulgrew had already left, and they seemed to me to be focused on trying to replicate her or kill the role. Ilene Kristen was there when I started, and one day I showed up, and there was Randall Edwards, playing Delia. You could not replace Ilene. Randall was a wonderful actress, but I would have loved to have had more scenes with Ilene. There were so many cast changes around me that I was aware of the instability. There were no complaints, but I think there was an awareness that you could be replaced. Not so much for Bernie Barrow, of course, but for the rest of us.

Karen Morris-Gowdy: I loved Randall Edwards. She was so sweet and so different than Delia, just as Ilene Kristen was. Ilene was a hoot, and I loved working with her as well. She kept you on your toes and was so good. That was a hard transition just because Ilene is Ilene and such a great actress. She was the big hit of the show between Jill and Delia and Mary at the time. People really missed Ilene, who had a huge following. I know Randall had a hard time stepping into Ilene's shoes. But she worked very, very hard. She was very quiet and kind of unto herself. She was not a group player but extremely dedicated. There was nothing not to like about working with Randall. She was always prepared, very kind, and she loved what she did. It was fun.

Ron Hale: It was tough when Ilene left. Randall Edwards was quite different—you were not going to get an Ilene. Randall had a different way of working and studying. She would go behind the set and sit there to work on her lines. We didn't spend as much time working together on scenes and hashing them out prior to doing them.

Randall Edwards: I had a desire to internalize in order to come more truthfully to a scene. I would spend a lot of time putting myself in that situation and imagining—and also running the lines in my head again so I could have them at the tip of my tongue.

When I first started on the show, Delia was extremely verbal—she talked and talked and talked. I had tons of lines to learn and often four or five days a week. I wasn't used to that. I also was not used to a teleprompter. I did not want to rely on it because I wanted to be in the imaginary reality. I never wanted to look over at it and take me out of character. I used to pay a high school girl to run lines with me at night. I would have them down and totally integrated so I could come in and say them more for myself and not have to rely on the teleprompter. I did that until I got used to memorizing that much dialogue each night by myself.

The year 1979 starts on a shockingly sad note. In a tragic accident, Edmund is killed in an explosion at the Coleridge beach house, and his mother, Jill, is severely injured trying to rescue him. This not only shocked the Ryan and Coleridge families, but the audience as well since it came shortly after Faith's miscarriage. The viewers never expected that they would blow up a child.

Karen Morris-Gowdy: That was devasting with Edmund. It was a tough storyline. I was a sidebar in that and not really part of it. It was very dark, and I don't think anyone in the cast loved it. By killing him off and Faith's unborn baby prior, it left the Coleridges childless. It was a family show and always about family, but there were hardly any children on it. The Coleridge siblings had no kids until the mid-eighties.

Despite not having his medical license, Seneca performs a life-saving surgery on Jill that threatens his future, but Roger and Faith come to his defense with the hospital board. Jill survives, but, despondent over the loss of her son, she becomes hooked on painkillers. Tom is recuperating from his surgery but temporarily loses his eyesight in the process. He is apologetic to Faith and wishes to set her free, but she remains at his side. She enlists Frank to help Tom with his immigration status and allows Tom to recuperate at her home despite her newfound closeness with Pat, who is a bit perturbed with the situation. Delia, meanwhile, is still making money in the commodities market using an unaware Maeve. A desperate Johnny, after giving a loan to his wife's family to keep their farm in Ireland from falling into bankruptcy, wants to make a quick buck, too, despite Delia's advice not to invest.

Jill beats her addiction and dumps the domineering Seneca, who always seems to know what is best for Jill. Frank shocks his family when he proposes to Rae. Some of the show's best scenes were with a disapproving Maeve unsuccessfully trying to hide her dislike of Rae and her disgust with the pending nuptials. Seeing Rae try to suck up to Maeve, who was not going to change her mind, and then confronting her future mother-in-law were some of the show's most riveting, well-acted moments.

Meanwhile, Johnny is playing the commodities market and loses not only his investment but also the bar. Enterprising Delia steps in and saves the day. At first insulted with a $50,000 offer from Rae to give Frank an annulment so he could remarry in the Catholic church, she counters with an offer of $83,000 (just enough to bail out Ryan's Bar). Rae gladly obliges. Delia is now the owner (unknown to Maeve and the rest of the family per Johnny's plea) and does her best to try to pretty it up, much to the consternation of Johnny and Kevin the bartender, who fight her the entire way. Delia becomes distracted when she eventually loses all her money too. Desperate to recoup it and not wanting to let her husband, Roger, know, she has sex with her sleazy, married stockbroker, Dan Fox (Peter Ratray), to make up her losses.

Louise Shaffer: I think Rae was a woman who really didn't have a moral compass of any sort. Maeve did in a good way—not self-righteous but just a woman who genuinely knew her values, knew what she believed, and knew what she felt was right and wrong. Maeve really had that locked down, and God knows Helen played that. I think that is very intimidating to somebody who knows in their gut that they really don't have that. They do what is expedient and what is pragmatic without any morals. On top of that, Helen Gallagher carries something with her that makes you want to please her. I suppose your persona bleeds into the character. I admired Helen greatly for the incredible career she had, to how smart she was, to the excellent work she did on that show. Perhaps that leaked out somehow.

Randall Edwards: When we did the commodities storyline, I went to a commodities brokerage firm and talked to somebody. At that time, I could really explain what the commodities market was and how it worked. This sprung the Crystal Palace storyline and the restaurant was modelled on Tavern on the Green. I actually got to go and talk to the managers there and got a tour of the bakery, the kitchen, and the offices. I loved being able to do all that research and bring some authenticity to Delia's storylines.

Malachy McCourt: This was a fun storyline, and I had a lot to do. But even here, my character had no backstory or any family members mentioned. On the other hand, do people really know much about the bartenders who are serving them? I used to throw in a communist line once in a while. At one point I adlibbed a comment about Karl Marx and Claire loved it. She asked, "What made you think of that?" I said, "Because I'm the left of Karl Marx." She thought that was very funny and kept it in but it never arose again.

For the 1978–79 season, *Ryan's Hope* would have another banner year, scoring wins in June for Outstanding Daytime Drama Series, Outstanding Direction for a Daytime Drama Series, and Outstanding Writing for a Drama Series. Unfortunately, its nominated cast members all went home empty-handed—Michael Levin for Outstanding Actor in a Daytime Drama Series; Nancy Addison and Helen Gallagher for Outstanding Actress in a Daytime Drama Series; Bernie Barrow and Ron Hale for Outstanding Supporting Actor in a Daytime Drama Series, and Louise Shaffer for Outstanding Supporting Actress in a Drama Series.

The Faith/Tom Desmond story chugs on. A girl named Poppy Lincoln (Alexandra Neil) is hired to care for a still-sightless Tom, who is unaware that Poppy is the spitting image of his former love, Teresa. Not realizing that Poppy is also a nutcase who wants her life, Faith invites her to live there until Tom's eyesight returns. When it does and he reveals that Poppy looks like Teresa, Poppy decides to impersonate her as much as possible to win him away from Faith.

Meanwhile, Pat has totally moved on from loving Faith to loving Nancy Feldman, who is commuting back and forth to her job at Frank's senatorial office in DC. The physical distance between them is not their problem, though—it's their disapproving, very religious parents. They are perplexed as to how this mixed-faith marriage can work. Delia is determined to get back on Maeve's good side after she learns how Delia used her to make her investment choices and inadvertently caused Johnny to lose his money and the bar. Meddling Delia then hatches a scheme to break up Nancy and Pat by constantly throwing her together with a new Jewish doctor at Riverside, the handsome Adam Cohen (Sam Behrens).

> **Randall Edwards:** Marriages of mixed religions was a big deal. For some people, it still is a big deal. I thought it was a relevant story to try to put out there and explore in front of an audience, hopefully shedding light on it with a more progressive outlook.

> **John Blazo:** I know the writers were writing for me. They saw this sensitivity I projected on stage, and that was what they saw in the audition scene. They wanted to see if that would work with Pat and get traction, hoping it would boost the ratings. The problem was, it worked when I was opposite Karen Morris and Tom McGreevy. However, when they later shifted the storyline to me and Nana, it just didn't. There were no fireworks overall.

The Faith/Tom/Poppy storyline comes to an abrupt close. As an obsessed Poppy does her neurotic best to imitate Teresa and to seduce Tom away from his wife, he still chooses Faith. Poppy, without putting up a fight, suddenly leaves New York, which is surprising considering how determined she was to win Tom. Amid Alexandra Neil's departure, the show once again recast two main characters. Kathleen Tolan was out as Mary Ryan Fenelli and was replaced by Nicolette Goulet, the daughter of crooner Robert Goulet. John Blazo was fired, and Robert Finoccoli took over as Pat Ryan. He lasted for about three months, until the writers decided to wrap up the Nancy and Pat story in the fall. Pat gives up on their romance due to the pressures put on them by their overbearing families, Nancy leaves for Texas, and Pat, after a change of heart, soon follows.

> **John Blazo:** I was there for a full year. My agent called me and told me that I was replaced. I will never forget it because we just bought that house in Brooklyn. My agent said that Claire would let me work one day into the next pay period so I could get paid for the next three months. It is always a shock when that happens, even

though you know you can be replaced. It was early in the morning, so I got dressed and went to the studio, which I was fairly certain people did not do. I went in and you had to pass by the mail slots, and my name was gone.

I walked into Ellen Barrett's office and thanked her for the opportunity. I then went and thanked almost every single person there. I even went down onto the studio floor, where they were rehearsing. The reason it is not done is because it is like you have leprosy and you are touching them. What I heard later is when they decided to replace you or let you go, they gave you a party and just did not shitcan you in the middle of the night. That was not the case for me or all the people who were replaced around me. But I was damned if I was not going to go into that fucking studio and say goodbye to people like Helen Gallagher, who I liked and know liked me. They were all warm to me, and it was like we are all in this together. I went up to my dressing room and sat with Danny Kelly and Bernie Barrow. Earl Hindman and I got along greatly. I was not just going to walk away with my tail between my legs.

I was never told why I was fired, nor did I ever hear from Claire Labine. I wrote her a letter thanking her for everything, and I never heard back. I was told that the actor after me was shorter with dark curly hair and was on for a few months. I deliberately never watched myself then and did not watch after I left. To this day, it still befuddles me, and I do not get that casting change.

I watched the show years later when SOAPnet reran it while I was working as a hospice nurse. I finally saw the scene when Pat gets drunk and ruins Nancy Feldman's family seder meal. They write scenes weeks in advance, and I thought, "That's my scene!"

Ruth Mayer: Claire did not like conflict, so maybe she just sat that one out. She always wanted to be adored.

Karen Morris-Gowdy: I was so young and had no idea what was going on. I am sure at the time I thought, "I hope I have a job," because everybody was getting axed around me. I don't know if they did not renew Tom McGreevy's contract a few months later or if he wanted out. Perhaps the writing was on the wall there, but we did not know it, so that is why they abruptly ended it with the character of Poppy. If they were not going to renew Tom, what were they going to do with Poppy? So, goodbye, Poppy.

Two staff members, Tamara Grady and Laura Rakowitz, joined the *Ryan's Hope* production team around the spring of 1979 to work behind the scenes. They would remain with the show (in various jobs) until its cancellation. Another staff member ABC Television hired a few months later was Art Rutter, a twenty-one-year-old fresh out of college, who became one of the show's two studio supervisors/coordinators. He reported to Broadcast Operations and Engineering at the network. Art joined Gary Donatelli in the same department at ABC. He had come aboard the year prior working as a camera assistant on *Ryan's Hope* and some of the other ABC soaps.

Gary Donatelli (camera assistant/technical director): I was a member of the union and worked as a camera assistant—a mere cable boy. I hopped between soaps. At *Ryan's Hope* I reported up to the technical director [George Whitaker], who was a real sweet guy. He managed the camera operators, the sound people, and the videotape editors. He was like the left arm for the director, and the associate director would be the right arm.

I remember coming into the studio where *Ryan's Hope* filmed. It was one of the smaller studios but homier than the bigger ones, and they served real beer from the bar's taps on Fridays! It always seemed nice and quiet in there, with the exception of someone like Ilene Kristen as Delia, who was yelling or crying. I remember approaching the stage for the first time—it is a wonderful place since you are in this dark limbo and then you see the set and the people on it as the characters and the bar and the big boom and the cameras behind it, and it all filters out into darkness. As I was helping someone move their camera up to the next set—we used to shoot the show in order, like live TV—I remember us rolling up and seeing Ilene and this other actor and thinking, "Oh my God. This is the real deal. This is the big time." In that point of my life, I was watching in awe.

Tamara Grady (production secretary/stage manager): I was not familiar with *Ryan's Hope* when I took this job. I had been working in an insurance company where one of the agents worked with the same accountant used by Claire Labine and Paul Mayer. I was leaving the company and wanted a job in the arts in some way. I didn't care if it was television, radio, theatre—anything. I contacted the show cold by sending in a letter. I really had no background in television, but I did have experience in management.

When I went for the interview, they told me I was overqualified for the job. I replied, "I know that, but I believe in learning the job from the ground up. If I start here, you will eventually promote me." The producer was Ellen Barrett, and she understood I was making a midlife career change because her sister had just done the same thing in her thirties. We just hit it off. I'm a Gemini; she's a Gemini. They liked the things I had to say, so I got the job.

As a production secretary, I oversaw getting out all the schedules and things like that. Mostly clerical work but I made changes to forms and such. I knew how to run things from my background.

Laura Rakowitz (production assistant/assistant director): After I graduated from Queens College in 1969 with a degree in English, I moved to Los Angeles. I couldn't find a job and, in those days, women were secretaries, nurses, or teachers. I went through the Yellow Pages, starting with the letter A, and then went backward from the letter Z. I got a job at Universal Studios as a secretary and quickly moved up to production assistant. I then became one of the first women to be promoted to producer. I was the associate producer on *Kojak*, *The Incredible Hulk*, and the short-lived show *Cliffhangers*. I also worked on *Columbo*, *McMillan and Wife*, and *The Rockford Files*. Some of the young, hip men at the studio kind of helped and moved me along. I was extremely lucky—no casting couch. I was truly blessed and worked on terrific shows. Television in the seventies was very prolific with big stars. The last show I worked on got cancelled. I was missing New York and my family there. I moved back and lived with my parents for a few months.

Through contacts, I wound up at ABC and *Ryan's Hope*. I had never watched a daytime soap and so it was a whole new world for me. I had to make a lot of adjustments before I even understood what was going on.

Ellen Barrett hired me, but I had to go through Claire Labine and Paul Mayer. They were very instrumental with me working there. I liked them and they liked me. However, Ellen was my queen and savior. She was terrific.

I started as a production assistant and worked my way up to associate director. I directed some second-unit footage on location in New York City.

Art Rutter (studio supervisor/coordinator): I was from Long Island, with longish hair and was kind of cocky but not arrogant. Everybody wondered how I got this job and thought I must be related to someone at ABC—I wasn't. A studio supervisor/coordinator was a studio manager, and the soaps had two: one would come in the morning for the light call and someone who would stay and reset the show for the next day. We would switch back and forth every few weeks. The job would entail getting in for the light calls, checking in all of the stagehands that were assigned to come in and fill out their timesheets. It was important to get them to respect you. These guys were in their fifties and sixties, and I was their boss at the studio. They had tons of experience and were a tough group of guys. They liked me because I was a real guy and did not act like a boss but would sit down and talk things out with them. The same applied for hair, makeup, wardrobe, the sound effects person, and the stage manager, who was DGA [Directors Guild of America]. Everyone else was IA [International Alliance of Theatrical Stage Employees, Moving Picture Technicians, Artists, and Allied Crafts]. I would oversee the people in the studio. I would stay on the floor for rehearsals and in the control room for the taping of the show.

I don't know if it was a financial situation or not, but the *Ryan's Hope* studio originally was in the old *Dark Shadows* studio in the Hell's Kitchen part of Manhattan. In those days, Hell's Kitchen was just that—it was a dangerous area. We joked that we were in the last outpost for television. *All My Children* was shot up on Sixty-Seventh or Sixty-Eighth Street in these huge double-size soundstages. *One Life to Live* was done on Sixty-Sixth Street between Columbus Avenue and Central Park West. They had very large dressing room areas and studio space. You could pass someone in the hall and not even know them. We were in a shithole of a studio, and everybody was in each other's face. It was like a New York apartment with everybody on top of each other. I think because we were away from everybody at ABC, that is why there was a lot of bonding at the time. Paul and Claire were never there that often, though.

Gary Donatelli: I worked a lot with Laura and Tamara. They were great. Part of what was so wonderful was that we all were excited to have jobs at a TV network, and as we got older, we realized how lucky we were. But the reality was on that kind of show and that kind of a schedule, you had to be good at what you were doing or you wouldn't be there the next day. It was really that simple. To be good at what you were doing was that you did your job but you also had a positive attitude. Laura and Tamara had that big time. Another thing I liked about working on the soaps was to be working in an environment where women were allowed and encouraged to be powerful.

A new mobster storyline was introduced in summer 1979 that would change the direction of the show for the next few years. ABC reportedly approved it but only if Italian surnames were not used. The network did not want to offend any Italian American viewers after the stir *The Godfather* movie caused a few years prior. Siobhan falls for the handsome Joe Novak (Richard Muenz), who owns a small fleet of fishing boats docked in Sheepshead Bay, Brooklyn. He is Jack's former friend and is a guest on investigative TV reporter Mary Ryan Fenelli's local news show about the alleged crimes of his uncle, Tiso Novotny (David Clarke), who is the proprietor of the Harborside Restaurant. After being introduced to Siobhan, Joe is immediately smitten and begins to romantically pursue the Irish lass. Tiso charms the Ryan family, especially Delia. However, as time goes on, they begin to believe the stories that say he is a mob kingpin, even while Siobhan and Joe's love for each other continues to grow. This story brought newfound excitement and danger to the serial. Siobhan and Joe became a popular star-crossed couple, and for some they even eclipsed Mary and Jack. It also attracted new, younger viewers that advertisers coveted, and the uptick in ratings proved it.

Malachy McCourt: Introducing the mob into the story in a way was truthful. New York had mobsters, and they would be in people's lives. Later, when they started bringing monkeys and that kind of nonsense into it, that was not part of *Ryan's Hope*.

Randall Edwards: David Clarke was a sweet man. Sarah Felder and I would hash out things about the story. I know that she wanted the whole abortion conversation to be more progressive than what the writers were comfortable with. I loved her face. I loved her performance. She was a wonderful actress. I did not know Richard Muenz very well, but he was a nice guy.

Art Rutter: David Clarke was an okay actor, but he could never get his lines. We did more pickups [re-filming part of a scene from a specific point in the action] with him than any other actor. On a Friday afternoon when you are trying to get out of there, if he was in the last scene, you knew he would never remember his lines and we'd go, "Aw, damn!" We would have to keep on extending and extending tape. There was a lot of moaning from the crew then.

Ron Hale: I became buddies with Richard Muenz. I loved working with Richie. He was such a character. However, I felt the mobster storyline had no reason being there. Once again, you are grabbing for straws. They brought in some good actors to do it. But again, it was like *why?* It was a soap opera. It was daytime TV where at that time probably 90 percent of the viewing audience was female. Over the years, women I met, just walking down the street, would tell me the same thing, "It's my half hour a day where I can put my feet up, give the kids a nap, and I can watch my story." So, what the hell, bringing in the mafia?! Obviously, they now wanted to reach an audience beyond these housewives, and it did work to some extent. But I think they began neglecting their core audience in the process.

In the fall, Senator Frank Ryan is headed to the altar with Rae when he gets trapped in an elevator with Jill, who is days away from relocating to San Francisco. When they emerge, he realizes he still loves her and wants to be with her—to Maeve's delight. A jilted Rae is furious, and hell hath no fury like a Woodard scorned. She helped Frank get elected and has the ammunition to take him down. She secretly uses it, and he is forced to resign his seat due to an influence peddling scheme because his signature is on papers incriminating him. He vows to clear his name.

Shortly after, the show saw the arrival of another new character. Turning up on the doorstep of Rae Woodard is her seventeen-year-old daughter Kimberly Harris (Kelli Maroney), an aspiring actress. While growing up in Kansas and in high school, Rae had become pregnant by a local boy. He went off to college in San Francisco. Rae gave birth to a baby girl and left her in the arms of her mother before relocating to New York City. It was there, while working as secretary in Woodard Enterprises, that she met and then married its founder, Bill Woodard. Even though she is now a wealthy woman, she did not claim her daughter. Troublesome, reckless, and self-centered, Kim has come to confront her mother and demand what she feels is owed her. Kim immediately gets into trouble when her purse is stolen at a coffee shop by a low-level drug dealer named Duke (William Converse-Roberts), and she is knocked unconscious trying to stop him.

Once awake at Riverside Hospital, she becomes smitten with her doctor, Adam Cohen, but her mother immediately puts a stop to it. Kim also meets Seneca, whom she finds interesting and thinks would be perfect for Rae. To get them together and help lose their inhibitions, the misguided teen laces a batch of homemade brownies with marijuana, sending Rae to the emergency room. A contrite Kim is comforted by an understanding Seneca and decides he is the man for her despite their vast age difference.

This would be the start of one of the show's most controversial storylines. Reportedly, it made actor John Gabriel, the father of two daughters, a bit uncomfortable and confused why the writers would take his character in this direction. But the professional that he was, he did his job despite his trepidation.

Louise Shaffer: I was only supposed to be on the show for a brief period. This was at the end of my two years there. What happened as I understood it (and again you must know how little I really knew of what was going on), there was a story needed. Jeffrey Lane, who was a friend of mine, was at that point writing after starting out as a production assistant. He was now writing damn good scripts. He was in a story meeting, and by that point I did want to stay on the show. Normally on a soap opera, I would do it for a year or two then leave. I had a lot of personal reasons why I wanted to stick around.

They knew that the show needed a sexy young girl—a nymphet, because ABC wanted them to bring in younger characters. My understanding is that Jeffrey suggested that Rae had a long-lost daughter. I guess they thought I was a good foil for the Ryans. Rae had this past, and it was a satisfactory solution. It was a way for me to hang on to the gig and it was a way to bring a younger character, which the network wanted. That is what brought me the longevity.

Laura Rakowitz: ABC wanted the writers to create a teenage character, although I never got the feeling they didn't like doing it.

Kelli Maroney (Kimberly Harris Beulac): I auditioned for it, just like everyone else. It just so happened that I'd only been in NYC for two weeks to go to conservatory school. I had no agent and one photo of myself and was sent to audition basically by an apartment rental lady. I know I'll be telling this story forever because it's so unbelievable. I'll live in gratitude for it for the rest of my life.

Louise Shaffer: I loved Kelli Maroney from day one. I thought Kelli has something amazing about her. She's just got charisma. It's really that simple. We were kind of old souls jointly, I think. We had the same total love of acting and at the same time an understanding of what you are up against if you are an actor. She had it quite young. We're both survivors—very tough in our own way. I think whoever did cast Kelli picked up something in both of us that was very much alike.

Kelli Maroney: Louise taught me everything I know. She could have had me for breakfast, but instead helped me with everything—playing an evil character, crying on cue, you name it. Her friendship is one of the highlights of my life. There is nothing I wouldn't do for her.

Ron Hale: I loved working with Kelli. She was such a sweetheart.

The writers skillfully integrate the Joe/Siobhan, Mary/Jack, Delia/Roger, and Kim/Rae/Seneca stories together over the course of 1979 and into 1980 and 1981. Jack volunteers to help Kim identify Duke and accompanies her back to the coffee shop. Later, after relaying Kim's story to Mary, she becomes intrigued, and they all return to the café with Kim, who sees Duke with the Man in the Green Hat (Harris Laskawy). Spotted, they run off as Mary calls the police.

On the personal front, Mary is still acting antagonistic toward Siobhan because of Jack, despite her sister's recent engagement to Joe. Johnny's distrust of Tiso comes to a head at an engagement dinner that Tiso throws for his nephew and Siobhan. The party is crashed by an irate Anna Pavel (Joan Lorring), whose husband works for Joe and now has disappeared. She all but accuses Tiso of having him rubbed out because of the $500 still owed him. Although Tiso tries to calm her and assure her he had no idea where her husband is, not all the Ryan clan believes him. A few days after, Jack goes to speak with Mrs. Pavel and her teenage son, Michael (Michael Corbett). She changes her tune, assuring Jack that her husband was paid the $500 owed and that he most likely ran off with another woman.

> **Michael Corbett (Michael Pavel):** I think a casting director saw me in either whatever stage show I was doing at the time or a TV pilot called *Coed Fever* with David Keith and Heather Thomas that I just did. I was offered this small role of this sort of tough kid from the other side of the tracks for three days work. My agent said, "You should do this. It will be great and your first TV gig." I went in and we shot. I remember doing my scene with big hair and a gray sweatshirt. My agent called me at the end of the day after taping and said, "They liked what they saw and want to expand the character. They want to put you under contract." That is how it started for me on *Ryan's Hope*. During this, I never had any contact with Claire Labine and Paul Mayer at all.

After watching Siobhan and Jack have an intense argument outside the Harborside after leaving the engagement party, Mary again questions what had transpired between Siobhan and Jack while she was working with Frank in DC. On the eve of her sister's nuptials, she confronts Siobhan regarding her true feelings for Jack. Unsatisfied with her answer, she asks her husband point-blank if he is in love with her sister. The next morning, she needs some alone time and promises to meet Jack at the church. She stops for a coffee at the same café where Kim went and notices Duke and the Man in the Green Hat again. She follows the latter to a warehouse owned by Tiso, where a drug smuggling operation is going on.

The wedding, meanwhile, proceeds without her, as the family thinks she is still upset with Siobhan. At the reception, Tiso is notified that a woman had stumbled across the operation, and he gives the nod to off her. Mary is later found in a car wreck with her neck broken. Barely conscious, she says goodbye to Jack and her parents. Before she expires, she mentions the Man in the Green Hat. Claire and Paul were finally able to kill off Mary Ryan, as they had planned two years earlier after Kate Mulgrew had left the show.

Michael Levin: I felt that none of the actresses who replaced Kate Mulgrew were right for the part. I do not know how the casting was done, but I thought it was a mess. Claire and Paul were taking suggestions from other cast members. They took Helen Gallagher's suggestion [Kathleen Tolan], and that was bad. They took my suggestion, which was bad, and unfortunately, I was not taking this recasting as serious as I should have. They seemed to have no idea for what they were looking for and they never did find it. I think it was a failure.

Karen Morris-Gowdy: I don't remember Mary Carney or Kathleen Tolan but I do remember Nikki Goulet. We became friendly. She was fun to work with and wonderful to have on the set.

Regarding Mary's death, I think Michael Levin may have had a lot of say in that since he was there from the very beginning. He made his unhappiness known every single day at work, which wasn't pleasant for everybody else, but we got through it. He was just grumpy all of the time (but a consummate professional) because he was frustrated. He put a lot into that character. He was dead set that they should not have recast Mary, and he was right. They were not going to replace Kate Mulgrew, and they never should have tried. After they finally killed Mary, I think the cast reached a point where we just wanted to move on.

Although Claire and Paul always wanted to end Mary, it seemed to be more difficult than they imagined when the time came to actually execute it. Claire Labine remarked in *The Philadelphia Inquirer*, "It took me something like eight days to write the funeral script." Mary's death, devasting to some viewers, was a one-two punch because another fan favorite, Tom Desmond, had been written off shortly prior. He almost dies after choking on an apple and then expires due to complications from surgery. A frazzled Roger, who is distracted by his marital problems with Delia, misdiagnoses Tom and then falsifies the medical records to cover up his blunder. The loss of her husband sends Faith into a lonely depression, which she tries to self-medicate with booze.

Karen Morris-Gowdy: The writers never discussed storylines with us. But I loved being able to play drunk Faith. I laughed and asked Paul and Claire, "Did I mess up at the Christmas party and that is why you think I should be playing this alcoholic?" But it gave Faith another dimension. Yes, she was a really good person and she was the youngest sibling to Roger and Jill, but she was more complex— and she had a lot of hurt there from the way she was treated by her mother. It allowed that character to not be just the goody-goody, which I can see why Catherine Hicks got sick of playing that.

Around this time, Jackie Smith became much more involved with the ABC soap story telling and casting than her predecessor. Her first order of business when arriving in her new position seemed to be promoting the network's soaps. Perhaps with her influence, the daytime chat show *A.M. New York* that followed *Good Morning America* produced a live, one-hour show from the *Ryan's Hope* studio on Tuesday November 27, 1979. Hosts Janet Langhart and Clay Cole were guided by Claire Labine through the various sets and introduced them and the viewing audience to Paul Mayer, Ellen Barrett, and the actors working that day. It was a fascinating behind-the-scenes look at the soap and the demanding work that goes into producing a new show five days a week.

For the ABC soaps in general, Smith created the highly successful "Love in the Afternoon" promos that usually highlighted two soaps with snippets from upcoming episodes in a thirty-second spot. They not only ran in daytime but during prime time as well. She was also able to work with ABC's popular game show, *Family Feud*, to offer a week of crossover competition featuring cast members from each of their five soaps with specials like "The Love in the Afternoon Super Feud Special" and "The Saints vs. Sinners Family Feud Special." These proved extremely popular with audiences and continued through 1983. Smith also spearheaded the popular *FYI (For Your Information)* hosted by actor Hal Linden. Viewers submitted questions that were answered during these sixty-second spots. They aired three times a day during the network's block of afternoon soaps.

The year 1980 began with Jack and the Ryan family still deeply mourning the death of Mary. Siobhan and Joe are settling in as newlyweds and are interrupted by Delia, who is thrown out of the Coleridge brownstone by her husband, Roger, when he learns of her tryst with Dan Fox to recoup her investment losses. Frank and Jill are moving in together, setting up a law practice (with former campaign worker Georgia Rothchild, played by Gloria Cromwell, as their secretary), and talking marriage. Kim shifts her focus from acting to landing the much older and married Seneca after her first play flops.

However, that quickly changes when powerful agent Paige Williams (Joan Fontaine) sees something in Kim and offers to be her agent. Kim is apt to agree until she has Frank read the contract details, and he advises against it since she would be almost indentured to Paige for the rest of her life.

Meanwhile, Kim discovers the evidence that Rae framed Frank to lose his Senate seat and, feeling that she owes him for his kindness toward her and wanting to punish her mother, turns over the written proof. This begins Frank's journey to clear his name. Rae is furious with Kim but is more worried about going to prison. She tries to reason with Frank before the Senate hearing in DC but finds Maeve instead. In one of the serial's most powerful scenes, all the animosity that has been building between the two women rises to the surface, and they have a huge blowout in the bar's kitchen. Neither holds back, revealing their ill feelings for each other. Rae astonishes Maeve when she says, "You're so very much like me. We are both powerful women, Maeve. And Frank loves power, and he wants both of ours. He wants heaven and earth, Maeve. And for a while we managed to give it to him. He kept his hands clean because I got mine dirty. It worked! Why could you not understand your own son?" Maeve demandingly responds, "Do *not* link yourself to me—not even in your mind. Now please leave my home."

Tiso has become enchanted with ditzy Delia. He pays a visit to Dan Fox and makes him an offer he cannot refuse to get him out of her life. Delia then learns from her brokerage firm that Fox went on an extended leave. Impressed with Delia's style and business acumen, Tiso offers to become her silent partner in setting up a fabulous restaurant in Central Park, à la Tavern on the Green, to be called Delia's Crystal Palace. She accepts, unaware that he had ordered the hit on Mary Ryan. When asked by Roger and the Ryans where she got the money to bankroll such an expensive venture, she lies and says that she had made another windfall in the commodities market. Also working with Tiso is Michael Pavel, who is hired as a busboy at the Harborside. Despite his mother's reservations, Michael pursued the job after being recruited by Tiso's enemies, who task him with assassinating Tiso after a machine-gun attack at Ryan's Bar had failed. Tiso survived, but one of his bodyguards was killed and Jack was injured. Michael successfully plants a car bomb in Tiso's limo outside the Harborside, but unexpected guest Delia and her broken high heel saves Tiso's life.

Randall Edwards: I loved the Crystal Palace storyline. It was my favorite. I worked a lot with Earl Hindman as my brother—what

a sweetheart. He was so low-key, so humble, so calm, and not pre-
tentious at all. He was just a kind man. Then a few years later, I see
him on the hit TV sitcom *Home Improvement* and it was like, "Hey!
That's my brother!"

Michael Corbett: I remember they told me that I was going to get
a mom. I was so excited because now I would have a family. It was
a challenging day the first time I shot with Joan Lorring. They gave
her a lot of lines. We had to do a few takes. You shot a soap very
differently back then than you do now. We would all go in in the
morning and rehearse everything. Then you would go up to the studio and shoot the show in order. It was done almost live on tape in
a sense. Joan was an amazing actress but had trouble with the lines.

Richard Muenz was just the sweetest guy and super great to
work with. What I remember about Sarah Felder was that she had
this long, thick mane of beautiful red hair. The entire cast I was
working with was terrific and could not have been nicer. I was loving what I was doing.

I liked [producer] Ellen Barrett a lot. She was a real straight
shooter. Again, I had no other point of reference. I remember I
would just go into her office, sit down, and say, "Hi, Ellen. How is
everything going?" I did not know any better to not interact with
her other than in a nice, casual way. She knew it was my first TV
job so she would advise me to learn my lines, do my work, and be
professional. We got along really well.

Kelli Maroney: Ellen was one of my greatest supporters. I'd never
met a real network television producer before. It was intimidating
at first because I didn't know how to behave around anyone—I
eventually realized she was in my corner and wanted me to succeed.

Louise Shaffer: Ellen Barrett was incredibly good to me. And yet
I will say I really don't know why Ellen did some of the things she
did. They were not choices I would have made, and I don't think
she made the best decisions. I really don't. In a strange way, with
people in charge, I did my damnedest not to get too involved. If
you have authority, you scare me.

At this point in the serial, one of its most infamous, wildly debated storylines began. The writers had already cribbed pieces of plots from the

movies *Jaws* (Siobhan almost becoming shark bait while swimming in the Atlantic Ocean on vacation with Joe in the Hamptons) and *The Godfather* (the machine-gun attack on Ryan's Bar). However, now they really went out of the box with the Prince Albert story. He was not royalty from England but a gorilla from the Central Park Zoo who is befriended by a lonely Delia.

> **Seymour Amlen:** I rarely sat in on creative meetings but remember I did early on. I had seen the remake of *King Kong* and jokingly suggested that we do a version of that on one of our soaps. I was surprised that they took me up on it and that it was *Ryan's Hope* that did it.

Amlen may have started the ball rolling and put this idea in Jackie Smith's head. Claire Labine told *The Cincinnati Enquirer* that she was talking with Smith about a previous story with Siobhan and the shark. Reportedly, Smith joked that after they ripped off *Jaws*, was *King Kong* next? In fact, Labine said she had been discussing, with her children, a *Beauty and the Beast* story featuring Delia because she "seemed just right for this kind of role. You know, she's unique on daytime television; there isn't anyone just like her. She's a woman whose self-image is especially low, and her childhood so bad that she feels isolated now."

Labine revealed that all the ABC executives (except Jackie Smith) thought they were crazy to run with this story. Her partner, Paul Mayer, did not want to write it either. Many had presumed ABC pressured Claire and Paul to write this, but they did not. In fact, it was even too outlandish for ABC at the time, proving that Claire had a hand in introducing fantasy elements into the standard soap that would become commonplace shortly thereafter and a detriment to her creation.

> **Rachael Mayer:** My sister Daisy said my dad threatened to quit over that storyline. He hated it. The fact that Claire liked it shows what a talented team they were because they disagreed about a lot of things, and they would come together. That was a real classic disagreement between the two. I think my dad liked stories that had a dramatic arc and deep emotional storytelling. He was never on board with King Kong.

> **Randall Edwards:** I was never given a heads-up about the Prince Albert story arc. I got the scripts and thought, "Oh, okay!"

Ron Hale: To quote the British, I was gobsmacked. I thought, "What in the hell is this?" I could not believe that Claire would come up with this. It was so off the wall. I blocked most of this storyline out.

Art Rutter: Some of the cast and crew, including me, thought that this story was stupid and idiotic. However, it was pretty cool and was the start of the soaps getting bigger and trying to top each other.

Ilene Kristen: If I was still playing Delia at that point, I would have told them that I am not doing it. To me, it distorted a real character with real neuroses. You are taking reality out of a show that had nothing but reality. Just because *King Kong* was a successful movie does not mean it belongs in a soap opera. It was ridiculous and not right for this show. The core audience of *Ryan's Hope* I think wanted that kitchen sink drama because it was like a real story to them.

After Tiso finds a location for the Crystal Palace, Delia oversees its transformation into her vision with help from her brother Bob, who agrees to be its manager. It is at this point that Delia (forlorn about her breakup with Roger) visits the gorilla cage at the Central Park Zoo on her way to the Crystal Palace and befriends its star attraction, Prince Albert (played by mime Donald Van Horn in a monkey suit). She learns all about him from his zookeeper, Owen Douglas (Jon DeVries), who is amazed with the connection the ape forges with Delia. The Ryan family had become used to Delia's daffiness, but her bonding with this gorilla had them all scratching their heads. They are all blind to her loneliness. The one good thing with this friendship, as Maeve points out, is that Delia begins spending more time with her son, who accompanies his mom a few times on her sojourn to the zoo.

Randall Edwards: Personally, I felt badly because Delia was such a bad mom in so many ways. I felt for Jadrien, the young person, and felt protective of Jadrien because my character was not the model mother. I always tried to be nice to him.

Jadrien Steele: I remember the Prince Albert story but not the nuances of it. It seemed a little strange to me.

Albert, however, becomes agitated when Owen is transferred, and the replacement zookeeper treats him badly. When he almost breaks free, he lunges for Delia, who tricks him to get back in his cage. Albert's behavior causes the zookeeper to aggressively punish him. The gorilla escapes a second time and heads to the Crystal Palace, where Delia is working late. Breaking in, he swoops the terrified blonde into his arms and takes her to Belvedere Castle in Central Park. After a police manhunt, a frantic Roger locates Delia, but Albert picks her up and climbs to the roof of the castle à la King Kong carrying Fay Wray to the top of the Empire State Building. Police sharpshooters shoot Albert with a tranquilizer gun, and in the last seconds on a Friday afternoon viewers see the big ape go groggy and then drop Delia. The episode ends with her screams and a look of fright frozen on her face as she plummets to the ground.

Randall Edwards: Donald Van Horn, the man in the gorilla suit, was amazing! The suit was very large and heavy. As you might imagine, it got pretty hot in there for him, and when someone would finally help him take the head off, during a break in shooting, he would be sweating. He never complained. The most remarkable thing was the fact that Donald really did "act," both with his body movements in the suit, mimicking a gorilla, and especially with his eyes, the only part of him that showed. He conveyed a lot with those eyes, which were surrounded with black makeup and shone through the holes in the costume head.

Ron Hale: We had a two-night shoot in Central Park in the winter. We did not start shooting until midnight, and the temperature was about twenty-eight degrees. I had to stand in the cold while all the production people were in their warm little trailers. I literally had to stand in one place while they were setting up the shots around Belvedere Tower. It was just brutal. I could do it without complaint if I was working in a film with Pacino and I was getting paid big bucks. But this was awful.

Randall Edwards: Yes, it was freezing. There was a wardrobe person who would throw a big coat on me whenever I was off camera. I remember the stunt double who actually did the fall off the top of the tower. I had absolute admiration and awe because I was petrified up there. Close-ups were shot on a set but the medium and long shots were done on location.

Laura Rakowitz: I did a lot of the location shoots in Central Park for this. We all thought this was very silly, but our Randall made it work in a big way. We sort of grew fond of Prince Albert . . . and enjoyed shooting it. I don't recall ABC inserting their influence at all. I think the network let the writers run with it.

Art Rutter: I did not have to work because they shot on location at Belvedere Castle and not in the studio. But I lived [near Central Park] on Sixty-Sixth Street and Columbus Avenue and said, "I'm going to this." It was freezing and so cold, but it was so much fun to watch. And on TV, it came across great.

Laura Rakowitz: For the outdoor shoots, I had to log in the scene shots and other information. We shot those scenes at night in the middle of winter. It was freezing but what was great about it, that I remember so distinctly, is that everybody had the cold breath coming out of their mouths, which always personifies a location shoot. I just love when that happens.

   I would then be in the editing room to make sure it was cut correctly. I had to make sure all the props were placed in the right spots.

Ron Hale: A couple of days later, after they started to edit the footage, some higher-ups came up to me and said, "My God, that was incredible, Ron. You had tears coming down your face just at the right moment." I just burst out laughing and said, "I was freezing my fucking ass off. Those were tears of me freezing." I should have kept my mouth shut and let them believe it was my acting. I blew it and had to be honest.

Randall Edwards: Honestly, I had some of my most personally emotional moments performing some of those scenes in the Prince Albert story. Even though with the guy in the gorilla suit there was a willing suspension of disbelief, the storyline and the intent were the need for a confidante. To me it was a yearning for acceptance and love, which was Delia's prime motivation for everything that she did. Delia was so insecure, and ultimately, she had to have Maeve accept and love her. That would fill that hole. Ironically, of course, Maeve did love Delia.

On the following Monday, lucky Delia lands in a safety net laid out by the fire department. However, the incident leaves her physically ill and traumatized. She is especially terrified of Roger. Dr. Adam Cohen uses hypnosis, and it is revealed that Delia had a past life as a maid for the Coleridge family back at the turn of the century. Her fear of a Coleridge ancestor was manifesting itself with Delia's current dread of her estranged husband. This arc did not last long and was quickly forgotten when Adam Cohen was written off the show shortly after it had begun. Also released was Albert. A tearful Delia says goodbye to the big ape, who is being shipped off to an upstate zoo where Owen now works.

> **Randall Edwards:** I don't know why that happened. I don't know if the story was too far out and they decided to back off of it. I was so disappointed because I was curious to find out where this was going to go.

When polled, fans named the Prince Albert storyline as one of their least favorites, although it does still have its champions. Even when originally aired, viewers were divided by it. *Daytime TV Magazine* ran some letters to the editors in its July 1980 issue, and the reviews were mixed. E. Tucker from Putnam Valley, New York, wrote, "Did somebody put LSD in the writer's coffee at *Ryan's Hope*? That story of Delia being kidnapped by a gorilla was as silly as something you'd see on Carol Burnett's show." M. F. Speers from East Orange, New Jersey, felt differently and remarked, "Delia's little romance with Prince Albert . . . really brightened my day. What a refreshing change of pace from the usual soap fare."

In 2009, Claire Labine still defended her story, remarking to Damon L. Jacobs at *WeLoveSoaps.com*, "Everyone always cites Prince Albert the Ape story as a mistake. But I'd do that again! I loved those scenes. It was a story about alienation. It was Delia relating to the one persona that she could relate to at that point. We were quite fascinated by all the ape research that was in the era when that was first being explored. We were really interested in that." The problem was that although some fans did appreciate what Labine was trying to convey—here was this beautiful young woman about to open a fabulous restaurant in Central Park and she felt she hadn't a friend in the world until she met Albert—most viewers found it silly and could not get past the fact that it was a man in a monkey suit pursuing the lovely Delia.

Laura Rakowitz: Randall Edwards was wonderful. She was the only one I knew who could act with a fake gorilla. For those of us who remember *King Kong*, Randall was such a delicate flower and reminded us of Fay Wray. Throughout most of the movie, Fay wore that flowing, almost see-through, sexy dress and we had Randall in that. With her features and blond hair, she looked a bit like the Fay Wray character. It ended up working, I guess, since people still talk about it to this day.

Helen Gallagher: In my opinion this was a fiasco. I thought it was ridiculous and my least favorite storyline from the show.

Art Rutter: This story was very buzzworthy and propelled *Ryan's Hope* into the conversation of being a cool, different kind of show. As I recall, Randall Edwards loved doing it from the beginning. Some of us came around and embraced it.

Randall Edwards: Early on they used to block the scenes to try to tape the show live. If you made them stop tape, you would cost the show money because then they had to edit. It was also like adding a whole extra layer of challenges for the directors and the crew. You would have a scene on a set with three cameras—one for a wide shot and the other two focusing on the different characters—and as the scene was ending, one camera would stay as the other two began rolling down to the next set. It was amazing that they were able to keep that up for so long. I think what changed was when soap operas began adding more elements of special effects, like with Prince Albert, so they had to give up that way of shooting. They would tape some sections in the morning that would get looped in later, like the locations stuff. I thought that was so interesting how soaps evolved that way.

During March, the show made a major change with its opening titles. The mellow flute and harp in the theme song was replaced with an array of instruments, including woodwinds and brass, and a jazzier, up-tempo beat. Gone were the dated photos of Helen Gallagher and Bernie Barrow with infant Jadrien Steele in Central Park. The new opening began with an aerial shot of the Empire State Building and the Statue of Liberty before zooming into various parts of the city featuring a variety of happy people—a young couple in the park, boys playing basketball, a high-class woman wearing a mink and her tuxedoed date descending a staircase to their limo—none of whom were cast members. Obviously, ABC wanted the emphasis to shift from the folksiness of the Ryan family to the excitement of New York City. The impetus for this change is believed to have been initiated by the network, but surprisingly Bernie Barrow may have been part of the cause as well.

> **Rachael Mayer:** Bernie was a tough negotiator. I think he decided that he was kind of the star and had an agent who was heavily pushing for more money. And I specifically remember that he wanted to be paid for being in the titles. Everybody was upset about that because it just didn't seem fair. Maybe that was out of the budget to some degree. They changed the titles without him [or any other cast members] because he lit that match.

> **Ruth Mayer:** And what a dumb thing to do in retrospect. You're in the titles and then you are no longer in the titles.

> **Helen Gallagher:** They brought in an actor they really liked and wanted to replace Bernie, but I talked them out of it. I was shocked and told them they would ruin the show because the audience is attached to Bernie.

Shortly after Delia said goodbye to Prince Albert, two new major characters were introduced to the story. Barry Ryan (Richard Backus) arrived first. A cousin from the Chicago "black sheep" branch of the family, he is a charming, suave talent manager who is immediately attracted to Delia. Unable to resist any man with the surname Ryan, Delia returns his affections. Barry's client is rock singer Ken George Jones (Trent Jones), who has a terrible secret and falls for Jill, even though she is making wedding plans with her live-in lover and law partner, Frank.

> **Richard Backus (Barry Ryan):** I initially had that stage actor's contempt for daytime drama. It used to be perceived as something where actors who couldn't get work on prime-time TV or the stage would go. There wasn't a lot of money [working on stage] even if you were on Broadway in those days. I had a family and told my agent, "You must get me on a soap opera so I can make a little money." Once I started doing soap operas, I came to like the genre and what it could do in terms of a long-form kind of storytelling.

My first soap role was Jason Sexton on *Lovers and Friends*. The show was produced by Paul Rauch. Harding Lemay was the head writer, and he was also working on *Another World*. He was writing one and a half hours of drama every day. It was too much for him to do, I think. The network felt there was not enough happening and it wasn't sinful enough. They decided to take it off the air to revamp it. Some roles were recast. They told some of the actors that they would not be coming back. They told some that they would like to have them back if they were still available. There were three or four of us who got paid in the interim to keep us available. That was a real boon and that lasted about six or seven months.

When it came back on as *For Richer, For Poorer*, Tom King was the head writer. It didn't last either. I don't know why it didn't catch on. It was a period when soap operas were booming but getting a new one started is always difficult to develop an audience to commit to watching it.

When *For Richer, For Poorer* went off the air, Paul Rauch, who was also producing *Another World*, brought me over to play Ted Bancroft. I did not have to audition. Beverlee McKinsey was great fun, and I really loved working with Paul Stevens, who played my father [Brian Bancroft]. He was a thoroughly lovely man and we played scenes together from time to time. Then Paul called me into his office and in a bright, cheerful voice said, "We are writing you out." I said, "Oh no!" I was quite disappointed to be written off, as I was moving from soap opera to soap opera. I thought my career was guaranteed.

I don't know if this is true, but for *Ryan's Hope*, I almost wonder if I didn't read for Barry and Ken George Jones. I cannot say for certain but Barry was the better part. He lasted longer and was a more fun character to play. I do recall reading with Randall Edwards, who was playing Delia at the time. I am almost sure Claire Labine and Paul Mayer were present, along with producer Ellen Barrett.

Trent Jones (Ken George Jones): I went to Yale Drama for a year, then did regional theatre and stage acting in New York City off-off-Broadway. That was enough to get an agent. Prior to all these, I had been in a rock band and played guitar. Since this was for a part of a rock singer, it helped that I was comfortable performing because that was part of the audition.

Most of the songs I sang on the show were composed by me. That gave me a leg up, I guess. It was one of the best auditions I ever had. It was taped, and I think it was only the director, whom I met along with Nancy Addison, who I was auditioning with.

Jackie Smith oversaw ABC Daytime. She did not like me, and she did not want me to be cast. The producers and the writers wanted me, but she did not. I had at least three or four different auditions. Finally, it was told to me that the show said to Jackie, "If you do not cast this guy, we will not do the story." Jackie gave in; however, she didn't really give in because before any of my shows were broadcast (there was a four- or five-week gap) she was forcing them to do auditions for a replacement.

Richard Backus: Not long before I was there, they did the King Kong storyline. I got the sense that people there were very unhappy with that. I remember very distinctly that somebody said to me, "With the arrival of Barry Ryan, the show is getting back on track and what the show should be doing."

Trent Jones: *Ryan's Hope* cast normal-looking people, unlike other soaps. I would watch and notice some days I looked good and some days not so good. I think it was a visual thing with Jackie. That would be my guess. I think my acting was on the line with the other actors, but it was more that she had an image of this rock star looking more like Sting or somebody extremely handsome. That is what she wanted in that part, and I wasn't that.

It was tough for me. This was the first soap opera I had ever done. Doing stage work I was used to four weeks rehearsal, here, you had maybe four minutes rehearsal. It was dispiriting, but Nancy Addison and the people in the studio were incredibly supportive, so that helped. Jackie finally gave up, probably because I was to be on for only six months.

Richard Backus: Trent was a lovely guy. He was easy to work with and genuinely nice. He went off and began writing soaps soon after this.

Trent Jones: Richard and I became friends off-screen. He came over to my house with his kids.

Richard Backus: I had some interaction with Claire and Paul, but they were usually busy, off writing. I saw quite a bit of Ellen Barrett, and I liked her a lot. I thought she was a particularly good producer. There were a lot of great people there. It was a very warm and supportive place to work.

More good news came *Ryan's Hope*'s way when it won another Writers Guild Award and two more Emmy awards at the June 4, 1980, ceremony for directing and writing during the 1979–80 period. Unfortunately, its nominated actors—John Gabriel (first nomination) and Michael Levin (third straight nomination) for Outstanding Lead Actor in a Daytime Drama Series; Ron Hale (second straight nomination) for Outstanding Supporting Actor in a Daytime Drama Series; Louise Shaffer (first of three nominations) for Outstanding Supporting Actress in a Daytime Drama Series; and Joan Fontaine for Outstanding Guest/Cameo Appearance in a Daytime Drama Series—failed to triumph. The two wins brought the total to eleven Emmy Awards in just five years. Although it was not the highest-rated ABC show, it was then considered the most prestigious, and Jackie Smith had a promo produced to tout the show's awards success and hopefully attract new viewers. It aired in the summer. Over snippets of Delia, Frank, Kim, Michael, Jack, Rose, Jill, Rae, and Faith, the announcer proudly hails, "This is *Ryan's Hope*, and it is a winner again. Now eleven Emmy Awards in only five years! This is *Ryan's Hope*."

Ruth Mayer: I remember when he went to the Emmys and we put up these signs that read, "Win or lose we love you, Dad." He would come home with all these Emmy Awards—it was like a fairytale. We had no idea if the show was going to be popular.

Rachael Mayer: They were enormously proud of their Emmy Awards.

Ruth Mayer: I will share one anecdote, which is one of my favorite childhood memories. It was at the Emmy Awards. I was sitting between Phil Donahue—big crush at the time—and my family. They were announcing either Best Drama Series or Best Writing. They were showing clips from the nominees, and they were typical soap opera scenes. They then showed Maeve talking to, I think, Siobhan. The room went silent and people started tearing up. It was like, what just happened? And then *Ryan's Hope* won. There

Claire Labine and Paul Avila Mayer, the co-creators, co-head writers,
and co-executive producers of *Ryan's Hope*, 1975. ©ABC

Portrait of the Ryan family (starting clockwise from bottom): Johnny (Bernie Barrow),
Maeve (Helen Gallagher), Mary (Kate Mulgrew), Patrick (Malcolm Groome),
Frank (Michael Hawkins), and Frank's wife, Delia (Ilene Kristen), 1975. ©ABC

Jadrien Steele (Little John Ryan) sitting on top of the bar,
with his on-screen parents (Ilene Kristen and Michael Hawkins)
and his real-life parents (Walanne and Jerry Steele), ca. 1975–76.
Photo by William R. Devine/©JPMorgan Chase & Co.

Wedding-day portrait of Mary Ryan (Kate Mulgrew) and Jack Fenelli (Michael Levin), 1976. ©ABC

Publicity cast photo, ca. 1977. Front row: Michael Levin (Jack Fenelli), Kate Mulgrew (Mary Ryan), Ilene Kristen (Delia Reid Ryan), Catherine Hicks (Dr. Faith Coleridge), Justin Deas (Dr. Bucky Carter), and Hannibal Penney Jr. (Dr. Clem Moultrie). Middle row: Malachy McCourt (Kevin MacGuinness), Bernie Barrow (Johnny Ryan), Helen Gallagher (Maeve Ryan), and Nancy Addison (Jill Coleridge). Back row: Andrew Robinson (Frank Ryan), Earl Hindman (Bob Reid), John Gabriel (Dr. Seneca Beulac), and Ron Hale (Dr. Roger Coleridge). ©ABC

Ana Alicia, Catherine Hicks, and Kate Mulgrew run lines off set, ca.1977. *Courtesy of Ilene Kristen*

Manipulative Rae Woodard (Louise Shaffer) truly loved Frank Ryan (Daniel Hugh Kelly) and he may have had feelings for her, but he surely loved her money and influence, which help propel him to the Senate, 1978. ©ABC

Hot-tempered Tom Desmond (Thomas MacGreevy) confronts his rival,
Patrick Ryan (John Blazo), about his feelings for Faith Coleridge,
while Georgia Rothchild (Gloria Cromwell) peers on, 1978. ©ABC

Barry Ryan (Richard Backus), from the Chicago branch of the family,
romanced Delia (Randall Edwards), who never could resist a man with the last name of Ryan.
He proved to be an even bigger liar than she was, 1980. ©ABC

Although she was engaged to Frank Ryan, it didn't stop attorney Jill Coleridge (Nancy Addison) from having an affair with her client, rock star Ken George Jones (Trent Jones), 1980. ©ABC

Conniving Kim Harris (Kelli Maroney) married older Dr. Seneca Beulac (John Gabriel),
but it didn't deter her from continuing having sex with studly Michael Pavel (Michael Corbett).
Who could blame her? ca. 1980. ©ABC

Feisty, sharp-tongued private eye Rose Pearse (Rose Alaio) became Jack Fenelli's sparring partner and first love interest since the death of his wife, Mary, 1980. ©ABC

Publicity photo of the extended Ryan family, ca.1981: Johnny (Bernie Barrow), Joe Novak (Roscoe Born), Maeve (Helen Gallagher), Siobhan Ryan Novak (Ann Gillespie), and Jack Fenelli (Michael Levin). ©Al

Harold Apter, producer Ellen Barrett, director Lela Swift, and Helen Gallagher in between takes while shooting on the streets of New York City, 1981. *Courtesy of Harold Apter*

Egyptologist Aristotle Benedict-White (Gordon Thomson) became obsessed with the recently jilted Faith Coleridge (Karen Morris-Gowdy), who strongly resembled the long-dead Egyptian queen, Merit Kara, 1981. ©ABC

In an interesting twist, quirky racecar driver Ox Knowles (Will Patton) teamed up with wacky Delia (Ilene Kristen) in an attempt to retrieve the Crystal Palace's air rights back from Hollis Kirkland, 1982. ©ABC

Filming of the new 1983 opening titles, refocusing on the Ryan and Coleridge families, took the cast on location around New York City. Pictured (left to right, top to bottom) Jill (Nancy Addison), Roger (Ron Hale), and Faith (Karen Morris-Gowdy) at the Plaza Hotel; Frank (Geoff Pierson), Siobhan (Marg Helgenberger), and Patrick (Malcolm Groome) at the Metropolitan Museum of Art; Delia (Ilene Kristen) on Fifth Avenue; Frank (Geoff Pierson) and Jill (Nancy Addison) in Central Park; Patrick (Malcolm Groome) and Faith (Karen Morris-Gowdy) in Heckscher Playground; and Jack (Michael Levin) on Columbus Avenue, 1983. ©ABC

Patrick Ryan (Malcolm Groome) is still in love with Amanda Kirkland (Ariana Muenker) who just returned from the cuckoo's nest and is unstable as ever, 1983. ©ABC

The mysterious Charlotte Greer (Judith Chapman) claimed to be Charlotte Greer Ryan
and accused Frank Ryan of jilting and swindling her while living in St. Louis
to finance his political campaign, 1983. ©ABC

was no comparison. It was different. It was quality—no offense to all the hardworking people who make soaps.

Ron Hale: I don't remember the episodes I submitted. However, this is going to sound self-centered, which I am not, but I blew it. You were allowed to submit three scenes pulled together from different episodes. I wanted to show my versatility, so I chose a comedic scene, a soft-feeling scene, and an anger scene. Both years that I lost—I will never forget and should have remembered the first time—that the actors who won [Peter Hanson as Lee Baldwin from *General Hospital* in 1979 and Warren Burton as Eddie Dorrance from *All My Children* in 1980] submitted over-the-top, dramatic scenes with yelling, screaming, and anger. At the ceremonies, they would show clips of each nominee, and they all had scenes like this. Not one of the other nominees did what I did to try to show some variety in my ability to play this character. I truly believed if I went that dramatic route—and I had plenty of scenes to choose from—I would have had a better chance. I was stupid. I guess they wanted *drama*! They wanted you chewing up the scenery.

The middle of spring saw the phenomenally successful launch of the Crystal Palace. As Barry promised, he delivers celebrity attendees, including producer/director Otto Preminger, movie stars Van Johnson and Betsy Palmer, and TV actress Shelley Smith—all playing themselves. Delia is stunning in her tight-fitting white evening gown, with Barry by her side almost the entire time. The Ryan family and even the Coleridge sisters cannot help but be impressed with Delia's masterful achievement, albeit it is secretly financed by Tiso, who is also in attendance. However, the night is spoiled by Little John's illness, which was made almost lethal by a drunken Faith, who gives the poor kid penicillin, forgetting that he is allergic. He lays in the hospital, teetering on death for a few days before pulling through. This near-fatal mistake is enough for Faith to admit she is addicted to alcohol and to get help.

As the summer began, the new storylines with Ken and Barry heated up, while a major one came to an end. Jack finally has proof as to who killed his wife. After he bugs Joe's office on his fishing boat, Jack hears one of Tiso's thugs, afraid that he would be rubbed out the same way as Larry, the Man in the Green Hat, relay to a shocked Joe what happened to Mary that day. As Jack plays the tape to a disbelieving Siobhan, Tiso arrives with a gun in hand. After blaming Mary's death on Jack for not controlling his wife, Tiso has enough chitchat and goes to shoot Siobhan, but Jack grabs a candelabra and lunges at Tiso. A shot goes off, and the screen fades to black.

When the soap aired next, Siobhan is caring for Jack's bullet wound while Tiso lays motionless on the floor. Joe arrives soon after and pronounces his uncle dead with a broken neck—just payback for Mary's murder. Joe begs Siobhan to run away with him, but she does not want to be part of his lies. Joe then runs off when the police sirens come closer. Later that night, his bloody vest is found at the crime scene, and the police surmise that the mob had killed him for letting Jack and Siobhan get away. His body is never found. For their protection, the FBI sends Siobhan and Jack to a safe house until it is secure enough for them to return. They do, and then Siobhan bids adieu to her family and departs for Texas to visit with her brother Pat.

Several reasons were batted around for why Richard Muenz and Sarah Felder were written out despite their popularity. According to columnist Jon-Michael Reed, "Richard had mildly bellyached for several months about his character turning into a mild-mannered milquetoast. Reports also filtered off the set that he felt stifled by the strong-willed, domineering Felder, who also raised ire among several of her other coworkers. Despite the troubles, both Muenz and Felder were dynamic presences whose absence will surely dismay . . . audiences."

Another possibility was Jackie Smith, who, despite her liking the tortured love story with Siobhan and Joe, finally got her way and was able to send Felder packing. Reportedly, she did not keep her dislike of the actress a secret. Allegedly, she felt she was not "soap pretty" enough for the role, despite Felder being a fan favorite. At one point, Sarah was even pressured to cut her hair to appease the network. It was not enough. ABC was now, obviously, going for a certain look when it came to casting.

Malachy McCourt: I remember some situations with Sarah Felder. But I understood the insecurity of actors. I don't know what it is about myself, but I didn't have that and never had. I grew up in poverty and had no training as an actor. I just have been lucky. I think because of this, actors felt comfortable with me. I got along pretty good with just about everybody. Half of my job was to be charming at all times. That's the way I am, so I always tried to make situations as funny, humorous, and compatible as possible. There is no point in having any kind of battles or personality conflicts with anybody. You can always get along with people.

Laura Rakowitz: ABC didn't like Sarah Felder. She was very unhappy with, not only the way they treated her, but the way they physically always wanted to change her all the time. She resisted, and it only enhanced the dislike of her. It ended up being a snowball that was rolling down the hill, getting bigger and bigger.

Richard Backus: I remember that when I first started, Sarah Felder, who played Siobhan, was let go. This may have been ABC-influenced because Siobhan had always been kind of wacky. After they killed off Mary Ryan, they decided to turn Siobhan into a more romantic leading lady. It was decided that Sarah didn't have the right qualities they were looking for. When they wrote her out, they threw a party for her and gifted with this silver circular box from Tiffany's that Claire gave out to the contract players when they left. It was engraved with your name, your character's name, the title of the show, and date of your first and last performance. It was genuinely nice of them. But Sarah was very unhappy. She was angry and upset and threw a fit. Claire and Paul were understanding and sympathetic.

Randall Edwards: I was aware of the way ABC was treating Sarah. It was too bad because she really had a look that was authentic. You could believe that she was Siobhan Ryan of Irish descent. She was not your typical soap face. I thought she was beautiful.

Art Rutter: I never heard anyone say that ABC felt that Sarah Felder was not hot enough or soap pretty enough.

Tamara Grady: When I started, it was Simon and Cuman doing the casting. They were not physically in our office because they were doing more than *Ryan's Hope*. I think most of the casting changes that occurred pre-ABC were by Labine and Mayer. Once ABC took ownership, there was a much different process. More people had to approve and look at the audition tapes. I don't really know if that had anything to do with the ratings.

Despite this setback, the show had to move on. To make Delia jealous, Roger dates a fledgling singer and airhead named Lily Darnell (amusingly played by Christine Ebersole, followed by Kathryn Dowling). She is uninhibited and just wants sex with no strings. Still hurt from losing Roger, Delia goes the honest route and tells Barry about her past two failed marriages to his cousins and her estrangement with Roger. She wants to take it slow. Barry agrees; however, it was only lip service, and soon he too is having a secret, carefree affair with Lily. After Tiso's death, Delia confides in Barry that he was her silent partner and had financed the restaurant. She is unnerved about what will become of the establishment now that he is dead. A level-headed Barry also convinces Delia not to file a malpractice suit against Faith for almost killing Little John by suggesting her vindictive behavior could anger Maeve and Johnny.

Ken, meanwhile, happens to be on the terrace of the Crystal Palace one night and witnesses a blowup between Frank and Jill regarding her reluctance to set a wedding date and how she went behind Faith's back to convince the head of Riverside Hospital, Marshall Westheimer, not to accept her sister's resignation. After Frank storms off, the charismatic vocalist, clad in tight leather pants, comes on to an outraged Jill. She softens a bit when Ken is persuaded to sing a song in the restaurant. After learning from Delia that Jill is an attorney, he decides he needs a New York lawyer to handle his legal affairs. He surprises Jill late that night in her office. After reminding her of who he is, Ken asks, "Are you smart and mean like Delia says? Or are you smart and warm and feeling?" An annoyed Jill responds, "Go with Delia." Jill then reluctantly agrees to rep Jones because she needs clients.

After experiencing Ken's exciting life in the music industry, she slowly falls for the personable singer and they eventually make love. Soon, an affair is in full bloom. Frank, meanwhile, is distracted helping a lonely, depressed Faith, who is trying to stay sober after her almost-fatal mistake while treating Little John.

Richard Backus: I had worked with Michael Levin during two summers at the American Shakespeare Festival, so I knew him already. I think because I had stage experience and was well-regarded in the theatre community, it helped me become accepted by the cast.

Trent Jones: The cast was interesting to work with and very professional. Nancy Addison was a total pro and supportive during the tough times and assuring me that she only wanted to work with me. I only had a few scenes with Daniel Hugh Kelly, and the thing about him that threw me was that he was one of these actors that give you nothing during rehearsal. He would sort of mutter, and I would be desperate to run lines. The minute the camera turned on—boom—he is in the moment, and he is there, completely natural and giving a superior performance. If I had more scenes with him, I might have been a little more forceful about my desire to work a little differently, but I wasn't in that position.

Helen Gallagher and Bernie Barrow were extremely sweet. I didn't have a lot of scenes with them either, considering that my character was breaking up their son's romance. My favorite scene with Maeve is when Ken came over to the bar and Little John was there. Somehow my character was to take out his guitar and sing an Irish ditty. I was charming Maeve by being able to do it. Helen is a great performer, and we got to sing together. That was fun.

Randall Edwards: Richard Backus was a lovely actor and person. He wrote poetry, and a bunch of us would get together and read poems. He is a such a nice man, and I loved working with him.

Richard Backus: Randall Edwards was a delight to work with. She was fun to be around and worked extremely hard. She really put her heart and soul into every performance. It was a real treat to act opposite her. Ron Hale was fun to work with too, but he seemed more nervous about doing the show.

Trent Jones: As for the directors, they were quite different, and I liked both of them. Jerry was a little more into character development. He was low-key and nurturing in the brief time we had to block. That was something I liked a lot.

Lela directed most of my concert scenes and was particularly good at that. She liked those types of scenes and did very well with it. I was happy with her because she had a clear eye on how she wanted to do things. Of course, we had very little time to do production numbers, and she'd come in very prepared to get done what she wanted.

Randall Edwards: Lela and Jerry were both excellent directors. Lela was very planned out, and she had a vision for everything. She was very thoughtful and methodical. You might want to argue something a little bit, and she might be a little bit flexible, but she basically stuck to her plan. Jerry was a little more collaborative. You could work together on things, for example. Not that he didn't come in with a plan obviously. Sometimes there was more conflict with the Lela Swift method than Jerry's approach with some actors, but they both worked, I think.

Richard Backus: I preferred Jerry Evans. I am not sure if he had an acting background, but he really understood actors. He could get emotions out of you and could say things that didn't hurt your ego. With Jerry, you understood why he wanted you to do something or move in a certain manner. He always put it in acting terms.

Lela could be very sharp at times. She directed the show very well, but she could say cutting things and did not have quite the bedside manner that Jerry had.

I used to joke when I first started doing soaps that soap opera acting combined the worst of film with the worst of stage. You had no rehearsal and no retakes. *Ryan's Hope* tried to shoot each episode as if it was live. They only had the tape machine from the network for a certain period of time and to reshoot cost more money. It was really set up like a live performance, and that put a lot of pressure on you.

Trent Jones: The scripts that Mary Munisteri and especially Claire Labine wrote were like one-act plays and were brilliant. I'd come from doing classics and felt I knew what a good script was. Some of the other scripts were decent and fine, but Mary and Claire's were amazing because of how character driven they were. Claire . . . was incredibly gifted. This was part of the positive experience for me, but it was frustrating too because I wanted way more time to work on the scenes because they were so good. You had to go with your gut. You know if you only have a six-month role, and it is your first, I was just starting to trust myself after a while and go with my first instincts and not try to dig into them. I was not a natural for this kind of acting.

Richard Backus: The writing was always so good. I think the show won Writers Guild Awards almost every single season they were on the air.

Randall Edwards: Claire and Paul were lovely, committed, beautiful, big-hearted people. They loved these characters. They loved the story. They loved writing and creating this world. They loved setting it in New York City, which they lived in. They also used their imaginations quite a bit—sometimes to the chagrin of the audience, I suppose. I thought that was very exciting and adventurous of them to create fantasy scenes and to bring in topics that were kind of testy socially, like abortion, and have that play out with conversations between Siobhan and her parents. And, of course, the crazy King Kong in Central Park storyline. I can never ever remember needing to go to them with something I was not comfortable doing or saying. I just loved what they were creating and went with it, including Prince Albert.

Two more new characters appeared on the scene at this time as well. A big-time law firm sent representatives looking for Siobhan, who was the potential heir to Tiso Novotny's estate. After his uncle's death, Joe inherited everything, but with Joe presumed dead, it would all go to Siobhan. Wanting confirmation that these men were legit and not hired by the mob, Jack meets with private detective Matthew Pearse (Tom Aldredge), based on a recommendation from Bob Reid, to look into it. Jack is impressed and hires him, unaware that his feisty daughter Rose Pearse Melina (Rose Alaio) is part of the agency. Sharp-witted and wisecracking, the Italian American beauty immediately butts heads with Jack, who does not think he can work with her. Unconventional in every way, Rose even calls her father, whom she is undoubtedly devoted to, by his first name only. Realizing it is both or none, Jack agrees to a trial basis after Rose demonstrates why she is a crackerjack private eye.

Rose Alaio (Rose Pearce Melina): I had an agent named Honey Raider who sent me on several interviews—I had never done television at all. I would get callbacks for the soaps, and that is where I learned camera blocking and all that good stuff. I had an interview with the casting director for ABC's soaps. I had watched *General Hospital* and there was an Italian character, whose name I cannot recall, on it. I remember telling this woman that if that actress ever leaves the part, please consider me.

A couple of months later, they flew me to LA to audition on camera. I hardly had any sleep, and I had to memorize this huge scene. When I got there, they cut that monologue, and I had to memorize a new one. I was exhausted. As we were taping the audition, I felt like my head was going to explode because I had forgotten the next line. I just exhaled and said, "Line!" And this voice came out of nowhere and gave me my line. I just looked at the actor I was working with and asked, "Did you hear that?" He said yes. And I said, "Oh, thank God." And the guy in the control booth, who gave me the line, bellowed, "*This is God!*" Gloria Monty was the executive producer, and she was wonderful. She took me all around the studio that day and gave me the greatest note telling me, "Don't trip over the wires."

I guess because I had callbacks for so many soaps, *Ryan's Hope* must have seen some tapes and called me in. I remember walking into the office on June 25, and there was Geoffrey Johnson, the show's casting director, and Ellen Barrett. I had met Geoffrey a few times before on other auditions and knew it was his birthday. I brought him flowers. I read for the part of Rose, and then they called me back to do a scene with Michael Levin. I remember that he came over to me and asked, "Are you nervous?" I replied, "No, not since the lobotomy." It kind of broke the tension. And I got the part. I never met Claire Labine or Paul Mayer at this point and presumed they watched my audition tape. I was also never given any history of the show or what they were going to do with Rose other than Ellen Barrett telling me that Rose "shoots from the hip."

We did what they called six packs every week. We would do a sixth show over two evenings every week so the studio could close down for all of August, and everybody had time off. We shot my first episode as part of the six pack, so it was done at night. I taught speech and have a New York high school teacher's license for it. After shooting, I walked out of the studio, and three or four people greeted me. I said hello, and one said to me, "We just want to let you know we work in the sound department, and we love you. There will never be a boom shadow in any of your scenes." It's called supportive tone, so that is why I could project my voice so well.

Back in Sheepshead Bay, although Michael Pavel got away with trying to blow up Tiso, he is now out of a job with the Harborside closing. A chance encounter with Delia lands him a bartending gig at the Crystal Palace. She hires him, totally unaware that his actions had almost killed her. The studly Michael then becomes a pawn of conniving Kim, who seduces him to make her older ex-lover, Seneca, seethe. They almost made it to the altar when Kim lied about being pregnant. Some manipulation by Rae, with assistance from Roger, helped Seneca learn the truth from Jill at the last moment. Both Seneca and Rae tell Michael that Kim is only using him to make Seneca jealous, but that does not stop him from proposing. Kim quickly rejects his proposal. Neither man is right for Kim in Rae's eyes, but she feels Michael is worse, so she bribes his mother, Anna Pavel, with a full college ride for her son if he stays away from Kim. Realizing Kim is playing him, Michael accepts. Shortly after, Seneca bails Kim out of jail after a bar brawl that she purposely instigated while with Michael. Knowing that he cannot fight his feelings for Kim any longer and his desire to protect her, Seneca proposes, and she accepts.

> **Michael Corbett:** When I first started on the show, I would go in and rehearse during the morning. I would see this woman with big glasses and a scarf around her hair in curlers. I'd go up on set later to tape the show, and I would see this beautiful woman like Grace Kelly—doors would open and you would hear angels sing as she walked in. I finally got up the nerve to say to her one day, "I am so impressed. You are so good, and you don't even have to rehearse in the morning." She replied, "Honey, that's me in the morning—the one with the glasses and the coffee." That is my first real memory of Louise Shaffer. It was such a gift to be able to work with these people who were so talented.
>
> Getting to work with and rehearse with Louise, who was the ultimate pro and just made everything look effortless, was such a learning experience. Louise was just so precise and so good.

> **Tamara Grady:** I liked Louise Shaffer. I was amazed by the fact that what she looked like in the morning when she came to the studio versus when she walked on set. In the morning without makeup, wearing glasses, and her hair in rollers, she was an average-looking person. But boy, when they did her hair and makeup, she was gorgeous. I was young enough then to not realize that could happen. Now I know better.

> **Kelli Maroney:** I loved working with Michael Corbett and was glad he was there. The perspective of an actor new to daytime TV is very different than that of the veteran actors. I so appreciated his friendship and just his being there. He was a newcomer but also an absolute pro.

Michael Corbett: I had so much fun working with Kelli. We'd be off in the corner between takes, hanging out. But it was a lot for both of us.

Kelli Maroney: [Director] Jerry Evans was easier for me to work with because he was more gentle and helpful. Lela Swift was energetic, brusque, and blunt. She'd been directing so long she knew just what she wanted and didn't waste any time on niceties. You couldn't take anything she said personally, or you'd have your feelings hurt all the time.

Michael Corbett: I loved working with both directors. Lela was a character. This is one of the biggest lessons I learned from her early on. She would say a lot, "If you can't say it, you can't play it. Learn your lines!" She would not let anyone get away with showing up and not knowing their lines. That has carried with me to this day. For me, being a young actor first starting out, I was absorbing everything like a sponge. If Lela told me to go do something, I would do it. I felt she clearly knows better than I do. I loved working with her.

Jerry was a little more easygoing and gave you a little more freedom. However, at twenty-one and doing your first TV show, I was welcoming Lela's guidance. Her approach did not bother me at all. I wanted to be told where to go and what to do.

Louise Shaffer: Their styles of directing were quite different. I think—no, I know—I worked better with Jerry. Lela had a wonderful sense of pictures and composition and the technical aspects. She was amazing in that way. I preferred Jerry because of the kind of actor I am, he was really interested in what I was interested in—motivation and what is going on way down, deep inside. If I were stuck, Jerry could come up with something to actually help me. And he had a profound sense of humor, which always helped.

Karen Morris-Gowdy: I loved having both of them as directors. I think it would have been very difficult if we just had one director. They had different styles, but they had the same goal. I attribute that to Ellen Barrett keeping it all balanced. Jerry was much lighter in his touch for sure. Lela was a hard charger, but I loved her. She was always so prepared and dead-on with her notes. When she gave you one, she would explain why—she was very succinct with that—and you could adjust. They never made you feel bad about receiving notes and were always very supportive. I remember Michael Levin would get very upset by receiving notes because he came in very prepared. You had to have room to move and adjust because we did not always know what the long-term storyline was going to be, so you had to take their notes and go with it and play with it. They knew the end game; we didn't. A lot of times actors want to know why they are doing what they are doing. We weren't supposed to. It was in the moment. And that was what was fun about soaps in the day. It was such an incredible opportunity to learn the craft.

Rose Alaio: Jerry Evans was a dream. He was wonderful and an actor's director. Lela was a nightmare. Tom Aldredge and I had a scene where we were in his office. We were arguing, and I had a line and then slammed the file cabinet. Lela said, "Rose, I want you to slam the file cabinet before you take your line." In my mind it did not make sense, but I agreed. When we went to tape, I didn't—I slammed the cabinet after I said the line. I said, "Oh my God. I am so sorry." Tom, in full voice so Lela could hear him in the control room, said, "Rose, your instincts are right on. Don't let anyone try to stifle them." He stepped in because Lela was a bully.

Louise Shaffer had a crying scene, and Lela told her not to let anything come out of her nose. *Hello?!* How do you control that? That's who she was. I had an opening scene where I had to look guilty because Rose lost Ryan. I had my eyes lowered, waiting for the countdown to start taping. My initial reaction was to look at Jack and the guilt would come. Lela stopped tape and told me that I should be looking at him. I replied, "Lela, for once could you just trust me, please?" I was told she always bullied the newbies.

Tamara Grady: Lela was kind of crazy. She was very loud and shrill. I will give two examples. If we were opening up, looking through the goldfish bowl, in the Coleridge living room, she would yell in my ear, "Cue the fish!" That was insane. Another time we had some sort of a fancy ball and she would say things like, "Tell that guy in the tuxedo to move camera left." I replied, "Lela they are all wearing tuxedos." She would do stuff like that.

Rose Alaio: That is funny because we had a similar scene in the office. All of a sudden, we had a water cooler, and she opened the scene through it. I guess Lela liked shooting through water.

Tamara Grady: Lela would also often overstep with an actor. I remember one time with Ellen Barkin, who came in as a day player. Lela gave her some sort of direction, and Ellen's response was, "Isn't that an actor's choice?" This had all the other actors thrilled that somebody had the nerve to point out that some things should come from the actor and not the director. Lela remarked to me that Ellen "would never work again." She said that a couple of times about actors who had exceptionally long, successful careers.

Rose Alaio: Danny Kelly kept everybody laughing constantly. He tortured Lela Swift. One time he was chewing gum just before tape. He took it out of his mouth and put it on the boom. It distorted all the sound. Lela was yelling, "What is that? What is that?" He just loved to mess with her. I loved him so much for that.

Art Rutter: Danny Kelly and I became quite friendly. We would hang out a lot after work and on the weekends. He was this tough, alpha Irish guy. He would do battle with Helen Gallagher many times, but they would always get along at the end of the day. Hearing that Danny was Helen's favorite Frank—I believe that. Whatever their relationship was, I think there was a lot of mutual respect. Helen certainly did not back down to anybody—neither did Danny. Maybe that was it.

With Kim now Mrs. Seneca Beulac, Michael turns his attention to his ex-girlfriend, Amy Morris (Kaye de Lancey). Unaware that she is mentally unstable, he helps her get a job caring for Ryan Fenelli (Kerry McNamara) while Jack is at work. She goes completely nuts when she thinks Jack's new girlfriend, Rose (the pair wound up making love, not war), is going to take her place and kidnaps Ryan, hiding out in a secret room that she accidentally discovered in the basement of the Crystal Palace. She imagines that Ryan is the aborted baby she had created with Michael. A manhunt is on to find them. When Maeve stumbles upon Ryan, Amy knocks her out and keeps her prisoner as well. After failing to get Amy to listen to reason, Maeve is able to set Ryan free—she is then found by Jack and help arrives. Amy recognizes her mental illness, apologizes to Jack, and is sent away to get treatment.

Rose Alaio: Kaye de Lancey was wonderful. I loved her performance, but I didn't have many scenes with her. This storyline was how Rose became closer to Jack.

The first actress [Kerry McNamara] to play little Ryan was not bad, but she never spoke. It was like her mother told her, "Don't say a word." I think they even had to dub in a voice of a little girl at one point. We were all concerned, and I think that is why they let her go because she was mute.

Michael Corbett: I remember that Kaye had very pretty blue eyes. Here's the weird thing about doing soaps for a long time and talking about them years later: I had completely forgotten about that storyline, and I vaguely remember it. Perhaps this was something to just keep Michael Pavel around. I guess after she kidnapped the baby and went a little cuckoo [and off the show], somebody sparked the idea to throw Michael to Rae.

Rose Alaio: One day Claire Labine called me and she said, "I want to thank you." I said, "Okay. Why?" She replied, "Because when Michael Levin shoots scenes with you, he's calm. He's normal." I had never met Michael before we started working together. He would throw fits, yelling or screaming during camera blocking or dress rehearsal. I would just laugh. Once he pulled me out of the room and asked why I was laughing. I said, "Because you are funny." We did get along, and I guess that kind of chemistry between us was good.

I also adored Tom Aldredge. We got along so well. We were like this comedy team. Rose called him Matthew the entire time until my last episode. Thankfully, Jerry Evans was directing and I asked if I could call him "Pop." He said, "Absolutely," and I did.

Michael Corbett: I do recall that Helen Gallagher would not work with me. She just felt that her character of Maeve would not interact with any character that was mob-related. She would not want to embrace them. My character got caught up in that. Helen was lovely. The crazy thing was that I had seen Helen in *No, No Nanette* on Broadway. I was very much into musical theatre, so to be working with her was so exciting. She was amazing. But I was bummed that her Maeve Ryan did not have interactions with my character, even though I would come into Ryan's Bar. They would get Delia to serve me from behind the bar. Randall Edwards could not have been lovelier.

Rose Alaio: Helen Gallagher took over for Ann Miller in *Sugar Babies* while Ann was on vacation. I remember watching Helen stretching and trying to see if she could still do a split. Of course, she went right down with no problem.

   I smoked, and I caught Helen looking at me a lot. She'd be getting her hair done, and I would be in my dressing room, with the door open, running lines with Michael, and she'd be staring at me. I thought she hated me. Finally, she told me she was doing a play and had to smoke in it so she was observing me because she was not a smoker. Helen was a doll—what a lady!

Although Ken George Jones was brought in to bust up Frank and Jill, Trent Jones played him so charmingly that you could not help but like him, especially after the viewers learn that he has a fatal disease. Ken has contracts to honor and goes on performing and singing his love song "Jillian" while getting weaker and weaker.

Trent Jones: Ellen Barrett was okay. I felt there was a creative difference when I had my final song called "Jillian" on the show. I had an extremely specific way I wanted to sing it, but she came into the recording studio and forced me to do it an unusual way. It wasn't disastrous but not what I had in mind. I thought to myself, "I am the musician. You are a soap producer. You really don't know what you are talking about here." There was no way to get around her. She was the boss.

Rose Alaio. Ellen Barrett was another nightmare. She told me I needed therapy. One time she called me to her office and I was standing at the doorway. She said, "Enter. Sit. Speak." I said, "When I feel like being a dog, I'll come back." And I left.

With Frank's help, Faith remains sober. That is, until she ventures out to the Coleridge beach house for some fun in the sun one fine summer day and discovers Jill and Ken making out on the deck. Stunned, she leaves without saying a word, but it sends her back to the booze, and all sorts of childhood slights with her sister came bubbling up to the surface.

   When Faith calls out Jill for having an affair with Ken, which she saw with her own eyes, and tells her she is throwing away her relationship with Frank, Jill responds, "I am not throwing away anything. What is happening between Ken and I has nothing to do with Frank. I love Frank." Jill's self-righteousness sends the aghast Faith into an explosive tizzy, and the sisters exchange harsh words. When Faith downs another glass of booze, she sarcastically asks Jill if she is going to stop her. Jill calmly walks over and fills up her glass. Faith then screams at Jill to get out. Their confrontation, which is the start of the Jill/Faith war, is *Ryan's Hope* at its most enthralling, from the acting to the direction to the writing.

On a lighter note, one day Barry feigns illness to spend the day frolicking in bed with Lily. Feeling bad for him, Delia unexpectedly drops by his apartment and Lily is forced to hide in the bedroom. Then Jill shows up looking for a missing Ken. With Jill's arrival, an eavesdropping Lily counts to three with the fingers on her hand. Christine Ebersole's perfectly perplexed look, signaling that Lily thinks Barry is boinking all of them, is hilarious. Unfortunately, it was her last appearance on the show.

> **Trent Jones:** One of my great disappointments was that when I started, Christine Ebersole soon left. I was there for her farewell party. She went on to do *Camelot* in a touring company with Richard Burton and someone else that used to be on *Ryan's Hope* [Richard Muenz]. I had been watching the show of course and thought this is a brilliant comedienne. She was just so good in that role. The girl that replaced her [Kathryn Dowling] was fine, but you could see Christine was a star.

> **Richard Backus:** I really loved working with Christine and Kathryn Dowling. Christine went on to become a hugely successful Broadway star. She was very funny, odd, and wonderful to work with. Kathryn was sweet and sort of ditzy.

Shortly after, Roger discovers that Lily's other paramour is Barry, who has just proposed to Delia. He decides to research his rival's past and uncovers his ex-wife Elizabeth Shrank Ryan (Pamela Blair), a dancer who sings like a canary when it comes to discussing her ex-husband. Not only is there no dead wife, but good ol' Barry has a string of ex-wives and former mistresses. Roger gleefully brings this info to Delia, who refuses to believe it. However, when she learns of Barry and Lily firsthand, in typical Delia fashion, she does not confront the truth head-on but throws an engagement dinner party where the guests are not only the Ryan family but also all the ladies from Barry's past, the goal being to embarrass and humiliate him. However, in a weird twist, the women all stick up for Barry and say he cannot help himself. Even Lily speaks up and confirms that Barry loves Delia only and no one else.

Confused as ever, Delia decides to take Maeve's advice and forgive Barry. As she is leaving the Crystal Palace to go to his apartment, she comes upon a soused Faith unable to start her car. She has fallen off the wagon yet again after discovering that her dear brother Roger had covered up Tom Desmond's death to protect his own butt. Trying to be a good Samaritan, Delia slides Faith over to the passenger seat and drives to Barry's while Connie Francis's song "Who's Sorry Now" blares from the radio. As she pulls up, she sees Barry outside kissing Lily while putting her into a cab—unaware that she is heading to the airport and a new life in LA.

Feeling that she was played a fool once again, in a blind rage Delia puts the pedal to the metal and runs Barry over. Horrified by what she has done, she goes to check on him. Thinking he is dead, quick-on-her-feet Delia then decrees, "Faith did it!" Since Faith got away with almost killing Little John, crafty Delia is sure that the Ryan family would rally around and come to her defense here as well.

She pulls Faith over to the driver's seat and then, in a beautifully shot scene, the camera peers from behind as Delia, clad in an aqua-blue gown, flees into the night, her high heels clickety-clacking on the pavement until she is well out of sight. A frazzled Delia races back home and thinks she will go to jail. After calming down, she realizes that no one saw her enter the house and that no one knew she was going to see Barry, so she can pretend to have a premonition about Barry and Faith. She strongly hopes that Maeve and Johnny will believe her since she actually had a real premonition a few days prior that saved Johnny from bat-wielding thugs. Her plan works and Delia is in the clear—for now.

Richard Backus: It was funny. I was on these shows at a time when they were doing remotes, and characters were being sent to South America and the Caribbean in these fantastically romantic places. I thought, "Why don't I ever get to do that?" Finally, I got to do a remote and where was it? On the street at night! The whole setup was super, though. They did an excellent job.

In the late summer of 1980, Labine and Mayer dropped a bombshell on the cast and crew when they sold *Ryan's Hope* to ABC. This had a profound, everlasting effect on the show. Speculation ran rampant with rising production costs and the pair's frustration with the network perhaps being the key contributors to their decision. However, it seems like, à la Uncle Tiso, ABC made them an offer they could not refuse.

Rachael Mayer: He sold it to be able to send his kids to college.

Ruth Mayer: My parents were so broke when we were little. My dad wrote army training films. We had the chewed-up furniture. My dad took a lot of pride sending us to private school, but when we would go to the pediatrician my mother would pay by check and say, "I hope it lands safely." They were scrappy. Selling *Ryan's Hope* was a miracle for our family. It was the first time we had any money.

Rachael Mayer: It was also the first time he felt secure that he could support his family and stop having constant anxiety attacks about finances.

Ruth Mayer: When they owned the show, they did not have a nest egg. Selling the show gave them that. My dad's father was a famous playwright and movie screenwriter in Beverly Hills, but he never bought any property, which is why our family had no money. He was such a communist. If only he had been a little less lefty, Dad would not have had to sell *Ryan's Hope*.

Rachael Mayer: Even though *Ryan's Hope* was successful, my father psychologically was on a thirteen-week cycle, and the show could go off the air. Every thirteen weeks, it got renewed. He still felt the show could get cancelled at any minute. That is what show business was like in his family.

Ruth Mayer: I remember one family dinner where my father and mother were working on shows [he was writing for *Where the Heart Is*, and she was playing Sarah Hanley on *Love Is a Many Splendored Thing*] that got cancelled the same night. That literally happened to them.

Rachael Mayer: The vulnerability financially—oh my gosh! When selling the show, we were at that point in high school, and he didn't have to worry about college. It gave him a little security.

During the eighties, several publications looked back on the first five years of *Ryan's Hope* and bestowed nothing but acclaim onto Claire Labine and Paul Mayer for their storytelling and superb writing. Rod Townley commented in 1984's *The Year in Soaps*, "Reality and authenticity were the qualities that first attracted viewers (and even critics) to *Ryan's Hope*." Christopher Schemering, author of 1985's *The Soap Opera Encyclopedia*, was even more praiseworthy and wrote, "The show was more interested in 'moments' than in story; long dialogue scenes between daughter and mother, lovers dreaming of their future; and brothers and sisters squabbling among themselves, remembering real and imagined slights and resentment. It was close to the original concept of *As the World Turns*, but with sharper dialogue."

With ABC now in charge, Claire and Paul were removed as executive producers and now were just the head writers. Ellen Barrett remained producer and was now the de facto executive producer but without the title. The cast became jittery, not knowing what ABC would do or how they would interject themselves into the show.

Rachael Mayer: Paul lost all creative control, and it was kind of heartbreaking.

Ruth Mayer: When he was executive producer, he was the captain of his own ship. That was just his personality. To take and follow orders was *so* not who he was. I can imagine that it was extremely hard for him.

Laura Rakowitz: I was working there for about a year when Claire and Paul sold the show to ABC. It was a surprise to me but I was never involved in that backstage gossip. I never knew any of the inner dealings. I felt that Paul and Claire wanted to divest themselves from the show, though they remained involved. I would go to all the production meetings, and if they weren't there in person, they were on the phone. Sometimes they would send in their notes separately, and often we would incorporate them. ABC did have a prominent role and they did have some silly network people present, like Jackie Smith. She was an enormously powerful lady, but not a very smart lady. There was always tension when she attended these meetings.

Rose Alaio: I was the last contract player under Labine-Mayer. I was kind of this pawn. It is interesting what happened. While we were off in August, they sent me scripts at the end of the month. When we returned to work, Michael Levin said, "I am so glad you're back." I replied, "Why? Where would I go?" He told me that they were trying to recast my part. I told my agent what was going on, and Honey said, "Oh, Rose. You have no idea the havoc that you wreaked." I asked, "What happened?" From what I gathered, with ABC now calling the shots, they pulled a power play and wanted someone new as Rose. Geoffrey Johnson stood up to them and said, "We gave you the *definitive* Rose." I remained in the part but Geoffrey quit shortly after.

Michael Levin: Unfortunately, some felt that Rose Alaio was miscast. That is all I will say.

Ron Hale: I really don't recall any changes at first. It was not overnight—then bam! Change. Ellen Barrett took more responsibility, though. I will never forget that sometime after Ellen became more in charge—this was just a brief time after women's lib and women were still fighting to be equal—that Nancy Addison and all of the women on the show were so thrilled to get a female upfront producer. It was a big step as far as they were concerned and within the industry. It proved that women were more than capable in running a show. We got along fine and I liked her.

Art Rutter: I don't recall any major changes after the sale of the show. However, I and other people thought it was very bizarre that Ellen Barrett was never given the executive producer title. In those days, the credits were much more protective than they are today. To me, Ellen was the executive producer. That's how she acted. It could have been as simple as that she just pissed off everybody and why reward her if they didn't have to. It also could have been Jackie Smith's way of wanting to push her out.

Tamara Grady: After the show was sold, it went from like a family to a corporation. I cannot put my finger on anything specific. I loved working with Claire and Paul. They were great people and thought the show was really very good. I hadn't watched soap operas since I was a kid and thought *Ryan's Hope* was far and above any soap I saw back then. We especially looked forward to Claire's scripts, which were often late but always brilliant.

Karen Morris-Gowdy: It definitely changed the complexion of the show. We were such a tightknit family, including the crew. And even though we were on ABC, we were our own unit. We didn't have the network dictating what storylines to do. It was run like a play every day because money was tight. You could not break tape. If you flubbed a line, you felt horrible because that was money to Paul and Claire. Then after a while, I saw the change with ABC, because now that the money was there, if someone did not come in prepared and did not know their lines and did not know their marks, they would just stop and retape over and over. The days became much longer, and it wasn't as fun. But as we went on, we got used to it. It was what it was. ABC wasn't going anywhere. Paul and Claire needed ABC, so we adjusted.

Kelli Maroney: I tried to stay out of that stuff as much as possible. I wasn't included anyway. I knew there was a thick tension in the air and that people looked unhappy. The little I did know I didn't understand because I wasn't part of the history and therefore had no frame of reference. I just wanted to mind my own business and do my work.

I knew that I was an "ABC character,'" as opposed to anything Paul and Claire had written or wanted to write. There was contention between them and the network as to the direction of the show, moving forward. But that's the sum total of what I knew. For me, it was one of those "Hey, I just work here!" moments. I never said it out loud, obviously.

Malachy McCourt: I indeed noticed a change when ABC took over. There was not a subtle but very drastic shift in the attitude because the thing with Paul and Claire was that they protected us from the network. They were on the front lines and took whatever crap was coming down the pike from ABC. We lost that.

Randall Edwards: I probably wasn't there long enough to notice a big shift. I do know we had some nice parties by ABC at the Plaza Hotel.

Richard Backus: As the show on a whole, I don't think I was aware of a particular change. However, I think it may have affected my tenure on the show later. The cast was a bit nervous. It felt like a family. A lot of people had been there for a long while and felt very secure in their roles. They felt appreciated and loved by Claire and Paul. Now with the network in charge calling the shots, they didn't know what might happen.

Rose Alaio: ABC was also not happy with my contract. They called my agent and asked that I take a cut in pay. I was making $425 a show, with a guarantee of one and a half shows a week. This was in 1980 and that was an okay pay—not great. They wanted me to go down to $400 a show and then give me a guarantee of more shows the second year of my contract. I told my father because he had been the secretary treasurer of a candy union, and he negotiated a lot for the workers. He suggested I tell them that you'll take it, but in the event that they write you out after the first year—which was our suspicion—they will pay you retroactively. I called Honey and she said, "Your father is a genius." She called ABC and then let me know they said never mind. That's when I knew my character would only be on for a year. When I told Michael what happened, he said ABC offered that to a lot of the contract players. The only one who accepted was Earl Hindman and, as a result, he was on for several more years.

The year 1980 closed out with Delia getting away with her disgraceful crime, although Roger has his suspicions. The story that she told Maeve and Johnny about something bad happening to Barry that night rings false despite her previous premonition. Guilt-ridden, but not enough to fess up, Delia only visits Barry once in the hospital to find out if he remembers anything about the accident—he doesn't—then stays away. She psychologically regresses back to needing Maeve's constant approval and fantasizes of being Mrs. Frank Ryan again. Delia, though, is right about one thing. As she predicted, the Ryan family pressures Barry not to press charges against Faith, who promises to sober up for good this time and enters into treatment.

Meanwhile, Ken languishes in the hospital, begging to die with dignity. Seneca, however, refuses to prescribe the drugs he needs to end his life, despite the pleas from Jill. A desperate Ken contacts a dealer, and Jill is arrested for his mercy killing because she is found holding a syringe at his bedside. She suspects that Barry gave Ken the drugs and is trying to pin the rap on her, so she hires an aggressive attorney who plays hardball with Barry. She is eventually exonerated when Ken's suicide note turns up in Little John's Ken George Jones notebook, where he revealed how he got the drugs.

Trent Jones: I knew the role of Ken George Jones was short-term and he was slated to die, but you always live and hope for remission.

Frank, who is now through with Jill, or so he says, spends more time with Faith, and it progresses into a romance—much to Delia's chagrin. Although Jill insists that she is not in love with Frank any longer, Maeve and Bobby (who has a special place in his heart for Faith) do not believe Jill and worry that the vulnerable doctor will get hurt in the end. Happier than she has been in a long time, Faith ignores their trepidations.

The Michael/Kim/Seneca story is the other major story that most suspected was spurred on by ABC. Kim is pregnant by Seneca, who is elated about being a father, just as she is cast in a Broadway play secretly financed partially by Rae. She decides to abort and persuades a reluctant Michael—still haunted by Amy's abortion—to accompany her. She later tells Seneca that she miscarried. It was a big deal in daytime to have a character actually go ahead with an abortion (they usually miscarried or changed their minds before going through with it), but the writers presented it with no moral or religious outrage. It was Kim's choice to go through with a legal medical procedure. The audience's disgust was not so much with the act but more with Kim lying and doing it behind her husband's back without his knowledge.

Kelli Maroney: The writers never discussed anything with me at any time for any reason. My attitude was then (and is still now) that I'm here to learn something when I get the chance. It never even occurred to me to want to discuss the writing and offer my input. I can't even imagine a scenario where that would have gone over very well.

I had to decide right away not to judge anything they had Kim do and at the same time try to grasp that I was on national TV doing it. One of my biggest fears was that everyone in America would think I was a bad person. But I realized that you can't inhabit a character and judge and reject them at the same time. Everyone has reasons for and justifies the things they do. Louise pointed out that playing "the girl you love to hate" was the best role in the show! I got to where I just enjoyed playing all of it and managing to justify whatever they threw me and having fun. It's much better to play the baddie than the good girl who gets stuck pouring tea and talking about what Rae and Kim had done that week.

As a reward for his help, Kim convinces Rae to hire Michael as her executive secretary. While Michael is enjoying the high life with a new wardrobe and is accompanying Rae to posh restaurants, an irate Kim is demoted to understudy. Seneca then pressures her to try for another baby, but Kim is determined to get her lead role back no matter what it takes. Her first steps are drugging the coffee of rival Connie Markham (Carolyn Hurlburt) to make her sick so Kim will have to step in during rehearsal and flirting with her producer Elliot Silverstein (Joe Silver). More shenanigans follow, and devious Kim is able to get Connie fired and regain her lead role.

The writers kept Kim and Michael at their conniving best going forward. Michael cozies up with Rae, and eventually the two hit the sheets. He now has to keep mother and daughter from finding out about one another since he has resumed his affair with Kim as well. Kim's luck juggling Seneca, Elliot, and Michael comes to blows when Seneca punches out an amorous Elliot, causing Kim to almost lose her job. She doesn't lose it, and Kim receives raves on opening night. A cast party is thrown at the Crystal Palace, and one of the guests is Christopher Reeve (now a movie star due to *Superman*) playing himself as a favor to Claire and Paul, who gave him his start on *Love of Life*. Michael also gets good news that evening with a promotion from Rae. The scheming young lovers end the year in bed together, celebrating their good fortune.

> **Louise Shaffer:** I reacted to this story as an actor the way Rae did. It is funny, when you are working, you try hard not to step outside the character but you sort of do. And in the same way that I really admired Helen and what Helen did, I thought it was amazing the way Kelli handled this storyline, given her age. That stuff is hard to play when you are young. They tossed her into that very quickly, and she didn't even get a year to settle in. Romance is one of the toughest things to play in the world, I think. Do any of us know what triggers that? It is hard as an actor to figure that one out and play it from the inside out. I used to watch Kelli and think, *Wow that kid really is handling something amazingly tough. She's doing it.* This was a complicated story. It was not doing Juliet on the balcony in acting school. Kim and Seneca's relationship was a difficult one to understand.

Kelli Maroney: John was wonderful to me. Here he was, saddled with a storyline that I'm sure he felt was not something his character would do, to say the least, but he separated all of that from working with me, the human being. He didn't blame me for the storyline, and if he was frustrated, he didn't take it out on me. He was patient with the reality that I was new, and he was nothing but encouraging to me.

Louise Shaffer: I loved John Gabriel. He handled everything with a great deal of charm. He was a particularly good and generous actor. I think that helped a lot with that storyline. There are actors who are there for themselves, and then there are actors who are collaborators and part of the team. John was one of the latter. You were always going to get good work from John Gabriel.

Ron Hale: John Gabriel and I became friends immediately because we used to do what I called the Yiddish act. John was Jewish. I do not know how we got into it, but one day there was something going on and I went into this whole Yiddish thing I was pretty good at. He came back at me. There were so many times after doing a scene he would look over at me and start the Yiddish act. We hit it off beautifully. Roger and Seneca had an interesting relationship over the years.

Rose Alaio: I got very close with Ron Hale. He was a doll and just the best. He invited me up to his upstate home where he lived with his wife, her sons, and their big standard poodle. We had a ball spending the day together. A new beer had come out and was not available in the city but was in Ron's town. We bought a case to bring back to the crew as a thank-you because we had a recent really long day of shooting.

Laura Rakowitz: Everybody was surprised with the pairing of Kim with the much older Seneca. Some were uncomfortable with it. I don't think Kelli Maroney and John Gabriel had much chemistry together. There was a triple whammy from it, but they kept it going for as long as they could.

Michael Corbett: I really did not work that much with John Gabriel, but he was always very nice. I like anybody who is in musical theatre, and John had a singing background. He was always very gracious and professional with me.

The people who stood out for me were Karen Morris-Gowdy— really lovely and very sweet. She was one of those people—knowing I was new—who would always ask me how I was doing and how it was going. She was very welcoming. Bernie Barrow was the ultimate professional and a great guy.

Karen Morris-Gowdy: I really liked Michael Corbett. I know what it felt like walking into that tightknit group, and everybody is looking at you up and down, waiting for you to show your goods. It is very intimidating, and in this acting and writing world, when you get a job like that, it is like the biggest day of your life. You have a paycheck. You're going to eat next week. There was no reason to act petty. There is room for everybody.

Ron Hale: Karen Morris-Gowdy *was* Faith—she really was. When I first got to know her a little bit, we just found out that she had been Miss Teen USA. One day, I ribbed her about it in a nice way. She turned around, gave me the finger, and said, "Fuck you." I fell in love with her on the spot. Karen was a very talented young lady with a wonderful sense of humor.

Michael Corbett proved to be the show's breakout star. An early article titled "Michael Corbett: *Ryan's* Best Hope for Sex Symbol" by Jon-Michael Reed was just the start of Corbett's press buildup in soap columns and fan magazines. Reed remarked, "The *RH* men have always been attractive, charming, top-notch performers. But they haven't sparked the libidos of the female audience as much as males on other soaps." Corbett changed all that, and Reed continued, "His boyish charm, mixed with an unsettling, subtly threatening street-punk savvy, made the ladies perk up." No doubt so did some of the male viewers. Corbett's surprise popularity delighted the network, but perhaps it was not what the old guard expected and accepted so easily. This off-screen drama would continue and come to a head in 1981.

3

The Ratings Rise,
Then the Writers Strike, 1981

Going into 1981, ABC's Jackie Smith now had an even bigger public voice in storylines and casting. She was credited for spearheading the rise in ratings for the other ABC soaps, so she was purportedly given the leeway to help boost the audience for *Ryan's Hope*. She commented to writer Tom Jory in *The Austin American Statesman*, "I think we are entering a Golden Age of Daytime, when the audience will no longer accept stories that do not have energy and humor. Agnes [Nixon] introduced the faster format. We've taken that and gone in the direction of suspense, high suspense, rather than the kitchen sink variety of story. In this search for quality and energy and distinction, we have given ourselves a terrible burden. We're eating up the material. A storyline that once ran a year now is done in three or four months. It's a lot of pressure on me because you say, 'How can we top this?' We have been topping ourselves, I can tell you."

Smith revealed to the *Ladies' Home Journal* that her immediate staff consisted of her and two other women, ranging in age from their midtwenties to midforties. She continued, "We're married, we're single, we come from different parts of the country; we represent a variety of points of view. But there is one thing that unites us—a passion for quality." She then went on to say how she began having focus groups, bringing together women to discuss the shows to see what was working and what was not.

Rachael Mayer: Paul spoke of Jackie all of the time. All I remember is that they were at odds.

Ruth Mayer: I remember that the executives at ABC were just a constant struggle. I think it was from the very beginning with the captain of the ship thing. My dad was probably arrogant and it was my-way-or-the-highway but it came from a place of total commitment. And I do think the executives were trying to make the show more like the others because it was the safe bet.

It is not surprising that this writing-by-committee strategy did not sit well with Claire Labine and Paul Mayer, who were used to only consulting with themselves, for the most part, regarding their storytelling. The writers clashed with Smith and the network even more moving forward. Many years later, Claire Labine opined to writer Tom Dorsey that when they sold the show, instead of sticking around, battling ABC, the duo "probably should have gotten out then and let them do what they wanted to try and then get us back when it was still salvageable." To some, the show was losing its realness—from the stories to the production design.

Ruth Mayer: I feel my dad would have said the opposite. He stood up for the integrity and quality of the show, and he was proud of it every time he did not compromise. ABC wanted to dumb it down and make it a more traditional soap opera. What elevated it was the things they fought for.

Rachael Mayer: I can give one example—the sets. He wanted the linoleum in the kitchen to be beat up and buckled. He wanted it to look like a real kitchen. And he wanted the taps on the bar to actually work. ABC did not want that. They wanted it to be pretty. Creatively, he was always fighting with them about those kinds of things. He wanted a diverse cast. The fact that they were Irish Catholic was a big no-no initially. Imagine how it went from there.

Ron Hale: We knew what ABC was trying to do. That was the major difference between our show and the others. When I started to notice all these changes, I just thought, "What are you doing?! Just because the other shows are doing this, it does not mean that we have to do it."

When we came on air and within the first six to eight months, I started to understand who we were and what we were about as a show. I remember just before a dress rehearsal walking onto the set one day into Ryan's Bar, and I just stood there. My mouth dropped because I had been so wrapped up in myself, trying to do the best I could with this new character that I was helping to create, that I just stopped and looked at that bar. The extras sitting there were guys wearing sanitation uniforms and cab driver caps. I just thought there was no other daytime TV show in the world that is real. We're real. This is about a real city—not Happy Dale or Sugar Grove with people named Lance—this is real. Look at Malachy behind the bar—*the* Malachy McCourt for goodness' sake! And he is serving beers to these actors. These were day players, but they were as much a part of it—they looked the roles and took them on beyond just being an extra standing there pretending to talk to somebody. It felt like a real Irish bar in New York City. It just made me go, "Wow!" *Ryan's Hope* began losing that at this time.

The resistance from Paul and Claire did not deter Jackie Smith with her thrust to get *Ryan's Hope* more in line with the network's other soaps. First, Smith pushed for the recasting of Siobhan and Joe and the resurgence of the mobster storyline. The Seneca/Kim/Michael/Rae plotline was also given prominence. Closer to the original nature of the soap was the Frank and Faith romance, with Jill hovering around them and Jack's attraction to the brash, opinionated Rose.

> **Laura Rakowitz:** I remember that ABC loved the character of Siobhan. They wanted to bring her back and have a romance. They continued the mobster storyline, which I thought was one of the best they ever had.

The year began, though, with an engagement party for Frank and Faith, which Roger uses to out Delia for the hit-and-run accident with Barry. Under prior hypnosis, Faith remembers the incident, but conniving Roger makes her forget what she recalled—that is until the next time she hears the Connie Francis song "Who's Sorry Now." Guess what tune Roger chooses to play on the jukebox at Ryan's Bar? The memories come rushing back to Faith, who fingers Delia as the driver.

Once again, the Ryan clan is disgusted with the deceitful blonde who tries to cry and excuse her way out of it, to no avail. Faith is so relieved to know the truth that she declines to press charges. Barry, on the other hand, needs time to think about it. Only Roger revels in Delia's chicanery and later tells a disbelieving Delia how impressed he was with her thinking fast on her feet and her ingenuity in framing Faith. Not surprisingly, Maeve begrudgingly allows Delia to remain a resident in her home despite her offensive behavior after a pathetic, weeping Delia throws herself at Maeve's feet, begging forgiveness. A contrite Delia is less successful with a stone-faced Barry, who will not confirm or deny if he is going to press charges and lets her squirm—even though he had already told Frank he will not. Going forward, his relationship with Delia remains frosty at best

Keeping Delia tethered to the Ryan family, especially Maeve, despite all her desperate actions and dirty deeds is what made *Ryan's Hope* different than other soaps, per John Genovese. Writing in *Afternoon TV*, Genovese so eloquently explained, "Delia could easily have degenerated into the 'bitchy' daughter-in-law mold (the Lisa-Erica-Rachel syndrome of the '60s and '70s) only to eventually break away from the core family altogether, but Labine and Mayer constantly produced trump cards which keep Delia somehow connected to the family fold . . . There is a definite psychological thread which binds Delia to this family . . . she is still a frightened child who never quite recovered from the childhood loss of her parents. Maeve is the mother figure she craves and adores." He said that this was an example of "fascinating, well-defined character relationships" that most other soaps were lacking. However, even some die-hard Delia fans felt she had finally gone too far and deserved a trip to the Big Doll House. The writers liked their characters to do the crime but not the time.

Randall Edwards: Wasn't that a terrible thing to do?! Even so, I did not think it was the end of Delia. For characters, there has to be repentance. The piper has to be paid. I knew at some point the truth would be revealed. *Who's sorry now?*

Laura Rakowitz: What I remember is the writers had arguments about "where to go" with this storyline and wanting to get it over fast. Delia was a naughty girl, but to have her do something so awful was just something they could not live with.

Richard Backus: It was fun to play a character like Barry, and I never questioned what the writers had him do. On *Lovers and Friends*, when they were trying to make things happen, my character had a brother who was the romantic lead in the show. He was a top photographer. I got a script where I break into his studio and smash all his equipment. I read the script and thought, "Oh my God! I am going to go to jail!" Not on the soaps you don't.

Randall Edwards: The bad girl gets to do so much dramatic, fun stuff, but there was so much comedy in the writing. It was a total joy and delight. Who can ask for anything more? You get to do all these devilish things but also be funny about it sometimes.

Rose Alaio: Richard Backus was divorced, and he had two kids. One day, he brought them to the studio when *The Pirates of Penzance* was on Broadway. I remember telling him that his children would probably like that show. I was a big theatre person, so I got tickets and we all went. We had a ball. Richard was an intellectual. He would tell jokes that he just knew no one would get because he dropped names of people no one heard of. Richard then invited some of us to a dinner party at his apartment because he was taking cooking classes. He made chicken livers with sour cream—it was actually very good. I went beforehand to help him set up because we lived about two blocks from each other.

During this Delia drama, Siobhan (now played by a blonde, Ann Gillespie) returns to Riverside and makes front-page news when she helps deliver a child on the subway as she is coming in from the airport. Her presence throws a wrench in Jack's relationship with Rose, who feels threatened by Siobhan despite Jack's assurances that there is nothing romantic between them. He even offers marriage, but Rose has a secret from her past that she is not willing to reveal. Siobhan, meanwhile, is receiving presents from a mystery admirer. Each day they get more and more extravagant, ranging from an entire fish to serve at Ryan's Bar to a white mink coat. After much speculation, Siobhan's gift-giver exposes himself. To her utter shock, it is her back-from-the-dead husband, Joe Novak (now Roscoe Born).

Roscoe Born (Joe Novak #2): I had heard of *Ryan's Hope* because I was familiar with all the soap operas. I never watched any of them, but my mother, sisters, and then wife watched soaps. I saw an ad in *Variety* and the description was for someone six feet tall and some other traits that I didn't have. I thought, "No way" and threw the paper on the floor. The next day, I picked it up and called the number listed for the casting director. I didn't even have an agent at the time. I went in and auditioned for the LA casting person. Then she came out, and there had to be at least fifty couples to go in and read. She got down to the end, and there were about fifteen of us left.

She said, "Sorry, we cannot see any more of you." I made some rude comment. She looked at me and said, "You have cajones." I got in to audition, and they flew me to New York. I had eighteen dollars in the bank.

Ann Gillespie (Siobhan Ryan #2): I didn't know any of the back-story until later, but apparently, they had been looking to recast the role of Siobhan for a while and had several sets of auditions. I was not a year out of acting school. I attended the ACT program [American Conservatory Theater] in San Francisco. I did not have a whole lot of experience on camera—just two TV movies includ-ing *Kent State*. I spent eight weeks in Gadsden, Alabama, which was where we shot the movie because you couldn't get anywhere close to Ohio. I then went without work for a whole month, which seemed like an eternity to me, but now I laugh. I begrudgingly told my agent I would go in on the audition for *Ryan's Hope*. I then wound up screen-testing with Roscoe Born.

Roscoe Born: I tested with Kirstie Alley and Ann Gillespie. I wanted Ann right away. Kirstie was weird, plus she was taller than me. I thought if they want her, I am not going to get the part. I was offered the role on my thirtieth birthday. I had a six-year acting apprenticeship in LA where I made maybe $5,000.

Ann Gillespie: I remember Kirstie being there. I saw her at other auditions as well. I know they were excited when they found me. Ellen Barrett, in particular, sort of took credit and a little bit of ownership over me because she felt like she discovered me. After a deal was set and I signed the contract, one of the requirements was that I dye my natural blond hair to brown so it would match closer to what Sarah Felder looked like. I was a bit horrified, but of course I went along with it. They sent me to some very expensive hair salon, and the stylist took one look at my hair and said, "I'm not dyeing that hair. People pay hundreds of dollars to look like that." The two of us colluded, and he put a rinse on it so it would eventually wash out.

Roscoe Born: Before we even started, Ellen Barrett, Paul Mayer, and Claire Labine took Ann and me to the 21 Club, which impressed the hell out of me. We had a two- or three-hour dinner with them. They said to us that it was a Romeo and Juliet kind of story. Afterward, Paul drove me home and said, "Don't re-sign when your contract is up." ABC wanted me to sign a three-year contract, but I was able to get a two-year pact because I didn't want to be stuck.

Ann Gillespie: When I attended that dinner at the 21 Club, I had the look of a brunette. It washed out in about a month, and nobody ever said anything about it again.

Rachael Mayer: My parents both loved soaps and thought it was a great incubator, but I think for actors, they felt they needed to reach the full height of their craft. If you need to make a living and need to be consistently on a show, it would be a safe bet and there's nothing wrong with that. I am guessing he may have seen some sort of star power in Roscoe Born, just like with Christopher Reeve. He was thinking that Roscoe needed to keep going.

Ruth Mayer: If my dad thought the quality was going down— which no doubt he did—his allegiance may have waned after trying to hold on to it.

Ann Gillespie: I thought Claire and Paul were lovely people, but I did not have a ton of interaction with them. But what I did have, I liked. They seemed very caring about these stories and these characters. I never watched the show, so I did not know any of the history or realize the title *Ryan's Hope* could have been about the character of Siobhan—but I do not really know. But I did feel they had a lot invested in Siobhan. From an actor's standpoint, that was pleasant, to have the writers care that much.

Rose Alaio: I loved Ann Gillespie. She and Roscoe Born were both great. It was torture how they taped *Ryan's Hope*. Everyone had to come in at seven in the morning for dry rehearsal and then camera blocking and then dress and then tape. We were there usually to seven at night. Roscoe's first scene was just him sitting at a table in a restaurant with a toothpick in his mouth. That was it. The rest of us went up to the greenroom and watched on the monitor. They were up to take five by then. Someone brought out a deck of cards and a bottle of wine was opened. It got to take seventeen, and we were laughing because this was one shot. Ellen Barrett was so obsessed with getting his first screen shot—let's do it with the toothpick in, let's do it with the toothpick out, let's unbutton your first shirt button, turn the other way. We were hysterical. It was a joke. We finally went back down to our sets and finished, and I don't remember what time we got out of there, but it was late.

Ann Gillespie: Roscoe and I hit it off immediately. We had instant chemistry and ended up becoming great friends. Doing soaps is hard work and how challenging it is remembering all those lines. Occasionally we would do two shows in a day. It meant you may have to remember two show's worth of lines in one day—that was nuts. They put our characters through all kinds of things, so it was great to have Roscoe's friendship to go through this together.

Behind the scenes, twenty-six-year-old Harold Apter joined the production staff and would progress to staff writer.

Harold Apter: When I was a teenager, I worked for Hal Prince. Then I was a stage manager in New York. I was horrible at it, so I decided I had to give up working in theatre, but I didn't know what I was going to do. I wrote to every single soap on the air. I got a rejection letter from *Ryan's Hope*, and then a few months later, I was working at an advertising agency. Nancy Horwich, who was the associate producer on *Ryan's*, called me to see if I would be interested in a gopher job. It is essentially a production assistant. I was about twenty-six years old and I said, "Nancy, if I can be you in five years, then yes." She replied, "You could be." I went in to interview with Nancy and producer Ellen Barrett. They thought I was okay, and they also—you could not do this now without getting in trouble—wanted a guy to carry around the copy paper because all of the scripts were copied in the back room at the studio. They hired me literally for the heavy lifting.

I knew nothing about the show. The only soap I had watched for a bit was *As the World Turns*. I began learning everything I could about *Ryan's Hope*.

Talented Roscoe Born was suave and full of charisma with an irresistible sexiness about him that elevated his Joe Novak and made him a fan favorite—despite his machinations. Joe easily wins over his friend Delia and slowly gets back into Siobhan's good graces, although her parents and Jack have misgivings. Ann Gillespie's Siobhan, however, was now being written in a different way versus when Sarah Felder played her.

The quirky, humorous parts of Siobhan's personality had dissipated, and she was written more as the beleaguered heroine with a personality shift closer to Mary Ryan—right down to her sister's impatience with Delia. In one episode, an out-of-character Siobhan yells at Delia to shut up and later tells her to mind her own business. Eventually, their friendship rekindles when Delia proves to be a big ally for Siobhan wanting to reunite with Joe.

Roscoe Born: I heard all the time from my sisters who had watched the show and some other women I knew that they missed Sarah Felder's quirkiness. But that's the thing when replacing characters. It wasn't Ann's fault, and they were writing it completely different. Ann was a straight-up type of actress.

Ann Gillespie: I didn't know the show at all ahead of time and didn't think it was important enough to do any research about it. Back then, I wasn't aware of this, but I was aware that the specter of Kate Mulgrew was everywhere. I did not know who she was, but I heard about her and that character. Now that this has been brought up, I think that is exactly what happened to Siobhan. In terms of the writing I did get—I don't know if it was very explicit—but Siobhan was very principled, later becoming a police officer and dealing with issues, ethical and otherwise, around Roscoe's character being in the mob. It makes sense now that they made that character more like Mary.

Joe swears (with his fingers crossed behind his back) that he has no ties to the mob. To that end, he needs a legitimate business to prove it. After revealing to Delia that he knew of her arrangement with his uncle, the Crystal Palace is coincidentally besieged with a union strike, led by waiter and secret mobster Orson Burns (Nicolas Surovy), and vandalism. Jack is doing his best to discredit Joe, and when Delia offers to let Joe live in the apartment on the upper floor of her restaurant, he is suspicious. Rose's investigating leads them to the truth that Tiso bankrolled the Crystal Palace, which Delia finally cops to, with plans (unbeknownst to Delia) to run a drug operation from a secret room in the basement. Of course, Jack shares this with the Ryan family.

Joe sticks up for Delia, claiming his uncle had a good side and that he genuinely was fond of her. It was a decent gesture on Tiso's part and a good business arrangement. He ends his defense of Delia by saying, "I can't help it. I like her." For which Johnny quips, "Seems to run in the family."

Shortly after, a smoky fire at the Crystal Palace almost costs Delia her life, but Joe strongly suggested to Roger that he go to the restaurant to check up on her. He finds an unconscious Delia in the smoke. After recovering, Delia is forced to claim bankruptcy. However, Joe rides in on his white horse to bail her out—taking part ownership while keeping Delia and her brother employed. This seemingly generous act gets him into the good graces of the Ryan family and back into Siobhan's loving arms.

However, Alexi Vartova (Dominic Chianese, followed by Leonardo Cimino, then Chianese again) has taken over from Tiso and is pulling Joe's strings. Now that he has the Crystal Palace back, Alexi wants Joe to enact revenge on Jack for his uncle's demise. Novak walks a dangerous line trying to keep the mob boss happy—instead of killing Jack, he will destroy his reputation as a journalist by setting him up for writing a false story and taking a bribe. To reach his goal, Joe needs the help of Tiso's former employee, Michael Pavel, who is now ensconced at Rae Woodard's newspaper. After a veiled threat from Joe, a scared Michael makes sure to get Jack assigned to the phony story Joe had laid out. Although the viewers were aware of Joe's deception, most still continued rooting for the charming mobster, even though he lied to Siobhan, stole the Crystal Palace from Delia, and was about to embark on ruining Jack's career.

> **Roscoe Born:** I wasn't concerned about Joe being likable. I didn't know anything about working on soaps, so that concept of trying to make your character likable so you don't get written off was not evident to me. I just wanted to make a full character and knew he was in conflict.
>
> [Joe] was in a state of ambivalence, trying to walk the line between a strong attraction to the goodness of the Ryan family on one side and the pull of loyalty to his mob family on the other, which he knew in his heart was evil. One day he goes over the line this way, and the next day he tries to balance it back the other way. I wasn't trying to play him sympathetically, but that is what made viewers feel compassion for him. I was just trying to play the full, rounded character that they had described to me.

Helen Gallagher: I was not a fan of the mobster storylines and did not think it particularly helped our show. However, if the family was involved in a family way, that is what the audience liked. I was very fond, though, of Roscoe Born.

Michael Levin: I can't remember if I liked this storyline or not. It was a soap opera so it had action, which they wanted then, although not particularly believable. However, Roscoe Born was a very good actor. He was also a nice guy and a pleasure to work with.

Randall Edwards: Our jaws dropped when Roscoe came onto the show. We would be hovering around the monitor, just watching him. He was a combination between Al Pacino and Paul Newman. We were just blown away. That is the thing about skillful writing with the right actor. They create characters like Joe that do dreadful things, but there is some element that you are still rooting for them.

Laura Rakowitz: Roscoe was such a terrific actor and played the part so interestingly with different layers to the role. Joe was one of those good guy/bad guy characters that you didn't have much of in soaps at that time. You did so more afterward. Joe was more dimensional than being completely good or bad, as compared to, say, Patrick Ryan who was always the good guy.

Tamara Grady: Roscoe Born was just gorgeous and such a good actor. You never saw him acting. He just became Joe Novak.

Rose Alaio: Roscoe was so funny. We were all in the greenroom one day, and he came in and announced, "I took this job because I am a big New York Mets fan. And what do they do? *They go on strike!*" [Luckily for Roscoe, the strike lasted only a week during spring training.] We all laughed. He was a doll and such a good actor.

Michael Corbett: Roscoe Born was such a nice guy and great to work with. He was a really good actor—very intense. Acting with him was one of those times where you are forced to up your game, so to speak. You had to act up to his level, which was great. We remained in touch for a long while after I left.

While the Siobhan-Joe love story remained extremely popular, so did two other plots. Faith is close to hearing her soon-to-be wedding bells despite

Little John's attempts to reunite his dad with Jill. She even flies in Frank's aunt, Annie Colleary (Pauline Flanagan), from Ireland for the nuptials. Seeing she has her son as an ally, Delia prods him along with his mischief making, but Frank remains stern with Little John, saying that he is marrying Faith—or so he thinks. Johnno is a big part of this storyline, and it showed that the apple does not fall far from the tree. He has inherited his mother's penchant for troublemaking.

Walanne Steele: It was an interesting touch when they brought in Maeve's sister. Claire originally thought Pauline was the right actress to play Maeve. When Helen Gallagher auditioned, Claire went in the other direction.

Jadrien Steele: I did not go to the studio in the mornings for the read-through and the blocking. I would come in usually around lunchtime. I was there for the rehearsals and then obviously the shoot. That way I was able to attend school half days, which made it workable. They did not block weeks of work time for me. I came in when I was needed.

I would run lines with my parents the night before. As an actor, you build that muscle of memorization and picking things up quickly.

Walanne Steele: I used to hang out in the makeup room. There was a television and I could watch what was going on downstairs. It was interesting. As a parent, it added another dimension to my life.

After getting mugged on a jog, Frank awakes to the fact that he is still in love with Jill. He breaks it off with Faith, practically leaving her at the altar. Fans expected Faith to take the high road, like she did when Pat ended their engagement to marry a pregnant Delia. However, the writers cleverly brought out a different Faith this time—she was a doormat no more. The almost-bride is livid not only with Frank but with her sister Jill as well, whom she claims did nothing to squash any romantic feelings left between her and Frank.

Nobody is safe from the wrath of angry, vengeful Faith. Faith even takes on Maeve in a wonderfully acted episode. Faith's first visit to Maeve after the breakup starts out cordial over tea, with Maeve allowing Faith to vent. However, when Faith goes too far and states that Frank purposely used her, Maeve reminds her that she reached out to Frank due to her drinking and that Frank made a mistake with her because he blocked his true feelings for Jill.

This sends Faith into a wild-eyed frenzy and results with the jilted bride yelling at a shocked Maeve to open her eyes about her "marvelous" son, who is by far no saint. Faith, however, directs most of her venom toward Jill. Audience reaction to this storyline was split, with some feeling that Faith never would have gone after her sister's true love while others reveled in seeing the Coleridge girls tear into each other instead of tag-teaming on Delia, as they did in the past.

> **Karen Morris-Gowdy:** I was so grateful that Paul and Claire started picking up on the nuances of the Coleridges. The Ryan family had their trials and tribulations, but they finally started to define the Coleridges as a family that had a lot of deep issues. I loved working with Nancy Addison—the silly scenes that we did and the dramatic ones. She was so much fun to play off of. I have two sisters, and I really loved those scenes. I adored Ron Hale and loved working with him. We had so much fun because Ron could be such a badass in our scenes.
>
> I loved working with Helen Gallagher as well. She was so different from her character. We all thought of Helen as our mom, but she wasn't. She was Helen. When working with her, you really had to be on your toes. She gave it to you and brought the best out of you. And I loved Bernie Barrow with all my heart—what a character. I came from a small town in Wyoming, and I didn't know a lot of people in New York. They became a family to me. Nancy became my sister, and Ron became my brother.

Kim and Michael, meanwhile, get careless with keeping their affair a secret. Kim suspects that Michael has a mystery sugar momma and thinks it is Delia, especially after the duo hit the disco dance floor at the Crystal Palace on New Year's Eve. Rae smells a rat when she finds Michael's gloves at Kim's place and then happens upon a Valentine Day's gift that her daughter gave Michael. She then plans an elaborate ruse to entrap Michael and Kim. It succeeds, and she finds them together in a hotel room. A weepy Kim pleads with her not to tell her husband, and Michael begs to keep his job, which gives him the lifestyle to which he is now accustomed.

Michael is sacked, and Rae keeps a nervous Kim guessing if she will rat her out. Needing stability with her career and her crazy personal life, Kim then hires Barry Ryan to be her manager, and he gets more than what he bargained for dealing with her lies and schemes. Womanizer Barry, however, is neutered, and Kim is the only woman in his life—strictly on a professional basis. A desperate Michael breaks into Rae's apartment to beg for his job back. At first she refuses but then recants after Michael calls it quits with Kim in front of her.

Malachy McCourt: I felt this storyline was a departure from the essence of *Ryan's Hope*, and I think it was a mistake. I do not know why it was happening. Like some of the cast, I thought it was not part of the traditional storytelling of the show. It had another element to it that was not *Ryan's Hope*.

Michael Corbett: I loved Randall Edwards. She was so much fun. I do remember that dance sequence. It was so *Saturday Night Fever*. At the time, I was hired as a John Travolta–type for an ad campaign for Anheuser-Busch beer. I was the disco guy who comes in and dances with a gal modeled after the one in *Saturday Night Fever*. We would do the disco number and then dance right out again. I think that is why they incorporated that into the show.

Randall Edwards: I really liked Michael Corbett. I remember doing that dance scene with him and that it was so much fun.

Richard Backus: I did know that the writers were having a tough time with what to do with my character. It was very frustrating going from being used a lot playing some interesting stuff to kind of being more like furniture. I was surprised that they didn't go in the direction of reuniting Barry and Delia in some way. There was never any talk of it.

Although the Kim/Michael/Rae plot line was not a hit with some cast members, it was with the critics and, more importantly, the audience. John Genovese summed it up best in *Afternoon TV* magazine regarding what made it work so well: It "produced new twists in the mother-daughter triangle formula. All three characters were users out to further their own ends and satisfy their own physical and material lusts, yet all three were, underneath, painfully insecure about themselves."

The spring of 1981 began with the departure of Art Rutter and tidings of good cheer in terms of awards and ratings. For the March 1980 to March 1981 season, the show received five Emmy nominations, including for Outstanding Daytime Drama Series. The others were for Outstanding Lead Actress in a Daytime Drama Series (Helen Gallagher); Outstanding Actor in a Supporting Role in a Daytime Drama Series (Richard Backus); Outstanding Actress in a Supporting Role in a Daytime Drama Series (Randall Edwards); and Outstanding Design Achievement for a Drama Series. It failed to get nominations for directing and, most surprisingly, for writing, after four straight nominations and wins. Most likely, the Prince Albert storyline still left a bad taste in many Emmy voters' minds. On awards day, *Ryan's Hope* came home with a single Emmy for scenic design. Well-deserved, the design team was led by Sy Tomashoff, who created the sets for *Dark Shadows*.

Art Rutter: ABC would rotate the studio supervisors/coordinators, so that is why I was moved to *All My Children*. I found the *Ryan's Hope* group overall as a family, with all of the warts and bitterness of a family. But I also felt a real warmth there. On *All My Children*, because it was a bigger group of people, it was much more impersonal. Everything was spread out, and it was shot in blocks, while *Ryan's Hope* was shot in thirty minutes from start to finish with some pickups. On *All My Children*, if you had some big sets, you shot out of sequence. I felt the continuity was a lot different.

The camaraderie was not as good and nice—it was definitely not a family feeling while I was there. The work was the same, but I had a lot more people to oversee—with two soundstages, there were two sets of staff for each department, so it was double the amount of people than on *Ryan's Hope*. This extra work didn't bother me, but it never became a family the way I liked it on *Ryan's Hope*. I was getting bored with the job by this point and was looking to leave anyway.

After working on *All My Children*, I was promoted to manager and later to director of program operations and administration, and I moved to the network offices. There were two Programming floors. My office was the floor with Josie Emmerich. She worked for Jackie Smith, who was in charge of all the soaps and whose office was on another floor with other executives. I never interacted with Seymour Amlen, but he was copied on all of my memos since he was the head of East Coast programming.

Richard Backus: Emmy nominations are somewhat random—I had come to soap operas from working on stage. I had always been very committed to ensemble acting and felt that everybody was important. When I got cast on *Lovers and Friends*, I introduced myself to the crew on my first day at the studio. The crew was startled because no actor had ever done that before. I got to know everybody. They liked me as an actor and got to know me as a person. On either *Lovers and Friends* or *Another World*, the crew would go out to lunch every day, and I was the only actor they invited to go with them.

This is a long way in saying that when your name comes up as a possible nominee—if you have a lot of friends on other shows, whether they know your current work or not—they'll vote for you. It gets you a nomination, and then after that, you must submit a tape. A group of your peers, who were not nominated, judge the performances.

I don't want to overstate this, but to some extent nominations are a reflection on how well you are regarded in that industry—the people you have gotten to know and if they like your work in general. I was sincerely honored to be nominated. I had a hunch Larry Haines [Stu Bergman on *Search for Tomorrow*] would win and expected that. I could bring a guest to the ceremony, and since I was separated at the time, I took my eleven-year-old daughter. Every time they presented an award in children's programming, the camera would focus on my daughter. She got on TV more than I did.

Randall Edwards: I don't recall what scenes I submitted, but there was a kind of a crazy story that happened to me on Emmy Awards day. The show's costume designers went out with me shopping for a dress because I was also presenting. We found this thousand-dollar dress made of silk with all this beadwork. I did not want anything tight so it was a little more elegant. The day of, I had to get to the studio early because they were going to curl my hair and help me with makeup and the dress. It went very well, although I did not win.

After the event was over, I got all my stuff and was still wearing the dress. I hailed a taxi to take home. When we got to where I lived, the driver became upset with me because I was taking too

long to get the correct amount of money out of my purse because
he did not have change for a twenty. I was starting to put my money
through the window, and he yelled at me and took off. I screamed,
"What are you doing?!" He went over to the West Side Highway
and started driving north. I had no idea if he was going to leave
the island. I am yelling, "I was paying you! Please stop!" Finally,
he pulled over. I dropped the money down and got out, thinking
I got away with my life. I am scrambling up the hill and had to
climb over a wrought iron fence and ripped my expensive silk dress.
I finally get up to West End Avenue and flagged down another taxi.
As I opened the door, I said, "Do *you* have change for a twenty?" I
just will never forget that—it was so frightful.

Ryan's Hope was, if not at its most popular, then very close to it. However,
a core set of disgruntled viewers (and cast members) were unhappy with
the new direction and missed the homier tone of the prior years. Even so, the
show had some of its highest numbers during this period, as did most of
the ABC lineup. Terry Ann Knopf wrote in the *Boston Globe*, "With a sub-
stantial increase in the daytime audience that included high school and college
kids, women as well as men in the 18- to 34-year-old age category, ABC capi-
talized on the changing demographic picture, leaving the other two networks
far behind." For newer viewers lured to *Ryan's Hope*, this was the show's heyday, as it arguably did a great job balancing the allure, glamour, and danger of
what New York City could bring with the hominess of the Ryan family.

In 1976, ABC had 4.7 million households, compared to 6.8 million
in 1981—an increase of 45 percent. During the same period, CBS lost
4 percent (dropping from 6.1 to 5.9 million), while the NBC audience
shrank by 27 percent (dropping from 5.4 to 3.9 million). Knopf gave credit
to Jackie Smith for establishing ABC's innovativeness and for swapping
the old-fashioned soap formula with long, drawn-out storylines for young
romance, adventure, and glamour. Knopf added, "What helps ABC
deliver a superior product is that the network exercises direct control over
its shows. Procter & Gamble, long a conservative force on the scene, owns
and sponsors six out of the thirteen soaps on television." For some *Ryan's
Hope* fans, this "one-size-fits-all" approach did not work.

Jackie Smith acknowledged that "extra edge of control," and added,
"Network ownership means a more direct line to the various program executives at ABC. There is less in the way of middlemen. I work with the shows

directly. I know how to get the PR department going. I really know what's happening on every show."

For *Ryan's Hope*, its increased popularity was mostly attributed to Michael Corbett and Kelli Maroney (although the star-crossed romance of Siobhan and Joe and the comical relationship between Jack and Rose undeniably helped). Not only was the duo being written about in the soap opera magazines of the day, but they broke out into the mainstream media when they appeared on the cover of *People* magazine. Kelli Maroney graced the October 27, 1980, issue with Genie Francis (Laura Webber Baldwin) of *General Hospital* and Kristen Vigard (Morgan Richards) of *Guiding Light* in a story called "Torrid Teens on the Soaps." Corbett was featured with Chris Bernau (Alan Spaulding) of *Guiding Light* and Alan Dysert (Sean Cudahy) of *All My Children* on March 9, 1981, in a story called "Soap's Lovable Cads."

Kelli Maroney: When that storyline took off, it was incredible. We were working so hard, and we just appreciated that people were enjoying it too. It was so amazing; we were just pinching ourselves. There isn't even a good word for what that experience feels like.

Michael Corbett: I noticed we got popular right away. I remember that in the first nine months of being on the show, I was on the cover of *People*. All of a sudden people are saying to me, "Oh my God! Your character is really a big deal." Our storyline started to heat up with the Rae and Kim triangle. Not having any point of reference, I thought this was all normal, and I started to do public appearances and magazine interviews. It was crazy, crazy press and fan mail. I did not know it was as big as it was because I thought, "Well, this is what happens."

Kelli Maroney: I have no idea how they chose us [for the covers], but I think they did quite a few soap actors that year. Teen storylines were hot. They were drawing a younger audience than they'd ever had before, during the summer especially, and the networks were over the moon. It was what they now call The Golden Age of Daytime Soap Opera, but it was also a dominant trend in all of our culture at the time.

There was a man who had a newsstand right outside my building. I passed by him every day on my way to work and back. The day the cover came out, I pointed to the magazine and said to him, "Look, it's me!" He looked at the cover and looked at me and said,

"Get outta here. That's not you." I looked so different with all that glamorous makeup. Even people who knew me and knew I was on the cover looked at it and asked, "Which one are you?" Seriously.

Another cast member getting the publicity push was Randall Edwards as Delia. She too landed on the covers of *People* ("Sex on the Soaps," June 1980) and *Us* ("Super Witches of the Soaps," January 6, 1981). Delia was always a popular character but, in the latter article, she was being grouped with the bad girls you love to hate. She received the honor due to her hit-and-run on Barry and then framing a soused Faith. However, Delia was less a villain and more of what they describe in the soap world as "the suffering antagonist." She does some vile things and stirs up trouble but rationalizes her actions with tears and a reason, albeit misguided, and still elicits empathy from a good portion of the audience who root her on. You had to have talented actresses, like Randall and Ilene Kristen, who understood the character to achieve this and make her lovable despite her dirty deeds.

ABC also began sending out *Ryan's Hope*'s actors to promote the show. They appeared as guests on local morning talk shows and made in-person appearances at malls throughout the country, usually paired with castmates or actors from other ABC soaps.

> **Ann Gillespie:** I was unaware how popular the show was . . . because I did not have any history of the show or watched it. I do remember people recognizing me on the streets, however. I never had that before because I never had that much visibility on camera. To be honest, that was also challenging for me to deal with. I guess I was convinced out of makeup, wearing glasses, in my sweats on my day off, standing in line at the bank, that I was unrecognizable. But apparently that wasn't true. I remember an interaction with a woman who spoke to me as if I was the character. She scolded me for what I did to my husband. Oh my gosh! That was sort of my first case, if you will, of that kind of fame. It made me uncomfortable, actually. I ultimately didn't enjoy it. In my private life, I really wanted it to be private.

> **Rose Alaio:** They sent us to a lot of places to do PR. Once they sent Michael Levin and me to Wisconsin. At dinner, Michael said we are ordering the chateaubriand and the most expensive wine since ABC is paying for it.
>
> Another time I had to do a mall appearance in Boston with

an actress from *All My Children*. We were on a stage, and during the interview I kept looking down, and there were about ten senior citizens in wheelchairs with their companions. After it was over, I found out that they were from a nearby nursing home. I said hello to all of them. The nurses with them watched *Ryan's Hope* religiously and just loved the show.

A couple of months later, I received a call from ABC sending me back to Boston to appear on a morning talk show with Michael Levin. I asked if it was possible for me to visit that nursing home after we did the TV interview. The PR person said that she would call them. She did and told me, "Rose, you have no idea how excited they were. They absolutely would love to have you and Michael. But you have to ask Michael, and he hates PR work." I pleaded with Michael and he agreed.

We did the television show in the morning, and we had a driver take us to the nursing home. They set up a tea for us with sandwiches and gave us a tour. We met the women who came to the mall. When we were on the second floor, a nurse came up to us and said that she rolls a woman named Agnes in front of the TV every day for *Ryan's Hope*. She said, "She doesn't look up or respond. But I know she is taking it in and knows what is going on." We went over to meet Agnes. Her head was hunched on her shoulder, and she was looking down. I knelt down so our eyes could meet and said, "Hello, Agnes."

And all of a sudden, her eyes lit up, her head came up, and she was looking at me, trying to talk. When she saw Michael, she got louder and more excited. The nurse started crying and said, "I knew she grasped everything that was going on." Michael was blown away. It was like this miracle happened before his eyes.

Ann Gillespie: To me, Michael Levin was so lovely. It was fascinating to me, coming into a system that was so established. So many of the actors had been on for so long and had ownership over these characters. What I remember about Michael's kindness toward me was that he really helped me understand what it means to be on a soap and how to best manage the day-to-day aspects of it, which was hard. I sort of remember feeling like they would write two months' worth of crying scenes and then two months' worth of happy scenes. And it felt like there was never any nuance. Michael was a kind of mentor to me about how to manage some of that—not just the acting piece but the psychology part. I really struggled working on the show. It was not easy for me on a number of levels. Michael was a very calming presence.

Rose Alaio: Ann Gillespie was a spitfire and I loved her. There were real stoves and sinks on the Ryan's Bar sets. Maeve would always be doing something because it was a restaurant. Most of the time it was string beans. A pot was on the stove, and Ann backed into it while wearing a bathrobe during camera block. Her robe caught on fire. The crew could not get over her swift action. She ripped off the robe and stomped on it until the fire went out.

Ann Gillespie: Yes, that was true. Thank God, my hair was up in curlers and that the bathrobe was terry cloth so it didn't burn very quickly! I remember how nice Rose Alaio was and the fond memories I have of her. But we didn't have much to do together.

Credit for the show's success has to go to Claire and Paul, who did a commendable job balancing what both ABC and new viewers wanted while trying to appease the core audience. However, it seemed that Paul did not feel very proud. In 1981, his daughter Ruth was attending an art and sculpture camp in Lacoste, France. She received a letter from her father stating his surprise with the rise in ratings for the show, which he felt was not at its best.

Ruth Mayer: As I said, my dad could be a bit of a snob, but he also took soap opera and *Ryan's Hope* and his writing very seriously. He took pride in doing something that was truly *good*, not the usual fare, and it was hard for him when he felt the show was no longer reflecting that quality.

I also think you can see . . . what a very sweet father I had. He had sent me to a fancy art camp and then paid for Cornell in full . . . because [he had] to work his way through the end of his college years and to start his professional life with nothing in terms of money.

Of course, all good things must come to an end, and for *Ryan's Hope* it began with the Writers Guild of America strike followed by CBS's decision to revamp its daytime schedule. Writers, with picket signs in hand, hit the pavement in April when their Guild could not come to an agreement with the film studios, networks, and producers regarding "compensation for the then new markets of pay TV and home video." Although this had no bearing on the soaps at the time, its loyal members (including the writing staff of *Ryan's Hope*) ceased writing their serials—or did they? There are various opinions as to whether Claire Labine and Paul Mayer crossed the picket line or not.

Laura Rakowitz: During this time, they were all the same writers. We would be in touch with them and were sworn to secrecy. There was not one writer still not working on the scripts. I am almost sure Paul and Claire were editing the scripts too. I was in LA for another writers' strike, and it was the same then. That is why the Writers Guild got so militant, because a director and an actor can't hide.

Roscoe Born: During the writers' strike, the writers were still involved. They still talked to the show through back channels.

Michael Corbett: I did hear that same rumor that it was Claire and Paul writing the show still using pseudonyms or something, but I cannot confirm that and really do not know. I was just trying to do my work and do my thing.

Ann Gillespie: The stories got so wacky. I believe I was told or assumed that Ellen Barrett wound up writing a lot of the scripts. One of the things we all talked about was that we felt we were living out Ellen's fantasies of what should be happening on the show. It was weird, and we thought this would not be the case if Claire and Paul were writing.

Rose Alaio: One day, Ellen Barrett said to me, "By the way, Rose had a daughter that she gave up for adoption." I thought, "Oh, how nice. Now I have to play that?!" We were all like "What the hell is going on?" during this time.

Rachael Mayer: I remember that my dad was so upset that they couldn't write. He was so frustrated and was going crazy with that. They were so pro-union—I cannot imagine him crossing a picket line. He was very left-wing. There is no way he was writing during it.

Ruth Mayer: I do not know for sure, but I cannot imagine it either.

Harold Apter: Paul was not writing the show, as far as I know, and I agree with his daughters that he would never have done it. I think Claire stayed out of it as much as possible. She was very involved with the Writers Guild for a long time. I cannot say for sure, but I don't think she was writing scripts either. Maybe she talked to Ellen Barrett, who kind of became the de facto head writer at that point. There were a bunch of other people, who shall remain nameless, that wrote the show. I just cannot see that Claire had any direct involvement.

The mob storyline continues on as Joe's plan works when Jack falls for the phony story handed to him, which is published in Rae's newspaper. When the defamed company files a lawsuit, Rae has no choice but to fire Jack, especially when $50,000 (presumed to be a bribe) turns up in his bank account (planted by Joe, with Michael's help). Aided by Rose and Matthew, Jack is adamant that he will prove that he was set up. Soon all roads lead to Joe Novak. Rose cozies up to a former high school friend, Lori Nuzzo (Anne De Salvo), who works as a waitress in a diner. She is also the girlfriend of Sal Brooks (Tony Schultz), a low-level mobster with ties to Joe and Alexi Vartova. Through an unsuspecting Lori, Rose is able to uncover helpful info. Jack, meanwhile, pretends to be down-and-out—even letting Ryan (now played by Jenny Rebecca Dweir) spend more time with Rose and live with Maeve and Johnny—as a way to get a pity job at the Crystal Palace so he can prove his innocence by keeping tabs on Joe.

With the mob storyline going like gangbusters, June saw the surprising dismissal of two of the show's most popular actors: Rose Alaio and Michael Corbett. This decision had many scratching their heads, wondering what was going on at *Ryan's Hope* and if the show was adverse to successful ratings.

Rose Alaio: I was called into Ellen Barrett's office, and she matter-of-factly told me that they were not picking up my option. I had expected this. She then said they would be throwing me a party, as was custom. They gave everyone silver boxes from Tiffany's with *Ryan's Hope*, your name, your character's name, and the dates you were on the show inscribed on it. I then went to see Nancy Horwich [associate producer], who was very sweet to me. She too told me about the party. I said that is fine, but I will not be there. Nancy was taken aback and said, "That is not very gracious of you." I retorted, "Well, it is not very gracious of you all for letting me go and taking away my livelihood."

Michael Corbett: I remember Kelli and I had just done a big promo tour with Tony Geary and Genie Francis. ABC chose a couple from each soap to do this bus tour. We just completed that, and Ellen Barrett called me into her office. She said, "Honey, I have some bad news. At some point in the near future, we're going to write your character out." I said, "Really?! Are you sure?" And she replied, "I'm sure, honey." And that was it. Ellen was great giving me the heads-up. She then said to me, "I am going to let you know what's happening." So, I knew a few weeks ahead of time.

Rose Alaio: I remember calling Michael Corbett after they let me go and giving him a heads-up about the combined going-away party that they planned for us. I did not think it was cause for celebration. He told me he would make sure that he was too busy to attend.

Michael Corbett: I thought Rose Alaio was great. She was such a nice Italian gal. I did not want a farewell party either.

Rose Alaio: They sent me my Tiffany's box. Louise Shaffer called me after that and said, "I'm calling on behalf of the entire cast. We want to thank you because the party tradition has ended."

While Rose is hanging out with Lori and Sal, he becomes suspicious of her and learns from Lori that Rose had gotten pregnant in high school. After some investigating, Sal connects her to Jack Fenelli. Rose then receives an anonymous tip regarding the whereabouts of her daughter, who is named Amelia. After watching her from afar on a playground, Rose skips town when Amelia's life is threatened by dim-witted Sal, who is unaware that the girl is now the adopted granddaughter of Alexi Vartova!

Rose Alaio: Tom Aldredge, who I adored and who was not under contract, called me after learning I was let go and said, "I'm not crazy about being on without you, so I'm not going back." They begged him because they had an upcoming storyline with Maeve. He called me and said, "Rose, they want me back." I said, "Tom, please. Go back for more money but go back."

Tamara Grady: Rose Alaio was popular. She was beautiful. I liked her.

Laura Rakowitz: I don't think the network liked Rose or her performance. They didn't like the pairing with Michael Levin. I distinctly remember thinking that they were sexy together. I personally was shocked that they split them up and that Rose left.

Rose Alaio: Other than that phone call from Claire, I had no interaction with her and Paul my entire time there. However, I saw them at a party thrown by ABC at Tavern on the Green for all the affiliates. This was just after they told me I was being let go, and I had a few more episodes to film. Paul came up to me and said, "I am so sorry, Rose. We wrote a quadrangle between Rose, Jack, Siobhan, and Joe, but it had to be a triangle." I saw it coming.

While Rose slinked off to Pittsburgh, Michael went out with a bang. Despite the promise that their affair has ended, Kim and Michael hit the sheets once again, and their interactions arouse Rae's suspicion. Irate and packing heat, she follows the lovebirds one night to Michael's houseboat and finds them in bed together. This coincides with Joe sending Sal Brooks to rough up Michael to guarantee his silence about Joe's involvement in setting Jack up.

The "Midnight Murder," as it was touted, lasted a whole week. It was riveting drama; a desperate Michael wants to keep his lifestyle with Rae. He pries the gun away from her, and it drops to the floor, as he keeps denying his feelings for Kim, who does not believe him. A wailing Kim throws insult after insult at Rae for being insecure about losing her looks and for being jealous of her and trying once again to ruin her relationship. She shares all the derogatory things Michael said about Rae. Fed up, a desperate Michael pushes Kim to the floor (and she lands near the gun) as he pleads with Rae to believe that he was going to break it off with Kim that night. Rae then reveals to a disbelieving Kim that Michael is sleeping with both of them. As Michael and Rae struggle, Kim picks up the gun and fires a shot, hitting Michael. Terrified that she has killed him, mother and daughter run off.

Michael comes to and is only injured but is then accosted by Sal, who is looking to move up in the mob. He finishes him off while going against Joe's orders. Too ambitious for his own good, Sal later turns up dead on the docks, discovered by Jack, who is framed for the murder. With Rose gone, Jack is left solo to clear his name of taking that bribe and now a murder charge.

Michael Corbett: [The Midnight Murder scenes] were very high-intensity stuff. We didn't see the scripts all at once. Every time we would get another script, it would unfold a little bit more. I think it wasn't until the last script that we saw that it was Michael Pavel who was shot, and we don't know who murdered him. I knew all along that they were going to kill me off.

My last day was a long, long day of shooting. I do not think there were many other people around. I remember leaving the studio quite late. The one thing I remember vividly was that the costume designer could not have been more fantastic. I was called up into the wardrobe room, and he said, "Honey, don't tell anybody, but order a couple of cabs and we are going to pack them with all your clothes." I did and had two giant cab loads of wardrobe that was all custom fit. Michael Pavel had an amazing wardrobe. I had tailored suits, fitted pants, and shirts that I wore for years—skin-tight clothing.

Rose Alaio: A very similar thing happened to me. The new costume designer was named Alex Tolken, who was wonderful. Thankfully, they fired Michele Reisch. She was the costume designer hired by Ellen Barrett—we looked like clowns, and her costume choices were awful. It was the day before my last taping. Alex said to me, "This came today." It was a notice stating that no costumes were to be given to actors who were leaving the show. Alex then said, "I am putting this under my blotter, and I am not reading it until the day after tomorrow, so you take anything you want." I thanked him.

Fans were surprised and outraged by Michael's death. There was arguably more of an outcry about his demise than when the show killed off Mary Ryan. By then, the audience had become weary of all the recasts. The media was also taken aback and could not believe *Ryan's Hope* would shoot itself in the foot and kill off a major fan favorite. *The Star* ran a half-page article titled "Soap Fans Are Shocked as ABC Fires Star of *Ryan's Hope* Love Triangle." Terry Ann Knopf, writing for the *Boston Globe*, asked, "Why remove a popular character from *Ryan's Hope?*" The show remained silent on the subject, so speculation ran rampant.

Knopf shared some theories: "Pavel was killed off because another actor was jealous and gave the producer an ultimatum; he was the target of the Moral Majority, which disapproved of his sexual escapades; Michael

Corbett himself had grown too big for his britches, thus becoming an internal liability."

Other alleged reasons bandied about included that producer Ellen Barrett did not like the character and wanted him gone. Also, some of the old guard playing the Ryans and Coleridges were not happy with Corbett's screen time and the promotional push he was getting from ABC. Whatever the reason, per Linda Dennison of *Soap Opera Digest*, irate fans immediately began writing to ABC, demanding Michael's return. They were "pleading that the powers-that-be bring him back as his twin brother or some other soap 'twist' by which popular actors are often resurrected." Other soaps may have heeded the call, but *Ryan's Hope* seemed determined to stay true to its core family and beginnings, so it moved on without him.

The cast, especially Corbett, and crew remained perplexed about why Pavel was killed off. Speculation quickly arose among them on why the show would do this and who may have made the decision to carry it out.

Randall Edwards: I was never in tune with the backstage stuff and never knew what was really going on. Everybody was lovely toward me. They were all great and supportive. I had no problems with anyone. A bunch of us, including Jerry Evans, would go out afterward and have a few beers at a bar down the street. We would hash out the story and think what could be better—just have a lot of fun.

Ann Gillespie: I don't remember any of this—I really don't. It could be because I was just not engaged enough to even know or care. But it makes me laugh to hear about it because it is like the soap behind the soap. I actually did not work with Michael, Louise, or Kelli very much. I knew them on set, and they were all pleasant to deal with—if a little bit aloof.

Roscoe Born: I was running as fast as I could to keep up because all I had ever done was theatre and small TV and film roles. I later did start realizing that folks were pissed off. All the regular actors were constantly complaining that *Ryan's Hope* wasn't what it had been. Some of the actors would say to me, "You should have been here a year ago." They were all not happy about things.

Tamara Grady: Ellen Barrett was an excellent producer and really knew her stuff. At that time, the producers didn't always get that information of how popular characters were with certain audiences. I think it just depends on your point of view. Ellen wanted good actors presenting good stories and perhaps viewers were more tuned in to these characters than expected.

Roscoe Born: I believe the story of the way Ellen Barrett fired Michael Corbett, but that doesn't mean she made the decision. It wasn't necessarily her fault, but that's the way she would execute that decision. She was tough. In her position, she "acted" like a producer.

Tamara Grady: In hindsight, [killing Michael off] probably was not the right thing to do, but I do not think Ellen Barrett did that unilaterally. I don't think any decisions were made without ABC's approval.

Kelli Maroney: I never heard what the particulars were. However, I'm sure that our storyline was a sore spot of some kind, but I don't know anything for sure.

Louise Shaffer: I was not shocked when Michael Corbett was fired. Again, I didn't know for sure, but I always felt there were a lot of decisions made at that time for political reasons and for egos. Decisions made had nothing to do with making good choices for the show.

I think too the whole thing went deeper than that. These were characters that came in when the power was switching on the show from the creators to ABC, and I think there were folks who really didn't want those characters on the show for a variety of reasons. I think that's what happened. It was part of the transition of power on the show.

Laura Rakowitz: Claire Labine may not have liked the idea of killing Michael off, and it may have come from ABC. She wouldn't have had any control over it.

Michael Corbett: It is a shame what they did [to Michael Pavel]. Obviously, I loved working there, and it would have been amazing to have kept going, but I guess it was the purity of the Ryan family that they wanted to keep focused on. I will never think of *Ryan's Hope* of being anything but an enormous gift. To be twenty or twenty-one years old and to be on a soap opera and become so popular and have such a track record within a brief period of time was an enormous gift.

I got hired by *Search for Tomorrow* right away—I think it was a matter of a few weeks. Paul Rauch was the executive producer at first, and then he was replaced by this amazing woman named Joanna Lee. She looked like Lucille Ball with flaming red hair, and she did a lot of nighttime TV in California. They brought her out to sex up the show. She was incredible. I loved her, and we had exceptional stories. She would come to you and say, "So what do you think about this? I am thinking of this story." She was incredible. Her contract was up, and they said we are getting a new executive producer—it was Ellen Barrett!

Rose Alaio: After I left *Ryan's Hope*, I was contacted by a writer in LA to talk about my time on the show. She then asked me if I could create my own character to play, what would it be? I said she would be a combination of Anna Magnani and Anne Bancroft with Mel Brooks thrown in. When I was on *Ryan's Hope*, if I could interpret a line as being funny, I did. The writers noticed and told me my comic delivery was great and that they were writing more in for me. I always tried to find humor in what they wrote and play it.

Shortly after, I get a call from my agent to audition for *Guiding Light*. I read the script, and it was for this fiery Italian, but funny, named Helena Manzini. She was created by Douglas Marland—God love him. What a nice, wonderful genius he was. When you screen-test, you sit in the makeup room while the other women are auditioning, and you can watch on the monitor. There was this one actress I had seen in this movie, and she was really good. I thought she could get the part. I remembered to catch myself and tell myself to "do the best you can—just do your Helena, and the rest is up to them."

When I got on the set, there was Michael Tylo, who played Quinton Chamberlain. I came screaming in as Helena—I grew up with women like that, but they were not billionaires. After it was over, I thanked Michael and felt so comfortable in the part that it scared me because she was so easy to play. I got the job, and it was like going from hell on *Ryan's Hope* to heaven on *Guiding Light*. The joy of working on *Guiding Light*! They had two studios—upstairs and downstairs. Sometimes you got in at eight in the morning, and you were out before noon. They would shoot your scenes in sequence. My favorite phrase was "We're dipping to black." You had *one* scene and it would pick up later on in the hour, but they would shoot all the scenes right then and dip to black to make insertions. It was a joy, from the actors to the directors—everything about *Guiding Light* was wonderful.

The missing piece to this "Why was Michael Pavel killed off?" puzzle was CBS. The Tiffany network had decided it was not going to sit on its butt and get whipped by ABC in the ratings any longer and decided to go on the offensive. The household Nielsen ratings for *Search for Tomorrow* had remained almost even with *Ryan's Hope* at 12:30 p.m., with NBC's *The Doctors* lagging far behind. CBS felt *Ryan's* (ranked seventh out of thirteen soaps) was the weak link in the ABC lineup. They pulled *Search* from its berth and moved up the start time for *The Young and the Restless* to 12:30 p.m. to go head-to-head with *Ryan's Hope*. *Search* was moved to 2:30 p.m., sandwiched between Procter & Gamble's *As the World Turns* and *Guiding Light*.

Trying to counter the publicity CBS was receiving, ABC may have decided that they needed a huge, exciting story on *Ryan's Hope* to attract the masses during the week of the time slot change, drawing attention away from *Y&R*. Hence the boneheaded decision to kill off Michael during the weeklong "Midnight Murder." An exciting promo ad was launched, with the announcer exclaiming, "Love turns to murder on *Ryan's Hope*." ABC ran it aggressively during daytime and prime time (on shows ranging from *20/20* to *The Love Boat*). The ploy paid off, and *Ryan's Hope* defeated *Y&R* that first week in the ratings and for a few subsequent weeks. However, the show could not sustain its momentum.

Arguably, killing off Michael Pavel was one of ABC's and the show's biggest blunders. No other actor or actress from the soap ever achieved the level of popularity that Michael Corbett did at this time. Yes, Kate Mulgrew was beloved, but she was not on the cover of mainstream magazines and did not generate the mainstream media buzz that Corbett did. He was liked enormously by women in the 18–49 demo, and he was loved even more by teenagers and the college crowd. He was young, handsome, and sexy.

They could have gone in many different directions with his character. Hell, if *General Hospital* could take rapist Luke and turn him into the soap world's most popular anti-hero, the talented, Emmy Award–winning writers of *Ryan's Hope* surely could have thought of stories to tie Michael to the Ryan family going forward. ABC, however, never gave them the chance. Instead, they sacrificed him for a short-term win in the ratings.

In 1987, Claire Labine was back as head writer on *Ryan's Hope* after a three-year absence. The following year, there was another writers strike. Recalling the prior one, she remarked in the *New York Times*, "There was a storyline involving an older woman [Rae] and a younger man [Michael], and when we returned, she unaccountably murdered him. [Actually, Rae took the blame for her daughter Kim.] It's a little as if you leave your children with a trusted sitter for the weekend and return to find them all juvenile delinquents and in jail."

Based on Rachael and Ruth Mayer's firsthand knowledge, Harold Apter's awareness, and this interview from Labine, it would seem that Claire and Paul were not writing any of the scripts during the strike and were just as shocked as the audience with the turn of events for Michael Pavel. Perhaps if she and Paul were there, they may have been able to prevent Michael's murder from happening.

After Michael was killed off, ABC blanketed the airwaves with a new promo for the show that was light years away from the *Ryan's Hope* of 1975. Per the announcer, "New York City—the glittering world of *Ryan's Hope*. The glamour and excitement. The romance. The intrigue. The danger. We've got the world where dreams are made of." The homey soap of the first few years was now replaced with shots of corks being popped from champagne bottles; a stunning Delia modeling a formfitting white evening gown; and clips of some of the cast, including Joe, Frank, Rae, Kim, Jill, Faith, and Siobhan at their handsomest and most glamorous. There was only one brief snippet of Maeve and Johnny.

ABC was flexing its muscles and announcing to the daytime audience that *Ryan's Hope* had a new look and theme. It tasked Ellen Barrett to keep the glamour up and hawkeyed viewers began to notice that the actresses were beautifully coiffured in elegant dresses, furs, and jewels when dining at the Crystal Palace. The strategy to reposition the show did attract many new and younger viewers, which advertisers coveted, but it also drove away a portion of the core audience, who longed for the hominess of the earlier years.

Ann Gillespie: I do recognize this shift. Obviously, I was part of it, having come in about the time ABC was taking over. I remember some of the push-pull in the air around what the show used to be, and Kate Mulgrew and her character of Mary was very emblematic of that. I think that is why I remember this so much. It was like I could not live up to that in a way. It was also the change in writing but more so the constant costume fittings. They were pushing us in a very specific direction. I was aware of the tension with some of the actors who had been there since the beginning.

Ron Hale: This was a few months into Ellen Barrett's reign. I suddenly noticed a lot of the ladies were getting teed off when notes were being given sometimes during dress rehearsal or with scenes stopping and Ellen coming out on the floor to talk with an actress—it was almost always the actresses. One time, Ellen was coming out while calling over wardrobe and hair. She did not like the way Nancy Addison's hair was styled and the way someone else's dress looked. Here is our Nancy, who would probably have been the greatest suffragette of all time during the turn of the century, saying, "Now we are getting notes on hair and wardrobe and makeup?! What about the darn scene?!"

Karen Morris-Gowdy: Ron is so right. All of a sudden, we had hairdos and glamorous clothes. As an actress and a young woman, it was heaven and fun. But at the same time, because of hair and makeup and wardrobe, a lot of times everybody was standing on set, waiting for the actresses to come down.

Ann Gillespie: I remember one day—and this is what bugged me about Ellen—she just waltzed into my dressing room brandishing a pair of scissors and said, "Today we cut your hair!" I was like, whoa! I called my agent and asked if she could do that. He replied, "You need a professional to do it, but yes, they own you and own your hair." There was a lot of emphasis—again I did not have previous experience on the show so I did not know what to compare it to—on hair, makeup, and clothes.

For the remainder of the summer, the stories kept moving on. Siobhan finally picks a career and chooses to become a police officer, to her husband's surprise. Due to her family connections, she is rapidly accepted into the police academy and starts training with handsome Sergeant Jim Speed (MacKenzie Allen), who is an old friend of Frank's. Siobhan's new vocation does not sit well with Alexi Vartova, who pressures Joe to make her quit. He has convinced Joe to launder money through the Crystal Palace under the guise of a charity casino in the restaurant's basement using "Delia Dollars" but where people in the know could gamble for real.

Gary Donatelli: By this time, I had worked my way up to cameraman, and one of the first interactions I had with Lela Swift in this position was a disaster. I had worked as a sports cameraman and had done some studio pedestal camerawork. When I was not on the road, I would fill in on the soaps. The difference in operating a sports camera and doing a soap opera is like comparing a dirt bike to a Harley-Davidson.

I reported to the set that morning, and one of the cameramen could not make it into work. They asked me if I could do it, and I volunteered because that is how you move forward. I rolled this camera out to the floor, and there was Lela in the middle of it all. It was this big casino scene at the Crystal Palace. There were many of the regular cast and tons of extras on the set for blocking. Lela turned around and asked, "Where is camera two?" I said, "That is me," as I rolled forward. She ordered, "Start over there above the card table and then roll across the gamblers and bring it over to these two."

I start rolling the camera over but had never operated this type of camera before in my life. I'm looking at some of the dials and controls on the side because I wanted to get a wider shot and wanted to change the lens. I hit something, and the camera just zoomed out. Lela yelled, "What the hell was that?! Who is this guy?" She then pointed over to Dick Kerr (who was one of the greatest cameramen of all time and taught us all how to become decent cameramen), and he rolled his camera to my spot. I tucked my tail between my legs and rolled my camera back to get out of his way and watch the master do the shot.

MacKenzie Allen (Sergeant Jim Speed): I knew several of the casting directors for soaps during that time, and that is how I got to audition for *Ryan's Hope*. It was such an incestuous group. Honestly, it was so political. I was dating a woman who was in casting, and her closest friend was the head of daytime at a network. It was such a back-biting kind of atmosphere, constantly running people down and criticizing them. Frankly, I got sick of listening to it—no matter where we went, all they did was talk and gossip about the business.

Michael's and then Sal's murders bring Frank and Jill back together professionally. Rae confesses to killing Michael and hires Frank as her attorney. He knows she is covering for her daughter. Jill is representing Jack. They begin piecing together clues to each case and recognize both murders are related. Meanwhile, Kim is delirious and remains hospitalized. When a second bullet is found on the houseboat, it clears Rae and Kim. However, Kim's troubles grow tenfold—she is pregnant but does not know who the father is. Seneca is livid with his wife's actions and vows to get custody of the baby if he is the biological daddy.

Faith does not believe for a second that Frank and Jill are not also a couple in the biblical sense and makes catty comments around them wherever she can. She is being romantically pursued by, in his laconic way, Bob Reid and also Jim Speed (when he is not putting Siobhan and the other recruits through physical training for the police officers' test). Jim also asks Faith to help out a friend's teenage son, Craig LeWinter (Paul Carlin), who is an alcoholic new wave rocker (the show trying to stay hip).

> **MacKenzie Allen:** The one early scene that I can't forget is at the police academy working out in the gym, doing calisthenics with a class of trainees, us all wearing Village People shorts and tube socks.

> **Ann Gillespie:** I remember that and hated it. It felt like this exploitive thing just to get us to show off our bodies.

> **Karen Morris-Gowdy:** I hated that part of the storyline with Faith in between Jim Speed and Bob. That wasn't one of my favorites. It was a hard one to play because she did not want to choose either. Faith didn't need a relationship at that point. She was just fine alone. That was kind of forced. However, MacKenzie Allen was a sweet guy, and I loved working with Earl Hindman—what a great actor and a crazy guy. You never knew what you were going to get.

> **Randall Edwards:** I had no issues working with Karen Morris-Gowdy and Nancy Addison. Karen was beautiful and wanted to leave to be a mom. Nancy—oh my God! Talk about gorgeous—such

a beautiful woman. She was extremely intelligent and sharp-witted. None of us hung out together, but I enjoyed working with them. They were very good.

Ann Gillespie: I remember having scenes with Karen Morris-Gowdy and Nancy Addison, who was a very seasoned soap actress. I watched her and studied her for her ability to handle the scenes so well. She was somebody who could hold it together. Karen was younger and newer at it all. They were both very nice but kind of in their own world.

Tamara Grady: Nancy Addison was an excellent actress and just so friggin' beautiful. I thought Michael Levin was a good actor and thought he should have gone further. Helen Gallagher and Bernie Barrow were wonderful. They were those characters.

MacKenzie Allen: Roscoe Born was very nice and so was Karen Morris-Gowdy. I had scenes too with Daniel Hugh Kelly. He was not particularly pleasant. I think because he was there for a while and one of the leads, he was a self-impressed and rather arrogant kind of a guy. Ann Gillespie was a preacher's kid, and I only remember that because her family was from the same town as mine in New Jersey.

Ann Gillespie: MacKenzie Allen was lovely—very warm and funny. I forgot we were from the same town. I enjoyed working with him enormously.

MacKenzie Allen: I liked Ann, but I was answering fan mail one day and she said, "You get fan mail as Jim Speed?" I don't think she meant it to come off like it did, but it was hurtful and has stuck with me.

Ann Gillespie: I am so sorry I said that. What a horrible thing to say. I think that had much more to do with me and my discomfort being on a soap. I didn't look up to soaps and thought they were beneath me. I am sure it had nothing to do with MacKenzie personally. I truly wish to apologize to him.

Roscoe Born: I liked working with Ann Gillespie a whole lot. Also, I didn't see the show that often. I didn't have a VCR, and I was always working. I didn't see anything wrong in what she was doing [as Siobhan], and I thought we were great together. But I saw how she threw quite a few fits. I wasn't a prince either in terms of my behavior regarding arguing about direction and the writing. I wasn't difficult in terms of my dressing room or that kind of stuff. All I cared about was the character, but I realized she was in trouble because of her temper and the way she expressed herself.

Randall Edwards: Ann Gillespie and I became really good friends. I loved her. We both had theatre backgrounds. We hung out and spent a lot of time together. She was a lot of fun.

Ann Gillespie: I loved Randall Edwards. I do not know exactly why we became fast friends, but we sort of had a sisterhood unto ourselves. Our off camera friendship was really pivotal, I think, for both of us, as we were trying to navigate that show and our lives and new relationships with guys and all of that. There was a real support system that was super helpful. Randall has just one of the biggest hearts on the planet. She takes things very personally, and she would get hurt by something somebody would say.

MacKenzie Allen: I was closest to Bernie Barrow. In fact, we were cast as father and son in a commercial for Tylenol. We shot it at a football stadium in New Jersey. Everybody was excited about it, and I figured I was going to make about $250,000 from it easily, and it was going to run forever. A week before it was going to begin airing, the Tylenol poisonings occurred. They pulled the commercial and took all their products off the market. They couldn't use the commercial because they had to repackage everything with safety precautions.

Roscoe Born: Bernie Barrow was wonderful . . . and a little bit like Johnny. He was great to me and asked if I played tennis after I had been there about a month. I said yes. He brought me to his indoor tennis club and . . . he beat me. I was thirty, and he was in his midfifties.

He was incredibly supportive and always a calming influence for me and the other young actors who would get frustrated. Our characters were confrontational. Our friendship helped because there was no animosity between us. Sometimes if there is animosity between the actors and their characters, it is unpleasant. But we could just wholeheartedly go at each other with no strings attached.

Ann Gillespie: Bernie was just the warmest man. He didn't seem like an actor to me; he just seemed like a dad.

Randall Edwards: Bernie and Helen were real sweethearts. Bernie was hysterical with a wonderful sense of humor. Helen came from Broadway, where she was a dancer. She always had that work ethic and that we are all in this together—we were a company. She was extremely generous to me as an actress and as a human being. She is a beautiful, beautiful woman.

Ann Gillespie: Helen Gallagher was the most amazing technician. I had been on camera in two television movies, but I had never worked with three cameras before. That is a skill unto itself. Then with teleprompters—I never could figure out how to do it. But Helen was masterful. She was just always aware. When a particular camera is on you, a light comes on. All three cameras are looking at you all the time. She could look at the teleprompter on a camera that wasn't on her, get the words that she needed, and she never dropped character or lost a moment. I could never do that. Helen was very skilled in how to do that kind of three-camera work with a minimum of stress. I was blown away by that because it was nothing but stressful for me and hard, having been shaped in the theatre, to figure out how to do it.

Helen and Bernie were just lovely, and they were veterans. I didn't realize actually, because I was so new to it all, that they rolled with the punches. They understood where to get involved, where not to get involved. I didn't know any of that stuff. I was very grateful that I got to work with them.

MacKenzie Allen: There was an undercurrent of uncertainty from the regular cast because of the writers' strike and the disruption of the storylines. They were nice enough, particularly Helen Gallagher, but I didn't become socially friendly with any of them. Some were there from the beginning. I don't know if it was that some of them had been an ensemble for so long that they weren't inviting when having somebody new come in. It was like they were a clique, and you had to break into it. Also, because I was new to the business, I wasn't as comfortable as I might have been. Maybe. That is what I felt and added to a lack of a feeling of harmony. But I don't want to impose thoughts that aren't deserved.

Joe and Siobhan reconcile and are living as husband and wife, much to the chagrin of both Johnny and Jack. To boost his restaurant's name recognition, Joe hires Barry Ryan to handle PR. However, for reasons never made clear, Joe is also trying to put Barry in debt using invitations to his weekly high stakes poker games.

Meanwhile, Delia catches Jack fiddling with a mirror behind the desk in the restaurant's executive office. Knowing the mirror has a secret compartment behind it, Delia (in her typical, conniving manner) negotiates with Joe for a bigger ownership percentage of the Crystal Palace in return for this information. This only adds to Joe's stress, especially after he learns it was the mob who had followed Maeve and locked her in a church's rectory to remind him not to cross them—or else. Although Joe tricks Delia into revealing the secret compartment and lies that he set up the video camera found in there, he still increases her ownership percent. As Joe anticipates, Jack and the FBI have him dead to rights on tape, revealing how he had set up Jack and how he was laundering dirty money for Vartova through the charity casino.

Richard Backus: I do not know where they were going with Barry. This was about the time that they brought in an actor named Paul Carlin, who was the son of Frances Sternhagen. He had a blue stripe in his hair. The minute the strike was over, he was gone. It felt like during the strike, the show was flailing around, trying to keep the show interesting.

Tamara Grady: Laura Rakowitz and I were responsible for Roscoe Born and Randall's first date. We knew there was chemistry there personally and when playing their roles. They were simply good actors.

Randall Edwards: Oh my gosh! I was close friends with Tamara and Laura. We are still in contact. They were great to work with. Tamara and Laura got tickets to a Peter Allen concert at Radio City Music Hall, and we all went. That is where my relationship with Roscoe began. Later, I did a Broadway show [Legs Diamond] with Peter Allen, so I invited Laura and Tamara to the opening night performance.

Harold Apter: I remember when Roscoe Born and Randall Edwards first started dating. That was interesting, and you couldn't tell anybody. That stuff was always a big secret and had to be kept on the down-low. I was delivering scripts to Randall at her home, and Roscoe showed up. They were good people.

Ann Gillespie: I was thrilled when Roscoe and Randall got together. I wasn't yet married to my then-boyfriend, Jeff Allin, who I have been married to now for thirty-eight years. We were all living on the Upper West Side and hung out. I've always had a piece of Randall walking around in my heart.

Roscoe Born: I loved working with Randall Edwards [whom he eventually married in real life]. She was so spontaneous and so funny. She is a great, great actor. She excelled in Delia's fantasy sequences, especially the *Hello, Dolly!* one.

Randall Edwards: The *Hello, Dolly!* fantasy scene was great and so much fun. There was one writer who I thought was absolutely amazing and am not sure if he wrote this episode. His name was Jeffrey Lane. He wrote wonderful scripts, and I thought he was second to Claire. He was a classic film buff, and he would bring elements from his wealth of knowledge of that material into his scripts. He was also very funny and wrote a lot of the comedic stuff. I believe the scenes with Christine Ebersole as Lily came from him.

Roscoe Born: There was never talk about romantically pairing Joe and Delia, though Randall and I would discuss it sometimes. But we loved playing that friend relationship. For Joe, she was critical, and that is why they wrote that relationship to give him this lighter side. I know they wanted to make him more likable by being sweet to this little waif.

Randall Edwards: I agreed that it would have been a bad idea to have Delia and Joe pair up romantically. We and the audience liked them as confidantes.

Ann Gillespie: It was not awkward at all for me working with Roscoe after he and Randall became a couple. We were all good enough friends to handle this. I was so happy for them. It was lovely, and they knew Jeff while this was all happening.

There were some love scenes that were uncomfortable anyway but to be able to do it with a friend—I know that sounds weird— made it easier. There was an acceptance among all of us—my husband is an actor too—that it was the requirement of the job. There was nothing like some of the ridiculous things that are on film now. They were always very careful to make sure sheets were taped to you. It was more of the intimacy of working with somebody as your husband on the show kind of thing. Then later we all moved to LA around the same time, so that was interesting.

Walanne Steele: I remember Bernie Barrow said that Randall Edwards and Roscoe Born were like fire and ice when they appeared together on television. I liked Roscoe very much. I thought he had a big future ahead of him as an actor. It never really took off as it should have.

Richard Backus: I don't remember much about Roscoe Born other than that I felt resentful because he was taking my place with Delia. I didn't like that.

[When told that Joe and Delia did not become a couple on the show] I thought for sure they eventually got together. I guess I am confusing real life with soap opera.

Randall Edwards: Roscoe was an amazing man. He was kind, sensitive, intelligent, and passionate. Perhaps it had something to do with the fact that his father was a newspaper editor that Roscoe was very well-read (books, newspapers, magazines) and intellectually curious about many subjects. He could talk about politics, history, art, film, and baseball! He loved to sing and play the guitar and write songs. He cared about people and social justice. Roscoe was a beautiful person, and the world lost a light when he left.

4

Soap Divas, Pesky Reporters, and Merit Kara, 1981–82

The writers' strike finally came to an end in July. Paul and Claire officially returned to their head writing chores and began cutting characters and creating new storylines for the fall. This had become a noticeable pattern for them. They lopped off storylines with a meat cleaver rather than letting them phase out. John Genovese of *Afternoon TV* praised the show to the hilt, but he also pointed out that, "There has been an irritating choppiness to the storytelling for the past few years. Story directions are too early altered, and stories too suddenly aborted." ABC may have been a factor in this as well. They kept a keen eye on whether a storyline was not working with the audience and how it affected the ratings.

Not surprisingly, the writers quickly dropped Paul Carlin as Craig LeWinter. More disappointing was the firing of the underused Richard Backus as Barry Ryan, despite his character owing Joe Novak a few thousand dollars. Barry informs Delia that some Hollywood producers have offered him a job and alerts her that his younger sister is heading to New York City. He then stops by Ryan's Bar to bid Maeve and Johnny farewell before he departs for Los Angeles.

> **Richard Backus:** At some point, they decided to write me out. I think it was [producer] Ellen Barrett who told me. Afterward I was on the West Coast . . . to try my luck in Hollywood. That is how I got my recurring role on *Bare Essence* starring Genie Francis. The villain of the piece was played by Ian McShane. I was kind of his right-hand man who did stuff for him. I don't know why *Bare Essence* didn't catch on. Genie Francis was lovely and

extremely sweet. She worked hard, so it certainly wasn't anything she did that I can see.

I came back to New York and was working steadily as a stage actor, but in some ways, I felt I was playing similar roles with less prestige, maybe. I wanted to try something new. When I thought about maybe not acting anymore, I initially thought I could act and write at the same time. The writing would just supplement my acting income. Once I started writing [for *As the World Turns*], I just loved it because it was so much fun. I let the acting fall by the wayside. I was writing for Douglas Marland when he died. Juliet Packer and I wound up taking over. I discovered head writing was not something I was good at. You need to be particularly good with coming up with stories. I was good filling out stories and finding nuances in stories, but creating stories was not my forte.

Based on the way they rammed through the Kim-with-baby storyline, you could tell the writers hated it. She has the shortest pregnancy on record and gives birth to a very premature little girl she names Arley, after her mother. Once Seneca is proven to be the biological father, there is a constant power struggle between him and Rae for custody of the infant. To escape the conflict, Kim runs off to stay with the Ryan family, and Maeve teaches her how to take care of her little one. She also is able to get a job at the Crystal Palace, despite Delia's protests.

Louise Shaffer: I don't have a clue as to why they did that. This was one of the times Kelli and I went with a willful suspension of disbelief. And looking back on it, I probably should have insisted on a clause in the contract where they cannot make you a grandmother. That is not a good thing to have happen to you as an actor.

Kelli Maroney: It was so funny we could never stop laughing, except at taping time. However, I did get to work with Helen Gallagher and Bernie Barrow. They were lovely actors to work with, and I was honored to get scenes with them. I respect people who've been in the trenches and know what they're talking about like they did. They could bring any actor up to their level. I had the utmost respect for both of them. Bernie was very kind. The man you want to have in your family to a tee. Helen was also kind, but more like "let's see what you're made of" [and] if I was up to the challenge.

Seneca is distracted from all the baby drama when he is hired by the soap opera *The Proud and the Passionate* to act as a medical consultant and gets romantically involved with the show's longtime leading lady, Barbara Wilde (Judith Barcroft, ex-Anne Tyler Martin, *All My Children*). After walking in on them together, Kim grabs Arley and skips town, leaving a note threatening her husband and mother not to come looking for them. Afraid of what she might do, Seneca respects her wishes, but Rae hires a private detective before changing her mind.

> **Kelli Maroney:** They wanted a return to the old ways and original characters, and I wasn't one of them. I would have been shocked to the core except one of the costumers tipped me off, so I didn't have a heart attack when I was told. I'm still thankful she did that.

Ratings-wise, *Ryan's Hope* survived the writers' strike still in very good shape. Per *Variety*, for the first week of September 1981, ABC had four out of the five top-rated soaps – *General Hospital*, followed by *All My Children*, *One Life to Live*, and *Ryan's Hope*. *Guiding Light* was the only non-ABC soap to crack the top five. *Ryan's* was still beating its chief time slot competitor, *The Young and the Restless*, on CBS as well as NBC's *The Doctors*.

Considering how well they succeeded with the storylines at the beginning of 1981, Claire and Paul surprised the soap press and the show's viewers with two new ones that were far afield from the show's roots. The forementioned soap-within-a-soap plot coincides with the arrival of bubbly, energetic, journalist-wannabe Elizabeth Jane Ryan (Maureen Garrett, ex-Holly Norris, *Guiding Light*), who blows into New York City and heads straight to Ryan's Bar to meet her distant Ryan cousins and find her older brother, Barry.

Within a few days, Jane, as she is called, begins a romance with Roger (a seemingly odd pairing until one remembers that Roger was originally attracted to the similar Mary Ryan when the show began), gets a job as a secretarial assistant to Rae Woodard at her newspaper, and sneaks into the Crystal Palace during the private anniversary party for *The Proud and the Passionate*. Jane is witness to when Barbara starts choking on an hors d'oeuvre and Roger performs an emergency tracheotomy to save her life. There is a complication, and Barbara requires surgery. When she awakes paralyzed, she threatens a lawsuit, even though her doctors suspect it was due to swelling from the trauma. Barbara does not believe her paralysis is temporary and, thinking her career as an actress is ruined, moves ahead with her $1 million malpractice suit versus Roger.

Barbara's paralysis, however, has a different effect on the actress's career. Her disability is written into the show, and soon her soap's ratings climb to everyone's surprise. Barbara is determined to keep her storyline on the front burner—even if it means faking being paralyzed. Suspecting that she can walk and wanting to get the goods on Barbara to help Roger, Jane finagles a job as the actress's assistant, which leads her to being cast as the private nurse to Barbara's character on the show. Jane's ruse comes to an end when jealous Delia sends an anonymous letter to Barbara outing Jane, unaware that her rival took the job to clear Roger.

The soap press loved "the soap-within-a-soap." Most enjoyed the irony and that the writers poked fun at the networks, producers, and actors who make soap operas. John Genovese of *Afternoon TV* magazine, opined that this story "has been well spun . . . with some wonderfully satiric scenes." It seemed that Labine and Mayer used this story arc to vent about the problems they had with ABC, especially their determination to write quality rather than copying what was appealing to the masses on other soaps. It is sort of surprising that ABC even approved it. Writing it may have been good for Claire's and Paul's souls, but unfortunately it was not what the show's viewers wanted to see.

> **Louise Shaffer:** I knew Judith Barcroft was on the show, but I don't remember much about it. To be honest, I was trying to pay off my mortgage. When they got rid of Kelli, I figured my days were numbered because it just didn't make any sense that they would keep me. In a lot of ways, I had stopped being Rae Woodard and became Kimberly's mother. I could not figure out how they were going to keep me when they had gotten rid of the two people who had been the basis of my storyline. The fact that they were doing a fake soap—I don't know what the hell happened with that story.

Arguably, another story weakness was Delia's consistent attempts to discredit Jane in the eyes of Roger and the Ryan family. There was one scheme after another that always seemed to backfire on the devious blonde whose shenanigans became tiresome. It was like watching the Roadrunner and Coyote cartoon. Also, for many, pesky Jane was written too sprightly and Pollyannish and came off as irksome. Not all felt this way though. John Genovese of *Afternoon TV* remarked, "Maureen Garrett's delightfully quirky interpretation of

Elizabeth Jane makes for a casting director's heaven." Jon-Michael Reed opined, "Garrett is a revelation as Jane; she was popular but perfunctory as Holly Bauer on *Guiding Light*. As Jane, she's animated, sparkling, and a fresh humdinger." The bottom line is that some of the audience did not agree, and the character did not become as popular as hoped. And, as always, it seemed Delia wanted Roger only when he was romantically tied to someone else and vice versa.

> **Randall Edwards:** I always thought that Roger and Delia were perfect for each other. Roger understood and accepted Delia despite (or maybe partly because of) her eccentricities. Delia needed that love and acceptance, yet didn't realize she had it in spades with Roger. Since Delia never did the self-work to heal from her childhood traumas and insecurities, she kept seeking wholeness from others which, of course, is impossible.
>
> Ron Hale always amazed me as an actor. He seemed to have such a good time all day, full of fun and humor, joking with the crew and everyone. Then when it came to taping, he was spot on— so effortlessly. My favorite memory of Ron was how every spring he would bring tons of lilacs into the studio from his garden and give them to everyone—my favorite smell.

The other new storyline had to have a major rewrite before it was launched a few weeks after the soap story. Claire Labine had recently become fascinated with Egypt. She crafted a *Raiders of the Lost Ark*–inspired story about an Egyptian queen named Merit Kara, who resembled Faith Coleridge, and how her hidden mummified corpse was being sought by legitimate historians and some nefarious folks. Her tomb contained an orb with a map to the River of Gold. Labine was to incorporate Frank and Jill into the mix to interact with a still-angry Faith, but she hit a snag.

> **Louise Shaffer:** I cannot confirm if this is true, but I heard third- or fourth-hand that Merit Kara was originally supposed to be a story for Daniel Hugh Kelly, Karen Morris-Gowdy, and Nancy Addison. After they invested all that money in props and costumes, somebody forgot that Danny had an out in his contract if he got a pilot that sold. Suddenly, they had to rewrite the story out of thin air because Danny's pilot, *Hardcastle and McCormick*, was picked up.

Tamara Grady: Yes, I know that the original story was to feature that triangle of Faith, Frank, and Jill. Merit Kara looked like Faith. And I know Danny left because he got *Hardcastle and McCormick*. But I do not know what they had in mind in terms of long story.

The sudden departure of Daniel Hugh Kelly left a gaping hole in the plot. Having Faith and Jill still at odds over the missing Frank diluted the drama and the friction between the sisters. At times it seemed the role of Frank was going to be recast (Don Scardino made a few appearances in the role), but it was not, and the story played out without him. Instead, the focus changed to new character, Egyptologist Aristotle Benedict-White. The writers were also able to incorporate the Joe/Siobhan storyline into this as well.

Gordon Thomson (Aristotle Benedict-White): The stupidest name ever invented. I think Claire Labine was able to bulldoze this storyline onto the show because after the writers' strike it was a sort of a "Garbo's back and Gable's got her" kind of thing. Here, I think it was "Claire's back and let's give her leeway on this."

What happened was, and it was a surprise to me, but Claire Labine and Paul Mayer had done some work with a director named Leon Major in Toronto. I had auditioned for Leon once or twice, but he never hired me. I don't know why because I am a decent actor. Claire had been to Egypt and had fallen in love with it. She was determined somehow to get this extraordinary culture on to her New York, Irish bar–set soap opera. She also realized that she needed somebody who didn't sound American, so she asked Leon. To my absolute astonishment, he recommended me.

I met with somebody from the show, but I cannot recall who it was. Then I did some form of test. Thanks to Leon, I found myself in New York, which was a dream come true. I'd been in Canada for about fifteen or sixteen years. I started as an apprentice at the Stratford Festival in 1965. That was my professional jumping-off point. Now I was in New York with this terrific group of actors, with this extraordinary story to tell, and with an insane name attached to the role.

I think I watched a bit of *Ryan's Hope* before I came to New York. I was intrigued and thought there was some particularly good acting going on. I wasn't unfamiliar with a lot of the faces I was working with, but I had not been a loyal fan by any means.

Karen Morris-Gowdy: Merit Kara came out of the blue after Claire returned from spending some time in Egypt. She always pushed the envelope. They spent so much time and money on it. The story was so out there creatively and got a lot of press. It seemed like the network loved it. I didn't love it at all, but I liked Gordon Thomson. He was a sweet man. They invested in a lot of new sets and costumes. The story went on for a long time. It was kind of like the Prince Albert story. They introduced these big, over-the-top storylines that didn't mesh with the show. I think all the actors were thinking, "What the hell is this?" But it's a paycheck, and you show up and do what you are supposed to do.

When *Ryan's Hope* launched this adventurous storyline, it was just following in the footsteps of other soaps. Around the time this began, viewers could find a Gothic Castle where people were tortured by a little person calling himself Mr. Big on *As the World Turns*; a Japanese serial killer picking off long-running characters on *Search for Tomorrow*; and folks stumbling on a supernatural cube in a cave on *Texas*. And, of course, the most infamous storyline came from *General Hospital* with its Ice Princess, the world's largest uncut diamond that was the key to building a powerful weapon that could destroy humanity if it fell into the wrong hands.

Jane Mayer of *The Wall Street Journal* wrote that the justification for these outlandish plots and a turn away from the standard soap story was because "the traditional audience for such fare, the young housewife between diaper changes, is waning. To reach out to other viewers, the networks are adding some new twists. Science fiction, fantasy, and strange special effects are growing common as networks try to lure more male and teenage viewers."

Back in New York City, attorney Frank Ryan abruptly departs for a job in St. Louis and to get away from the feuding Coleridge sisters. Shortly after, Jill is contacted by a former archaeologist named Spencer Smith (Lester Rawlins), an old friend of her deceased father, who lives in an elegant brownstone with his manservant, Thomas Mendenhall (former stage manager Dick Briggs).

In ill health, Smith wishes to get his affairs in order. Oh, and his life may be in danger because thirty-feet beneath his house is hidden the mortuary shrine of Merit Kara, an Egyptian queen. The shrine has remained untouched because Smith believes it to be cursed since his father and his secretary both died shortly after the shrine arrived in America. Smith wants Jill to investigate the credentials of a young Egyptologist named Aristotle Benedict-White, who has invested many years learning about Merit Kara and desperately wants to get involved with Smith's proposed museum.

Laura Rakowitz: I liked Gordon Thomson. He was a great guy. Our original stage manager before Tamara Grady was Dick Briggs, who played the butler, Mendenhall. He was delightful.

Tamara Grady: Yes, I took over as stage manager from Dick Briggs. I never had to go to the dry rehearsal that was in the rehearsal hall. I didn't pick up until the actors came to the studio floor for camera blocking. It was my responsibility to get the actors to the set, to make sure there was quiet on the set, and to make sure all the other departments had done their jobs, like confirming props were in place. I am the person who counted it down—five, four, three, two, one. I also threw the cues.

When the show began, it was shot in order. They used to call it "go intos," like Ryan's parlor goes into Ryan's kitchen. I don't remember exactly when they stopped doing it this way, but then they started to shoot by set. They would shoot all scenes from one set and go on to the next set. It would all be put together in editing. I think the new way was probably easier for everybody except for the editor. It certainly saved time because we weren't repositioning constantly. The equipment would get to one set until the scenes were shot and then move on to the next. And I am sure the actors found it better too because if all their scenes were done in the morning on one set, they could go home.

Jill meets White at Lem's Chinese restaurant to discuss his taking the job. Unbeknownst to them, they are watched by Faith, who slips away without a word. She then brazenly lets herself into Jill's apartment with her key. Jill is furious for the unwanted intrusion, and another argument escalates when Faith taunts her about Ari. She vindictively tells Jill that she saw that same look on her face every time she would see Jill with Ken. She warns her sister not to hurt Frank again. Jill calls Faith delusional and tells her off. She advises her younger sister to worry about her own life, and Faith storms out.

Meanwhile, in arguably the show's best and strongest storyline from this period, things are going downhill for Joe after Jack shares the tapes from his hidden camera with the Task Force on Organized Crime. The Feds make a deal with Joe. In exchange for immunity, he helps them nail Alexi Vartova. Joe only cooperates with the stipulation that he keeps his wife, Siobhan, at a distance for her own safety. To reach that end, Joe and Jack make sure that Siobhan overhears Joe talking to his cohort in crime. An astonished Siobhan leaves Novak and moves back in with her parents. She tries to understand her husband's actions, but steely-eyed Joe pushes her further away.

The Ryan family is furious with Joe for what he has done. Bob Reid quits his job at the Crystal Palace and cajoles Delia to come with him out of loyalty to Jack, but she refuses. Infuriated at what is being asked of her, Delia hisses at Jack, "You do nothing but cause me trouble. Working here, you were a pain. As a brother-in-law, you were nice maybe five minutes out of the year." Rightfully owing Jack nothing, she refuses to give up her investment in the Crystal Palace for him. After confronting Joe about what he did, Delia understands why based on her own experience about lashing out at others who wronged her. After getting assurances from Joe that he will leave her the restaurant if anything happens to him, Delia sticks by her friend and is determined to keep Bob working there as well.

Joe wins over Vartova's trust, and although he kills one of Vartova's right-hand men and gets shot sneaking into his office (Roger mends his wound on the sly), he is able to retrieve notebooks showing how the crime lord is laundering money. Vartova is arrested without suspecting Joe. Thinking his debt to society is over, Joe is livid to learn that the Feds are now forcing him to go undercover to prove that Aristotle Benedict-White is dealing in stolen artifacts, especially since Spencer Smith decides to choose Ari as his successor. Joe's contact in this sting is Jim Speed. When a satisfied Ari returns to his hotel room, a gunshot startles him. He tackles the intruder, and it turns out to be his unhappy girlfriend and business partner, archaeologist Yvonne Kaheel (Patricia Triana), whom Ari deserted in Luxor to come to New York. After making love and promising to share the shrine of Merit Kara with her, a satisfied Yvonne returns to Egypt.

After overhearing Jill tell Maeve about an upcoming Egyptian costume ball thrown by the museum connected to Spencer Smith, Delia immediately calls the museum's curator, Jonas Roving (Michael Wager). After she mentions Ari's name, he quickly agrees to have the fundraiser event at the Crystal Palace.

The sumptuous Egyptian Ball was probably the most elaborate party scene *Ryan's Hope* ever showcased. The production values were top-notch, from the costumes to the hair and makeup to the sets. All the show's main female characters (Jill, Faith, Delia, and Jane) and many background players were clad in exotic Egyptian gowns and headdresses. The Crystal Palace's waiters and a few of the male guests wore tunics. These episodes were expertly directed by Lela Swift and Jerry Evans, who surprisingly didn't earn Emmy nominations that year. The production design team did, though, which was well-earned due to the opulence on display.

Gary Donatelli: Lela Swift was an amazing director. At that point in my career, I was in such awe of her because I wanted to grow up and be a director. I would watch her and Jerry Evans (their directing styles were completely different) in the middle of this incredible fray, and by the end of the day, they would put out an entire episode. You could really feel the story being told, along with the sound effects and music. I remember at that point they had a system of three cameras across—a left, a right, and a wide. The rule was always start wide and then go to close-ups. In order to time things out to what was going to be seen on TV due to the primitive editing, everyone who was involved in act one would be on their sets—the people in the bar, the people in the restaurant, the people in the hospital.

I remember this one time watching this great opening scene with these actors, and what would happen is that when they began going into the close-ups with cameras one and three, camera two, along with one of the two booms, would try to quietly roll away from that set over to the next set. We would get set, and when they finished up over at the other set, it would come to us for the wide shot on this new set. Then those other two cameras would move over to left and right positions. It was a very beautiful dance. I remember more than once in these kinds of situations that the actors from different sets would see each other's performances. They would turn to each other and say, "That was great. We can do better!" There was a great camaraderie on their part. You would feel the build of the whole scene as if the writer had intended shooting this way.

Karen Morris-Gowdy: There was something exciting when the stage manager would cue us to start scene one, and we would go straight through to scene five. We would stop for the commercial inserts, the cameras would move to the next set, and then we started up again. You had to be prepared and hit your mark. It was nerve-wracking but so much fun. After ABC owned it, we filmed, say, all of Faith's scenes in her living room in one swoop. That change wasn't as much fun for me.

Gordon Thomson: I liked Lela Swift a lot. I liked Jerry Evans as well but thought Lela was much more exciting because, to me, she was a bit off and very vigorous. There were even fewer women directing then than there are now in television and movies. For me, she was probably more fun to work with than Jerry.

Walanne Steele: Lela Swift and Jerry Evans were extremely nice to Jadrien, as was the stage manager, Richard Briggs.

Harold Apter: Jerry Evans was great and a wonderful guy. Lela Swift was insane, but she was one of the first female directors in television. She wanted to rewrite everything. I remember I got very upset because she put stuff into the dialogue that I knew was really dumb. She rewrote me, and that really pissed me off.

MacKenzie Allen: Jerry Evans was a man who was very encouraging and warm. He was very easygoing to work with.

Tamara Grady: I agree about Jerry. He would try to make everyone feel comfortable. He was very relaxed and would often change things to suit the actor. He also had a quality about him that I thought was remarkable in that he would take the time to shake every extra's hand and learn their names, which he would remember. Therefore, so many people loved working on our show with him. It was an incredible skill. I could never remember anybody's name, which is not good, and used to call people "honey," or "sweetie," or "dearie." Jerry had the skill to identify someone that would click in his mind and remember their names. It really is a skill.

Ron Hale: It started happening early on, which threw me for a loop, that directors were not really directing in daytime anymore. I would call them choreographers because they blocked out the show for their cameras, for their booms, etc. You had to be here at this point because camera two is going to pick you up, and then you have to move over there for camera three. I don't want this to sound bad because they both interjected with their thoughts.

Gary Donatelli: I would second what Ron said, and he is one thousand percent right—the goal became to rush things through. When I was a young cable kid on the show, they ran *Ryan's Hope* just like a stage play. They would come in and do a table read in the morning, then go on the floor and do a dry rehearsal with the cameras. We would then break for lunch and come back to do a full-dress rehearsal. Then they would pull out red canvas chairs. The whole cast would sit down like a theatre piece, and the director and ADs would give everybody notes.

When I became a director later [on *One Life to Live*], we were still doing one show a day, but we weren't doing that many rehearsals. We were doing the segmenting [shooting all the scenes out of continuity on one set and then moving to the next set] but then they upped it and wanted us to do six shows in five days—then almost seven shows in five days. All of a sudden, we were getting rid of dress rehearsals or taping dress rehearsals to save time. Of course, doing this, you lose something, and what we lost was a chance to rehearse scenes a couple of times. I held on to rehearsing each scene twice as long as I could. Bob Woods and some others would call me "Gary Two-Times." I wanted to run it once to discover something. Then let's play with it again for a minute, and I will see you up on the floor later. A director became more like being a traffic cop. It was maddening at times. My longest day at *One Life to Live* was shooting 165 pages. It was crazy.

Gordon Thomson: Ellen Barrett wasn't unpleasant, but she was not an easy woman to get along with. I remember at one point there was a kafuffle upstairs and Helen Gallagher saying, "I love that girl." Nobody else seemed to love Ellen. I had enormous respect for Helen, and after she made that comment, I thought, "Wow, if you love *that* girl, there must be something there."

Ann Gillespie: Ellen Barrett most certainly ran the show, and she ran my show. I defiantly revolted against that. I remember Paul and Claire being soft and kind, and I don't really remember that about Ellen. She was much harder, and she had this kind of proprietary attitude toward me. It was like, "You're mine, and I am going to keep you on the straight and narrow" kind of thing. I wasn't the most mature person anyway in my professional career or even as a human, but that didn't sit very well with me.

Roscoe Born: I pulled a prank on Ellen Barrett that finally got her to warm up to me. She was crazy about Perry Como. She had put out a memo about kissing. It was in everybody's box. It was talking about tongues and wanted us to watch old movies to see how they kissed. Everybody thought this was absurd. I had her assistant Mindy write up a memo with her name on it and exactly in her format. It said the Perry Como special was going to air, and it was required viewing for everyone in the cast. I put it in all the boxes. I told everyone what I did, and they were laughing their asses off. She got furious and finally got Mindy to confess that I wrote it.

I went back to my dressing room, and my pants were missing. The show was still being taped. I went to her office wearing a shirt over my underwear, and she wasn't there. I found out she was down on the set. She was sitting on this bed, talking to someone, so I just walked over and stood right in front of her. She gasped and fell backward onto the bed. She then started laughing loudly. From then on, I got along really well with her. She had stolen my pants and had them in a drawer in her office.

Harold Apter: Ellen Barrett was a wonderful mentor and friend. She encouraged me and was the first person I showed a sample script to. I had been promoted to production secretary number two and had read everything, from the long story to the outlines to each episode's script. I sat down and wrote a script in one sitting because I was afraid if I stopped, I would not finish it. It took me an entire day to complete. I gave it to Ellen, and it took her about a month before she called me into her office. This was just after the writers' strike. She had a habit of making people sit on a footstool. It made you look so juvenile. She looked at me and said, "You are a writer. Do one more and then give them to Claire." That's what I did. Claire had asked me a few months before if I wanted to write, and I said no because I was terrified of it. Claire read the scripts, paid me for them, and made me a writer for the show. I was simultaneously writing the show and being production secretary.

Jill accompanies Ari to the ball. After Ari tries to learn the shrine's whereabouts from her, Jill promises if he stops prying, she will get Spencer to make sure he reveals the location. Jonas Roving stops by to speak with them and promises to share the townhouse's blueprints with Ari and Jill. Ari, however, becomes distracted when Faith arrives on the arm of Jim Speed and is the spitting image of Merit Kara. Not able to take his eyes off of her, Ari asks Jill if she knows who that woman is. Jill reveals it is her sister, Faith, and flippantly tells him, "Don't hesitate to introduce yourself. Tell her Jillian sent you."

Meanwhile, Delia's plot to flirt with Orson Burns to get Bob worried enough to stick around at the Crystal Palace goes very wrong. They struggle upstairs in Joe's apartment when Delia refuses to give in to his advances. Orson throws her to the ground, and she dislocates her shoulder. Delia's screams draw Joe and Bob, who come to her rescue. Roger and Jane follow, and Roger treats a shaken Delia while Joe tells Orson to disappear for a while. Although he sees right through her ruse, Bob agrees to stay on permanently as manager to keep an eye on Joe.

Ari introduces himself to Faith and begins to tell her the story of Merit Kara, who loved the same man as her sister. Without telling Jim Speed, a spellbound Faith allows Ari to whisk her away from the party and to Spencer Smith's house so he can prove to her how much she resembles the long-dead queen. Faith is astonished with the similarity and even more so when she learns that the queen lost her true love to her sister, just as Faith lost Frank to Jill. The next day after Ari fills Jill in on why he left the party with Faith, she goes to her sister and warns her to stay away from Ari because he is obsessed with Merit Kara. Faith interprets Jill's concern as trying to take something from her yet again. Describing Ari as the most exciting man she has met in a long time, Faith demands that her sister back off and not ruin this budding relationship.

Ari convinces Faith to let him photograph her dolled up as Merit Kara at Spencer Smith's house. She hesitantly agrees. Glimpsing Faith dressed as the Egyptian queen is too much of a shock for Spencer, who suffers a fatal heart attack. Before dealing with the consequences of Smith's sudden death, Ari, despite Faith's warning, heads to the Crystal Palace first to look at an Egyptian artifact in Joe Novak's possession (given to him by the FBI). Ari is impressed with the artifact and pays Joe the lowball price of $7,500. Joe informs Jim Speed that everything went as planned. While Ari badgers Jill for permission to look for the Merit Kara shrine, Faith rejects Jim.

Later, she gets cozy with Ari at his hotel room after he gifts her with a gold ankh—the Egyptian symbol of life. They are interrupted when the door opens, and Faith sees a black-gloved hand. Ari runs out into the hallway, but the intruder has fled.

Harold Apter: The first episode that I wrote was when Spencer Smith died in his house. I named his physician Dr. Apter. The reason I knew I could be a writer was because it had a scene between Maeve and I think Delia. There was a monitor in front of my desk at the studio. I was watching the rehearsal, and the words came out of Helen exactly as I heard them in my head when writing. I knew then I could write. I guess that is why I wrote as many episodes as I did because I was able to pick up the voices of the characters.

I bought my first VCR, which cost $600 at this time, to tape the show. I still have all the VHS tapes with recordings of every single show that I wrote. I never missed an episode. I read everything, but for me it was more about hearing the show in my head and understanding the characters and where they were coming from. That has served me in good stead this past forty years.

Claire was my teacher. This was the first time I ever wrote anything professionally. Since then, I have had a lengthy career writing in television and feature films, but Claire taught me how to write dialogue. She took great pains to teach me and was wonderful. She did that with a lot of us. She would find somebody she felt had the chops to do it and take them under her wing. She did the same thing with Jeffrey Lane and Rory Metcalf. That was quite a wonderful experience for me.

My memory of Paul Mayer was that he was a decent human being and always very nice to me. However, most of my interaction was with Claire. The thing about being a writer in general is that it is mostly an awful experience because the kind of criticism you get is not fair and is not kind—or at least it feels that way. With the two of them it was not like that.

They would get together every day at Claire's home, where they concentrated on the long story. They had breakdown writers who would come in. At one point Mary Munisteri was writing breakdowns, but I think that was later. It was their show and only a half hour. It is a lot different if you are doing an hour and need a lot more material. They also both wrote scripts. If Claire really liked a particular outline or wanted to introduce a new character, she would write the script. They were very involved.

The year 1981 ends with the Merit Kara shrine still unfound. Ari's romance with Faith begins to heat up, which helps his mood. The most profound change at this time came with Siobhan's departure. This deeply affected Joe, who has a lonely Christmas, ostracized from the Ryan family. Early in the new year, he is unaware that Siobhan has upped and left town to stay with Frank in St. Louis. Considering that Rose Alaio had been let go because the writers wanted a triangle and not a quadrangle, this unexpected development definitely threw a monkey wrench into the plot.

Gordon Thomson: The people I worked with were lovely—they really were. I got along with everybody, and I usually do. I loved my job and have ample respect for people who do it well. They appear to respect me in return. Very rarely have I met somebody whom I would call a cunt, and you can quote me. There were one or two, but I am not going to name them. Not a one was on *Ryan's Hope*. They were really a wonderful, unique group of people in a medium I was unfamiliar with.

I remember being especially fond of Nancy Addison. I thought she had one of the most exquisite faces and a wonderful acting intelligence. This is not to diss anybody else, such as Karen Morris-Gowdy, who I worked with much more. I liked her a lot, but Nancy had a special thing—I don't know what it was. And I was horrified to learn that she died so young.

I was working with either Nancy or Karen on a particular scene. When we finished, Helen Gallagher, who is not Miss Hyperbole and must be herself—Irish to the backbone—said, "Good acting." Well, I practically fell over. I thought, "This is wonderful." And thanked her. That was one of the nicest compliments that I ever received. It still resonates to this day. It is such a lovely, simple thing to say, and this from a Tony Award–winning actress means a great deal. She was quite extraordinarily talented. We didn't have many scenes together, but she is good at her job and I am good at my job. It was just two professionals working.

Ann Gillespie: We were doing two shows in a row. It was the end of the day doing the second show, and I had some long, emotional monologue. I was having trouble with it—stumbling and not making it work apparently. For better or for worse, I could hear in the headset of Dickie Briggs—who was the stage manager and standing about four feet away from me—the voice of Lela Swift yelling, "No! No! No! That's all wrong!" I just lost it. I looked into the camera and said, "Fuck you, Lela!" Of course, the producers and ABC execs were watching. Ellen Barrett and I had had enough run-ins at that point, so I think that was the moment they decided to let me go.

Roscoe Born: I was not surprised that Ann left the show. I recall that day when she was having trouble with the dialogue, and they said something to her over the PA. She said something to the effect of "If this wasn't such shit, maybe I could remember my lines." Everything just stopped, and we were at a total standstill. There were these big stage doors. We heard them open and then this loud stomping. It was Ellen Barrett coming in. She took Ann by the arm and marched her out.

Ann Gillespie: I'm glad that Roscoe remembered it as I do. And I think I did say that about the writing and really struggled with how to make that dialogue work. And yes, Ellen came storming down to the set. It was such an iconic moment in my life, and I wondered how it affected other people who witnessed it. Poor Roscoe was standing there, basically responding to me but looking like he was pulling for me. I can see it in his eyes saying, "You can do this! You can do this!"

Roscoe Born: Randall Edwards wasn't working that day. When I got home, I told her that I think Ann is going to get fired. Two or three days later, they did just that.

Ann Gillespie: It was fascinating, as I recall, because in the few days after that, I felt like the crew, who I gathered did not like working with Lela much, respected me more. But within two days, I get called into Ellen's office on a day I was not working. I knew what this was. I walked in and Ellen asked, "Are you happy here?" I replied, "Frankly, Ellen, no." And that was the end of my time on

Ryan's Hope. My therapist at the time was very proud of me because I stood up for myself in a way that I never had.

However, I still had work to do on the show. The interesting thing was that I think in Ellen's eyes I was being the bad, rebellious child to her authoritarianism. In the meeting where I was let go, I felt like we were equals for the first time ever. When she asked me if I was happy there, I was not going to bullshit and I told the truth. It was clear they were going to fire me, but ABC owed me vacation pay and time. I asked Ellen if she could make these things happen and sure enough, she did. She got me everything I was wanting and owed. In a bizarre way, it righted our relationship. I was gone about two weeks after that blowup on set.

Obviously, in retrospect, I wish I had handled my discomfort and my displeasure with the conditions of the writing and whatever in a different way. But it was a significant moment for me on another level in terms of my own development. Then, I undervalued soaps because it was not part of my family ethos, which was much more academic and upper crusty. I had some conditioning that did not serve me in serving the soap. I had stuff in my head that got in the way and contributed to why I was only on the show for a year. I have no regrets about any of it and am glad I got to do it. Good lord, it was a learning experience.

It was freeing for me to be let out and to do other things. One of those things was the prime-time soap *Beverly Hills, 90210* [recurring as Kelly's alcoholic, socialite mother Jackie Taylor beginning in 1990]. It was such a better experience than being on *Ryan's Hope* on so many levels. By that time, I was married and had a child. I had my second kid basically on the show since they wrote my pregnancy in. I was in such a different place as a human and an actress.

After Ann Gillespie was let go as Siobhan Ryan, columnist Jon-Michael Reed opined in the *Los Angeles Times*, "The show has lousy luck in casting replacements . . . Perhaps it's better that the writers create new characters, rather than struggling with actor replacements who obviously don't spark the writers' imagination as vividly as originating performers."

The way roles were cast also changed, and theatrical backgrounds took a backseat to attractiveness and looks, though it does not mean that the actors were any less talented. Daytime television began becoming a bastion of pretty people in glamorous, glitzy settings surrounded by drama and intrigue.

Ratings-wise, *Ryan's Hope* lost its lead to its main time slot competitor *The Young and the Restless*, and CBS's strategy seemed to be working. For the last quarter of 1981 (September 28 to December 13), per *Variety*, *Ryan's Hope* ranked fifth, now tied with *The Young and the Restless* with a 7.0 household rating and 28 share. *General Hospital* was tops with a 11.8 rating and a 39 share, followed by *One Life to Live* with a 9.8 rating and a 35 share. *All My Children* followed with a 9.6 rating and a 35 share, and *Guiding Light* with a 7.7 rating and a 25 share.

Perhaps realizing their new storylines were not drawing new fans and were not popular with the old ones, the powers-that-be wrote off all the characters from the soap-within-a-soap after it wrapped up in early 1982. Most expected the Merit Kara story to be cut short, but it continued playing out.

> **Harold Apter:** There were always thirteen-week story projections, so a story would last at least that long. They might bury it a bit, but that is the way everything was laid out. I guess since Claire and Paul still had total control over the writing, they could screw around however they wanted to. One of the first samples I wrote was the introduction of Ari. I thought the stuff with the tomb was intriguing.

> **Gordon Thomson:** I liked my storyline because I liked my work and loved the job, but it was way off base. Personally, I thought it was a foolish attempt on Claire's part to inject this exotic story into it. *Ryan's Hope* was basically the bar, like *The Golden Girls* was basically the kitchen, *Cheers* was the bar, and *Frasier* was the radio station and the living room. When shows with that essential nest range go beyond that in terms of story, I think they run a very big risk of bewildering an audience. They were probably thinking, "Where are Johnny and Maeve? This is not Ryan's Bar. This is Egyptology. There is Faith Coleridge, and she is dressed up as Merit Kara?! Good God!" Why did these people get involved with Egypt? There was no reason except for Claire's passion for the country.

> **Walanne Steele:** As with a lot of soap operas, as time went on, you run out of believable plots to have happen. This Egyptian story was

far-fetched. They were running out of things to do and drifted from the real interesting part of the show. It got too far afield.

Karen Morris-Gowdy: You kind of knew Paul and Claire didn't have their hand in it as much as they did at the beginning. We were part of the ABC Daytime machine now trying to keep up with not only *All My Children* but *General Hospital* too. They didn't need to have these types of storylines because we had such incredible actors.

Roscoe Born: I hated the Merit Kara story—everybody on the show hated it! We just felt foolish, and we all made fun of it constantly. I never knew what was going on behind the scenes, so I can't vouch that ABC forced an adventure storyline onto the soap or not. The soap-within-a-soap didn't work either.

Gordon Thomson: I suspect Helen Gallagher was one of the big disapprovers of this storyline. I am not quoting anybody, but I have a hunch because of her nature and role in the show and iconic status at the time in the New York theatre world.

Laura Rakowitz: I don't remember the storyline that well other than it was a fun adventure plot, and we loved being in the mummy room.

Harold Apter: It was crazy at first doing double duty as a production secretary and a dialogue writer during Merit Kara. They would hand me an outline—at that point I think only Claire and Paul were doing these—with about a week's time to write the script, but I was very quick. Since I was still working in the studio, they would give me the outline on Thursday. I would take the day off on Friday and deliver the script on Monday. I had to deliver forty pages of dialogue, usually. It came back to me on Tuesday, after Claire edited it, then I had to make copies to distribute.

Roscoe Born: My feelings about the story aside, Gordon Thomson was one of the greatest gentlemen I ever acted with. We later worked together on *Santa Barbara* and a very strange Canadian soap called *Family Passions*. It only lasted twenty-six weeks and was filmed in Toronto. It was a Canadian-German coproduction. The studio was in this weird building in the industrial part of the city.

Birds would swoop in through holes in the ceiling and fly through the scene. But Gordon was always a consummate professional.

Gordon Thomson: After that—Roscoe was a son of a bitch, and I hated him! Seriously, Roscoe was heaven. It is unusual to me to find somebody who was as striking to look at as Roscoe and who was also a truly sensitive, profound actor. That was a talented guy. It is one of the nicest compliments I have ever heard from him. I had no idea.

The year 1982 began without any of Maeve and Johnny Ryan's children on the canvas. The roles of Frank, Pat, and now Siobhan remained vacant. All hope was pinned on cousin Elizabeth Jane Ryan after the soap-within-a-soap arc ended. Desperate to clear Roger, Jane turns to Seneca for help, and they are able to expose Barbara's fakery by tricking her to get out of her wheelchair—witnessed by an impartial observer. Cornered, she drops her lawsuit against Roger, and Seneca ends their romance.

The Ryan family and Roger hail Jane as a hero. Jane and Roger grow much closer, which infuriates Delia. He even buys a souped-up sports car to please her, and Delia vandalizes it. But Jane, who worked previously as a mechanic, is able to repair it. Another scheme to embarrass Jane for being sent to reform school backfires when Jane reveals that her father was abusive. After beating her up one too many times, she and her then-boyfriend Ox Knowles hopped in her father's car to get away from him, and he reported it stolen. All are sympathetic to Jane, but Delia still believes there is something not right with the too-good-to-be-true journalist.

When Rae approves Jane's story on racecar driving, the reporter borrows Roger's car and drives to a New Jersey hangout. There, she runs into Charley, an old friend and Ox's former pit crew member. He has a look of concern on his face when Jane tells him of her engagement to Roger. She then heads over to a diner to talk with a driver. His back is toward her as she approaches, and when he turns around and removes his sunglasses, she freezes in her tracks—it is Ox Knowles (Will Patton)!

Randall Edwards: Maureen Garrett was cool. Again, she was not your typical soap opera–look person. I always liked when they made those choices and picked somebody who was not only a magazine face—somebody who was more authentic. Maureen came to my wrap party when I left the show, wearing a mustache!

Harold Apter: Will Patton is great. I remember his audition when he came in and watching it. He nailed the character, and it was always easy to write for him, unlike some others. I hated Seneca. I liked John Gabriel—and I even went to see him before his cabaret act—but Seneca was an asshole.

Randall Edwards: I think this was Will Patton's start. I remember that his head was always at an angle. We were like, "Wow! That is so curious." He was interesting and odd as an actor and continues to be an interesting actor. Again, not your stereotypical choice or mode of performance for a soap.

The Merit Kara story plays out with the opening of the tomb, which Faith accidentally discovers when she stumbles down a secret passageway. All interested parties are in attendance, including Maeve and Johnny. Intrigue grows when it is discovered that the shrine contains an orb with a map to the River of Gold. After getting blood poisoning from a scratch from a bracelet found in the tomb, Maeve confesses, on what she thinks is her death bed, that Jill is actually the biological daughter of Ed Coleridge. This makes her the half sister to Roger and Faith, who throws another hissy fit, accusing Jill of taking another man from her—this time her father.

Two Middle Eastern countries want to get their hands on the orb, as does the FBI and Ari's greedy girlfriend, Yvonne, who has returned from Egypt and will let no one stand in her way. The story comes to a climax in a warehouse in Brooklyn. Yvonne and her henchman, Mischa, threaten to kill Faith if Ari does not hand over the artifact. Unknowingly tailed by the cops and the Feds, Yvonne is surprised by Joe as she is about to kill Faith.

Ari grabs the orb and makes a run for it, but Yvonne, now composed, shoots him dead in the back. The orb rolls across the floor, and Joe picks it up. Yvonne demands it back, or she'll shoot Faith too. Joe tosses it to her, and when she goes to catch it, he grabs her arm with the gun, and it drops to the floor just as Jim Speed and Jonas rush in. Jonas, it turns out, is an undercover FBI agent. He wants the orb, but Joe, realizing how dangerous it could be for the world, tosses it into the fire. Yvonne is arrested and a shaken Faith thanks Joe for saving her life.

Harold Apter: During this storyline, I was production secretary number one. I had graduated from number two. We got a call in the studio one day from a woman who was absolutely hysterical.

She yelled, "They're going to open the tomb! Don't let them open the tomb! I just saw *Raiders of the Lost Ark* and everybody's going to die!" I said, "Ma'am, we shot that two weeks ago. It's okay." She still went on and on about it. Before I finally got off the phone with her, I suggested that she get help. My memory of Merit Kara is keyed to that personal moment.

Once back home, Faith apologizes to Jill and realizes she got caught up with Ari's warped obsession with the Merit Kara shrine, which got him killed. Now knowing that he just used her, Faith returns all the gifted artifacts. She loses Ari, and Jim Speed's interest in her wanes as well. He disappears from her life, and so does all the anger and spark she displayed. Instead of building on that and turning Faith into the show's newest villain, a challenge Karen Morris-Gowdy had already proven she could have risen to, they morphed her back to the selfless heroine—hell, she even remained sober. The Ryan family is grateful to Joe for rescuing Faith, and Maeve tells her ex-son-in-law that perhaps in the near future they can trust him again.

MacKenzie Allen: I might have left the show because I wanted out—you would think that would be something I would remember. I wasn't interested in renewing the contract and wanted to do something else.

Gordon Thomson: I was given about a two-week notice, so clearly the story was not a considerable success. Ellen Barrett wanted to give me a little party. I said, "Please don't. I would be embarrassed. I haven't earned it." I begged her, and she finally acquiesced. I think I had been around for one or two of those beloved-characters-leaving-the-show parties. I didn't get one nor did I want one. They gave me a little round silver box from Tiffany's with my name and the character's name and the dates I was there. That is all I have, and it is fine with me.

MacKenzie Allen: About a year and a half later, I worked with Randall Edwards again on an episode of *Tales of the Unexpected*. The lead was played by Carol Lynley. She was not unfriendly, but she was a bit reserved and aloof when she shouldn't be. I gave up acting a few years later.

Gordon Thomson: I was unaware of any network scrutiny while on the show. Somehow, I made their radar. I was sent to John

Crosby at ABC, which led directly to Aaron Spelling, which led to a screen test with Joan Collins, which led to the show *Dynasty* that changed my life.

At the time I was thirty-seven years old. I never looked as old as I am. When I was approaching the soundstage to do my screen test with Joan, she was coming out of the stage door. I said, "I'm Gordon Thomson. I am to test for the Carrington son." She replied, "Darling, you're much too old." It took me about four years to understand what a truly unpleasant thing that was to say.

That job changed my life. Many months later, we were chatting one day, and I said, "Joan, was that really such a big deal?" She replied, "Yes, darling, because as an actress I never had children more than twelve or thirteen years old." Well, on *Dynasty* she had four of us who all could vote. That was a big blow to her vanity. I don't think she had the clout at the time to axe hiring me. I looked thirteen years younger than I was.

In the script the character was described "as a young man of twenty-four." I think that was mostly for Joan's ego. The camera doesn't lie. I did the screen test with Joan. She knew then that this young man could act. And she also knew how important it was to have good actors doing this Richard and Esther Shapiro material. If the script is not absolutely first-rate—and most prime time isn't and *Dynasty* rarely was—then you better get people on board who really know what the hell they are doing. I did know what I was doing because at that point I had seventeen years in the business and had learned a great deal. I had done Shakespeare, Noël Coward, and all that stuff. I had a big fat resume, and I loved acting.

Dynasty was an incredibly happy set. John Forsythe was utterly professional. The only combination that didn't work was Joan and John, and Joan and Linda Evans to a degree. Joan is very protective. She is vain, and why not? She is so beautiful and always has been. If anybody was screwing up, somebody would say something to them very quickly.

[After *Dynasty*] I played Mason Capwell on *Santa Barbara*, and I think the writers liked writing for him. The best writing that I ever came across in front of the camera was on *Santa Barbara*. I had thirty-five pages a day, five days a week. All I was concerned about was getting to work, doing the work, going home, having a light supper, going to bed. For that reason, I enjoyed it more than *Ryan's Hope* because so much more was demanded of me. The peripheries, which I should care more about, don't mean that much to me because I love my job of acting.

I was hoping to retire as a patriarch on a daytime soap. It is a genre I really like. I don't think *Santa Barbara* was cancelled by the network [too many affiliates stopped airing it]. I do know at the end we had an executive producer by the name of Paul Rauch, who was one of the most unpleasant, dictatorial assholes that I ever worked with. He was something else. He made us work every holiday— Labor Day, Fourth of July. That is un-American. Today, I would just not show up for work.

The Roger/Jane/Ox storyline plowed on. Delia finally gives up trying to break up the couple, even though her suspicions about her rival are soon proved correct. Perhaps realizing the audience was not taking to goody-goody Jane, the writers wisely pivoted in a more interesting direction. Jane is revealed to be a master liar, just like her dear ol' brother Barry, when it comes to her prior love life. She keeps quiet about once being wed to Ox, who calls her "EJ." Actually, they are still married, since Ox is alive and he never filed the divorce papers. Jane gives him a Coleridge family necklace to hock (replacing it with a fake, which she continues to wear) so he can divorce her and get himself out of trouble with Leopold Osquillo (Ernesto Gonzalez), the leader of some South American despots he owes money to. He does neither, but it does not stop her from continuing her sham plans to marry Roger.

5

Kirkland's Hope? 1982

After the Merit Kara plot was wrapped up, ABC once again felt what worked on its other shows would on *Ryan's Hope*—hence the introduction of the Kirkland family. Explaining the reasons, Claire Labine told *Soap Opera Digest* writer Nerissa Radell, "The network wanted a new family on the show. And I have to say this in all justice—philosophically, it was a viable decision. We had worked the veins of the Ryans at this point. ABC had breathed new life into *One Life to Live* by bringing a new family in. But the problem here was that Paul and I had been doing the show for seven years, and we were making up a new family on demand. We didn't feel the need for it."

This was the final straw for co-creator and co-head writer Paul Mayer, who decided to leave after six and a half years. Claire Labine was now the sole head writer. When asked by Joanna Coons of *Rona Barrett's Daytimers* magazine why Paul had departed before their contract was up, she responded, "Paul wanted to do other things ... I wasn't ready to leave *Ryan's Hope* yet. I felt as if there was still a lot to do, and the torch was not in very good shape to be passed." Claire also mentioned that she stuck around because she adored the characters. However, she admitted that she preferred the original characters because they were around longer than the new ones. This remark was very revealing and may explain why some cast members felt like outsiders. At the same time, while losing Paul Mayer, the show gained a new staff writer.

Harold Apter: At this point, ABC demanded that I make a choice. I either accept a contract as a full-time writer or I stay with the show in production. I chose writer.

To get the show back on track, *Ryan's Hope* recast two of the Ryan children in March. A talented, fiery, redheaded newcomer named Marg Helgenberger became Siobhan #3, and the boyishly handsome Patrick James Clarke became the fourth actor to play Pat. As a bonus, Kelli Maroney was rehired to reprise her role of Kim. ABC gave this a big publicity push via their "Love in the Afternoon" promos: "Siobhan's back! Patrick's back! Kimberly's back, and you know trouble can't be far behind! *Ryan's Hope* weekdays on ABC!"

> **Malcolm Groome:** ABC contacted me about reprising the role of Pat. We went into negotiations with Jackie Smith, and it fell through. Jimmy Clarke was then hired to play him.

> **Kelli Maroney:** I wanted to come back. I didn't want anyone else to play my character except me. It was childish and probably not the best career move, in retrospect, but that's how I felt at the time.

Pat (sans Nancy Feldman since their relationship fizzled in Texas), Kim, and her ill baby, Arley, wind up on the same drama-filled flight from LA to New York. The pair had never met before. Arley gets sicker, and severe weather prevents the plane from landing in New York. Arley, who has viral meningitis, slips into a coma, and a determined Pat tries to keep her alive. Knowing the baby could die, the pilot decides to go for the landing, and the plane crash-lands at JFK. All are safe, and Arley is rushed to Riverside Hospital, where Seneca cares for her. She makes a full recovery. Grateful for keeping her granddaughter alive, Rae helps fund Pat's idea to set up a 24-hour community clinic for the poor. Kim and her baby move in with Rae, but not before Seneca serves her with divorce and custody papers. Kim then becomes romantically interested in Pat, who is distracted by his drive to open the clinic.

Siobhan surprises her family and shows up at Ryan's Bar on St. Patrick's Day. She wants to get right back to policing. Delia tips off Joe that his ex-wife has returned, and he immediately makes plans to win her back, even though he had accepted the recently departed Alexi Vartova's inheritance of his legitimate businesses (including real estate and the Dixon Trucking Company). He puts his inheritance to effective use and leases one of the vacant buildings to Pat for a dollar a year for his clinic, which impresses Siobhan.

Helgenberger and Roscoe Born clicked immediately as star-crossed lovers Siobhan and Joe. They steamed up the screen with their physical chemistry. Siobhan was still being written as the show's main heroine, and the talented Helgenberger had such a likeable presence that viewers began to forgive the lack of quirkiness in the character when she was first introduced in 1978.

Roscoe Born: I think perhaps Siobhan's original quirkiness had to do with Sarah Felder. Sometimes if the actor doesn't have those qualities, it won't work if you try to force them into it.

I was crazy about Marg and was very attracted to her, so that may have had something to do with it. Plus, she is a great actress. I think I tested with about twenty or thirty women up for the part. When they brought Marg in, I knew within one line that she was a quality actor and should get the part. It was instant. I think everybody else recognized it too. She was still in school at the time, and it was midsemester for her. We started shooting after she finished.

Laura Rakowitz: Marg was magic and even more so with her pairing with Roscoe Born as Joe. Marg is one of those unusual people who are just organically made to be an actor. She is smart, and acting is something that just comes naturally to her. She fell into the Siobhan character in such a beautiful way, and when paired with Roscoe they burned up the screen. They were delightful to work with. What was great about them was whenever they had to have a conversation with a director about a movement or an emotion, they would both be on the same page. It was fascinating to watch them work as a team. When they were not on screen, I missed them. They had great storylines and were just terrific together.

Tamara Grady: I loved Marg Helgenberger. She was absolutely the best Siobhan. I am still really good friends with her. No matter how high up she got in the business, she never ever got too uppity to keep me in her life, which was always nice.

Roscoe Born: I took Marg out to lunch before we even started shooting, and I told her that she was going to be in prime time or movies so don't re-sign. I totally meant it, and it was not a come-on or anything. I then let her know that was what Paul Mayer had said to me.

During this time, the serial lost the very popular Randall Edwards. At Roger's bachelor party held at the Crystal Palace, Delia is the surprise guest jumping out of a big cake and performing a song-and-dance number for him. It is the last time the audience saw the beloved Randall in the role because she refused to renew her contract. It was reported in the tabloids that ABC offered her "the sun and the moon to stick around as Delia." As fate would have it, Ilene Kristen had been playing Georgina Whitman on *One Life to Live* for a few months when she was told that her character "was going to be taken in a different direction," and she was let go. She was now available to reprise her role as the show's popular resident schemer, Delia.

Randall Edwards: I don't recall ABC offering me a lot of money to stay. I was determined to do theatre [*Biloxi Blues* with Matthew Broderick in 1985 and *Legs Diamond* in 1988] and film. My leaving had nothing to do with the character of Delia—she was great to play—it was wanting to do other things. I next did *As the World Turns*, where I temporarily [for two months] played Annie Stewart. The actress who had the part [Julie Ridley] left to have a baby. I don't have a sense of the differences in the two soaps in terms of production, but the character was so totally different than Delia. It was more of a straight leading lady–type. I thought, "I could never play this character for any long period of time." I just had the joy of playing Delia, and nothing could compare.

Shortly after that, I worked again with MacKenzie Allen, who was such a charming guy, and Carol Lynley in an episode ["The Gift of Beauty"] on *Tales of the Unexpected*. It was a small production company that put this TV show together. We brought our own clothes for costumes. I was in awe of Carol Lynley and thought she was amazing. I could not believe I was doing a TV show with her. We did not have a lot of social interaction, but she was very professional and was like what people have said about me—internally doing their work and staying in this little bubble. She was absolutely lovely.

Ilene Kristen: I started to see this holistic doctor who took me off my thyroid pills. I also got third-degree burns from an ointment I got from a dermatologist to get rid of some white spots that were on my skin. I then had to go on cortisone, and between that and not taking my thyroid pills any longer, I put on ten pounds. On my small frame, it looked like thirty pounds. I then got hired by *One Life to Live* to play Georgina Whitman, even though my neck was swollen and I couldn't fit into any of my clothing. I managed to play Georgina for six months, but I wasn't happy. They then fired me.

The next day I get a call from *Ryan's Hope*. I went to meet with Claire, Paul, and Jackie Smith, who was running daytime for ABC. Jackie was an anorexic, neurotic, conniving mess. She said to me, "Darling, we want you back as Delia, but you have to stop eating." I said it had nothing to do with what I ate and explained my situation to her. My whole tenure at *Ryan's Hope* the second time was fraught with problems.

Ilene's first appearance was on Roger and Jane's wedding day. She has a very amusing comedic moment trying to motivate Little John to get dressed for the ceremony and then gives up in typical, uninterested Delia fashion.

Shortly after, newcomer Hollis Kirkland (veteran TV and film actor Peter Haskell) arrives in New York City. The mogul, nicknamed Kirk, has a past connection to Rae Woodard, and his appearance rattles her. It also coincides with a mystery company called WB Realty Corporation buying up old buildings (including Spencer Smith's townhouse), displacing the residents. Then they would knock the buildings down. They also purchase the air rights to many buildings, including that of the Crystal Palace. Not surprisingly, ruthless Kirkland is behind the company, and he immediately acquires enemies in Jack, who is doing an investigative series of columns titled "Death of a City" for Rae's newspaper, and Delia, who is trying to obtain full ownership of her restaurant. Kirk tries to use his history with Rae to get her to call off Jack, but she refuses.

Harold Apter: I didn't realize then, but it is possible Claire could have based Hollis Kirkland on Donald Trump, with him being a real estate mogul buying up air rights.

Roscoe Born: Peter Haskell was interesting to play with and against. He was an old-school actor. He went to Harvard, so he was extremely bright but had this machismo attitude as a person and as the character. There was always a front there, but he could be witty and humorous.

Tamara Grady: Peter was a bit of a Hollywood guy. Most of the original cast were artsy actors from New York. I can understand why there might not have been any camaraderie between them.

Laura Rakowitz: I had worked with Peter Haskell in LA on another television show. I was extremely excited to learn that he decided to come from Hollywood to New York and that we would be working together again. I always liked him.

Kelli Maroney: Peter was wonderful. At first, I didn't know what to make of him. It didn't occur to me that, even though he'd had a huge TV career already, he probably felt a lot like I did when I first got there. Peter had a huge presence about him, and he seemed so "Hollywood" to me—as if I even knew what that was. I couldn't have been more wrong. We stayed in touch sporadically over the years, so I got to see him a couple of times before he left us. He had a light in his eyes and seemed the picture of health and energy. I think we all expected he would still be here now.

Louise Shaffer: I loved Peter. He was charming and smart. God love him, he decided he was going to go back to school to become a lawyer while he was acting on the show. He didn't last awfully long with that, but he really thought he could do both. That's the kind of can-do, high energy, great guy he could be.

Ilene Kristen: Peter Haskell was fabulous, and I loved working with him. I always liked watching him on nighttime television and thought he was a super choice to play Hollis Kirkland. We became close, and I actually saw him, oddly enough, about a month before he died. We had lunch, and he looked great. I was in shock when I heard he died a few weeks later.

Roger and Jane's wedding day is a bust. The ceremony does not take place because the guilt-ridden, still-married-to-Ox Jane gets cold feet and flees from the church, leaving an embarrassed Roger standing at the altar. Delia encourages an enraged Roger to enact his revenge on Jane and Ox—especially when Delia tells him that Jane hocked the Coleridge necklace, which Jane later admits. Roger eventually softens toward Jane and wants to reconcile. However, he is hellbent on keeping Ox away from her, but she refuses to stop spending time with Ox.

Harold Apter: I got to write a lot of the Jane and Ox Knowles story. I remember writing their first scene together. Jane was always supposed to be kind of tomboyish and the counterpart to Siobhan. But I do not remember the character taking a turn.

Louise Shaffer: I thought Maureen Garrett carried something incredibly special. A lot of the *Ryan's Hope* cast really did. Will Patton did too—just a fabulous actor. The show really had wonderful actors. I think that was one thing I really liked about the show. The guys were remarkably talented. You often get talented women in daytime. I think *Ryan's* had equally talented men.

Roscoe Born: Will Patton was great to work with. I only had a few scenes with him, but what an experience. Claire brought him in, and I am sure the network didn't want him. Will was not a soap actor. He was real. When I had scenes with him, I felt like we were just talking to each other. He was great, and they should have kept him on the show.

We shared a dressing room. Everybody in the cast thought he was odd except me. I didn't think he was weird at all, but maybe because everybody thought I was weird. People would come up to me and ask, "Does he ever say anything?" I'd say, "Yes, we speak all the time." Sometimes I would find him reading Kierkegaard [a Danish philosopher and theologian] in the dressing room. Maureen Garrett was good too, but a lot of the core cast didn't like her either. They seemed to not like most of the new people brought in.

Helen Gallagher: I do not think that was true. The word out in the business was that *Ryan's Hope* was the only soap that you could go on . . . and feel welcomed. This was because we actors were very welcoming.

Laura Rakowitz: I liked Will and Maureen. They were sort of outcasts, not only on the show but in real life too with the old-timers. Both were good actors with great timing. They were delightful to work with. They handled their storyline very well and were always interesting to watch on the screen especially Will. He was very quirky. I enjoyed that about him. Ellen Barrett liked him because he brought an oddity to the show, which I think she liked. And he was pleasant to work with.

Kelli Maroney: Maureen was charming to work with, and I liked Will too. He was definitely there to work—not there to make friends. If he was a method actor that could've been a factor. I felt like an outsider most of the time myself so I didn't see it as unusual.

Roscoe Born: The whole time I was there, it seemed that there was this testing period for whoever came in. But that happens on all soaps. Actors are afraid they are going to lose their storyline or worse. "Does this person mean I am going to get killed off?" Daniel Hugh Kelly pulled me aside after I was on the show for three months. They were starting to build a triangle between Jack, Siobhan, and Joe. He said, "I have to tell you anybody that has ever worked with Levin has gotten killed off." It was all this bullshit intrigue that I didn't want anything to do with. But it was that way on every single soap I ever worked on.

Delia, meanwhile, is distracted from the Roger/Jane/Ox drama while trying to get full ownership of the Crystal Palace. Touting Ilene's return, one of the "Love in the Afternoon" promos proclaimed, "She's beautiful. She's charming. And she's full of surprises. She's Delia Coleridge on *Ryan's Hope*."

Ilene and Randall each took a different approach in playing Delia. It was obvious to their castmates, the audience, and the creators. Claire Labine opined to Neena Pellegrini, "Ilene is an earthy, fundamental, desperate Delia. Randall's is more of a mercurial, high-comedy figure. I loved both of them. We had the best of all possible worlds because the actresses are so good but so different." She went on to say that she wished Ilene would play Delia for another three years and then have Randall come back after that.

Ilene Kristen: I did see Randall Edwards in the role. I thought she did a good job. A lot of people loved what she did with the role.

Randall Edwards: Since I had never watched the show, I was not familiar with the way Ilene played Delia. I just went at the character as an actress like you would with a play—trying to understand the character's motivation and where they were coming from. Why they were doing what they were doing. What they wanted in this story. I loved that and really sunk my teeth into it. It was not until later that people were letting me know that I was doing something very different than Ilene had done and that both interpretations worked and were interesting and hopefully entertaining to the audience. That was the feedback I was getting. It is also a testament to great writing how they showed the progression of Delia.

Helen Gallagher: I liked Randall Edwards very much. I thought she was quite good. In fact, when Ilene came back, I think she had a tough time taking over that part because Randall had really made it her own.

Roscoe Born: It was totally weird because I had never seen Ilene Kristen as Delia. For me, Delia was Randall. It was a big adjustment. They had vastly different energies, so I felt it was like two different characters. A lot of people who had watched the show from the beginning never accepted Randall. But from my experience on working on other soaps, that is what happens most of the time.

Ilene Kristen: I thought Roscoe had that winning combination of charisma and talent. He was hardworking, and he never seemed to have a false moment. It was a little challenging at the start to connect with him because he was involved with the actress I replaced. I am sure that was a difficult thing for him, but we eventually bonded—mostly about music. He was a very talented musician and songwriter.

Laura Rakowitz: Randall and Ilene played Delia so differently it was like two separate characters. Both were enchanting. They both brought their personalities to the character. Randall was more vulnerable. Her Delia was always making the wrong choices at the wrong time. Ilene's Delia was more conniving, and her actions were more thought out and calculating. They brought out interesting dimensions and aspects to Delia. It was fascinating to watch.

Kelli Maroney: I loved what each one of them did with the role. It was like playing with two different characters because it *was* playing with two different characters. Each actor brings themselves to the role. It's always going to be different, and I think that's what Roscoe was saying. It was so much fun the few times they wrote scenes for Kim and Delia.

Ron Hale: I absolutely agree that they played the role as if two different characters. Randall was more—well just as a person—more psychoanalytical. She had to, I think, break down every scene, every line, every word to make sense to her. Ilene went on instinct, as all good actors do. I am not saying that Randall was not a good actor—she was! It was just her whole approach to the character was very deep.

Karen Morris-Gowdy: I can see why some people felt that way. And you know what, people may have felt that about Catherine Hicks and me. I don't know if I was a totally different Faith than they remembered. That is what's hard when you replace someone. But the difference was that Catherine hadn't been there that long after two prior Faiths. I don't think the audience—as much as they may have liked them—were really embedded with them. But everyone was with Delia, who was such an unusual character. And Ilene was so out there. But Randall worked very hard.

Ann Gillespie: When I was on the show with Randall, I recall that she had a lot of crying scenes, and those were just awful. I did not know how to do those and was never good at it. She had a ton and would spend all day long in her dressing room, making herself so depressed that she could do it. I have to say it was a little confusing to me as a friend because she had to withdraw so much to be able to do what she needed to do for the scene. Sometimes I needed to talk with her, but she was unavailable. That was just a small piece because she was mostly totally available. She had so much integrity about her acting. I like to think I did too, but she would leave me in the dust in terms of the preparation and the authenticity that she strived for in these ridiculous things we were being asked to do.

Malachy McCourt: I had a different relationship with Randall Edwards. It was not the same as it was with Ilene Kristen. There was not the merriment I had with Ilene, who was very professional and all that, but she did not take it too seriously. She knew it was a soap opera, and we were there to have fun. I liked Randall. She was nice and professional, but there was no fooling around and she was more serious. I would still try to play around and throw in lines here or there that they would have to cut.

Tamara Grady: I was good friends with Randall Edwards. At that time, I thought she was the best Delia. But she and Ilene Kristen attacked the role of Delia differently. I thought Randall brought more humor, and her Delia seemed to have more places to go than Ilene did. Ilene's Delia was either funny or a victim.

Malcolm Groome: I watched some of the show when Randall Edwards played Delia. It was a totally different interpretation than Ilene's. Randall was a good actress and gave an interesting depiction of Delia.

Harold Apter: Claire Labine complimented me on how well I wrote Delia. When Ilene Kristen took over Delia from Randall Edwards, she had her own ticks, which I incorporated into my scripts. Claire liked that.

Going forward, Claire's long story centered on the breakup of Roger and Jane, with her determination to help Ox win his big race and Roger's attempts to bring him down; Joe trying to win back Siobhan, who resumes her job on the police force; and a desperate Kim, who turns to Orson Burns (now played by Robert Desiderio) to bilk millions out of her mother. They concoct a fake kidnapping of Arley and Kim to extort the money from Rae. After sneaking the baby out of Rae's apartment, the plan proceeds as planned until greedy Orson turns the tables on Kim and tries to ice her out. She discovers his deception and tries to outmaneuver him, but it puts her and Arley's life in jeopardy.

Seneca and Rae bring the cash to a deserted building, where the drop-off is to take place. It goes askew when Seneca and gun-toting Orson scuffle, and he drops the gun. It is picked up by Rae, who shoots Orson. Just before Orson loses consciousness, he tells Seneca that Kim formulated the whole scheme. After making sure his daughter is okay, Seneca goes back to Orson, who is gone. At home, while Kim gives the performance of her career playing the terrified kidnap victim to reporters and the police, Seneca immediately instructs his attorney, Jill Coleridge, to help him gain full custody of his daughter so he can rid himself of Kim.

Meanwhile, a frantic, injured Orson begs Delia for help. For $10,000 and a passport, he will give her information on how to get back the Crystal Palace. After she pays him, he reveals Kim's part in the kidnapping and that it was Joe Novak who masterminded the waiters' strike, vandalism, and the fire at the restaurant, causing her bankruptcy. Delia refuses to believe that her friend would do that, but when confronted, Joe confesses to her, Bob, and Siobhan. However, he tells Delia that he never changed the deed, so legally she still holds sole ownership. After he hands it to her, she hisses, "Thanks for nothing. All you did was give me what was mine in the first place."

Delia's anger toward Joe softens quickly as she plots to get her air rights back. To reach that goal, she needs Rae Woodard's help with Hollis Kirkland. She tricks Kim into admitting that she concocted the kidnapping scheme and secretly records her in her office at the Crystal Palace. Delia then tries to blackmail Rae with it, but the sneaky publisher steals the tape. After watching it, Rae is appalled and forces Kim to sign custody of Arley over to her instead of facing jail time. Later, Seneca and Rae reach an agreement to share custody.

It was great fun to see schemers Delia, Rae, and Kim interact with each other more than usual. One particularly funny moment happened at a charity function for Pat's clinic. One of the announced prizes up for bid is dinner for two at Delia's Crystal Palace. Snarky Kim says to Pat, "What is she serving, poison apples?" Delia just happens to walk by and responds, "No, cooked goose."

> **Kelli Maroney:** Those kidnapping scenes didn't start out to be comedic, but Bob Desiderio was so hilarious, it was almost impossible to keep a straight face. I'd have to avoid eye contact with him. I struggled many times to not break and just crack up during taping! Having him in the storyline—the short time he was there—was so refreshing.

> **Ilene Kristen:** Louise and Kelli were great to work with. Louise was wonderful as Rae. I liked Kelli a lot and we are still in touch.

> **Kelli Maroney:** I wish they had given us more to do together as Kim and Delia.

In spring 1982, the Daytime Emmy nominations were announced, and the Academy's love for *Ryan's Hope* continued to wane. Although it received another nomination for Outstanding Daytime Drama Series, it only scored two additional nominations—Outstanding Actress in a Supporting Role in a Daytime Drama Series for Louise Shaffer and Outstanding Achievement in Design Excellence for a Daytime Drama Series. This would be the first year since the soap began that it left the ceremony empty-handed.

As for the show's ratings and popularity, it was a mixed bag. It rebounded with the college crowd. During a survey of students on eleven campuses across the country in April 1982, 28 percent of the respondents admitted to watching *Ryan's Hope* at least once a week. The show placed fifth behind *General Hospital* (73 percent), *All My Children* (58 percent), *One Life to Live* (45 percent), and *The Young and the Restless* (29 percent).

Per the researchers, young people liked the ABC shows best because "they use more on-location footage and innovative production techniques, tend to feature more college-age characters, and have a higher sexual content." *Ryan's Hope* did not abide by this formula, so it is a testament to its writing staff and cast that younger people were still invested in it.

Unfortunately, remaining popular on campus did not translate into bigger household ratings as officially tabulated by A. C. Nielsen. In May 1982, the show's ratings fell to 5.8/26. It was now being beaten outright by *The Young and the Restless*, and its NBC competition got stiffer because at the end of March, *The Doctors* was moved to noon to make way for the former CBS soap *Search for Tomorrow*, which changed networks. *Ryan's Hope* was now ranked seventh behind *General Hospital*, *All My Children*, *One Life to Live*, *Guiding Light*, *The Young and the Restless*, and *As the World Turns*. There was a bit of good news, though. In the key women 18–49 demo (attractive to advertisers), *Ryan's Hope* ranked fourth, with 3.2 million viewers, behind *General Hospital*, *All My Children*, and *One Life to Live* and ahead of *The Edge of Night* and all the CBS and NBC soaps.

At the end of June, Claire Labine left the show, and the head writing reins were turned over to her longtime friend and associate, Mary Munisteri. Labine commented to author Mary Ann Copeland in 1991, "There were choices and they were clear choices, business and creative choices, after we sold the show. Soap opera took a different direction after *General Hospital*, and then ... management of daytime at ABC wanted *Ryan's Hope* to be different." Just before Labine's departure, there were other changes to the writing staff as well.

Trent Jones: In my personal life, I already had one child who was born before I acted on the show, and then my wife was pregnant with our second child. I had to pull something together. I was in the greenroom at *All My Children*, where I was doing day work to keep my insurance up. They had *Ryan's Hope* on the TV, and I had not been watching because I was pissed that they killed me off. But what was showing was the Egyptian story, which I thought was interesting. I am a sci-fi fan and like all that shit and thought this was different. I knew how to lay out a script, so I went home and typed up a sample script doing two stories. I imagined where the Egyptian plot was going and a romantic story—action and nonaction. I knew the characters I was writing about.

My agent at the time, Honey Raider, also represented Louise Shaffer. I gave my script to Honey, who gave it to Louise, who gave it to Claire Labine. It sat on Claire's desk for months. However, she finally did read it and gave it to Mary Munisteri, who was running this development program for new script writers. Mary called me, and I got into the program. One of the first things Mary said to me was, "This isn't for everybody. David Mamet wrote briefly for *Ryan's Hope* and was fired. It requires a certain kind of talent." She would give me a breakdown, and I would write a script. She would then edit it and talk with me about it. She was extremely sweet and very perceptive. This went on for a few months. I finally got an actual on-air script, which led to me being hired.

Harold Apter: I left *Ryan's Hope* right before Mary Munisteri became head writer. They fired me, and to this day I am not exactly sure why. I think ABC was not pleased with what I was doing. I remember a comment about whiny dialogue. Somebody there didn't like the way I wrote Roscoe Born's Joe because he told Delia he was feeling depressed. Joe and Delia liked each other as friends and would have these conversations to help each other. I liked making it real and the reality that Claire brought to it. I may have made it too real for ABC's taste. But shit happens in show business.

It's an interesting world because a writer's style to some people's ear is one thing, and something else to another. It is the hardest thing, and not taking it personally is even harder. It is always a question of somebody's taste, and if you are a head writer or a show runner, you want people who are going to do it in a way that hits your ear correctly. It sucks, but it happens all the time. I never watched the show again. I said, "I'm not going to watch that shit anymore." I was devastated—*it hurts, man.* It's an emotional investment working on a show.

Trent Jones: Claire was still the head writer and editing all on-air scripts. I remember I wrote one scene that had one extremely good line in it. When I got the edit back from her, she kept that one line but completely rewrote the rest of it. It was Maeve's memory of growing up in Ireland, and Claire's words were just beautiful. After the script had gone into tape, there was some in-house party, and somebody came up to me and said, "That was just an amazing scene you wrote." I said, "Thank you." You really couldn't write Maeve, especially if it was an intimate and revelatory type of scene. Maeve was Claire, and her genius came out even more with this character.

Harold Apter: After getting canned, I remember sitting in my bathtub and thinking, *What am I going to do?* That is when I decided to move out to LA and try for the big time, which I did. I never wrote for a soap again and only worked on prime time [*Star Trek: The Next Generation; Walker, Texas Ranger; The Sentinel; Earth: Final Conflict,* etc.]. I missed the characters. It was like leaving my family because you are working with these same characters every day for an extended period of time. Working freelance in prime time is not quite the same. Storytelling is completely different. The way you write dialogue is different. For a soap, it is basically pages and pages of dialogue. When you write for film or prime-time television, it is more about what the camera does, so you have to be much more economical in writing dialogue. What Claire did for me is that she taught me how to write dialogue in a way that was easy for me to adapt to what I had to do in prime time.

Trent Jones: I recall being asked after I started working, "What do you think is the most important attribute a script writer has?" I said, "Stamina—you need to have enormous stamina." A little later, I was having a conversation with Claire, and she asked how I answered. I told her. I said what did you say and she exclaimed, "Amazing talent!" I thought, "Oh shit. I failed that test."

Mary Munisteri's first order of business as head writer was to wrap up the Roger/Jane/Ox triangle. In a surprise move, fickle Jane breaks it off completely with Roger due to his vindictive behavior toward Ox, including having him arrested for the stolen Coleridge necklace. Jane helps Ox (bailed out by Rae) build his new racing car, and then he wins the Grand National race. Ox pays off his debts and accepts a job as the spokesman for Hollis Kirkland's car and tire company. Ox and Jane try to reconcile, but after catching him twice in compromising positions with his producer, Sydney Galloway (Marilyn McIntyre), Jane heads to LA to join her brother, Barry.

Hollis Kirkland then became a force on the show under Munisteri's reign, with his renewed romance with Rae despite being married to Catsy Kirkland, who is residing in Arizona; the discovery that Kim is his biological daughter and helping with her custody battle with her ex-husband,

Seneca; his control of the Crystal Palace air rights, putting him at odds with Delia; and the arrival of his fragile daughter Amanda (Mary Page Keller), who is haunted by a past memory she cannot fully recall and falls for Pat after a chance meeting in Central Park.

With Jane gone for good, Ox falls into Delia's arms, making Roger jealous. To escape all the family drama in her life, Maeve begins ballroom dancing with a man named David Newman (Robert Brown), which makes Johnny jealous. Sister Mary Joel (now played by Jacqueline Brookes) reappears and is now running a shelter for prostitutes, some of whom are found murdered, causing Siobhan to go undercover as a call girl to stop the ringleader, Ace Landrace (Vyto Ruginis). Overprotective Joe shadows Siobhan but has his own issues as mobster China Pollard (Lee Kirkland) wants him dead and a returned Orson offers to do the job. Loser-in-love Faith makes another poor choice when she begins spending time with Siobhan's gruff blue-collar boss, Detective Mitch Bronski (James Sloyan). Jill's continued support of Seneca during his child custody fight reignites feelings between the ex-spouses.

> **Trent Jones:** I thought Mary Munisteri had a co-head writer. There was a guy who I really liked. We didn't write by storyline but by script. The one character that stands out for me was Detective Mitch Bronski. I liked James Sloyan as an actor, and he was good. They had some exceptionally fine actors on here.
>
> I also remember being assigned to do a script that featured Amanda Kirkland and something to do with Alice in Wonderland. Will Patton as Ox was a wonderful actor too, and we knew he was going places. He was great.

In October, the quarterly ratings for July through September were released, and the show received some good news. With the beginnings of Munisteri's stories just unfolding, the ratings had ticked up steadily to a 6.2/26. This was most likely due to teenagers and college students being on summer vacation since the show performed better with younger audiences. Soon after, things soured when criticism began that the show was being too Kirkland-centric, even though Munisteri continued to intermingle the Ryan and Kirkland/Woodard families. Maeve, Pat, and Siobhan Ryan all had front-burner storylines, as did Delia. If anything, the characters of Jack and the Coleridges were not used as much as in the past.

Pat and his romance with the troubled Amanda Kirkland, who is plagued by a childhood trauma, was featured. Kirk did his best to keep the incident buried in her mind. All Amanda can recall was walking into a room as her father and his business partner argued. Shortly afterward, he disappeared with money that he allegedly embezzled from her family's company. Pat tries to help Amanda regain her memories. Patrick James Clarke, who had a disarming smile that lit up a room, and pretty newcomer Mary Page Keller became very popular in their roles.

Kelli Maroney: Jimmy Clarke was great! Peter Haskell had kind of taken him under his wing, and we all hung out quite a bit after work. We all really liked him and the audience did too, I think.

Ilene Kristen: I love Malcolm Groome and, in my heart, he was irreplaceable as Pat. With that said, of all the replacements, I liked Jimmy Clarke best. John Blazo was a very lovely guy but not right for Pat. The guy after him was some Italian kid with curly hair [Robert Finoccoli]. That was such odd casting. Jimmy had a glint in his eye and an adorable sexiness about him. He oozed Irishness. I really liked what he did in the part.

Karen Morris-Gowdy: I thought Jimmy Clarke had a more boyish way about him. Malcolm's Pat had a lot more wounds.

Maeve continues practicing with Mr. Newman for the big dance contest, making Johnny feel quite resentful. Defending this story, Mary Munisteri told *Soap Opera Digest*, "Maeve has lost her own sense of independence. She's not quite in touch with who she is apart from Johnny. She's a woman who's never been to the movies alone. She just doesn't go places alone except to church or to her Irish dance group. Aside from that, she's part of a couple. And it becomes increasingly clear to her that she's never had cause to think of herself as an independent or so unusual woman. When she feels alienated from Johnny, she feels so frightened she has to pause."

Despite putting Maeve and Johnny on the front burner, this storyline did not sit well with the audience or Helen Gallagher. Maeve and Johnny were the tentpole couple that were supposed to be indestructible amid the romantic turmoil of their family. Even though Maeve's relationship with David is a platonic friendship with the love of dance at its core, any threat to her and Johnny's sacred marriage ruffled the viewers' feathers. Hence, the story was wrapped up quickly.

Helen Gallagher: I thought this story was foolish. It just did not fit the storyline for Maeve. She was not a dancer; she was just a woman who owned a bar. I heard the audience was not happy with it either.

Laura Rakowitz: I do remember that the fans didn't want to see Maeve with anybody else but Johnny.

Soon grumblings from unhappy cast members began to slowly leak to the press about their dissatisfaction with the show. Many felt there was too much focus on Hollis Kirkland and the characters connected to him. Some actors even began calling the show "Kirkland's Hope" in interviews. It seemed to be a repeat of what transpired with the Michael Pavel/Kim Harris situation the year before, but here some of the cast found the courage to voice their opinions publicly. While other soaps could introduce new families as they saw fit, it was a bit more difficult for *Ryan's Hope* since the show was named for its core family. Having this new wealthy family take attention and airtime from the Ryans rankled some loyal viewers. But after seven years on the air, the show needed some new blood to shake it up. And at least the Kirklands were not as outlandish as many of the wealthy families introduced on competing soaps at the time (i.e., *General Hospital*'s Cassadine family). Hollis Kirkland was focused on buying up real estate in New York City rather than taking over the world.

Louise Shaffer: I heard that "Kirkland's Hope" moniker around the edges. I knew there was a lot of anger and rumbling about this storyline. Working on a soap opera, there usually is. Again, this was one of those times where there was a lot of tension behind the scenes, and I didn't want to know about it. I was just trying to pay off my mortgage.

Ron Hale: I think the term "Kirkland's Hope" was fair, oh yeah. I was there and a part of it. It was like, "Who are we? What are we doing here?" Once again, if the moves are made that make sense and are thought out about how to make the show better, fine. Here it seems they just decided to add another family. So, we called it "Kirkland's Hope." I used it more than once. I wasn't happy and not because I wasn't working as much. It was more, "What are they thinking?!"

Karen Morris-Gowdy: I remember this. Ron had been there from day one. He was probably like, "Okay, now what's going on with these Kirklands?" I know it bothered him and others. I was still young, so it really didn't affect me. And I did love working with James Sloyan. It was a fun storyline because of working with him.

Kelli Maroney: I could understand why the rest of the cast felt like they weren't getting their due. But it isn't fair to blame actors for their storylines.

Laura Rakowitz: I remember the cast complaining that the Ryan and Coleridge families were put on the back burner in favor of the Kirklands. This was the first time I heard the phrase "back burner" being used and now understood what it really meant. The old-timers were not happy with the Kirkland storyline at all. It didn't matter how much they were paid or how they were treated, they were unhappy with this. I can't confirm what they said to the press, but I guess that is how some of them handled it.

Roscoe Born: I didn't care about the Kirklands, but I know a lot of the actors were all pissed off about it. The core actors who were there from the beginning were really anti-Kirkland. That seems to be a pattern on all soaps when a new family is introduced.

Michael Levin: I remember the Kirkland and then later the Dubujak families but not fondly. It was just a move by ABC to get the show in line with its other soaps and was just par for the course.

A delightful surprise was the romantic pairing of Ox and Delia. Both characters were quirky to the max, and the actors played off each other quite well. Delia gets Ox to put Little John in his TV commercials for Kirk's company. He also aids Delia with her wacky blackmail plan to get her air rights back after she learns Kirk's big secret—he is Kim's biological daddy. She gets hold of a letter confirming it, but Roger snatches it, and it goes through a roundelay of hands, remaining unopened. Desperate, Delia begs Jill and Jack for help in trying to get Kirk to back off from using the air rights to build his skyscraper. When Kirk tells Jill that he did not realize Delia had so many friends, Jill assures him that Delia is no friend of hers, but she admires the success she has made of the Crystal Palace and that it is unfair for Kirk to take it away from her.

The aforementioned letter winds up with Kim, who finally opens it and learns the truth. She confronts her parents. Kirk wants them to unite as a family, including Kim's half sister Amanda, but his plan hits a major obstacle when his wife, Catsy (Christine Jones), arrives in town.

Kelli Maroney: Mary Page Keller and Christine Jones were welcome and exciting additions for me. New actors coming in, with no baggage, was fantastic. It was so fun and different for me to have Kim thrown completely off-balance by these strange new relatives. Both the actors and the characters were such a positive shot in the arm and bright, fresh energy.

Ilene Kristen: Well, I had a terrible crush on Will Patton. I idolized the man, but he was out there. He wasn't your typical soap actor, but I loved working with him. Our storyline together was interesting. I was so excited when they had Ox not be with EJ anymore and hooked him up with Delia. Maureen Garrett was a lovely person, but it was like "No, no, no! I want Will Patton!"

Mary Munisteri was the one who paired Delia with Ox. I don't know why, but I was sure sending out vibes that I wanted to work with Will more. Not that I didn't love working with Ron Hale. I did. However, I wanted more and more of Will Patton!

Ron Hale: I truly blocked this entire storyline out, but I remember Will Patton because Ilene just *loved* Will. She just thought he was the greatest thing since ice cream. I liked working with him too.

Walanne Steele: I remember Jadrien working with Will Patton, who played a racecar driver and he got a racing suit to wear. This was a busy time for Jadrien as he was also appearing in the Broadway musical *Nine*. Ellen Barrett was very accommodating about it. I remember when Jadrien performed with the cast on the Tony Awards broadcast, she called to say how wonderful he was on it.

By the end of December, the soap's ratings plummeted almost ten points to a 5.3/21 share. Its rival, *The Young and the Restless*, hit its highest rating ever, up to that point, with a 7.9/31, totally crushing *Ryan's Hope*. CBS's aggressive plan had worked, and its soap had steadily eroded the ratings of its competition. ABC, however, had no intention of following suit to counter the juggernaut that was *The Young and the Restless*.

Seymour Amlen: We had game shows in the morning and soaps in the afternoon. *Ryan's Hope* had been on the air for quite a while at 12:30. It had never been big in the ratings. It had a good crew and a talented cast from Broadway and off-Broadway, so there was no reason to be unhappy with it.

Ryan's Hope would never be a hit unless we moved it to a later time slot. At the time there was no chance of that because *Ryan's Hope* was a half hour. Our major shows were all one hour. Up to the late seventies, all the soaps were half hours. Once one of the networks stretched a soap out to an hour [NBC with *Another World*], the rest followed suit. ABC expanded *All My Children* from 1:00 to 2:00 p.m.; *One Life to Live* from 2:00 to 3:00 p.m.; and *General Hospital* from 3:00 to 4:00 p.m.

Laura Rakowitz: I didn't pay attention to ratings talk until the late eighties and felt that ABC thought of *Ryan's Hope* as the stepchild everybody wanted to forget. I don't know why it was. I don't know if Claire Labine did or said anything that pissed them off. I think ABC wanted to see *Ryan's Hope* fail at this point, so they didn't do anything to help us out.

Ilene Kristen: I never concerned myself with ratings. I just concentrated on learning my lines. That is all I could think about. But I do feel that ABC did not promote the show enough. All attention was on Luke and Laura from *General Hospital*, but I don't think that in itself was a detriment to *Ryan's Hope*.

ABC seemed to put most of the blame for the ratings erosion on Mary Munisteri. They seemed to be listening to the "Kirkland's Hope" contingent and critics such as Jon-Michael Reed, who found the show to be "in shambles." Arguably, Munisteri did a good job balancing the domestic drama of the Ryan family with the uber-rich Kirkland family that ABC had wanted injected into the show. The Pat/Amanda, Siobhan/Joe, and Faith/Mitch romantic pairings were all on the front burner, along with Kirk's involvement with Rae and Kim. The financier's determination to destroy the Crystal Palace made delightful, strange bedfellows out of Delia, Jack, and Jill, who joined forces to save it. The call girl serial killer plot brought suspense and intrigue with a touch of humor when a meddling Delia and undercover cop Siobhan get arrested together for being hookers. However, in daytime television, it is all about the ratings and ad rates. Obviously, a good portion of the audience was not happy with the direction the show was going.

Kelli Maroney: I thought Mary Munisteri was incredibly talented and a great writer. She wrote some exceptional stories and scripts. I don't know who was pinning the blame on her, but it's unfair and unrealistic to blame one person for slipping ratings for an entire program.

Karen Morris-Gowdy: I loved Mary Munisteri. Some of her scripts were my favorites. She was a very fine writer.

Ilene Kristen: I had a wonderful relationship with Mary Munisteri, and she is a great writer. I had a big storyline so I was enjoying it. But there is no doubt that the creators made the show a fuller experience. They probably would never have let the Kirklands happen, but there was probably pressure from the network. Mary knows how to write and knows how to be a head writer. Sometimes head writers are not allowed to write what they want. Claire and Paul could when they owned the show. Once the network is involved and steps in, then you have to obey.

Trent Jones: I was living in Long Island City and would get about a week to write one script. I would just do draft after draft with my wife reviewing. I really did not know the politics going on. All I know is that Mary didn't last awfully long as head writer, and they demoted her.

Not willing to shuffle their schedule the way CBS did, ABC removed Munisteri as head writer and then called in the big guns. A drastic change was about to begin.

6

Enter Charlotte Greer, 1983

Believing they were in a desperate situation, ABC lured Claire Labine and Paul Mayer back to take over as head writers and, as Trent Jones stated, demoted Mary Munisteri, who remained on staff. Remarking on one reason she returned, Labine told Nerissa Radell, "I hated to see it battered and bloodied." This move won praise from the soap press. Columnist Jon-Michael Reed remarked that the show "grew steadily less interesting. The show's very title and theme seemed on the brink of extermination . . . The return of Labine and Mayer . . . will hopefully result in a better-blended drama."

Better? Perhaps. Blended? No. As they did when returning from the writers' strike in fall 1981, Labine and Mayer wielded a meat cleaver, writing out nine cast members and abruptly ending storylines instead of trying to integrate at least some of them. Labine and Mayer also had some demands before they would agree to sign on. Claire explained to Radell that one of their mandates was to rehire Shirley Rich, the duo's original casting director, who worked on the show in 1975.

The pair had another requirement that was a bit more sensitive. Claire explained, "We also wanted to have Malcolm Groome . . . come back because he's great and because his presence on the set brings such joy to everyone who works with him. There was a perfectly lovely actor, James Clarke, who was playing the role, but he wasn't Malcolm." This latter change prompted Jon-Michael Reed to remark, "The switch is sure to cause mixed emotions for *Ryan's Hope* fans. Groome is an accomplished young actor, but Clarke, a charming performer, was just beginning to develop into an interesting characterization."

Geoff Pierson (Frank Ryan #4): I had to test for Frank. What is interesting about *Ryan's Hope* is that I got called in to read for the part of Frank Ryan in about mid-1982, but nothing came of it. Danny Kelly had played the role and had gone to LA. They did not have a Frank Ryan, but I think a couple of actors substituted here or there, but nobody was hired for the role. I was not aware of all this backstory at that time.

Then, that December, I got called to come in and read for a part, but it was for a different casting director named Shirley Rich. I read in her office, and I do not recall any other actors being there. Turns out it was again for Frank Ryan, and I am not sure if I put that together at the time that I had already auditioned for it. I think there were some callbacks, and then I tested with Nancy Addison and Karen Morris-Gowdy. They made us do some scenes. They had several actors testing for it at that time.

I met Claire Labine and Paul Mayer the day of the test. When I walked out of the soundstage after doing the two tests, Claire and Paul walked down from the booth where they were watching my audition and came out into the hallway as I was leaving. This is unusual because the way the acting profession works is that you audition and then you leave because if they want you, their producers will have to negotiate with your agents. Claire was so excited—I do not know how else to put it. She was in glee and thrilled. I guess maybe she already got permission from the ABC network people who were watching it too. I do not know.

Malcolm Groome: Paul and Claire came back as head writers, and one of their conditions was to bring me back. That is when I came in to replace Jimmy Clarke. We crossed paths just a little bit. He was a great guy, and I really liked what he did on the show. It was an interesting direction for Pat to go in. I thought he deserved better than being written off.

Karen Morris-Gowdy: I was so delighted when Malcolm came back, and I had the opportunity to work with him as a little more seasoned actress at the time. I had just started when he left. It was wonderful.

Geoff Pierson: When I started, John Gabriel came up to me and said in jest, "You are here to save the show." I guess it was known to the cast that the ratings were declining. The role of Frank had been vacant for almost a year and a half. I think that was just John's way of welcoming me.

To tell you the truth, it was an extremely exciting time. I started filming around the holidays in late 1982. When I received the offer to do the part, I started watching the show, and I was very confused. I thought Peter Haskell was like Johnny Ryan, and the Kirklands were the main family. Peter and Mary Page Keller as his daughter—who I later did a movie with—were wonderful and exceptionally good in it. I could not figure out, though, who the Ryan family was to the show.

Mary Munisteri's stories came to a quick close. The prostitute killer is revealed to be mobster Ace Landrace, who is killed by Joe Novak in a gun battle that also takes the life of Mitch Bronski. Loser-in-love Faith Coleridge has her third straight romantic partner end up in a body bag. Thinking she needs someone with money to help her save the Crystal Palace, Delia dumps Ox, who leaves town, and tries to cozy up to Roger. That ploy fails, and she winds up bankrupt and alone. Amanda Kirkland remembers the horrid memory she has been repressing, which results in a breakdown. Her parents then ship her off to a sanitarium in Switzerland. Thinking Pat has the audio recording of Amanda's psychiatric session in his briefcase, Rae pushes a work cart into him at Riverside Hospital, knocking him unconscious but also starting a fire. However, he had already passed the tape on to Jack, who gave it to newly arrived Frank Ryan, who now has the goods on Kirk.

Amanda's repressed memory reveals that Kirk is actually the embezzler, and when Will Brader threatened to expose him, they fought. Young Amanda then shot and killed Brader, thinking he was going to hurt her father. Catsy knew what Amanda did and helped cover it up, but she thought Brader, not her husband, stole from the company. Now facing jail time, Kirk is forced to jilt Rae, remain with Catsy, and go off to Switzerland. Kim splits town too, leaving baby Arley with Seneca. She is going to make a movie in Australia (secretly financed by Rae after Seneca threatened to reveal what she did to Pat). The blossoming romance between Jill and Seneca comes to a complete halt with Frank's reappearance.

Rachael Mayer: The story I heard was they wanted to inject Claire and Paul to save the show, but I think it was futile.

Ruth Mayer: My dad was married to an actress, and he knew how painful it was for actors to lose jobs. It was also part of the business that Claire, when they were in charge, would leave to him to do the heavy lifting, and she would keep the beautiful relationships. I think later it was the network who would fire people.

Cut from the show were Will Patton, James Sloyan, Peter Haskell, Christine Jones, Patrick James Clarke, Mary Page Keller, Kelli Maroney, Jacqueline Brookes, and Vyto Ruginis. The firings even extended to the writing staff. Commenting to S. Ezra Goldstein, Paul Mayer admitted, "We're losing some very fine actors, but what do writers have to draw upon but their own childhoods, their own fantasies? And those characters came out of other people's fantasies, not Claire's nor mine. We just didn't feel comfortable with them." Later, he remarked to Nerissa Radell, "It wasn't the performers' fault, but if you look at those other characters, they were all nasty people, grubbing for money. We write a very sentimental show about love and sex, things we're interested in. We wanted to go back and build the stories around the family, which meant we had to lose some of the Kirklands."

Mayer's statement was not completely accurate. Yes, *he* did not create any of the Kirkland family members, but Hollis Kirkland came aboard while the show was under Claire's tutelage. And together they decided to recast Amanda, who was created by Mary Munisteri, and introduce her older sister, Leigh Kirkland. With both on the canvas, it was a bit mind-boggling why they could not have at least kept their father on the scene. Kirk was by far a more realistic tycoon than what was to come.

To the soap press, it did not matter, and the firings were called "a spring bloodbath." And to the viewers it was jarring. Labine and Mayer seemed to not consider that *Ryan's Hope* accumulated new and younger viewers from 1980 on. There were many fans of these characters, the mob storyline, the intrigue and glamour, and the faster pace. Instead of trying to find a better balance and improve upon what Mary Munisteri attained, they axed many characters, slowed things down considerably, and transported the show back to 1975—which elated the critics and many longtime fans. However, the eighties were not the seventies in terms of what many newer soap viewers wanted and expected. The lack of glitz (Did they really have to make Delia lose her fabulous Crystal Palace?), coupled with longer, drawn-out scenes may have turned off some of these newer audience members.

Laura Rakowitz: At the production meetings, I remember Paul and Claire calling in and voicing their displeasure with the Kirklands. They were happy to write them off because they didn't like the people, they didn't like the storyline, and they didn't like the fact that ABC inserted themselves into those storylines.

Geoff Pierson: When I first started working, it was a tumultuous time as they were literally getting rid of Peter Haskell's story and his family—Christine Jones, Mary Page Keller, and Kelli Maroney. They got rid of Jimmy Clarke as Pat Ryan, and Malcolm Groome came back about the time I started. It literally was a day-to-day basis for me to figure out what was really going on. Some of the storylines go back for years, and you must catch up to know what has been going on.

Kelli Maroney: Peter Haskell and Jimmy Sloyan called it the St. Valentine's Day Massacre. I remember telling Ellen Barrett they would write me out, too, and she said, "No, they wouldn't do that again." But they did. They asked us all to not take our vacations so all the characters would be available for what they wanted to write. I was so mad that I declined and took my vacation. I wasn't about to help them write me, and everyone else, out of the show.

Louise Shaffer: The "great massacre" is what I called it. They wiped out all these characters like in one day. All the actors that I was involved with were let go. You get thirteen weeks, and then they can dump us. I was like "Oh my God! I got through this." It really was like living through a massacre.

Kelli Maroney: Peter [who fought to keep Hollis Kirkland on the show] was someone who didn't take things lying down. But I'm sad to say that by that time I considered it folly to try to reason with anybody there—having seen this cycle play itself out a number of times already. If it was happening today, I'd like to think he would have had me as backup in there, taking a stand with him. But back then I was just over it.

Tamara Grady: Of the firings, I was most surprised about Mary Page Keller. I thought she was the best of the bunch, but of course she was still young and green then too.

Louise Shaffer: I was okay in terms of how much longer they will choose to keep me on the show, but I thought I would be talking to Rae's portrait or my reflection in the mirror. This is a perfect example why a lot of us tended to not know much because if you really did know what was going on, you would not be able to do your job. Acting must really be about something you love. You can't love something if you spend most of your time wondering, "When am I getting the ax?"

Kelli Maroney: Since they had written me out for the second time, I didn't expect they would write Kim anymore, and it would be crazy for me to put myself through that "ABC character" stuff again even if they did.

[*One Life to Live*] had a much bigger studio and a bigger cast, [so it was] a completely different experience. As the stories and technology evolved, it was beginning to be more efficient to plan to shoot on one set and one storyline at a time, the way they still do now. Since it was a much bigger production, it was a lot more obvious how fast technology was changing daytime drama forever. I loved getting the chance to play a different character [Tina Clayton] and seeing what it was like on those bigger, hour-long shows. It was amazing to work with that incredible cast. Those actors were daytime megastars of the time. I always felt like we were in Texas and not a soundstage on the Upper West Side. The Buchanans [Philip Carey, Clint Ritchie, and Robert S. Woods] were these three larger-than-life cowboys, and it felt like being on the Pondarosa! It was all that broad masculinity. Those guys really lived those characters and loved making you break up laughing.

Trent Jones: At this point, I am in Los Angeles. I was still acting and doing a show out there. I was still writing scripts via Federal Express. New head writers worked on ego. You would come in and say, "Oh, this is why it is not working" and write out who you thought were terrible characters from the prior writing regime. When Claire came back, I think she, to reassert control, was writing more scripts, and I was getting fewer—maybe one every other or third week. With Mary, I got a script a week. I was getting paid for one a week but doing less. In retrospect, I should have thought that was a good thing, but I didn't. My show was over, and we came back. About a week after, I get a call from Paul saying they are letting me go. I was not pleased with the timing of that.

As a writer, I was more attuned with Mary than I was with Claire. I was able to give Mary more of what she wanted than with Claire. Because she left so soon after I was hired originally, Claire and I hadn't created any kind of rapport. I was a newcomer to her and was representative of what was going wrong in 1982.

I eventually got hired on *Guiding Light*, and it was quite different there, beginning with the atmosphere. Pam Long and her co-head writer Richard Cullerton were young, though he left after a month or so. There was more energy, and we had writer meetings that were a lot of fun. It was challenging work going from a half hour to an hour show. At one point in 1983 or 1984, they had a talented team there. We were all script writers and competitive but in a cooperative way. It was more involving, and we did crazy stories. *Guiding Light* hit number one in the ratings briefly during this period. Pam Long was on and off, but when she was on, she came up with some remarkable stories.

A big blow to the show during this time of transition was the loss of Roscoe Born. After a second machine-gun attack on Ryan's Bar that sends Maeve, Johnny, Frank, Jill, Faith, Delia, Jack, Siobhan, Joe, and Bob ducking for cover, Joe realizes there is a contract out on his life for killing Ace Landrace. His mere presence is putting his ex-wife and her family in danger. He journeys down to the Caribbean to meet with mob boss Mr. Bruhn (Jerry Orbach) to beg for his life. After agreeing to Bruhn's demands, Joe never returns.

Roscoe Born: I had a two-year contract, and they asked me to stay. I only agreed to stick around for eight more weeks, and they almost doubled my salary. I just did it for the money.

Shortly after, I met with the producer of *Paper Dolls* at the Plaza Hotel. I got the job [as David Bailey] just from that meeting. There were way less pages to memorize on a prime-time soap versus daytime. Maybe six to eight pages the most in a day. Sometimes less than that. It was harder, though, because you were sitting around all day. All I had done before that were small parts on shows, and they sort of knew when they wanted to use me. It was a much harder process for me compared to daytime because I didn't know how to gear up for it.

Ilene Kristen: I was not surprised that Roscoe left. I always sensed that he was never satisfied. I would sit with him and say, "You have to look at the positive side of this job. You have your weekends free and can do as much music as you want to do. You have a natural audience from doing this." I think he felt that this wasn't a good enough job for him even though he had a fantastic part, and it wasn't stereotypical in any kind of way—and *he* was not stereotypical. He was very good-looking in a unique way and very charismatic. What he projected on screen cut right through the screen.

To emphasize that the Ryan and Coleridge families would be the show's only main families again, ABC filmed a new title opening. Instead of featuring anonymous people, some of the scenes were reshot or new ones inserted with the current cast of actors, underscored by the same musical theme. The ending shot has the Ryan family in the park, which was reminiscent of its original opening from 1975. Although ABC invested money in this and still featured *Ryan's Hope* as part of its "Love in the Afternoon" campaign, the network did not publicize the show as much as it did its hour-long serials in the soap press.

Per longtime soap opera journalist Connie Passalacqua Hayman, "I started as editor at *Afternoon TV* in 1981. In the two years I was there, I don't think we ever did a *Ryan's Hope* cover—not that we didn't love the show! I know we did *The Edge of Night* [a Procter & Gamble–produced soap on ABC] and lots of other New York shows [on the cover]. Honestly, no one at ABC ever did a lot of campaigning for *Ryan's Hope* ... I really don't remember any favoritism toward *All My Children* over *Ryan's*, but then again, *All My Children* (and *One Life to Live*) always had their own publicists. I can't remember anyone in particular who was assigned to *Ryan's Hope*."

In a shocker of an interview from around this time in 1983, Jackie Smith revealed to journalist Kelly Scott that the writers wanted unlucky-in-love Seneca Beulac to come out as homosexual. The short-sighted executive previously stated that she thought it was unlikely that daytime television would ever have gay characters, so it is no surprise that she vetoed it. "We all went, '*Not* Seneca!' I steer people away from homosexual stories because they are not romantic to our viewers. We try to be in touch, but I have not seen evidence that anyone wants to see Seneca Beulac become a homosexual."

True, but perhaps the writers chose the wrong character to tamper with? Arguably, a better and more believable choice may have been Delia's brother, Bob Reid. Perpetually single, he was enamored with his best friend, Frank Ryan, and was always mooning over Faith Coleridge, who just considered him a friend. This was the character who could have come out as gay, although it is unclear if actor Earl Hindman could have pulled it off.

Story-wise, Pat languishes in his hospital bed for a while with the ever-faithful Faith at his side. Shortly after he recovers, Amanda (recast with Ariana Muenker, formerly Marianne Randolph on *Another World* and Melinda Gray on *As the World Turns*) flies in from the cuckoo's nest after checking herself out. She swears she is recovered and hates her father for what he did. She surprises her newly arrived older sister Leigh Kirkland (Felicity LaFortune) frolicking in her boudoir with an embarrassed Jack. Leigh came to town pretending to be Leigh Marshall and was looking for information on what transpired with her family. This led her to Jack, and they instantly fall into bed together. When he later uncovered her deception, the hotheaded reporter was furious. Amanda's return coincides with their reconciliation after Jack accepts Leigh's reasons for lying about who she was and admitting that she truly is interested in him.

> **Malcolm Groome:** I particularly liked when Pat was in the hospital and became aphasic. Then Claire wrote in my astral body leaves my physical body and walks around the hospital. Whenever they would introduce spiritual things like that, I really appreciated it. I loved that they did that. Whenever I was given something like that to play—I was more of a character actor on stage—I liked it. But Pat was usually just written as this mild-mannered, namby-pamby nice guy. But when they gave me something to sink my teeth into, that was my favorite because I was able to play something interesting.

> **Ariana Muenker (Amanda Kirkland #2):** I had to audition and, thinking back on it, my experience was interesting. I had always gone up for parts before, but here, no one told me that I was replacing an actress and stepping into someone else's creation. It wasn't until I got the job that it was revealed to me that I was taking over a character already on the show. First, I was really shocked and

thought, "Why didn't you tell me?" Then I got a little apprehensive. I had not watched *Ryan's Hope* and didn't know anything about the former actress playing that role. I didn't know who the character was, and now I must step into someone else's shoes, hopefully to connect with the audience enough so that I can make it seem reasonable for this new actress to take over the character. However, I had no idea how the character was created. I was always able to leave my mark when creating a role from nothing. It's your baby. I wasn't sure how this was going to work out.

I had a funny moment that I only realized later. It happened after the screen test. Mary Page Keller was in the hallway, and I didn't know who she was. I was waiting for the elevator, and she was standing nearby. We looked at each other and smiled. I thought to myself, "I wonder if she is auditioning for the part too." At that point I still did not know I was replacing anybody. I didn't know if she knew anything. I cannot imagine they kept that a secret, although the TV business is not about cherishing people. It really is about ratings and making money.

Malcolm Groome: When I came back, I had a bit of an overlap with Mary Page Keller. I thought Hollis Kirkland was a great character. Mary Page was replaced with Ariana Muenker. I liked her a lot, and we worked well together.

Ariana Muenker: I did know there was a recent change on the show and felt there was some pressure put on these new characters or at least the replacement actors like myself to make this really work. Otherwise, why did they let the other actors go?

I was never involved with the politics of things like that. I pretty much stuck to myself, though I connected with a few people on the show. There were longtime cast members and a small bunch of newbies. I felt kind of removed because I replaced someone, and there was a stigma in my mind in that I did not know what the cast felt about her. I didn't know why she left or what happened. It was not a clean experience for me, so I did not know how to navigate it.

I had no idea that Malcolm had originated the role years before and came back. He was already there when I started. That is probably why I never realized he was the first Pat and was gone for whatever reason and came back. Malcolm was darling. He took a brotherly approach with me and was extremely kind. His whole persona mirrored his character. That's who he was.

Malcolm Groome: Claire and Paul were still approachable, but I think they did not have as much power. It seemed like they had to make more concessions when they no longer owned the show. They still had the long story they were following, but it did seem like compromises had to be made.

Ariana Muenker: My interaction with Paul and Claire was nothing above or beyond what cast members are exposed to, like seeing them at an event or holiday. They may have been at my audition, sitting in the control room, because I did have to do a screen test. They didn't take me under their wing or anything. I do remember meeting Paul but never Claire. He was exceedingly kind.

I was told nothing about Amanda Kirkland or what my storyline would be. They kept me very much in the dark and in fact made me transform my looks. I had long blond hair. I had to darken my hair to a medium light brown and cut it short. They wanted me to have a similar look to Mary Page Keller so there was not so much of a physical difference. I was just crushed when they made me cut my hair. I hated that hairstyle and thought I looked like a mousy little mom-girl.

Pat resumes his romance with Amanda, who is as unstable and paranoid as ever and made more so by Faith lurking on the sidelines, mooning for Pat. Despite his proclamations of love for Amanda, she bemoans to Leigh about how Faith makes her feel insecure with her relationship with Pat. This story had shades of the Delia/Pat/Faith triangle of the late seventies, right down to Amanda's out-of-control jealousy of the time Faith spends with Pat at work. Amanda, in a rage, even trashes Faith's office one day.

This would not be the only retread Labine and Mayer would serve up during this period. Another was the Delia/Frank/Jill triangle. With Delia losing the Crystal Palace and her exciting life around it, the writers regressed her to being the aimless waif wanting to be a Ryan. She sets her sights on Frank, yet again, but he only has eyes for Jill. To sway him, she uses Little John's troubles to spend time with him as a family, and in a despicable move even for Delia, resorts to setting her son up to be accused of stealing money from Jill's wallet on St. Patrick's Day. Needless to say, her plan backfires big time, and a regretful Delia gives up her designs on her former husband.

Delia soon disappears temporarily from the screen with the character off on holiday in Florida.

Surprisingly, the writers were cognizant of repeating themselves. Regarding Delia/Frank/Jill, Paul Mayer commented to Nerissa Radell, "The outlines were ten days ahead of taping, and we really thought that in all honesty, Dee, who'd lost everything, would go after Frank when he came home again. Having written this for eight years, we used up a lot of our fantasies. It's sometimes hard to find things that are fresh." They even rehashed Delia using her son to get closer to Frank, just as they did in early 1981. The only difference was that other actors were playing the roles. As for the Amanda/Pat/Faith triangle, Labine admitted, "This is where we are in danger of being on worn ground."

> **Malcolm Groome:** They continued the Pat/Amanda love story, but I agree that it became a recycled Delia/Pat/Faith triangle.

> **Ariana Muenker:** The thing for me with my acting career in those early days always seemed separate from my life. However, I think you draw on the things you connect with. It's not that I personally had daddy issues since my father and I were close, but my dad was not very demonstrative. In retrospect, I think it was probably an awkward and difficult idea for me to wrap that around my head. I really didn't know Amanda's backstory because they really didn't give me much, as if they purposely didn't want me to know. I think they wanted me to play her fresh and new. I was only told Amanda is in love with this guy who is not going to respond back. It was unrequited love and all the drama that comes out of that. This young girl having to process what it means to love someone and not have it returned.

> I knew that Pat and Faith had been connected, but of course the character of Amanda thought that was over. People are not rational when they fixate and have an obsession. It was beyond love for Amanda. She was obsessed with Pat.

> I had a lot of compassion for Amanda. She was a perfect fit for me. One of my favorite scenes is when she goes completely crazy in Faith's office. Amanda just loses it, smashing everything in sight and throwing things off the tables. That was a joy to play because it gave me an opportunity to act out, which I never did in my real life. I was a good girl because I was a professional actress since I was

ten. I never went through that rebellious teenage period. I rebelled in my twenties.

Ilene Kristen: Even having Delia treat her son so badly, the fans still loved Delia. I would sometimes get a "tsk, tsk" when recognized in the street, but most of the time it was love.

Ariana Muenker: I got along well with everybody I interacted with on the show. Felicity LaFortune played my big sister. She was a sweetheart. Ilene Kristen was one of these hippie wild girls—that is what she seemed like to me. Karen Morris-Gowdy was truly kind and pretty. I didn't have a friendship with her probably because of the age difference.

I didn't have many scenes with Helen Gallagher or Bernie Barrow. They were quiet, nice, and incredibly wise, but rather authoritarian. They had a bit of this aura that they were the king and queen. I didn't feel like I had to go connect with them. I stayed around people closer to my age or people from my storyline.

Ilene Kristen: I was put on the back burner because of my health. I was not back on the thyroid pills yet, and I was pushed aside. I was not even on screen for a few weeks because I had to go down to the Rice Clinic. I lost the weight and came back. I was not taking my thyroid medication, and the cortisone had filtered out of my body.

A delightful surprise for longtime fans of the soap was a week of dream sequences where Kate Mulgrew, as the deceased Mary Ryan, appears to her husband, Jack, and her mother, Maeve. With Jack's romance with Leigh Kirkland proceeding, he develops guilty feelings of being unfaithful to his dead wife. Maeve Ryan is also having thoughts of her daughter. Mary appears to help them overcome their grief and move on with their lives in extremely well-written, poignant scenes. Regarding her short-term return, Mulgrew told columnist Jon-Michael Reed, "It was a little awkward coming back . . . but after the first day, I enjoyed it. It was delightful to work with Michael Levin again in tandem with those superior scripts by Claire Labine."

Helen Gallagher: This was one of my favorite storylines. Mary was dead, but we had scenes together as Mary and Maeve in the kitchen. I loved that whole sequence.

Ariana Muenker: Of all the actors, the person who stuck out for me most was Kate Mulgrew. I was floored by her and thought she was fabulous. Though she was there for a brief period, she left such an impression on me. There was something bigger than life about her.

In late March, ABC finally named an executive producer. Probably to her grave disappointment, it was not producer Ellen Barrett but new hire Joseph Hardy. He was a well-respected theatre director and had prior television experience producing soap operas and prime-time series (i.e., *A Flame in the Wind, Love Is a Many Splendored Thing, James at 15/16*, etc.). He overlapped with Ellen for a very brief period. She either quit or was let go, and associate producer Felicia Minei Behr was promoted to producer. This move by ABC immediately raised warning signs among the cast and crew. They knew the times were a-changing. However, it is likely that none of them expected how much would change later in the year and in 1984.

Geoff Pierson: I do have a funny story on how we heard about Joe Hardy. Ellen Barrett called the whole cast that was in the studio and the crew together after a day's shooting. It was already night-time. Ellen made the announcement that there was a new executive producer. She said that he was an esteemed theatre director and went on and on with the compliments. Finally, she said his name— Joe Hardy. Earl Hindman, who played Bob Reid, was standing next to me. Earl then says very quietly, "Oh no, not Joe. That is the last person we need." I looked at him and then he laughed, admitting he had no idea who Joe Hardy was and was just joking around.

Malachy McCourt: Joe Hardy gathered all the actors together and told us what was happening. He was giving a speech and said, "We will all get along together and be one big, happy family."

And then I commented, much too loudly, "You don't fire your family! You can't! You fire actors, not family."

He took quite an exception to that and, after my remark, he wanted to prove you can. I was then told I was no longer needed. My smart-ass mouth got me into trouble again.

I had one time asked for a contract, and the network said no, but I don't know why. I was always a week-to-week player, so they could easily let me go anytime or just stop calling me, which they did.

Joseph Hardy: I had an extensive background working in theatre and on television. I do not know why it happened that they offered me the job at that time. I knew about *Ryan's Hope*, and I liked watching it before I had anything to do with it. I liked Claire Labine, but ABC had taken over the show and wanted changes made. The network wanted me to modernize the soap. That is why they brought me on. I think that worked well.

Laura Rakowitz: I don't know if Ellen Barrett left on her own accord or was fired. When Joe Hardy arrived, it was a shock to the system. He liked the show well-lit and brought a kind of prime-time film look to it. However, I am not sure if he was a better producer than Ellen. Joe certainly had his hand in all aspects of the show. He was an interesting guy, and I learned a lot about video tape editing from him. I personally will always be grateful for that.

Tamara Grady: I didn't like working with Joe Hardy, frankly. To me, Ellen Barrett had more heart.

Joseph Hardy: *Ryan's Hope* was set up very well in the beginning with the family situation and placing it in New York City. The characters were medium level regarding the situations they were put in. My goal coming in was to give the stories a little more zip to have it work better. I also hired people who seemed to be a little more up-to-date as actors.

Labine and Mayer's main long story arc centered around new character Charlotte Greer (Judith Chapman). It seems the writers bet the farm on this one storyline, hoping it would bring back core viewers who had abandoned the show in the last few years, appeal to the current audience, and attract new fans.

Once Frank runs Hollis Kirkland out of town, he is persuaded to run for political office again. The day he officially announces his candidacy for Congress to the press at Ryan's Bar, a glamorous woman appears calling herself Charlotte Greer Ryan. She claims that she was married to Frank in St. Louis and that he ran off with her money. The fact that she has written proof and knows so much about the Ryan and Coleridge families creates suspicion that there is some truth to what she is saying, despite Frank's vehement denials.

Others suspect that Rae Woodard is behind the smear campaign enacting revenge on Frank for ruining her relationship with Kirkland. Frank is forced to drop out of the race (Jill replaces him) and becomes obsessed with proving Charlotte is a fraud—even going to extremes (such as kidnapping and torture) to get the truth from her. Frank's unorthodox methods puts him in direct conflict with Siobhan, who calls him out and tries to stop him, causing even more family turmoil.

> **Geoff Pierson:** Judith Chapman was great. I did the tests with the actresses up for that part. I think there were fourteen of them. They looked at a lot of women. I did not know who she was, but she did other shows [*As the World Turns*]. She was great in the audition so you could almost tell that she would get the part, although some of the other actresses were good too. Judith really stood out. I figured they would hire her, and they did.

> **Judith Chapman (Charlotte Greer):** I was in California, and I got a call to audition. They flew me back to New York. I had lived there and had a lot of friends there. I asked one girlfriend if I could stay with her because I was auditioning for *Ryan's Hope.* I went to the audition, and after it was, "Thank you. Thank you very much." I was on my way out of the building, and Joe Hardy comes down to the lobby from the soundstage. He looks at me and says, "Do you have to leave?" I replied, "Nooo." And he said, "Because I would like you to start tomorrow." I replied, "We can do that, Joe!"
>
> I only got the sides for the audition, but Joe was very forthcoming in telling me the whole storyline with the love affair in Ireland between Charlotte's father, Neil, and Maeve, who left and wound up marrying Johnny Ryan. I thought it was a great idea.

> **Ariana Muenker:** I knew Judith Chapman from our time together on *As the World Turns* in 1978. I idolized her as an actress and thought she was amazing. She was so beautiful and had this tremendous charisma.

> **Louise Shaffer:** Judith Chapman is a good actress, and I thought she was wonderful in the role.

> **Judith Chapman:** I had very little interaction with Claire and Paul. They were off in their cubbyholes. However, I was very grateful and appreciative that they thought I captured what they envisioned, so it was very exciting.

Geoff Pierson: Frank was written very much so in shades of gray. I had never seen the previous actors as Frank, so I do not know how they played him. The way I reacted to the writing is the way I played him. I agree Frank could be self-righteous, hypocritical—he had a temper, and he did not always treat everybody in the most sensitive way. There were many shades of gray to him, as I said. I saw that as just the way the guy was—first starting as a policeman and then going to night school to become a lawyer. He was a working-class type of guy. I acted the part the way it struck me. I know Claire liked my portrayal, and she told me that the way I played him was what she had in mind.

Malcolm Groome: When I came back, Geoff Pierson was Frank Ryan. He was an excellent actor but a bit distant and cooler as compared to Andy Robinson.

Ilene Kristen: Geoff Pierson has a better career than all of us. Boy, was he solid as Frank.

Judith Chapman: Acting is instant intimacy. You come on the set—you may or may not know your castmates—and then you start working with them—sometimes even doing a love scene. Geoff Pierson was not hard to look at or deal with. He is fantastic and was wonderful to work with. He was just so giving. He was *there*. He was prepared. He had made choices prior, so it was not, "Now what are we supposed to do?" We knew instinctively what to do. I have worked with actors where we just did not have the chemistry and just didn't lock. It definitely locked with Geoff.

Ron Hale: I don't recall who was the head of daytime [then], but when they hired Geoff, it kind of got around that somebody up top did not think he had that leading man, daytime look. Well, talk about a good actor. Our characters hated each other. One day out of the five acts, Geoff and I had three of them. The other two may have been one-minute scenes. Our three scenes were nose-to-nose anger and almost getting close to throwing punches. The way the schedule was set up, our scenes were to be shot at the end of the day for some reason. In the morning after we blocked everything, I can't remember if it was the director or one of the producers, but they came up to us and said, "I have a big request of you." One of the actors in the other scenes was ill or running late, and they wanted us to do our three scenes right at the beginning of taping. Again, Geoff and I had run it a few times. He knew his lines. I knew my lines. And we did not want to blow it rehearsing it too much. We wanted to keep it fresh.

Geoff looked at me and said, "Are you ready?"

I replied, "Yes, are you ready?"

We went and did it and did not stop once. We kicked butt. I will never forget that because, again, you have to rely so much on the person you are working with to give you what you need to come back and reply. If you are working with what I call a lox, which I had to do many times in my life, where you have to make it all up yourself and act like that person is giving you what you need to bring on anger or tears and they are not giving you crap, it is difficult. Geoff just kicked my butt, and I think I kicked his back. We had mutual respect for being professional.

Geoff Pierson: Ron Hale is a great actor and is still a great friend of mine to this day.

Judith Chapman: I got along with all the actors I worked with. We all have our own little bag of tricks, quirks, and idiosyncrasies—especially if you are doing an ensemble piece like a soap opera. You have your little quirky things, and once in a while a snit fit, but then you get down and just do the damn work—no divas allowed. Of the cast, I loved Helen Gallagher. During my time there, Helen decided that she was going to do a show about Tallulah Bankhead at the Manhattan Theatre Club. I had great fun going to see her in it, and many years later I played Tallulah Bankhead just before COVID hit.

Springtime brought a few pleasant surprises to *Ryan's Hope*. In an ironic twist, the show won its sixth Writers Guild Award for 1982 and the Emmy Award for Outstanding Writing for a Daytime Drama Series (which included Harold Apter and Trent Jones, who did not share in the Writers Guild Award) for March 1982 to March 1983. *Ryan's Hope* was only nominated for one more Emmy Award for Outstanding Actress in a Supporting Role in a Daytime Drama Series for Louise Shaffer, who emerged triumphant as well. She was the only cast member, other than Helen Gallagher, to ever take home an Emmy. However, not all the winners were happy about their victories.

Louise Shaffer: I won, and they didn't televise it! [CBS refused because ABC swept the nominations in the soap categories.] I was nominated twice before, and I always chose my own tapes. This time my husband [writer Roger Crews] said he wanted to see what I selected. He and my agent Honey looked at the choices I made, and most of them were based on how fat do I look? Did the costume make my hips look big? Literally, that was my main concern. Roger looked at me and said, "Sweetie pie, every single scene you have chosen features the other actor. You haven't picked one scene that shows you. In most of them, you are listening to somebody and trying to hide your hips." He and my agent then chose for me.

Harold Alpert: They originally omitted me from the nomination list. I called Claire and said, "Claire, I was part of the team." Then they corrected it. I was not surprised we were nominated but was surprised that they left me out. I snuck in under the wire. I only found out we won by reading it in *Variety*. I read it daily. Somebody gave me a good piece of advice when I moved out to LA. He said that I should read the trades every day, and you'll feel part of the business.

Trent Jones: I was still in the pouting stage, and it was probably before I was picked up as a writer for *Guiding Light*. I didn't go to the ceremony and didn't care. I would go on to win five more Emmys.

With the focus back on the Ryan family, it looked like the *Ryan's Hope* of the seventies was here to stay. Paul Mayer remarked to S. Ezra Goldstein, "It's easy enough to make fun of the soaps. There are some shows, comic book soaps, where I don't think the writing is very good. But we're not embarrassed by *Ryan's Hope*. It's a class act. We're trying to do something good." However commendable it was to try to present an adult soap opera, to go fully in that direction may have not been the right decision. Those "comic book soaps" were snagging big ratings and favored by the youth audience. Although the ratings for *Ryan's Hope* did tick up a bit, they quickly fell, and the show was now down to a 5.0 rating.

There was a bright side. Despite *Ryan's Hope*'s diminishing household ratings (per the *Los Angeles Times*, the show in 1983, "fluctuated between the middle and the high teens for its place among all 25 programs"), Jackie Smith announced that its serials' schedule would not change for the upcoming 1983–84 season and remarked to the press, "If it's not broken, why fix it?" It seemed the soap was still doing extremely well with women under age fifty-five (who the advertisers catered to), remaining in the top five along with *General Hospital*, *All My Children*, and *One Life to Live*. Seymour Amlen contended that with this audience ABC had "a 29 percent advantage over CBS and delivered twice the number of NBC viewers." With *Ryan's Hope* holding its own in the desired demos, it is not surprising that ABC would not juggle it schedule to boost *Ryan's* household ratings in fear of jeopardizing its other shows.

The Charlotte Greer story unfolds (loved by the critics and most of the audience) in an unfortunately predictable fashion at first. Frank is telling the complete truth, and Rae did hire and pay Charlotte to ruin Frank. There was no nuance to the story for the audience to question otherwise. Arguably, it would have been more interesting if there was some truth in what Charlotte was claiming about Frank, or if instead of Rae it had been Faith running the dirty tricks department. The anger she had for Frank and Jill could have resurfaced, and she would have enacted her revenge on Frank for jilting her days before their wedding. Perhaps these surprises would have had more of a shocking and lasting impact rather than the one presented.

As most new executive producers do, changes were immediately enacted on the show per Joe Hardy's instructions. Production-wise, he brightened the show with precise lighting. He said to Joanna Coons of *Soap Opera Digest*, "Before you couldn't see people's eyes very well." Story-wise, he surprisingly ended the Pat and Amanda romance.

Desperate for Pat's attention, Amanda fakes a suicide, but it goes awry and she almost drowns in her bathtub after miscalculating and taking too many pills. When she recuperates, she swears it was an accident but realizes it was an extreme way to win Pat. She vows to change and thinks it is best she goes back to San Francisco but promises to return. She never will.

Ariana Muenker: Amanda's attempted suicide left a huge impression on me personally as a human being to this day. That was a big, scary scene to do. Actually, the entire time frame leading up to it, where she sort of loses it after realizing that she is not going to be loved and then basically doesn't want to live, sticks out for me. For the bathtub scene, I had this tiny little bathing suit on because I was supposed to be naked, taking a bath. Then taking the pills and slipping under the water. We had to rehearse it up to a point, but

I could not get my hair wet. If I did, we would have had to dry and style it and start all over.

That day was a big deal on the set and for me. I remember thinking from an actress standpoint that it was the only time on the show that I was by myself. I felt alone doing that scene because I had to be and I wanted to do it well and do it authentically. I was excited at the same time because it was a big acting deal to have to play that kind of a scene. When I was on *As the World Turns* the second time, my character Melinda dies in the water, so this was a sort of a call back to that experience.

Malcolm Groome: I liked Ariana a lot. We worked well together, and I was extremely disappointed when they wrote her off. I think she was kind of devastated at the time. When I moved back to LA again, I ran into her at a Trader Joe's. It was fun to see her.

Ariana Muenker: I never understood why my part was terminated. I was heartbroken and was having fun with the character. For some reason, I cannot recall how I found out that Amanda was being written off or if I was ever given any concrete reason why she had to go. I signed a three-year contract with incremental increases in my pay over a period of time, which was standard in the business. However, there was a clause that after every thirteen weeks they cannot renew your option and let you go. I was on for six months through June. I do recall them saying that they might bring me back as Amanda in the fall. If that were the case, why would they have me gone for two or three months, only to bring me back with a renegotiated contract? They don't do that, so I knew it was a false promise. In my heart of hearts, this taught me how hard it is to take over a role and make a new connection.

I was back on *Guiding Light* in 1987. I played Christine Valère [the former fiancée of Johnny Baur, now in love with ex-prostitute Roxie Shayne]. On *Days of Our Lives*, I knew going in I was replacing another actress [Patsy Pease]. She was having a personal issue that made her unpredictable in terms of showing up on set. It wasn't anything that she had control over. She was beloved by the audience. I was grateful when I got the role. And I was equally disappointed when it was done. That was another job where I had a three-year contract, and after six months, they let me go. I really wanted this to work since I was a young adult living on my own. It was at the point in my life where I was transitioning from one path to another but didn't know it.

The big reveal in the Charlotte Greer storyline was that Charlotte was actually using Rae to further a truly nefarious family plot. It comes to light that Charlotte is the daughter of Neil (Roy Poole) and Una (Kathleen Widdoes) MacCurtain, who were part of a long-standing feud with Maeve's family back in the old country. Neil was an ex-suitor of Maeve's, and a dispute had erupted between their families that left his brothers and father dead, inadvertently due to Maeve's father. Although she loved a good revenge plot more than most, even Rae is taken aback when learning that MacCurtain's plan is to kill Frank and Pat. She threatens to warn the Ryans and Neil stabs her with a sword and leaves her for dead in Charlotte's apartment.

Judith Chapman: The storyline was only for six months, but it was just so special. The wonderful Kathleen Widdoes, who I was just in awe of, played my mom. She was great fun and always up and positive. Roy Poole was my dad. He was in a wheelchair [off camera] most of the time. He was not in good health. It was this whole Irish vendetta. They had groomed this young girl, their daughter, to wreak vengeance on the Ryan clan. Unfortunately, she did fall in love with Frank a little bit.

Geoff Pierson: I thought this story was bizarre in a way, but I did not know what to compare it to. I was not familiar with the types of stories done on daytime television, with the long-form serials with stories going on for many, many months. This was an explosive storyline and to me seemed exotic—who is this mysterious person? And she is connected somehow to something that happened in the old country. It had a vendetta and the IRA—it was an overly complex story. It took months to unfold. We never knew, of course, what the conclusion would be and just went with it at the time. I would have to say it was my favorite storyline because it was so disruptive to Frank and the Ryan family, right to the end with the vendetta against his parents.

Judith Chapman: I knew this storyline was front-burner, even for a short period, but I don't think I understood the gravity of it and the motivation behind it. In hindsight . . . , it was a huge deal. One of my favorite parts of it is that Charlotte's goal was to seduce Frank Ryan. We had these fantasy scenes in eighteenth-century Ireland, with these classic clothes with the laced-up bodice and pushed up bosoms. And he was in this gorgeous frilly white shirt. We were in this cabin, and the love scene started—no clothes ever came off— but it was very erotic.

We have laughed about these scenes since. What I loved about it was that the network called Joe Hardy and said that the show had gone too far in the sexual nature of this. ABC threatened not to air it. Joe easily could have agreed to appease them, but he fought and said, "To hell with you. You will put these scenes on." And ABC did. I loved and respected Joe anyway, but I was very impressed and really respected him after he stood up to the network. I was almost in a banned sex scene on a soap!

Tamara Grady: I loved this storyline. I loved working with Judith Chapman and Roy Poole. They were such good actors. This was just a pleasure to work on. I don't know how the audience felt about it, but I loved it.

Judith Chapman: Our scenes were seamless. The directors gave me and Kathleen and Roy just so much freedom to do what we were brought on to do, but in the confines of getting the show done. I was thrilled with the direction from Lela Swift and Jerry Evans— no objection whatsoever to their directing styles.

Louise Shaffer: I thought the Charlotte Greer story was an obvious attempt to pull the show back to its kind of Irish roots and bring it back to what the show had been. I don't think it worked. Part of *Ryan's Hope*'s charm when it first went on the air was that it was about immigration. Maeve was not even first-generation American. However, from the network's point of view (and I have never been a fan of networks) their needs had moved on, and they needed to make money. Advertisers wanted that young demo, and those kids could not be less interested in this one Irish story. If you wanted to write that warm, wonderful Irish show again, then you needed to find another venue that wasn't going to be supported by toothpaste. They wanted the kids, and the kids could not care less about that storyline. It was one of the times where I thought I really let myself get outside of what I was doing and thought to myself this is a mistake. The story came out of left field, and it wasn't doing the job of what the show needed to do.

The plot climaxes as Neil holds Frank and his mother at gunpoint in an underground garage. Past animosities between Maeve and Neil surface. As a deranged Una eggs on Neil to shoot them, she realizes Neil still loves her nemesis. Just before he can pull the trigger, Neil suffers a fatal heart attack and drops the gun. Una picks it up and fires. She misses Maeve and critically wounds Frank. Una is taken into custody while Charlotte flees the scene and is never heard from again, leaving the audience befuddled.

Judith Chapman: The way they wrapped up the storyline is the one thing I was disappointed with. I said, "Really?!" After my father dies and my mother shoots Frank, Charlotte just runs up the stairs and out of the parking structure? That was a little unsatisfying for me, and I am sure for the audience as well. Wrap it up! Arrest her! Kill her! But I guess they decided to leave it open-ended for a possible return or whatever, which, of course, never happened.

I went back to LA and worked on a number of soaps [including *General Hospital*, *Days of Our Lives*, and *The Young and the Restless*] after this. *Ryan's Hope* was only a half-hour show, with a smaller cast, so it was a very intimate experience, far more so than any other I have worked on. It had a nicer feel than any of the soaps I did in LA.

Tamara Grady: I think the change in regime hurt this. Usually if a story ends abruptly or in a way that is not satisfying to the audience, it is because somebody has it in their head they don't like it. These shows were run by committee. Nobody makes unilateral decisions. It depends where you are on the totem pole and who puts pressure on who. This too is a function of low ratings. When your ratings aren't good enough, everybody is trying to fix what they think is the problem.

The only long-term effect that the Charlotte Greer story had on the plot was that it was the impetus for Frank and Jill to finally wed. It happened in his hospital room while he was recuperating from his gunshot. Fans were elated that they finally tied the knot but totally disappointed that they were denied a big, fancy wedding. And Rae Woodard, who survived her stab wound, is once again allowed to roam free with no repercussions after ruining Frank's political career a second time.

> **Geoff Pierson:** As I recall, there was a conversation about Frank and Jill's wedding. They really thought it was extremely anticlimactic and probably a mistake. Not a mistake getting them married but having the ceremony in the hospital room. It must have been a huge disappointment for the fans, considering all the time and buildup to it.

Fresh faces new to the scene around this time included Sergeant Bill Hyde (David Sederholm), a studly detective who partners with Siobhan. Delia drools over him (however, Bill and Siobhan eventually hook up). Jill's newly discovered family hits Riverside straight from the trailer parks of Kansas. Her biological mother is Bess Shelby (former film star Gloria DeHaven), a beer-guzzling, hash-slinging waitress. Her half sister is Maggie, a scheming gold digger. When Maggie reads about Jill's life in New York City, she decides to head to the Big Apple to cash in on her sister and claim the life she thinks she was robbed of. Maggie was similar to the character of Kim Harris, who was introduced to stir up trouble for her mother Rae, while Maggie will cause much turmoil for her sister Jill.

> **Ilene Kristen:** I loved working with Marg Helgenberger. We had some funny scenes together. I liked her a lot. Our characters were gaga over David Sederholm. He was a hunk and a half and a very nice guy.

> **Geoff Pierson:** Marg was a complete doll. She came before me, I think right out of Northwestern. It was always fun working with her. We had a real, natural relationship.

> **Malcolm Groome:** After Mary died, Siobhan sort of took her place. They had similar love stories with each daughter's lover (Jack for Mary and Joe for Siobhan) not initially welcomed in the family. For me, Sarah Felder *was* Siobhan. She played her very quirky and very real. However, I loved Marg in the role, and we had a great relationship playing siblings.

> **Cali Timmins (Maggie Shelby):** I was living in Toronto and had been acting for a couple of years. The casting director—I think it may have been Mary Jo Slater, but I could be wrong—came to

town, and I met her to audition. I got a callback, and then they put me on tape. I was then flown to New York to do a screen test. I know I tested with somebody, but I can't recall who it was with. I do know that they had been looking for someone for a long time and met with a lot of people. It kept being brought up to me, but I am not sure why, that it was a big part on this top show.

I remember feeling very good and positive about the test but not expecting to get it because they had been looking for a while. When I did get it, there was a rush to get me a visa so I could work in the States since I was Canadian. That ended up being a huge, scary undertaking since it was so last minute. I was scheduled to work the next day and the visa still had not come through so there was a possibility that I was not going to be able to do the job. Obviously, though, it worked out.

I don't recall if Claire Labine and Paul Mayer were at my screen test or if I met them for the first time afterward. I had heard a lot about them. Claire was lovely to me, but I got to know her much better many years later when she was out in LA working on *General Hospital*. At the time, I was not personally aware of the writers and everybody behind the scenes. I was just focused on doing the job but was aware of the directors and Joe Hardy. I really didn't know at that time the history of the show.

Louise Shaffer: Joe Hardy was the end of me because he brought in Gloria DeHaven, who was his friend. And they didn't need two over-the-hill divas at that point. I knew then I was out.

Karen Morris-Gowdy: When Joe Hardy came in, it was when the show fell off the map. Joe was not warm and fuzzy, that is for sure. At this point, I wasn't as invested in the show—no question. Going to work every morning wasn't as much fun, and it was like, "Get me the hell out of here!" I would come in as prepared as I used to be, but my heart wasn't in it. I think we all felt that, and it was really sad because we were so grateful to be working. We loved the show and had a great entity. We had worked really hard for it collectively.

Laura Rakowitz: Gloria DeHaven was a delicious addition. I love old films and she was part of that old Hollywood.

Ron Hale: I loved Gloria DeHaven. She was the wackiest. She had a challenging time with the lines and was no spring chicken. It was a whole new world for her, but she worked hard at trying to be the best that she could be. She did a lot of wonderful work on the show. She would spend time up at my house and at Nancy's place in Bucks County. I am so sad that she is gone. She was just a wonderful lady.

Cali Timmins: I had a wonderful relationship with Joe Hardy. He was great and excited to bring Gloria and me on at the same time. They had a fun relationship and lots of banter back and forth. I do not have any bad memories of Joe—only positive ones. He was very supportive of my work. He would make his little comments and then, seeming to be pleased, walk away.

Most of my scenes were with Gloria DeHaven, so we were very close. Gloria was obviously old-school. It was great to come onto the show with her because—yes, there was a lot of attention on me—but her as well. We were coming from completely different backgrounds. I was like a white piece of paper ready to learn and absorb, and she had already been doing her thing for many years. In some ways it was harder for her, so that made me more confident.

And to have this experienced person and celebrity who people looked up to sometimes struggling with her lines sort of put me at ease, although she was great fun to work with. Her challenges were different than mine. She wasn't used to pages of dialogue and not having retakes. That was not my challenge because I was very good memorizing the dialogue. If anyone went up on the lines, it was usually Gloria. I was happy to just do it again. We helped each other through it. She was very aware of everyone around her and always smiling and joking between takes. I was more serious and intense because I wanted to do it right. Off-screen, she loved to rehearse lines. I would go to her apartment, and we would have dinner. She had lots of stories. I probably would be more interested in her stories now than I was back then. She was just a lovely woman, very supportive and warm but not what I would call nurturing because she was struggling with this new medium, as I was. It wasn't like the people who had been there for a while who could offer pearls of advice.

Most exciting was the return of Joe Novak (now played by newcomer Michael Hennessy), whom Siobhan briefly spots in New York. She tracks him down and they make love, but Joe insists they cannot see each other anymore. He explains that to save both his and Siobhan's life, he was ordered by mob boss Bruhn to steal the very rich Jacqueline Dubujak away from Bruhn's nephew and get her to marry him instead.

> **Laura Rakowitz:** I didn't like Michael Hennessy at all. Of course, it may have been since I had such a big crush, in a mature way, on Roscoe Born. I never thought anyone could replace Roscoe as Joe. I thought Michael was not good in the role. There was nothing sexy about him, and Roscoe just oozed sex. Joe was an interesting character but needed that quality. I felt it was one of the worst casting decisions ABC and the producer made at that time.

> **Tamara Grady:** Michael Hennessy was a terrible actor. Nobody really could replace Roscoe Born, ever. He was just gorgeous and such a good actor. You never saw him acting. He just became Joe Novak.

During this time, a big story was brewing between newlyweds Frank and Jill versus Delia for custody of Little John. Then, out of the blue, Rae, as a favor to Frank, gets a friend to offer Delia a job managing a restaurant/club in San Diego. Delia decrees that Frank and Jill would make a wonderful home for her son, packs her bags, says a quick goodbye to Maeve, and flies off to the West Coast. To say the audience was stunned with this chain of events was an understatement.

> **Ilene Kristen:** I had come back from the Rice Clinic and was down to 110 pounds but was not on the right dosage of thyroid medication. At the clinic, they took me off [of it] and when you are in an environment eating only 500 calories a day, you can do that. But when I came back to New York and on thyroid meds (which I was on since I was eighteen years old), I started gaining weight again. They never really talked to me about it. Jackie Smith was very bizarre, and she was obsessed about my weight. It was her decision to let me go, and maybe Joe Hardy had something to do with it also, although Joe said to me "I was your friend, Ilene." I knew him from the seventies. They didn't like the fact that I couldn't keep my weight, even knowing it was a medical condition. I was not treated well, and I was fired in a very hurtful way. It was not right, and by today's standards it would have been a lawsuit. And I have to

say that I wasn't treated well by Claire and Paul. They never called me, but I think they were very upset and couldn't. Actually, no one from the cast reached out to me, other than Malachy McCourt. It was very strange.

Rachael Mayer: What happened to Ilene makes me sad. My mother struggled with her weight, so my father would never want to hurt an actress around their weight.

Ruth Mayer: But I also remember him talking about having to tell actors, "You've got to lose ten pounds." He had a lot of heart, but it was also a business. If the viewers are saying, "What happened to so-and-so?" I do not know what happened or what the feedback was with Ilene—but it was all a business at the end of the day. It was tough. Can you imagine telling an actor that they have to lose weight? And your livelihood is on that? But he loved and adored Ilene. I am sure that was painful for her and painful for Claire and Paul as well.

Laura Rakowitz: ABC thought Ilene was too heavy. This girl went through her paces to lose weight. I personally didn't think she looked bad on camera anyway. Ellen Barrett fought for her, and then left. I am not sure about Joe Hardy. Bottom line that is what happened. I was appalled by it. Ilene, who is one of the healthiest people I know, is always working out and in tune with her body. She still looks fabulous, and she is not a youngster.

Ilene Kristen: I still remember that day I was fired. Joe Hardy phoned me, and I knew something was up since I wasn't on the call sheets. I knew I was going to be fired because my astrologer told me. I was ready for it.

Joe: Ilene, I didn't know you lived on Seventy-Eighth Street.

Ilene: Yes and you used to live on Seventy-Eighth Street.

Joe: Yes, I did.

Ilene: You used to live with David Rounds.

Joe: Yes, how did you know that?

Ilene: Well, I know these things.

Joe: Well, we are sending Delia away to San Diego.

Ilene (I was so ready for this): Are you sending her away with two weeks' pay or six months?

He went silent. I hear paper shuffling and he says, "Six months." I said bye and hung up. I was already scheduled to do this show *Strange Behavior,* so I thought, "Oh fuck it. I have money to do comedy." But it was not right, and it was not good the way they treated me. But I think Joe Hardy had a bigger idea, and he wanted to make his mark on the show, so that is when they introduced Cali Timmins as Maggie Shelby and Gloria DeHaven as her mother, Bess. Maggie was sort of the new Delia but not in the eyes of the audience. I could have sued, but I am glad I didn't.

Cali Timmins: When Ilene left, being young and myopic, I was not aware of how horrendous it was. I just thought Ilene chose to leave— honestly, I did. When I learned what really happened, it disgusted me and I don't get it. Like anybody gives a damn about that. *Ryan's Hope* was not *Dynasty*—it wasn't what the show was about. Ilene would joke with me that I was hired to replace her. I said, "Wait, what are you talking about?" I never thought of that being my role because Maggie was nothing like Delia, except that we were both blond and conniving.

Ron Hale: I didn't think Maggie was the new Delia either. I loved Cali. When she first came on, she had a lot of work to do as an actress. It was all new to her working on daytime. She worked her butt off. She would come to my dressing room and ask, "Can we run the scene? Can we run it?" We would rehearse the scenes over and over. Cali really improved and just grew into the character.

Ilene Kristen: Claire didn't want to give Delia a long goodbye because the audience would have gone after her with pitchforks. The fans went crazy when I left.

Arguably, for the next few months *Ryan's Hope* was at the top of its game despite Ilene Kristen's Delia being sorely missed. It was a time when Labine and Mayer seemed to be combining what they thought the show should be with aspects that ABC demanded. Storyline highlights included the renewed romance between Siobhan, who was now living with Bill Hyde, and the married Joe. They have to keep their trysts secret from not only their loved ones but also Joe's father-in-law's right-hand man, Stamford "Hutch" Hutchinson (DeVeren Bookwalter), who eyes every move Joe makes.

Another very good plot development was the rivalry that emerged between media maven Rae Woodard and Leigh Kirkland, who purchases a TV station so Jack can become the star news reporter. Leigh's defense of her mother and her happiness that her parents reunited also riles Rae. With meddling from vindictive Rae, Jack and Leigh's romance fizzles, and Jack finds himself attracted to his glamorous producer, Sydney Price (Robin Greer).

The standout story, though, was the machinations of the calculating Maggie Shelby. After coming to New York City and meeting Jill, Maggie makes sure to insinuate herself into her life. First, she exaggerates an injury she sustained while volunteering at Jill's campaign headquarters. Faith invites her to recuperate at the Coleridge brownstone and then (in typical annoying, selfless Faith fashion) suggests to Jill that she, Frank, and Little John move in as well. Maggie then begins lying that her mother is a world traveler. Roger sees right through her ruse, but he is attracted to her and helps her craft phony letters from her mother in exotic locations while they romp in bed. Maggie's fairytales start to unravel due to Bess's arrival.

Duplicitous Maggie blackmails her mother into pretending to be Betsy Trailer, and she is hired as the Coleridge housekeeper so she can be close to Jill without revealing her true identity. Then Maggie's ex-boyfriend Dusty shows up in the city and threatens to reveal the truth unless he is paid $10,000. Sensing that Bess's appearance is making Maggie jumpy, Frank and Faith suspect something is afoot.

Cali Timmins: I was very lucky. My character got right into the main storyline with the Coleridges and the Ryans, although I did not get to work with some of them because Maggie was not in the bar much. It was amazing and incredible for me to work with Nancy Addison, Geoff Pierson, and Ron Hale. That is where I learned everything. They were all extremely supportive, especially after they got to know me and saw that I wanted to learn from them. I was open to everything they had to say. They were so great in what they did, and I wanted very much to prove myself and to show I was worthy to be there. I worked hard, and I think that they saw that.

They were also such wonderful people. Ron was fun. They were like family and loved each other. It was a great group to be a part of. I adored Nancy, and she was an amazing role model. It made my job easier because they were such pros. I probably didn't realize how great I had it until later in life when I worked with people who weren't great. They had their characters down and knew what they were doing. I sound like I am exaggerating with all these nice things to say, but it was such a positive experience, especially these early years.

Ron, Geoff, and Earl Hindman would sometimes go to a neighborhood French restaurant for lunch. One day they invited me, and I became part of the group. They were fantastic actors and human beings. It was just so much fun.

In late November 1983, ABC fired Claire Labine and Paul Mayer. At the time, *Ryan's Hope* ranked 14 out of 26 network daytime programs. They were not on board with the additional changes the network wanted to make. Agreeing, Jackie Smith felt that Labine and Mayer "had outgrown the show." Claire told author Mary Ann Copeland, "We left at that time without rancor. It was really clear that they wanted to do something so profoundly different ... We had all the Sturm und Drang, we've had all the fights, all the blood on the floor, and at that point they said they knew what they wanted it to be like, and they did what they needed to do." New head writer Pat Falken Smith was brought in to bring a "fresh viewpoint."

Rachael Mayer: Claire and Paul were fired on a Friday. Claire was hired back a few years later, but Paul was not. That's a mystery. He was very unhappy with the show first after they sold it and then after they left. He was sad to see what happened to it and thought it just fell apart.

Ruth Mayer: I remember when he was fired. There were probably only a few times in my life where I saw tears in his eyes. I remember him saying, "It's like being kicked out of your own sandbox."

Laura Rakowitz: Joe Hardy did not get along with Claire and Paul, so it was no surprise that they left. Claire and Joe were like oil and water. I was a witness to some verbal confrontations over storylines. Joe was very sarcastic and very cutting. I don't know how Claire and Paul handled that. Claire was the more assertive one, and Paul stayed more in the background.

Claire and Paul deserved all the kudos and accolades they received for creating and writing such an exemplary and ground-breaking soap. Its first five years was kitchen sink drama at its best—real people with real problems the audience could relate to. However, when the 1980s began, their determination to keep that kitchen sink vibe they had been doing did not fit with where soaps were heading. The younger audience increased due to Luke and Laura, the Ice Princess–type stories on *General Hospital*, and the glitz and glamour seen on super-popular prime-time soaps such as *Dallas* and *Dynasty*. It was now the decade of excess, and the networks wanted it incorporated into their serials.

Arguably, when Claire and Paul worked in tandem with ABC and created a balance, such as in 1980, the first half of 1981, and even in the first half of 1982 with the introduction of Hollis Kirkland, the show rocked. But when they dug in their heels and fought ABC (Did they really think the audience would be more interested in aging soap opera actress Barbara Wilde than teenage vixen Kim Harris?), the show veered off course. However, nothing they did would prove to be as egregious as what ABC would serve up during the next year. It is a shame Claire and Paul could not work out a compromise with ABC moving forward in 1983 and save the viewers from what was to come.

Rachael Mayer: Paul went on to write for *Search for Tomorrow* and then moved to California to work on *Santa Barbara* [he never officially wrote for the show] before giving it all up to go to graduate school in his fifties. He worked as a social worker and therapist for the last thirty years of his life.

Ruth Mayer: Dad's famous line was "I never watched a television show that I wasn't paid to watch." As far as I know, he never saw *Ryan's Hope* ever again.

Geoff Pierson: It was not encouraging for the cast that was there because we all had tremendous faith in Claire and Paul. I was still a newcomer even at that time, compared to the original actors like Helen, Bernie, Ron, John, and Earl. There was a close bond between them and even me with Claire and Paul, especially Claire. It was her show. Whenever you have a change like that, losing the person you have confidence in to lead and write the show, and then you get someone new, it obviously will be of concern. Will it get better or will it get worse? What is going to happen?

Cali Timmins: Claire and Paul leaving was huge, but I do not know how it affected me personally because I really did not have a relationship with them. But I remember there was lots of real concern and worry of what this would mean to the integrity of the show and where it was going to go.

Ron Hale: Of course, after Claire and Paul left with their open-door policy, the door slammed shut when the geniuses at ABC took over and started throwing in whomever as producer or writer. It was awful. You had to fight tooth and nail or have a temper tantrum and throw a chair across the rehearsal studio floor and walk out, which many actors did. They'd say, "I'll be back." They'd walk out onto the street to cool off because of the stupidity of the people in charge. Most times the actor wanted a minor change—not to change the entire scene. It was like, "The way you want my character to say this is so stupid, and they would never say that."

Michael Levin: I was one of the chair throwers, and it was a low point for me. I was called on the carpet for it. I apologized and regretted doing that. It was a momentary reaction to the nonsense that was going on.

It was somewhat surprising that ABC named Pat Falken Smith as the new head writer for *Ryan's Hope* given the bad blood between them. She had a successful run head writing NBC's *Days of Our Lives* from 1976 to 1978, even winning an Emmy Award. She then wrote for *General Hospital* for two and a half years and was most famous for developing the controversial rape of Laura Webber Baldwin by thug Luke Spencer. She and her team quit in a huff in fall 1981.

The main reason was the infamous Ice Princess plot. Smith was dead set against it, but Monty and Jackie Smith pressured her to write it. She tried to keep it grounded, but then the writers' strike happened. When she returned, it was a sci-fi adventure, complete with the freezing of Port Charles. Though the writer hated it, the audience did not and the ratings soared. Not wanting anything more to do with the show, she asked to be released and was. The animosity started afterward, when, allegedly, Monty was telling cast and crew that she had fired Smith. *Days of Our Lives* quickly hired Smith back in October 1981, and she departed the following April.

Aided by *Ryan's Hope* staff writers Mary Munisteri, Nancy Ford, Judith Pinsker, and B. K. Perlman, Smith continued Labine and Mayer's stories.

Some interesting characters connected to Joe Novak were introduced. The roles of his spoiled, insecure wife, Jacqueline, and her powerful father, Max Dubujak, were cast with Gerit Quealy and Canadian film star Daniel Pilon respectively. Fred Burstein was cast as Joe's cousin Laslo Novotny, who turned up in Riverside to warn Siobhan and the Ryan family that Joe was in danger from his mob family.

Gerit Quealy (Jacqueline Dubujak): I had gone to the William Esper Studio for training, and I had been doing a lot of theatre, not only in America but Japan and other places. I finally got an agent, and they sent me for the part. I watched *Ryan's Hope* long before I ever auditioned for it. When I went in to read, I thought I was going up for an Irish part, being Irish myself and all. I was disappointed that I wasn't in the "family."

It was a huge casting call. There were girls just all over the place. I thought, "Oh well. I won't get this anyway." I kept getting called back, and the room of girls got smaller and smaller. Finally, there were four of us for the screen test. I remember that they didn't like the dresses that I brought and gave me a dress they liked better. I had about nine dollars to my name when I got the audition. I had no idea how I was going to pay my rent. I cannot recall how I survived with that little money from the audition to getting my first paycheck.

Fred Burstein (Laslo Novotny): I really did not have acting experience, but it was something I thought about. My brother lived in Los Angeles, so I was able to go out there and have a place to stay. I had no credits. I met a guy named Leonard Kantor who wrote *The Untouchables* and became my manager, not my agent. He said, "I will tell you where to study and what to do." He helped me get into SAG.

In 1982, Leonard went to New York to work on the soap opera *The Doctors* as head writer [with Barbara Morgenroth]. He created this part [Ken Lucia Robinson] and wanted me for it. I was a football player who was in a car accident and in the hospital. My face was totally wrapped up in gauze except for my eyes. I was wearing short pajama pants and that was it—no shirt. My character would just moan, "Oh gee, I hope I still look like myself when the surgery is over." I did not understand the emphasis on his face. He was a football player—not an actor. To boot, there was a picture behind the hospital bed of me just before I had the accident. They wanted me to copy the Burt Reynolds seminude photo from *Cosmopolitan*. I went to a photographer they lined me up with, and we took a lot of pictures. They chose a photo of me leaning on my elbow with only a small towel over my midsection.

Finally, there was the big dramatic moment for the big reveal. Of course, the cameras were on the actors looking at me. The doctor takes off the bandages, and the nurse I was in love with gasped. You did not know if I looked like something out of *The Twilight Zone* or if I looked like me. I looked like I look. It was fun to do.

After *The Doctors*, I had a short-term part on *All My Children*, then an author I knew from Los Angeles named George Baxt introduced me to his friend Joe Hardy. He set up the meeting, and I went to Joe's office. I gave him some tapes of me. We hit it off and became friends. We are still friends to this day. At one point he told me there was a part coming up—a cousin of one of the main characters [Joe Novak]. He said, "If it works out, it could go for a while. If it does not, it will be a couple of shows." I said sure, but it was not like they had a hundred actors come in and audition. It was just let's see what happens. It worked out well.

Gerit Qualey: Tamara Grady was the stage manager on my first day on the set. When we went to shoot my first scene, Tamara yelled out, "Five, four," then held her hand up for three, two, one. There was this long pause and Tamara said, "Gerit?" I replied, "Oh I'm sorry. I thought someone was supposed to say 'Action.'" Everybody started laughing.

With a new head writer in place, it was not surprising that some of the cast had to go, and 1983 came to an end with two longtime favorites being given their walking papers. Exasperated with Jill, Frank, Little John, and the Shelbys residing with her in the Coleridge brownstone that she once occupied alone, Faith accepts a job in Minnesota to get away from the chaos. Just before Christmas, the welcome angry Faith re-emerges, showcasing Karen Morris-Gowdy's underused talent. She vents to ex-fiancé Frank about the living situation, tells off Jill and Roger, and then splits town without saying goodbye to her current romantic partner, Pat.

Unlike Morris-Gowdy, who got an entire final episode, Louise Shaffer's

Rae Woodard just vanished from the screen. One of her last episodes has Rae delivering news from troublemaking Delia in San Diego to Frank and Jill before she heads off to Roger's apartment. The next thing the audience learned was that Rae had relocated to California.

Karen Morris-Gowdy: Joe fired me, and I was like, "Oh, thank you." I was so unhappy—we were all unhappy. He was tanking the show. It was like, "What the hell is this?" I know Joe liked me, but I think he was caught in the middle because I was young but not an ingenue like Cali Timmins. Faith was a character they could still play with—throw me in and throw me out. I think he liked that. He needed that character, but Cali's Maggie kind of took over. I didn't think they were able to find a way to work the two characters together. Also, he knew I was not happy and found going to work laborious. I was grateful, but at the same time I wish I had the courage to have said, "Joe, I am going to give you my two weeks' notice." I wish I had had the guts to do that because when you get fired, you feel shameful and think you did something wrong.

Ron Hale: With Joe Hardy, just like with other producers I have seen over the years, they come on, take over, lift their leg, pee their territory, and fire two or three people immediately—exactly what he did.

Michael Levin: I didn't like Joe Hardy. He obviously did not place much faith in me. He was trying to use me as a steppingstone for his ideas and for other actors' (that he brought in) purposes. It was a negative relationship but not necessarily a big deal. I felt that I had to protect Jack from Joe Hardy.

Malcolm Groome: During this time, I was not afraid of being fired, but it was a disappointment to come back to the show, then be relegated to a minimal part. What was awful for the cast was to see so many good actors let go when Pat and Joe came in. Either one or both were involved in writing off Faith. I was terribly disappointed when Karen was let go. I remember, though, it was never wise to confront Joe about anything.

Ron Hale: I felt lonely after this. They wrote off Roger's sister and his best friend. With Karen, I was like, *What?!* She was such a delight and so good as Faith.

Louise Shaffer: Contrary to some reports, I was fired, and I was not demoted to recurring. They really didn't do that in those days. But if you were fired and they wanted to bring you back for a bit and you didn't have anything else going on, you could negotiate as a day player.

I was incredibly angry. My Emmy hadn't even come back from the engraver yet, and they dumped me. I felt very pissed off. In all fairness, the network's job is to make money. Their job is certainly not to produce a good show, but to produce a show where they can guarantee a demographic that they need. You can't get mad, really, when they are doing their job and you are trying to do your job, which you do because you love it. I don't care about demographics and ratings. What I care about is if Rae is being properly motivated at this moment. Can I find the hook in this scene where I personally can identify? Those are my concerns, and they have nothing to do with somebody who must explain to her bosses why the show is not making the kind of money *General Hospital* is making. I guess the sad thing is that the people who lose are the audience.

Laura Rakowitz: I think Joe Hardy liked Karen Morris-Gowdy more than Louise Shaffer. He honored Karen's character of Faith by letting her have that final episode. He did a wonderful thing for her but didn't for Louise. I thought Louise and her character Rae were very smart. Louise had a lot of questions for Joe, and I don't think Joe liked being questioned. I don't think he disliked Louise, but there was a personality disagreement there. As for Karen, though Joe liked her, I don't think they saw any more storylines for Faith. These may be the reasons why Karen got a send-off and Louise did not. That is my perception.

Louise Shaffer: Unlike Karen, I did not have a last big goodbye episode. I think I got shipped off to somewhere on the West Coast. As every new administration does, I think Joe Hardy really wanted to put his own stamp on the show. He had people he had worked with and liked for a long time and wanted to bring them in. For Rae, it was almost a kind of sneaking-off-in-the-middle-of-the-night sort of thing.

Laura Rakowitz: I liked Karen and thought she was always underestimated. However, this was a girl who fell into acting and was a very personable gal. I don't think she was sorry when they let her go. She was a good wife and wanted to be a mother. Personally, I think she rode off into the sunset and was happy to do that.

Louise Shaffer: When I was fired, Ellen Barrett was working on *Search for Tomorrow*. She knew I needed a job. I do not know why Marie Cheatam left, but Ellen saw to it that I replace her [as Stephanie Wyatt]. I have every reason to be grateful to Ellen.

My favorite story working with Peter Haskell [playing Lloyd Kendall] happened there. They had a scene where they brought in some dogs. I can't remember why, but they were needed. To make the dogs snarl menacingly, this son of a bitch—who was their handler and I hope is rotting in the depths of hell—forced this poor, scared dog to climb to the top of this ladder. A lot of the actors felt this should not be happening. Peter was our union rep. It was made clear to us there was no way we should complain about this because we were going to go into overtime. Peter walked off the set and over to the phone that was in the hallway in those days ... called our union and told them about this fucker abusing this animal. The show got stopped until they found another way to do the scene.

7

Goodbye Ryan's Bar,
Hello Greenberg's Deli, 1984

The new year began with the introduction of Dave Greenberg (played by the disarming Scott Holmes), who took over from his parents as the owner of Greenberg's Deli, a nearby establishment where the Ryans and Coleridges would sometimes eat. It now had a modern look to it and a young vibe. This was the start of the show's transformation away from the Ryan family to a gaggle of forgettable teenagers and young adults. First to arrive was Richard Berk as Rico, a homeless teen who tries to attack Maggie. Feeling sorry for his situation, Dave takes him in and officially shares custody of him with Frank Ryan. Rico begins working at the deli when not in school. He was quickly followed by Flash (Melcourt Peoux), Dave's African American friend.

Although Joe Hardy had no say in hiring the show's new head writer, he did have the authority to add a staff writer to Pat Falken Smith's team. Her name was Martha Nochimson. A wife and new mother, she had just finished getting her PhD from CUNY. While home with her child, she became fascinated with soap operas and developed an interest in writing for one.

Martha Nochimson (staff writer/consultant): My sister, who works in the industry, told me the Writers Guild was sponsoring a workshop for aspiring soap opera writers. I watched *Ryan's Hope* carefully and wrote up a spec script, expanding on the stories in progress. When I called the Guild, however, I was told that Nancy Ford had finished with the workshop, but I could send the script to them and they would send it to her. I did.

After three weeks, I gave up hope of ever hearing back about it, when suddenly I received a phone call. I picked up the phone and heard these words, "This is Nancy Ford. You can do this." Shock. Amazement. Joy. She had some comments to make and offered to come to my house and edit with me. When I rewrote, she gave me Joe Hardy's address and told me that if I hurried, I might get her job. She was being fired. (Even more unbelievable . . . when I met up with Nancy about twenty years later, she said she had never said that to me, but she did.)

I sent Joe the script on a Friday and the next Monday, the phone rang. It was Joe Hardy. He said, "Darling, where have you been all my life?" He gave me twenty minutes to get to the studio. I drove like the wind. After a brief interview, he told me he was going to give me two Writers Guild contracts, one as a script writer and one as a consultant to the head writer, Pat Falken Smith. Crazy.

"Joe," I said, "How can I be a consultant? I don't know anything. I've never done this before."

Said Joe, "The greener, the better."

Alice in Wonderland. But I was thrilled. Needless to say, I signed on the dotted line, and I took a leave of absence from my appointment as an associate professor in the English Department at Mercy College in Dobbs Ferry to write for the show.

Max Dubujak, with his eyes on Jill, relocates to New York to get to know her. To that end, he contacts Seneca about donating a new wing to Riverside Hospital and hires Jill to be his attorney to handle the details. Jacqueline has her butler, Lawrence Prince (Stefano LoVerso), keep tabs on Joe, and he reports back that he is seeing Siobhan, who disappeared after she stood up Laslo. Of course, Jack insinuates himself into the situation to help find Siobhan despite Joe's pleas to let him handle it. Meanwhile, a mystery man (à la Deep Throat from Watergate—complete with secret meetings in dark places) is providing undercover agent Bill Hyde information about the connection between the mob and Max. Bill is teamed with detective Kenny Graham (Corbin Bernsen, later of *LA Law* fame), who is unaware of his new partner's actions. After Jack, with support from Sydney, Leigh, and the Ryan family, goes on air reporting Siobhan's disappearance (she purposely dropped out of sight to meet with Laslo in secret so the mob would not find out), all hell breaks loose.

It was around this time that the decision was made to entirely refocus *Ryan's Hope* to try to reach a new audience. Whereas Claire and Paul brought the soap back to 1975, ignoring popular soap trends in their storytelling, ABC went the opposite way by shifting the attention to a gaggle of new, younger characters and pushing the core families almost to the background. These wild swings in storytelling clearly hurt the show and had viewers perplexed. To achieve this new direction, the holdover writing team from the Labine-Mayer years was finally let go, as Nancy Ford had predicted. Only B. K. Perlman survived. They were replaced by Peter Brash, Maura Penders, and Betsy Tooker.

> **Martha Nochimson:** It was a transition time for the show. I believe Joe was new. . . as producer and the old stalwarts were leaving. Writers were coming and going through a revolving door. The old team called the new team "the impostors," but they seemed to like me and told me I was the best writer of the new crowd.
>
> When Mary Munisteri left the show, it was clear that Joe Hardy wasn't planning any kind of farewell ceremony, which I thought strange . . . Mary had been on the show since the beginning, and the main female character, Mary Ryan, was named after her. I decided I would organize a little party for her. Yes, not exactly what newcomers to a team do. But I was just as reckless and risk-taking as Joe. When he got word of what I was doing, he announced that he was going to do the honors. And he really was extremely gracious about it. He took the writing team to Orzo, a lovely Italian restaurant on Restaurant Row that is no more. We had the most gorgeous champagne I have ever tasted, and he gave Mary a bottle of it as a parting gift as well.

To signal the change in the show's focus, the writers had to come up with something big. To most of the audience's horror, they blew up Ryan's Bar. You could not have done anything bigger or made a bolder statement than destroying the heart of the show, where most of the interaction between characters took place for the last nine years. Soon after, the action officially shifted to Greenberg's Deli.

> **Martha Nochimson:** When I knew Joe Hardy, he was in a mood to take risks and to try new ways to upgrade running a soap opera. He was very excited about having a staff writer who had a PhD, and he talked about that all the time. He asked me to write the weekly synopsis for the show, which I think ABC kept on file and various

magazines used. He was so proud to be able to submit text that he considered really well written. I wouldn't have mentioned it to anyone on the team if I had my druthers. It was reckless and a mistake. Of course, everyone hated me because of my often-mentioned degree. At that time—maybe now too, I don't know—people in the industry disliked and distrusted academics.

I think I recall getting some idea from Joe that Pat was not his choice [for head writer]. But he tried to be positive about the experience she brought to the table . . . Since I was Joe's hire, not Pat's, I have no idea how he presented his decision to her. But she never considered me a person she wanted for her team. He was well aware that she was unstable and difficult. Nancy remarked to me that Pat wasn't bringing anyone she had worked with before to the team and that said a lot. It did. But, after all, I could understand that she felt that I was there to babysit her and perhaps even to spy. Or worse—to take her job once I had the lay of the land. It didn't seem promising for a long-term professional partnership. And it wasn't.

Joseph Hardy: I tried my best to make the show a little less folksy and a bit more "television-y."

Martha Nochimson: I was quite involved with the whole delicatessen thing. If I remember, I created Dave's nickname, and they wanted me to do other inventing for the story. But I really can't recall knowing who decided that we'd go in that direction. I do seem to recall that Joe Hardy got bored with it after a while. I clearly remember walking onto the set of the remains of the bar after it exploded and hearing someone from the crew say, "Those Ryans know how to party."

On soaps, it's always a mistake to torch the past; soap is about continuity or it's about nothing at all. Sadly, once people like me started talking about the genre and gave it respectability, the networks began to take an interest, and they were always wrong about what they dictated. They didn't read what we were saying, and they thought that an upgrade meant making soap more like nighttime—disaster! They didn't understand they had an exciting, unprecedented way of telling stories in the traditions of soap. And, of course, the genre has all but imploded.

Joe and Maggie are trapped in the rubble of the bar. Most suspect that the Novotny crime family did it to get revenge on Joe, while Jacqueline suspects Hutch set it up because he is jealous of the increased business responsibilities Max gave Joe. Saddened by what he thinks his family did to the Ryans, Laslo goes to Maeve with a wad of cash in retribution.

Fred Burstein: I remember that scene when Laslo went to the destroyed bar and saw Maeve. He had money and was saying excitedly something like, "Please, please take it. This wasn't me. I had nothing to do with this. Take the money and fix up the bar." She hissed, "Take your Novotny blood money and just get out of here!"

After we shot that whole scene, Joe Hardy said to me, "When somebody is yelling at you like she was, you go the other way. You calmly, quietly talk to her completely opposite than the way she is speaking to you. Do not take your cue from her and use that same kind of voice and urgency." Basically, he felt it was not my best scene, but he was trying to help me and offer advice—don't do what the other actor does. A lot of times when I was on the show, I would speak in a calm, low-key kind of voice. Then the director would come in after one take and yell, "Faster! Faster! Talk faster!" Some of the shows are now on YouTube. I watch myself sometimes. And. I. Am. Talking. Like. This. Who knows—maybe if I could see when I thought I was good, it could be worse?

Maggie is quickly released from the hospital, but Joe languishes with his injuries. Seneca informs Jacqueline that he needs plastic surgery. Trying to give Joe some good news, she lies to him and Max and says she is pregnant. She learns that her father had arranged her marriage to Joe and demands to take her husband's place in the organization if something happens to him. Jacqueline then desperately offers Laslo a lot of cash to impregnate her, but he declines. After Hutch sends a thug to make another attempt on Joe's life, Jacqueline moves him to Sweden (tailed by Bill Hyde under orders from Bob Reid, the mystery agent) to recover. The car he is riding in plunges off a cliff while bursting into flames. He is presumed dead, and the last scene the audience sees is a bandaged Joe peering from the bushes.

Geoff Pierson: I remember once Roscoe Born left the show, they had a tough time recasting Joe. I had some dealings with Michael

Hennessy, and I did not think he was probably the best person for that role. I did not have to work with him a lot.

Gerit Quealy: Who didn't have a crush on Roscoe Born? When I came on and knew I was going to be paired with Joe, I was so excited. When it wasn't Roscoe, I was like, oh. Okay. I think Michael Hennessy was already cast, and I didn't test with him. He was a strange guy and didn't make a lot of friends there. He was problematic, and there were odd situations. That is all I will say.

Fred Burstein: Shortly after I came on, Michael Hennessy's character went into the hospital. Off camera, he said something to me like, "They are killing me off. You are just starting. I won't be here for long. I hope you have it better, and it goes well for you." We had a few scenes together when Laslo would go visit him.

Cali Timmins: There were certain cast members who would come and go. It wasn't so much a personal issue, but the character did not meld and the people did not either. And they usually did not last that long. I believe Claire and Paul created Joe and think only they could have cast it right. I think Michael just was not the right fit.

Gerit Quealy: I loved DeVeren Bookwalter, who played Hutch. He was a great ally and fun. Behind the scenes, he was very sarcastic . . . making sly remarks but always in a good-natured and funny manner. If there was friction, I think he was one of those people who had been in the business for a long time and knew how lucky anybody is to be working. I thought he did an excellent job with his character, and maybe it is partially due to that his character was an ally of Jacqueline's. There was a natural camaraderie for us there. We and Daniel Pilon also bonded over what became a difficult situation with Michael Hennessy.

Geoff Pierson: I did work a lot with Daniel Pilon and liked him very much. Our scenes were quite limited, but we became friends that lasted after the show. I thought Gerit Quealy was wonderful as his daughter.

Fred Burstein: Gerit Quealy played my love interest for a while. Whenever Max would pronounce her name, it was "Jacques-lean."

But Laslo would ask, "Where's Jackie?" I liked Gerit. We talked and rehearsed together but that was it. It was fine working with her.

Gerit Quealy: I thought Fred was a nice guy and had a lovely wife.

Ratings for the first two months of 1984 under Pat Falken Smith's tenure were announced in March, and not surprisingly the numbers were disappointing. Per *Variety*, *Ryan's Hope* dropped to a 4.8 rating and 16 share (up to that point in the season, it was averaging a 5.1 rating and 17 share) versus a 9.3 rating and 32 share for *The Young and the Restless*, which had blown past the struggling soap. The news got even grimmer for *Ryan's Hope* as it lost the Women 18–49 Demo for the first time to *The Young and the Restless*. This is ironic, considering ABC infused the serial with a gaggle of teenagers, thinking it would boost the younger audience, but instead it had the opposite effect.

As for the Emmy Award nominations, despite the mesmerizing performances delivered by, in particular, Geoff Pierson, Judith Chapman, and Helen Gallagher, not a single cast member received recognition. *Ryan's Hope* received a lone nomination for Outstanding Writing for a Daytime Drama Series. Despite its lack of nominations, the show triumphed, winning the Emmy for the Charlotte Greer storyline. This was the sixth and final Emmy Award for Claire and Paul writing *Ryan's Hope*. Curiously, Pat Falken Smith and her team were not listed on the ballot for their contribution to the show afterward. Claire and Paul, with their writing team, also won the Writers Guild Award. It was their eighth and last win together.

> **Judith Chapman:** There is no doubt that Claire and Paul deserved the Emmy. Although I was young then, I had some acting chops and experience in knowing what good writing was and what good writing could do. And what good actors and a good director could do. It was just soap opera gold—that's all there is to it. I'm glad they won. I didn't win, of course, because I wasn't nominated. Actually, I have never been nominated for an Emmy, which is neither here nor there. But I would have been very proud to have been nominated for playing Charlotte Greer.

Smith's stories continued to plow on. Dave Greenberg is smitten with Maggie. He not only gives her a job as a waitress while she is still pursuing her modeling aspirations but also offers to rent the loft above his restaurant to her so she can leave the toxic Coleridge townhouse—an atmosphere she helped to create with her actions. He also promotes her modeling career whenever he has the chance. However, Maggie has developed deep feelings for her brother-in-law, Frank, who seems to return the affection, but their guilt about Jill keeps them at arm's length.

Two new characters were introduced in March. Lauren O'Bryan as Maeve and Johnny's granddaughter Maura Thompson, now going by the name of Katie and a wannabe dancer, shows up at what was left of Ryan's Bar on St. Patrick's Day. At least Pat Falken Smith kept with tradition and allowed Maeve to sing "Danny Boy," as she did in the previous years.

Helen Gallagher: I always sang "Danny Boy." The kids hated it and would say, "Here she goes again!"

The other newcomer was Elite model Traci Lind (billed Traci Lin) as hayseed teen runaway Pru Shepherd. She is in NYC looking for her long-lost sister, Dawn. Arguably, she was one of the worst major characters created during the eighties or ever to appear on the show. Both Katie and Pru get jobs slinging pastrami at the deli and eventually share the upstairs loft with Maggie. They soon are joined by newcomer Grant Show as brooding bad boy Rick Hyde, Detective Bill Hyde's rebellious younger brother. Show was originally cast as Maggie Shelby's sibling Ben, but since he so resembled actor David Sederholm, the character was changed. To say the decision to move the action from Ryan's Bar to the deli and its denizens did not sit well with the viewers and some of the cast is an understatement.

Joseph Hardy: I would meet with Jackie Smith and other ABC executives on a regular basis to discuss plots. They were usually agreeable, and Jackie was fine. There was a point, however—not I and not particularly she—but some of the ABC executives wanted the show to go in this different direction.

Martha Nochimson: Joe decided that we would have weekly writers' meetings. I thought it was a great idea. And it worked well for Joe. I gave him a lot of ideas that he used on *Ryan's Hope* and even more that he used when he met with the other soap executive producers. But I had hoped that the meetings would create a community, and they didn't. As I said, the other writers hated me as an academic intruder . . . Pat and Joe did not have a good relationship, but I never was privy to specific arguments.

Ron Hale: The world that you were working in and took pride in is now just moved around by the bean counters, because that is what they are. It's all about ratings. The fact that this show was good for a reason—they didn't care. *General Hospital* is doing better than *Ryan's Hope*, so we have to make *Ryan's Hope* more like it. The other excuse that I always loved for changing things was "because we have to bring in a younger audience." I heard that all of my adult life on daytime television. Every head of programming spewed it.

Malcolm Groome: Pat and Joe wanted to reshape the show in their image, put their own stamp on it—hence they blew up Ryan's Bar. That pretty much says it all. It felt to some of us originals that the show was losing its heart [and] we felt off-put by that at the time. In their defense, I think they were tasked with improving the ratings.

Helen Gallagher: When they blew up Ryan's Bar, the new writers never consulted us. We were just told it was going to blow up. I thought they were ruining the show. Even though I felt this way, I never gave any thoughts of leaving—I never left a show in my life. And I did not this time either.

Michael Levin: I had very little to do at this time, and I did not have much of a storyline then. It was a bad decision to blow up the bar, but what are you going to do?

Laura Rakowitz: Every one of us missed Ryan's Bar, though we did like Scott Holmes. Once they made that decision—it no longer was *Ryan's Hope*. It just lost that taste and that feel. Though it was still set in New York City, it just wasn't the same thing.

Cali Timmins: Scott Holmes was a great guy and easy to be around. Nothing against him, but I didn't love the Dave and Maggie storyline that much. I didn't get it. Dave was a nice, safe place for Maggie, but it wasn't something that excited me as an actress. Neither did interacting with Pru and all the rest. It became less fulfilling for me as an actress.

Tamara Grady: Grant Show was always a good actor. I thought he was better than David Sederholm, who played his brother. We used to call Bill and Corbin Bernsen, who played Kenny, the "Easter cops" because they always wore pastel shirts for some strange reason.

Cali Timmins: When I worked with Traci Lind and Lauren O'Bryan, I was not into the show and was going through the motions. But again, I never thought of my character or myself as being part of that group. I was thrown in with them due to my age. That was the only connection. To me, they were all doing their own thing and experiencing the nightlife. It was the eighties, so there was lots of partying going on. That's how I kind of felt about them also on the show as Maggie. They were fun and cute, but we did not have much in common. I do not want to speak for her, but I think doing a soap was not Traci Lind's dream. It was just another gig.

Tamara Grady: The actors were young, and it was tough. It was like herding cattle, but I was extremely strict and everyone was afraid of me, especially the younger actors. It seemed to me almost every summer from that point on, we did teen storylines and then went back to more adult stories when the kids went back to school.

Malcolm Groome: When Joe Hardy came on the show, he took me aside in the hallway of the dressing rooms and he said, "I want to make you the youth of the show." I was thirty-four years old and thought, "I am an adult and Pat is a doctor." I resisted that and said Pat was too mature, which is one of the biggest mistakes I made. I should have run with it and taken advantage of that opportunity. That's when they brought in more youthful characters and the main stories centered around the "kids" at Greenberg Deli, which supplanted Ryan's Bar as the hub of the show. I probably would have had better stories if I had said, "Yes whatever you want." However, I thought it would have been creepy to put Pat with any of the teenage girls brought on.

Joseph Hardy: I felt a little bit of resistance from the older cast, but it was not my doing; it was ABC. I had to sort of work that out. I did some new casting after that. I also wanted to make the look of it more up-to-date and ABC went along with that too. It was fine.

Helen Gallagher: I knew Joe Hardy before he came onto *Ryan's Hope*. He tried to change a lot of it, but he did not succeed. The cast tried to push back but not verbally. We did with our performances. We would stick to the ways we used to do it and not go along with how they were doing things on *All My Children*.

Malcolm Groome: Going back to the early days when we all felt like a family and the Ryans and the Coleridges were the heart of the show, we were very protective of that. And maybe even a bit elitist about it. We felt entitled, and it was our show. As much as I love Joe, it felt like he was taking that away maybe because he had to make his mark on the show. He was almost destroying the Ryan/Coleridge connection a little bit. He totally revamped the show. It was unrecognizable to us.

Fred Burstein: I heard some of the actors complaining about the changes—not, however, Bernie Barrow or Helen Gallagher. I thought Bernie was great. He was an extremely sweet, nice man. Helen was too, but we never sat down and talked or laughed together. I heard others complain that once Joe Hardy came in, they were not getting any stories or doing much. I never became friends with anyone on the show.

Gerit Quealy: Joe Hardy came in and changed the whole regime. Joe was a bit remote and had a very specific idea in what he wanted the show to be. I think it was tougher for the actors who had been there from the beginning to cotton to the changes he was trying to make. Certainly, the entrance of the Dubujaks was a big part of that.

Fred Burstein: Michael Levin was genuinely nice and a good guy. He thought with Joe Hardy in charge the show was not doing as well as before. He felt he was not getting much work, and the ratings were not as good.

Gerit Quealy: At the time some of us were the new kids on the block, though I was a happy puppy wanting to be friends with everybody. I came into a kind of—*turbulent* is too strong a word—more a sense of friction of some kind that I was only aware of in a peripheral sense at first. The longer I was there, the more obvious it became. I am grateful to Joe because I wouldn't have gotten on *Ryan's Hope* otherwise.

Cali Timmins: There was concern. I felt it, but they were professionals. They showed up and did their job. There was awareness the show was going this way instead of that way. I was in that group and not with the young, new additions. I hung out with Nancy

Addison and Gloria DeHaven. I was invited to Ron Hale's family home on the weekends. I was privy to those conversations more than the new, younger cast members, even though I was younger. It was not as if it was not a lovely place to work. You just felt their frustration. I understood it. The storylines were going crazy as compared to when it started with long emotional scenes with such good actors. Now it was getting very silly. There was talk about the ratings and what stories were not working. However, this was part of every show. Helen Gallagher was Helen, of course—the epitome of professionalism. She set the tone for everybody, and she was never unpleasant. There was no ego on this show from anybody. It was unique in that way.

Gerit Quealy: I loved Ron Hale and thought he was so funny. I also like Michael Levin a lot. We were doing this huge party scene that took days to film. I was wearing this wig that looked terrible and had a life of its own. Michael Levin walked in, and he didn't have his normal toupee on. I was taken aback and had no idea. I loved the old guard—I really did. Bernie was a warm guy. Like Maeve, Helen was the matriarch of the show. She was a very classy lady who could give her opinion and yet never sounded snotty. It was always like, "I don't know why they are doing this." There was something elevated about her.

To show the audience that they were watching a new *Ryan's Hope*, the opening sequence was partially refilmed. The theme music was altered, and a few shots of the Ryans and Jack (interestingly Roger was cut from the opening) were now intercut with the new characters—Maggie, Dave, Pru, Katie, Rick, Jacqueline, and Max—dominating. Rather than ending on a shot of the Ryan family, as in the prior opening, it finishes with a solo Maeve.

The exploitation factor also kicked up a notch or two during this period. Prior, *Ryan's Hope* was a bit demure compared to the other soaps, although Michael Levin and Michael Corbett flashed their physiques a bit and the show seemed to love getting whoever was playing Joe Novak into a Speedo. Now the young actors were shirtless much more frequently, and some of the actresses were scantily clad and made up to the hilt. This was no doubt in keeping with ABC's overall daytime goal to play up the sex appeal of the cast to reach those desired younger viewers.

Gerit Quealy: David Sederholm was a very lovely man and a nice guy. Grant Show too took his shirt off a lot. They were aware of what was going on too. In the beginning, I was often wearing lingerie, and there were all kinds of problems with that. I remember I had one crazy little outfit where too much was showing, so they put these little cotton balls on me instead and that made it worse. Another time I was wearing a negligee while reading a letter or something. I could hear this chatter on the walkie-talkie and then people come rushing down and start taping me [with double-sided tape]. There was a lot of flesh revealed, even if it wasn't on screen. Sometimes it was so embarrassing.

Cali Timmins: I liked looking at Gerit. She was gorgeous and a lovely person as well. She was a classic beauty and reminded me of the movie stars of the Golden Age of Hollywood. I remember Joe Hardy brought in this makeup artist to glamorize us more. I was called into his office with Gerit and remember thinking she needs nothing because she is so beautiful—not that I needed much either. Joe was very complimentary but still wanted to glam up our looks. I am not sure if it was at this point, but they made me wear a fall on the back of my head to give me big hair, which I did not have. It looked so ridiculous. After a few months, I took it off.

In one of the better storylines of this period, Sydney Price begins a romance with Jack after he officially calls it quits with Leigh Kirkland. A handsome friend from Leigh's past named Jeremy Winthrop (Herb Anderson, the brother of *Dynasty's* John James) turns up in New York during this time after she sells half her share of the television station to him. When they receive an anonymous photo of Sydney and Max together, they begin to suspect that Sydney has a past connection to Max and that she is hiding some of his dirty deeds. They set out to trap her.

Maggie now becomes the show's central selfless, victimized heroine (every soap had to have one). Her departure from the Coleridge brownstone does not stop Roger from harassing her. Roger, in a misguided character assassination by head writer Pat Falken Smith, is turned into a stalker and voyeur. Maggie confides in Frank about Roger's actions.

Cali Timmins: I don't ever remember meeting one-on-one with Pat Falken Smith. I don't have memories of me asking, "Why are you making Maggie good now? Or what's happening?" This does not mean those discussions did not take place. I do recall, however, thinking, "Wow, the show is really changing."

Martha Nochimson: Pat also was constantly coming up with ideas that dramatized violence against women. She was said to be the author of the infamous rape of Laura by Luke on *General Hospital*. Some said no. But that would have been typical Pat. Some of the violent scenarios were used, others not. She especially had it in for a pretty blond character called Maggie. When Pat talked to us about the show, she would sometimes tell us to take off our feminist hats and just think about telling a good story.

Ron Hale: They would do anything to advance a friggin' storyline when the network took over. Let's have Roger rape the nineteen-year-old. To hell with the character and to hell with his history through the years. Just throw his character to the dogs because we need this storyline to move in this direction. I was very passionate about my character, as you can tell. I fought with them about what they were doing to Roger. If they wanted to take Roger down this dark path, I pushed them to make excessive drinking the reason for his abnormal behavior. They agreed.

Geoff Pierson: As I recall, Ron disliked how they pushed his character to almost raping Maggie. He did not think that was a good idea at all.

Cali Timmins: Ron Hale may have voiced his displeasure of what they were doing to Roger, but he had such a wonderful sense of humor that he would play that character off camera, lurching about, being a creepy guy. He was making fun of his character and himself. There was lots of that kind of humor, even though I am positive he didn't like what they were doing with his character. Ron liked to work a lot and loved to act. He also loved working with Geoff.

Geoff Pierson: The up-and-down relationship between Frank and Maggie was dictated by whoever was the head writer. There was a certain amount of wishing they would make up their minds. There was a certain inevitability that they were going to have to work that out between Frank and Maggie to get Frank and Jill back together.

It was ultimately what they did because I think it had to be for the long-term sustainability of the show. Although they flirted with all kinds of different things at the time and made it interesting.

Cali Timmins: Maggie to me was just a young girl who goes through good and bad times. I never thought of her as an evil character—she was manipulative, a survivor, and she learned from an early age how to get by. God knows what she experienced living in a trailer and working at a factory. I never, ever thought of her as anything but a good person who maybe sometimes had bad judgment and went about things the wrong way because of her lack of sophistication and self-esteem. So, when she became *good*, that was part of who she was. Once she had love in her life and saw the experience of the loving Coleridge family, she was able to incorporate that. At the time, I really did not dwell on this as I was mostly concentrating on doing my scenes.

Laura Rakowitz: I thought Cali Timmins was terrific and much better as the bratty tramp. She was more interesting and I was disappointed when they turned her into a good girl. Cali was another one who had a great innate talent for acting. I am sorry we haven't seen much of her recently.

Cali Timmins: I was very close with Tamara Grady and Laura Rakowitz. I was hanging out with them a lot. I could not get enough reassurance that I was doing okay. And they gave that to me. They saw that I was working very hard, and they were very indulgent that way. Sometimes I would ask if we could do my scene again. They would say, "No, it was very good. We have a deadline and have to move on." I would beg: "Please!"

After Maggie has another encounter with the obsessed Roger, who snuck into the loft, Frank comes to look after Maggie and to tell her that he informed Jill about her brother. They don't know that an inebriated Roger is also up there, creeping around, and overhears Maggie confessing to Frank that because she is in love with him, she cannot be with Dave. This sends the unhinged Roger over the edge. He comes rushing out of his hiding spot, screaming, "No!" and pushes a wooden structure onto the pair, just missing them. A fight then breaks out between Roger and Frank.

During their violent struggle, Roger falls down an open elevator shaft and is rushed to the hospital.

Ron Hale: We knew where this storyline was going, and I think we had an idea what was going to happen in a week or two. There was enough of a lead time for the actors to shape up what we were doing. It led to Roger getting into a fight with Frank and Roger falling down an elevator shaft. After all these years, I am saying this publicly for the first time. Malcolm Groome came to me one day and knocked on my dressing room door. He asked if he could talk with me. He said, "I overheard something. You have to know this. Joe Hardy wants Roger to go down the shaft and never come back up." Malcolm saved my butt because after he told me that—although he would not tell me where he was or where he overheard it—he looked at me and said, "This is the truth, and he doesn't want Roger to survive."

I contacted Jackie Smith and went to see her. We talked and I said, "You have to be honest with me. I know my source is 100 percent trustworthy." I told her. She looked at me and said, "Interesting." I asked if she knew about this and she said, "Oh yeah." I said, "I just want you to know that I am very angry." She said, "I am glad you came and am glad you heard about it. I will deal with it, Ron. Don't worry." And that was it. Malcolm did not have to do that because if somebody found out, he could have lost his job. He was man enough to warn me. I do not have a clue why they wanted to kill Roger off.

Art Rutter: Jackie Smith was a star at the network. I always thought she was cerebral (although some would disagree about that) and a larger-then-life character. She never seemed to get her hands dirty and just kind of oversaw everything. Her fury was evident when you started to fuck with daytime, like when ABC News would cut into the soaps. That was part of my job in programming, and Josie Emmerich would come into my office or perhaps go to Seymour Amlen's. Jackie would get on the phone directly with Roone Arledge, the head of ABC News, or yell at Fred Pierce, the head of ABC.

Perhaps Ron Hale being absent from the new opening was an intentional sign that he would not be around for much longer? Either way, Jackie Smith came through for him. Roger survives the fall but injures his hand, jeopardizing his career as a surgeon, and then causes lots more trouble. Frank comforts a shaken Maggie, and they share a kiss. The pair fret that Jill (and Dave) will learn of their indiscretion from Roger, who does not disappoint. He lies to Jill that he caught them making love, and she informs Dave.

It is surprising to note that throughout these major character assassinations and adjustments to *Ryan's Hope*, Pat Falken Smith was an enigma to most of the cast. It seems she never spoke to them regarding their characters or the storylines she had in mind.

> **Fred Burstein:** I was at a party with Pat Falken Smith and Joe Hardy once. She had, I think, about a sixteen-year-old daughter. She said, "I watch my daughter, and if she is watching closely, I know those are the characters that I have to give the most attention to. If she is not paying attention, like combing her hair or is distracted when other characters are on, I do not give them as much airtime." It seems this one girl controlled who got to be on screen more.

> **Geoff Pierson:** I do not recall any interaction with Pat Falken Smith or being enlightened by her on any storylines. In fact, I do not even remember meeting her.

> **Gerit Quealy:** I never met any of the writers, and we really weren't allowed to. Perhaps they didn't want us to influence them or they influence us. They didn't want the actors asking to do certain things. I did this thing with my eyebrow. When I opened a script one week, it said, "Jacqueline raises her eyebrow." I thought, "Oh, they are actually watching."

> **Tamara Grady:** Pat Falken Smith changed the show a lot. I really didn't have any direct dealings with her. I did like some of the new characters that came through, such as Dave Greenberg and Flash. I remember having a lot of fun on the set with the actors because they both had great senses of humor. To me that was helpful on days that could be trying. Smith brought a totally distinct perspective to the show.

Unlike the cast, staff writer Martha Nochimson worked with and got to know Pat Falken Smith for over a year and, unfortunately, it was a very unpleasant experience for her. Perhaps the cast dodged a bullet that Smith never reached out to them.

Martha Nochimson: Pat was talented, experienced, but jaundiced, bitter, jealous, and suspicious. To be fair, and I was very conscious of this at the time, she was a battle-scarred veteran of the Hollywood studio system. I can't find any movie credits for her on IMDB, but she was twenty years old in 1946, and I think that's when she began working—she probably was never given an assignment that would get her a place in the credits. She told stories about being in Hollywood that made it clear that she was always marginalized by a male-dominated industry. It didn't make her sympathetic to other women in the business. She was fiercely protective of her prerogatives and position and [was] sure I was there to sabotage her. I wasn't.

She said on occasion she couldn't understand why I didn't try for a job as a head writer. I told her that I had a lot to learn before I could do that, and I really was there to learn. She wasn't there to teach, however. She did everything she could to humiliate me. I thought it was funny because I knew I was going back to teaching. She really didn't have any actual power over me—but not for want of trying.

I had to go to her apartment every day I wasn't working on my own scripts, and she would often meet me in pajamas and a robe—very disrespectful of me as a professional. And she really didn't let me do any work. She asked me to answer her fan mail—also disrespectful. She took the writing team to lunch once and asked me to pay the bill using her credit card—secretary much?

And at the same lunch, she behaved in such a despicable way to Barbara Perlman [aka B. K. Perlman], a lovely and accomplished person, that I could never respect her afterward. When we were almost finished eating, Barbara suddenly passed out on the table. The rest of us got very busy reviving her. We wanted to call an ambulance, but Barbara refused. She was all right after that. Pat just sat there like a stranger, and when Barbara came to, she said, "Aren't we wonderful?" She said nothing to Barbara—not, "How are you?" or anything resembling that. The "we" she was referring to clearly meant her and, yeah, the team members who had been taking care of Barbara too. Weird, for sure, and much worse.

The show, with these changes, rambled on. Katie is trying to land a gig as a dancer on one of those teenage dance programs. Thankfully, this came to an end when Lauren O'Bryan was let go. Shortly after, Julia Campbell took over as Katie, and the character became more mature and appealing. Pru is paired with Rick Hyde, after he has a brief fling with Katie, and her missing older sister Dawn turns out to be Sydney Price.

One story that had interesting potential was a possible romance between Jacqueline and Laslo, whom Max loathed, after Joe's supposed death. She confesses to her father that she pretended to be pregnant. He forces her to fake a miscarriage to save face. She does and seethes when discovering that Siobhan is having Joe's baby, despite her denials and engagement to Bill. Later, Bill and Jacqueline stumble upon a secret surveillance room in the Dubujak mansion and are treated to a tape of Joe and Siobhan making love. Jacqueline turns to Laslo for support. The writers, however, could not make up their minds if they should romantically pair them up or not. Siobhan, meanwhile, finally admits the truth about who had fathered her baby. She gives birth to a boy and names him Sean Novak.

Gerit Quealy: I think it was Felicity LaFortune who said to me, "We expected Jacqueline to be very angular, with a sharp haircut." I thought, "OK, that's not me." I think it took me time to grow into being a mean character. I didn't see her that way because I felt that she had been manipulated from the very beginning by her father and by Joe. I had a huge amount of sympathy for her. Later, I never felt she was selfish, but it is an interesting trajectory to see somebody who is constantly manipulated by other people that she loves. There are ways you can go, and one is to be bitter and try to manipulate back. I don't think her trajectory was necessarily wrong, but it just took me a while to grow into it. I think the writers were trying to make her more of an Erica Kane kind of character. It took me a while to figure that out.

Laura Rakowitz: Daniel Pilon was an interesting fellow who was full of himself. I thought he played Max Dubujak very well, and the character was interesting. However, I don't think his castmates were happy with him because he thought of himself as the star of the show, and he was not. Perhaps he was treated like one. I do know that Joe Hardy liked him a lot.

He got along by the seat of his pants. Gerit Quealy would help him out with lines, and that was kind of her to do that because I don't think any of the regular cast would have helped him.

Fred Burstein: Daniel Pilon always looked at the teleprompter. He never bothered to memorize his lines. There was one time when I had to get somewhere after taping, and we were in a scene. He kept saying to the director, "I want to do it again. I want to do it again." I said to him, "What are you going to do to make it better? You've done it three times. You keep looking at the teleprompter. That is fine. We all want to get out of here." He was friendly, and we had some nice chats. But he thought he was the best actor in the world and was always talking about some movie he made with some famous actor.

Gerit Quealy: Daniel and I developed a very warm relationship. He comes from film, so I think the daily grind of memorizing lines every day was more of a challenge for him. I would often, while underneath the camera line, remind him of blocking—come toward me, go that way. Later on, I started to wonder if I should be more selfish as an actor and worry about my own thing. I tend to be, in general, a whole picture kind of person. I don't know if that is the best way to be as an actor because the director is there to be the whole picture kind of person.

Tamara Grady: That whole Max Dubujak story didn't add anything to the show. Daniel Pilon was very egocentric. He wasn't a particularly good actor and had a tough time remembering his lines, so there were a lot of delays. We were still using teleprompters at that time. But he was nice to me and once gave me a ride in his private plane. He flew me to Martha's Vineyard, which was great.

Fred Burstein: I am not sure if Daniel Pilon had trouble memorizing his lines (or even tried), but I know I did. I am not a good memorizer. The director would tell me, "You say this. Then you move over here behind the couch. Then you sit on this chair and then you go back behind the couch." I am like, "Okay, we walk into the room and then?" I would spend a long time going over the lines with my younger brother Bob, who I lived with in Brooklyn. It was a half-hour show, and I had a small part, but we would go over and over the lines. He would say in frustration, "You just did it five minutes ago! Don't you remember?" I'd reply, "Bob, don't get me upset. Just read me the lines and don't tell me how to say them."

Sometime in spring 1984, the controversial James Reilly joined the writing staff as a breakdown writer. He had previously held the same position on CBS's *Capitol*. He would go on to be the head writer on *Guiding Light* and *Days of Our Lives* and created the notorious soap *Passions*.

> **Martha Nochimson:** I remember James Reilly being brought in, but either it was later than May 1984 or he was in deep cover until later. All I remember is that I thought he was a terrible writer . . . Pat praised him as a writer, though I don't remember her being enthusiastic about his ideas for the show.

Around the same time, disheartened longtime fans finally had something to cheer about when word leaked that the show was bringing back Delia. However, instead of Ilene Kristen (ABC claimed she was unavailable) or Randall Edwards reprising the role, it was recast with Robin Mattson from *General Hospital*, no doubt as a ploy to attract fans from that soap. The third actress to play sociopath Heather Webber, she was so wonderful that she made the role her own. Unfortunately, that did not happen with Delia. The role was played previously by petite blondes, and Mattson was an attractive, statuesque brunette, making it visually off-putting for the audience. Also, her character was badly written as a blathering buffoon and given a dismal storyline to boot.

With typical Delia fanfare, she sends anonymous party invitations to her family and friends. At the designated spot, Delia reveals herself and that they are there to celebrate her fourth trip down the aisle—this time to a rich, older oilman named Matthew Crane (Harve Presnell). However, Delia is also carrying on a secret tryst with poor artist Steve Latham (Franc Luz), who followed her back East. Delia spends her honeymoon with Steve, forgetting to give Matthew his heart medication, and he winds up in the hospital. A panicky Delia frets that she will be charged with attempted murder.

> **Ilene Kristen:** The show never contacted me at this time to come back as Delia. If that is what they said, it was a lie.

Ron Hale: Ilene *was* Delia. I had to try to adjust to a few of them . . . knowing that none of them were going to be Ilene's Delia. It was up to me to pretend that they were and that they were the Delia that Roger had been dealing with all these years.

Laura Rakowitz: Robin Mattson was very miscast. However, there were times where I thought she was interesting, though I can't remember any specific moments. She wasn't totally off but just not right for the part.

Tamara Grady: Robin just wasn't Delia. It was not a good recast. As much as I liked Robin as a human being, at the time she was extremely nervous. She would hold on to her script right before the countdown. She just wasn't secure in that role.

Ron Hale: Robin Mattson was a fine actress and a nice gal, but she brought a totally different approach to the role. She was also physically wrong for the part. Ilene was this little whirlwind of a person. Her physicality was all part and parcel of the character with the jittery way she moved. Then you get somebody who is almost five feet nine inches and a couple of inches shorter than me. It was off-putting. Just asking the audience to accept it was tough.

Jadrien Steele: For the most part, I felt lucky to work with the actors who played my parents. However, for the life of me, I do not remember Robin Mattson playing my mother.

Geoff Pierson: I remember when Robin Mattson and Harve Presnell were there. Harve used to fly up from Virginia. He had his own plane and would land in New Jersey. He was not on that often and recurred for a few months. I so enjoyed working with Harve. Later, I did a TV pilot with him.

The return of Delia coincided with *Ryan's Hope* being evicted from its 12:30 p.m. time slot, its home since 1978. It was shifted to noon. This change was all due to Agnes Nixon, arguably the woman the show's fans hated the most. Her newest not-well-received soap, *Loving*, was floundering in the ratings in its late-morning berth, and she demanded the 12:30 time slot to have her creation be the lead off to her other soaps, *All My Children* and *One Life to Live*. The noon time slot, however, was undesirable because a lot of the affiliates aired local newscasts at the time. *The Doctors* on NBC was moved there in 1982 and withered away before being cancelled a year later.

Seymour Amlen: Agnes Nixon wanted to become a producer. She came up with a demand that ABC take her new show *Loving* and put it on the air. Jackie Smith did not want to lose her, so we did it in the late morning or at noon in some cities. A lot of the stations did not carry or delayed airing it because they had news shows on. They ran it late at night or early in the morning. Anyway, it was not doing well.

Then Nixon demanded ABC move *Loving* to 12:30 p.m. and *Ryan's Hope* to noon. The other networks were after Nixon to come join them. It became up to management to decide what to do. I argued strenuously not to do it. If we had to lose Nixon, so be it. Jackie was sort of on my side but a little ambivalent because she wanted Nixon to stay. Fred Pierce, who was the head of ABC at that time, and who I worked with previously in research, came down on the side of keeping Nixon. The time slot switch was made. And, of course, that was the end of *Ryan's Hope*. It was also ironically the end of *Loving* because it did far worse at 12:30 than *Ryan's Hope*.

Art Rutter: I was still friendly with people working on *Ryan's Hope*, and they were very unhappy about the change. I also heard a lot of bitching and moaning about this from the programming people who worked on my floor at ABC. I can see Seymour's point, but Agnes Nixon was Jackie's meal ticket. ABC had a very successful run with her soaps, which were huge then. Nixon was such a superstar that Jackie was afraid to lose her for obvious reasons. Could other people have stepped in? Sure, but why?

A friend of mine had gone from working in ABC prime time to the number-two guy at NBC daytime. He reported to Brian Frons, who was recruited [in 1983] to beef up their daytime schedule since they were not doing well in the ratings. Brian was a very aggressive guy—a pit bull. He may have been whispering in the ear of Agnes Nixon because that is something Brian would do. It could have been a one-two combination from Agnes of "this is what I want, and if I do not get it, I'm leaving." NBC was welcoming stars with open arms then because they needed to counter ABC, which was so powerful in daytime.

Ron Hale: We knew exactly what was happening. Agnes Nixon was pulling a power play. She did not like Claire Labine because Claire came out with a show that just kicked everybody's butt. It was so much finer than "All My Kids"—from the reality, the honesty, and the quality of the acting. It was no secret how Agnes felt about Claire. If there was a function and the two of them were in attendance, Claire would nod her head, and Agnes would just turn and walk away. There was no love lost there, and I think it mainly came from Agnes.

Helen Gallagher: The time slot switch was the undoing of our show. Agnes Nixon wanted our time slot because in the Midwest that is when they would take lunch. She wanted her show to air when we did. She got it, and that was the start of the end for *Ryan's Hope.*

Laura Rakowitz: We were all miserable about the time slot change—not only miserable but furious. We thought that was the death knell. In those days it took a long time to get a soap opera off the air. We didn't know how much longer the show was going to last. The minute ABC acquiesced to Agnes Nixon (who I don't hold anything against because I understand what she wanted to do), it was the beginning of the end for *Ryan's Hope.* It was a terrible thing to have happened.

Geoff Pierson: The time slot change was—I do not want to say a death knell—but considered a particularly challenging move in a negative way for us. Everybody was aware of it, and everybody thought they were—I do not want to say sabotaging the show—but ABC was putting the show in a downward spiral. It was going to be almost impossible to compete there at noon. That was the consensus among us anyway. Perhaps some felt that maybe we would do fine there, but even so it was not a positive move for the show.

Tamara Grady: We lost many viewers then because a lot of stations had newscasts at twelve. We dealt with fear of being cancelled for about five years. Once they switched the time slot, that was the prevailing mood. There was no shock when we finally did get cancelled.

Malcolm Groome: This was the early death knell for the show. We lost a lot of our markets when they moved our time. We felt bruised by that. ABC was favoring Agnes Nixon and all her shows as well they should have. She was a big moneymaker for them, and we knew it was her power play they got us moved. *Ryan's Hope* got pushed to the side because of it. We were not happy about it. Our ratings went down because we were not nationwide anymore. However, our ratings were still high where we were shown, and especially in New York, where we were always popular.

Ron Hale: We were not dumb and knew that our time slot was a great lead-in to *All My Children*. Once they moved the show, we all said that the handwriting is on the wall and we aren't going to be around much longer. We knew it was just death.

Gerit Quealy: The morale was not good. Everybody was very upset about the time slot change, and rightly so. That was when we started to lose our audience because they couldn't or had a tough time finding us because we were on in various times in different markets. I know it was on after *General Hospital* in some places. That is when the foothold was really lost.

Cali Timmins: I almost felt that ABC was giving up on us. It felt like the fight was over. Everybody was devastated about this change. At the time, I did not understand what this really meant, but it was definitely a dark day when we found out. The fan base was so incredibly loyal for so long, even until this day. ABC just didn't get the show's audience. Once they made the switch, every day the cast was aware that *Loving* was not doing as well in the ratings. I, personally, never checked ratings once the whole time I was there. I think Ron Hale did, though.

Fred Burstein: My wife had my daughter shortly after the time slot change. She was in the hospital, and the nurses recognized me. One said, "Now that the show is on at noon, we can watch you every day." That was neat. I never heard anybody say to me that they used to watch but couldn't any more due to the switch.

In the middle of the year, Joanna Coons, of *Soap Opera Digest*, interviewed Pat Falken Smith, who defended her creative decisions. The head writer revealed that all her major changes to the soap happened because "ABC conducted a

In 1984, ABC foolishly transitioned the show away from the Ryan and Coleridge families, which was reflected in the new opening titles and its promotional photos. Pictured are (left to right, top to bottom) Maeve (Helen Gallagher) and Johnny Ryan (Bernie Barrow) on a tandem bicycle; bad-girl-gone-good Maggie Shelby (Cali Timmins) and Dave Greenberg (Scott Holmes); Jill Coleridge (Nancy Addison) with her biological mother, Bess Shelby (Gloria DeHaven); detective Bill Hyde (David Sederholm); tycoon Max Dubujak (Daniel Pilon) and his headstrong daughter, Jacqueline Dubujak Novak (Gerit Quealy); Katie Thompson (Lauren O'Bryan), Maggie Shelby (Cali Timmins), and Pru Shepherd (Traci Lin) roller skating; hayseed Pru Shepherd (Traci Lin); and glamorous TV news producer Sydney Price (Robin Greer), 1984. ©ABC

Laslo Nivotny (Fred Burstein) was Joe Novak's cousin with ties to his crime family
so Laslo's motives were always in question, ca. 1984.
Photograph by Michael Weisbrot. Courtesy of Fred Burstein

Ron Hale, associate director Laura Rakowitz, lighting director John Connolly, and unidentified crew members working on the Greenberg's Deli set, 1984. *Courtesy of Laura Rakowitz*

Duncan Gamble, as sleazy manager Tiger Bennett, and Cali Timmins, as the scheming Maggie, attend a charity costume ball, 1985. *Courtesy of Laura Rakowitz*

Bernie Barrow, Helen Gallagher, and Malcolm Groome in costume at the charity event, 1985.
Courtesy of Laura Rakowitz

Scott Holmes (Dave) and stage manager Tamara Grady with Marg Helgenberger (Siobhan),
Grant Show (Rick Hyde), and Yasmine Bleeth (Ryan Fenelli) in the background, 1985.
Courtesy of Laura Rakowitz

Felicity LaFortune (Leigh Kirkland) and Michael Levin (Jack) make a handsome couple at the ball, 198
Courtesy of Laura Rakowitz

Executive producer Joseph Hardy clowns for the camera, ca. 1985. *Courtesy of Laura Rakowitz*

Fans were thrilled when Roscoe Born reprised the role of reformed mobster Joe Novak, who returned to Riverside in 1988 when he suspected that Max Dubujak survived the fall into the raging river the year prior. ©ABC

Christopher Durham's last scene as Dakota Smith exits his office and the show, 1988.
Photo by Laura Rakowitz. *Courtesy of Christopher Durham*

Ron Hale and Ilene Kristen shooting Roger and Delia's second trip down the aisle, 1988.
Courtesy of Laura Rakowitz

Bernie Barrow and Helen Gallagher on set for the wedding of Roger and Delia, 1988.
Courtesy of Laura Rakowitz

Catherine Larson
(Lizzie Ransome)
and James Wlcek
(Ben), 1988.
*Courtesy of
Laura Rakowitz*

Group portrait from the last day of filming *Ryan's Hope*. Clockwise from bottom left: Michael Levin, Karen Morris-Gowdy, Frank Perkins, Earl Hindman, Ron Hale, Malcolm Groome, Laura Rakowitz, Helen Gallagher, and Bernie Barrow. *Courtesy of Laura Rakowitz*

Jason "Ash" Adams (John Ryan) with makeup artist Michele Bruno
on the final day of shooting *Ryan's Hope*, 1988. *Courtesy of Laura Rakowitz*

Ryan's Hope's last cast photo, 1988. First row: Bernie Barrow (Johnny), Helen Gallagher (Maeve), Yasmine Bleeth (Ryan Fenelli), Michael Levin (Jack), Caroline Wilde (Grace Coleridge), Felicity LaFortune (Leigh), Ilene Kristen (Delia), Rosemary Prinz (Sister Mary Joel), and Tichina Arnol (Zena Brown). Second row: John Gabriel (Seneca), Maria Pitillo (Nancy Don Louis), Lois Robbins (Concetta D'Angelo), Malcolm Groome (Patrick), Nancy Addison (Jill), Karen Morris-Gowdy (Faith) Ron Hale (Roger), Barbara Blackburn (Siobhan), and Casey Biggs (Fenno Moore). Third row: Brian McGovern (Chaz Saybrook), Diana van der Vlis (Sherry Rowan), unidentified woma Catherine Larson (Lizzie), James Wlcek (Ben), and Jason "Ash" Adams (John). Fourth row: Keith Charles (Dowd), Malachy McCourt (Kevin), Steve Fletcher (Matthew Strand), and Lydia Hannibal (Chris Hannold). Fifth row: Earl Hindman (Bob), John Sanderford (Frank), and Irving Allen Lee (Dr. Evan Cooper). Sixth row: Michael Palance (Rob Rowan), unidentified actor and Dick Briggs (Mendenhall). Top row: Frank Perkins (Father McShane). ©ABC

rl Hindman, Thomas MacGreevy, Ilene Kristen, Malcolm Groome, Ron Hale, and Jason "Ash" Adams in Los Angeles, ca. early 1990s. *Courtesy of Ilene Kristen*

Ilene Kristen, Claire Labine, Joan Barrow (Bernie Barrow's wife), Karen Morris-Gowdy, Helen Gallagher, and Nancy Addison, ca. late 1990s. *Courtesy of Ilene Kristen*

Paul Avila Mayer and Brian McGovern in Los Angeles, ca. early 2000s.
Courtesy of Brian McGovern

focus session and the apathy of the audience was tremendous ... The consensus: *Ryan's Hope* was an okay show, but nothing much happened. That's death!" Smith admitted that her plots and focus on new, younger characters caused a stir with the audience. She stated, "They either love what I am doing or they hate it—but they are passionate about it and that's good." Based on the declining ratings, this was not good, and the passionate fans were tuning out.

Other than the Matthew/Delia/Steve triangle, the remainder of 1984 was dominated by the convoluted storyline that Smith dished up involving Maggie insinuating herself into Max's life when Jack asked her to spy on him. Dubujak is involved in a mysterious plot called Operation Eagle, which involved collecting portions of an old coin. Maggie agrees to keep tabs on him mainly to keep Max's attention from Jill, even if it jeopardizes her romance with Dave. She selflessly does this because of the guilt she feels for loving her sister's husband, despite Jill tossing her out on her ear.

As this played out for six months, Jacqueline and Jeremy Winthrop begin a romance that makes Laslo jealous and that Max wants to use to his advantage; Sydney's identity is revealed to all, including Pru, and she warns Maggie that she is playing a dangerous game with Max. Jacqueline's butler, Prince, is murdered; Jack discovers a portion of the coin that Max desperately wants. Dave calls off his engagement to Maggie, who takes one for the team and hops in the sack with Max to prove her loyalty, and Frank agrees to help Jack nail Max and free Maggie from his clutches. In the height of lunacy, the audience is supposed to believe that Maggie can send Dave cryptic messages via the daily newspaper's crossword puzzle.

Cali Timmins: I really did not understand the Maggie/Max storyline. This was probably the hardest time on the show for me because it got a lot of airplay. I remember Geoff Pierson saying they are sort of redoing the movie *Gaslight*. It was very convoluted and mixed up. I was very frustrated. I had been working with Geoff— and nothing against Daniel Pilon—but he had a different style of acting than I was used to. He was not interested in finding out what the heck is going on in the scene, as I was, and making it make sense. You want to make it as real as possible, but that was hard in those scenes. I didn't get what was going on, and I was getting annoyed trying to justify my character's actions being around some dangerous people. And being afraid of and being intimidated so much by this guy. I knew Max was rich, but I could never figure out if he was a nice guy or a bad guy or what. It was the only time I thought my storyline was going off the rails.

The show suffered another blow when it was put on hiatus for a few weeks because ABC purchased the broadcast rights to the 1984 Summer Olympics. Seeming to confirm where it stood with the network, *Ryan's Hope* (along with the other two half-hour soaps, *Loving* and *The Edge of Night*) was preempted for the entire time, while ABC's three hour-long shows were not. This contributed to audience deterioration, which had already begun with the time slot change a few months earlier.

When the show resumed airing, the Maggie/Max story begins to wrap up. Dave learns why Maggie is doing what she is doing with Max and explains it to Laslo and the dumbfounded audience: "He's [Max] out to corner the gold market. That's the only reason Maggie's there. To stop him. The night she was supposed to meet me at St. Pat's—she heard how he was going to frame Jill and Frank if the Feds got wise to him. So, she stayed to get proof . . . to save them."

When Jacqueline realizes Maggie is spying on Max, Laslo and Dave kidnap her, and she eventually falls into bed with Laslo. After Dubujak's jet blows up, passengers Frank and Maggie are presumed dead, as is Max, who had bribed an airport official to state he was on board. Frank and Maggie escape from the burning wreckage and spend the night on a deserted beach. Max discovers that Hutch had killed Joe and planted the bomb meant for him. Max tosses the coin into the river and admits to Jack that he was only going along with Operation Eagle to find out who killed his son-in-law. Rather than face the music for his crimes, Hutch commits suicide. Once the survivors are found, Maggie rebuffs Max and runs into Dave's arms, while Frank refuses to reconcile with Jill after catching her in a clinch with Max.

> **Fred Burstein:** Scott Holmes was a singer and working on Broadway while we were doing the show. I had a scene where I am alone in my apartment and I had to think some things over. Jacqueline came to my door, and then I pick her up with one arm and carry her into the bedroom. Scott called me up that night and said, "I do not usually do this, but I had to tell you that your scene was great." I said, "Wow, thank you. I will never forget that you said that." And I haven't and I won't.

Gerit Quealy: You can get a script one day and not like something. I did balk when they had Jacqueline go after Laslo, and she was supposed to sleep with him. I was upset about that because I felt my character wouldn't do that. Though, looking back, I should have accepted it and just figured out in my own head why she would do that. It was confusing and tough for me at the time. It shouldn't have been, though. I wasn't happy about it, but there you are.

Cali Timmins: When Frank and Maggie were in that plane crash, there was this whole complicated scene with Frank trying to rescue us, and he had to open the plane's door. He is pulling on it to open, and the whole door came off. They never edited it out.

New stories included Sydney writing a book about Max that he wants stopped and Siobhan investigating the Santa slasher. The one most appreciated by the core audience was the reopening of Ryan's Bar on Thanksgiving Day. After months of being subjugated to scenes at Greenberg's Deli, the entire Ryan family is front and center, celebrating the holiday in their renovated establishment. Changes included an all-tile kitchen, a brand-new bar, and a new half wall dividing the bar area from the dining room. The show had not seen all the core Ryan family characters together like this for a long time.

By the end of 1984, ABC's overall daytime ratings dropped from a 7.2 rating, 24 share for 1983 to a 5.5 rating, 19 share. The network also hemorrhaged female viewers, losing 450,000 viewers in the Women 18–49 Demo and 420,000 viewers in the Women 25–54 Demo. As for *Ryan's Hope* individually, it averaged for the year a 5.0 rating, 12 share. It was down almost 2 ratings points and 5 shares from the prior year when it aired at 12:30 p.m. in most parts of the country. This decline should not have been a total surprise to the network due to its boneheaded decision to save *Loving* and switch *Ryan's Hope* to the undesirable noon time slot, where it lost affiliates. And Pat Falken Smith's wonky storylines did not help the situation in the least.

With the ratings sinking, ABC finally realized that what was transpiring on screen was not working and was not what the audience expected from *Ryan's Hope*. Characters that Smith created were slowly being phased out. First to go was Rico, whose biological mother thankfully showed up to reclaim her annoying son and take him away. The character of Jeremy Winthrop had potential, but he was unfortunately sent packing, as was Laslo, who just temporarily disappeared from the show, leaving Jacqueline without a romantic partner. Despite a new romance brewing between Matthew and Bess Shelby, and Delia now wanting her husband back, the storyline was cut short. It was adios to Delia, Matthew, and Steve Latham. It was reported that Robin Mattson did not cotton to the East Coast (just as most of the audience did not cotton to her), and she and Delia returned west. Frustratingly, the pathetic Pru Shepherd still remained on the canvas.

Moving forward, Joe Hardy and his writing team needed to make some drastic changes in 1985 if they wanted to save the show and rebound in the ratings—or at least not hemorrhage any more viewers.

8
The Ryans Rise Again, 1985–86

I t seems Joe Hardy finally took charge in the direction of *Ryan's Hope*. As he said, when he was hired, he was asked to implement whatever changes in the show that ABC dictated. Audience unrest and dropping ratings proved that the viewers were not interested in what the network served up. Perhaps finally realizing that *Ryan's Hope* could never be *General Hospital*, they let Hardy take the lead to revitalize the show. The first change was the exodus of head writer Pat Falken Smith. She was replaced by former actress Millee Taggart (ex-Janet Bergman, *Search for Tomorrow*, 1971–1982) and Tom King. Taggart became a writer for *Search for Tomorrow*, and King had worked on *For Richer, for Poorer*. They both worked together on *As the World Turns*. As head writers for *Ryan's Hope*, they did not have carte blanche, however, as ABC executives still interjected ideas and had a say over storylines.

> **Joseph Hardy:** I don't recall anything special about Pat Falken Smith other than that she did not last very long. I fired her.
>
> **Tom King (co-head writer):** On *As the World Turns*, I was paired up with a guy named John Saffron. I didn't like him, and I didn't like working with him. I would go to his apartment and he had no books, and I thought, "This is not my kind of person." I also did not think he was a very good writer. When I talked about the soap characters, they were like real people. He would be like, "On this date, John boffs Lila." I thought it was disrespectful to the characters and destroyed my fantasy of what we were doing.
>
> I was about to quit when he was diagnosed with a brain tumor and had to leave. I was now in the position of head writing the show

by myself, which I didn't like to do for an hour show. It is just too much work. I had gotten to know Millee Taggart when we were both script writers. I found her funny and talented. I called her up and asked, "How would you like to be the co-head writer?" I cleared it with Procter & Gamble and the producer, who I think was Mary Ellis-Bunim at the time. We went ahead from there, and Millee was delightful to work with. I enjoyed it.

Millee Taggart (co-head writer): *Ryan's Hope* was my favorite soap opera. I loved it because it was in the manner of *Guiding Light* and *As the World Turns*—character-based family drama. There were no explosions or people buried alive like some were doing at that time. I was so thrilled to get this offer and could not wait to start. I had worked with Joe Hardy before and so had Tom King. He hired us. I loved working with Joe and absolutely adored him.

You have to have a great deal of trust and hire writers who were meant to write *Ryan's Hope*. For me, it was the kind of soap I just loved writing. However, it had lost its humor. It lost its personality. Soaps had become cash cows. It was awful, especially for a show like *Ryan's Hope*.

Tom King: I had watched *Ryan's Hope* because it was touted as a different kind of show, and I was curious. I liked it and thought it was good. And it was different. It was more like a play.

Seymour Amlen: I would not say *Ryan's Hope* was a better-quality show than *Loving*. How do you judge that? Any new soap you put on generally took a long time to generate an audience, regardless how good or bad they were. It was just the nature of the beast.

Tom King: I thought it was a mistake by the previous writing team, who took the focus off the Ryan family. Some soap head writers are very egocentric and thought they could save the world.

Millee Taggart: At our first story meeting with ABC, one of the network people who was hired to pep up *Ryan's Hope*—not Jackie Smith—sat at the conference table and said, "I see a woman in a padded cell." I asked her, "What is she doing?" She responded, "You take it from there." That was my introduction to the family-driven *Ryan's Hope*.

Tom King: Jackie Smith and I got along very well. She was hated by writers—they just despised her. I liked her, so I don't know why that was. I thought she was good at what she did and never gave me any problems.

Millee Taggart: Our relationship with Jackie Smith was great. I liked working with her. She was a wackadoodle, as we all know. One thing I loved about Jackie is that she would wear the same outfit to work every day for a week. Usually, it was a white skirt and a white sweater, possibly with different jewelry. I once asked her why and she said, "First of all, no one will know if I stayed out overnight, and I do not have to think about what to wear each day because I always know what it will be." I am sure she had several of these same outfits. She never interfered with our storylines.

Tom King: It was funny how those executives were. Her second-in-command was just horrible. She took over for Jackie Smith when she developed a brain tumor. I will never forget what Jackie said when she had to have a second operation and refused to have it, which meant she was going to die. Claire Labine said to her, "Jackie, what in the world?! Why don't you have the surgery?" Jackie replied, "Because I can hear the drill."

Millee Taggart: I, too, have erased Jackie's colleague's name from my memory bank. She was the one who came up with the woman in the padded cell. I know she had black hair, medium length. It was not Josie Emmerich.

Tom King: Joe Hardy was good to collaborate with. He was very open. The only thing I did not care for was his taste in casting. It seemed to me if you had five finalists for an actress job, he was always in favor of my least favorite. I did not like his taste in actors. Millee was usually in agreement with me. I would be in favor of one, and he would always want someone else. It was strange.

Millee Taggart: I did not have that same experience with Joe Hardy with casting. He was a very strong man. He always stood between Tom and me and the network. He did that too when we all worked on *Loving* later. If Joe liked you and believed in your work, which he did with us, then he had your back.

Joseph Hardy: I would meet with Jackie Smith and other ABC executives on a regular basis to discuss plots. They were usually agreeable, and Jackie was fine. I know there were storylines that I wanted to do that ABC said no to, but I cannot remember exactly what they were.

Cast firings at this time included Robin Greer as Sydney Price, who took a screaming header off Max Dubujak's balcony while she was snooping for juicy intel on the tycoon for her upcoming tell-all book. This set up a murder mystery that would last throughout the summer. Veteran Earl Hindman was let go, and his Bob Reid relocated to San Diego to be closer to his sister, Delia. Shortly after, original cast members John Gabriel as Dr. Seneca Beulac and Jadrien Steele as Little John Ryan departed without much fanfare. Jadrien just disappeared from the show with only a mention from a disbelieving Frank that his son opted to go off to live with Delia in San Diego.

Tom King: It is not always the head writers' decision to get rid of somebody. Quite often with a character like Seneca, the actor does not want to re-sign, and you would have to recast. Sometimes if the character was very emblematic, you just decide to kill them off or have them leave town.

Eventually, most of Pat Falken Smith's writing staff, including Martha Nochimson, were let go too. This is not a surprise since most head writers want to bring in their own team, who they know and feel comfortable working with. However, her firing had more to do with Joe Hardy.

Martha Nochimson: I knew my days were numbered on the show when during a writers' meeting I said something—I can't remember what it was—and Joe lashed out at me ... And it was over just as suddenly as it began. But I knew that Pat was really trying to get rid of me and that she had done an Iago on Joe, stoking his suspicions about me. When he fired me, he graciously said that no one could have done the consulting job I was contracted for. I appreciated that. And it was also true that I couldn't stop myself from trying all kinds of experimental things in my own scripts. I had gotten a lot of good feedback from the cast, but all in all, I wasn't useful to Joe in the way he expected.

My time on *Ryan's Hope* changed my professional life. It was a springboard to numerous academic opportunities [Her books include *No End to Her: Soap Opera and the Female Subject* and *Television Rewired: The Rise of the Auteur Series*, and articles for *Film Quarterly*, *Cineaste*, etc.] as well as television writing opportunities. Mary Munisteri invited me to join her team when she became the head writer of *Guiding Light* [in 1986]. Joe Hardy changed my life by taking a risk on me. I doubt he would remember me, but if he did, it would be a negative memory, I feel quite sure. However, I remain grateful to him. It isn't always the people you love who get you your breaks in life. Pat was a living textbook for me. She really impressed me with what the industry could do to a smart, talented woman. I think things are better now, and, maybe in her day, were better for other women.

With what transpired on screen in 1984 under Pat Falken Smith's head writing tenure, it was unsurprising come Emmy Award time that *Ryan's Hope* did not receive a single nomination for the 1984 to 1985 period. This was the first time since the acclaimed show began that it was totally snubbed by the Academy. To say that ABC and Smith, and to a degree Joe Hardy, had tarnished the show is an understatement. Ratings-wise, *Ryan's Hope* tumbled down to a 3.4 rating from a 5.0 the year before. With the network's cancellation of *The Edge of Night* in late 1984, *Ryan's Hope* was now ABC's lowest-rated serial.

The Dubujak family would dominate the show for the next nine months. Laslo Nivotny reappeared and a new character on the scene, sort of, was Ryan Fenelli (now played by Yasmine Bleeth). Last seen as a six-year-old, Ryan contracted Soap Opera Rapid Aging Syndrome (SORAS) and emerged as a fifteen-year-old who flees the Catholic boarding school that she is attending. Jack allows her to stay in Riverside, and she pals around with teen delinquent DJ LaSalle (Christian Slater, son of actor Michael Hawkins and casting agent Mary Jo Slater) while lusting after the older Rick Hyde. He has ditched Pru and is attracted to Jacqueline, who is way out of his league. Even so, a romance blossoms, but it falls apart when Rick suddenly leaves town to secretly attend the police academy.

Tom King: Aging children used to be commonly done. We needed network approval before we could do this. Usually, you would trot child actors on, and they would say a few lines and then they would be trotted off again. You couldn't do much with them.

Millee Taggart: Everybody wanted a young storyline, but you cannot do much with a character between seven and sixteen years old. People were used to this sort of thing. Yasmine was wonderful. She was beautiful and insightful and vulnerable. She never disappointed. She never threw tantrums. I just loved her. I've been an actor myself and am very sensitive to people's work. She was a joy. After I left the show, I was in touch with her after we both moved out to California. She was gorgeous but still vulnerable and having a challenging time making her way.

Tamara Grady: Aging of children happens a lot on soaps, and it is ridiculous. I happened to have loved Jenny Dweir. She was adorable. I don't know whatever happened to her. Yasmine Bleeth was a good little actress, though.

Laura Rakowitz: They eventually need to age these young characters. I understand they want to attract the young adult audience who may have been watching with their mothers when they were children. I get that, so the SORASing of Ryan and later Little John didn't bother me so much.

Malcolm Groome: What can you do but accept that? Interesting that they age them so quickly. Yasmine was so precious on the show. We understood it and moved on.

Michael Levin: Yasmine Bleeth was very sweet and pretty.

Fred Burstein: It is funny. I really did not make any real connections with any of the actors. Christian Slater was about fifteen when he came on the show. I think his mother was a big agent. I used to talk with him sometimes. I said something to him once, and he brushed me off.

I overheard Yasmine Bleeth once say, "Why do I have to work with Laslo? Why do I have to work with that old man?" I was, like, thirty-four. She wanted to work with Christian Slater.

Millee Taggart: We knew that Christian Slater would become a star because he was such a good actor. We cast Christian and Yasmine together, but he was a kind of a hard sell. We wanted him because he was not traditionally handsome—probably still isn't. In those days, they wanted Barbie and Ken. But Christian could act. I thought their storylines were wonderful. We really loved having him on the show, and DJ was a great character. Christian could take a sentence and make it matter. I can't recall why he left.

Tom King: I had no interaction with Christian. He was a good actor, but he got into some trouble, so he was written off the show.

Since he had motive and Sydney was pushed off his balcony, Max is arrested for her murder. He hires Jill to represent him, unaware that her estranged husband, now working in the district attorney's office, is assigned to prosecute. During this period, Siobhan keeps dreaming of a mystery lover. When she realizes it is Max, she accepts a date with Laslo to try to shake her feelings for the tycoon. It does not work. At a fancy charity costume ball, Siobhan dances with Max, and the romantic sparks fly. This was one of the soap's most elaborate set pieces since the Egyptian Ball from back in 1981. The cast was costumed to the nines in outfits ranging from nuns and flappers to leprechauns and Henry VIII. All heads turn when Maggie arrives dressed as Cleopatra on the arm of slick, fast-talking Tiger Bennett (Duncan Gamble), costumed as Mark Antony, her new boss at the cosmetic company where she is now modeling.

> **Duncan Gamble (Tiger Bennett):** I had previously met Joe Hardy a few times out in California. He was a really good guy, but I am not sure if he specifically asked for me to audition or if my agency at the time submitted me in for the part. I was living in LA, and I had been an original cast member on *Capitol*. I tested with this cute young girl named Cali Timmins. It was one of those really fun kinds of scenes where I was this big, hot shot, rich guy who wanted to represent her because I had a modeling job for her, but only if she slept with me. I then seduced her while we are talking about her upcoming wedding to Dave Greenberg. The scene was such a riot because Tiger was such an asshole but a nice guy. We just got right into it. I thought, "This is way too fun."
>
> After we finished the scene, Joe and Felicia Minei Behr came out of the booth, laughing. I got the part and had real fun with it. Later I remember meeting Millee Taggart and Tom King, who seemed to be open in receiving actors. Tiger was such an interesting

character the way they brought him in—this very rich guy throwing his money around.

When I got the job, I was very excited, but I had very straight, thin hair. I decided to go to a salon to get a little body added to it. Somebody recommended a hair stylist on Madison Avenue, and I went. I asked for a light perm. I was always fighting with my hair because it was so thin and just laid flat. The stylist left the product in too long, and I came home with a frizz because he couldn't get it out. I did what I could to straighten it out and cut it shorter. I showed up for work on my first day, which was the costume party episode, and Felicia Minei Behr looked at me and asked, "What did you do to your hair?!" I was so embarrassed and humiliated. She laughed and said, "Fortunately, you are playing Caesar, so it will really work."

When Max is found not guilty, the verdict sends Sydney's grieving sister, Pru (who was temporarily staying with the Ryans), over the edge. Wild-eyed and out of control, she swipes Siobhan's gun and holds Max at gunpoint after crashing a party at his home. She was ready to show him some country justice. Max is gently able to talk her down, and Siobhan is impressed with this sensitive side of him. With nothing keeping her in New York City, Pru returns to Dogpatch or Hooterville or wherever she supposedly came from. The character was finally, and thankfully, written out.

Millee Taggart: Siobhan was a wonderful character, and Marg Helgenberger was an excellent actress—very quirky. I remember that we talked about how she was everything that Daniel was not and vice versa. Max was sleek and European and cosmopolitan. Siobhan was a no-nonsense, redheaded Irish girl who grew up living over a bar. I love opposites falling in love.

Laura Rakowitz: We thought the pairing of Max and Siobhan was like the Aristotle Onassis and Jackie Kennedy love story. Siobhan was on the rebound too. I was a little surprised with this romance, but Marg was so good she made it work. Daniel didn't. Most of the cast didn't like this story, but I didn't mind it as much only because I loved watching Marg with a character nobody else liked or wanted to see her with. She made it believable.

Dave Greenberg, meanwhile, ditches the pastrami and rye to concentrate on his music career as a songwriter. This brings him closer in friendship with Maeve and Johnny's granddaughter Katie, who is pursuing her theatrical dreams too. They then find themselves working together on a stage show. Believing in his talent, Katie crashes a recording session for Johnny Mathis to demo one of Dave's songs. Impressed, the vocalist agrees to record it and include it on his next album.

Katie finds herself falling for Dave, who is smitten with her as well, although he and Maggie are still engaged to be married. Maggie, meanwhile, has been neglecting Dave as she enjoys the glamorous life as a model and traveling with Tiger. Although she has rebuked Tiger's advances in the past, this time they have a fling while away on a shoot. Tiger then plots to steal her away from Dave for good. Maggie confesses to Katie what she did, unaware that her best friend is in love with Dave.

> **Duncan Gamble:** Cali Timmins and Scott Holmes were great to work with. Cali was a very sweet girl. I was about thirty-seven, and she was in her early twenties, I think. I remember her talking about her aspirations and dreams. Scott was just a salt-of-the-earth type of guy. I had met Gloria DeHaven in California. She was just down-home people and wonderful to work with.
>
> There was just a good vibe about the whole company. They had a real quality about the work. Everybody in the cast was very nice to me and took me in right away, even though I was an out-of-town guy from California. The cast was an ensemble, and it was like all-for-one. It was not like the big stars were over here, and everybody else was over there. They made you feel like you were part of the family.

Although she knows they are through, Maggie is too prideful to give up Dave to her rival, so she lies that she is pregnant. The June wedding remains on the calendar while Maggie scrambles to get with child. Roger volunteers, but Maggie picks Tiger. He agrees, even though he is mad that she chose to marry Dave. They hop into the sack again, but scheming Maggie fumes when a spiteful Tiger announces he has had a vasectomy. Roger then suggests she pretend to be pregnant and fake a miscarriage after the nuptials— probably recalling what his devious ex-wife Delia had done to Pat.

It was at this point that, not surprisingly, the criminally underused Felicity LaFortune as Leigh Kirkland was given her walking papers. Her character returns to San Francisco to get married. Maggie weds Dave and, taking Roger's advice, goes one better and ropes in an unsuspecting Katie to make it look like she had pushed her down a flight of stairs during an argument. However, the plan goes aslant when Katie takes the tumble, not Maggie. All is good when Katie awakes with no memory of the accident. Roger offers to make her short-term amnesia permanent if Maggie makes him her manager. She agrees, and he performs hypnosis on Katie. Dave and Pat suspect something is afoul when Maeve informs them that Roger and Maggie keep hanging around Katie's bedside. After learning that Roger is now Maggie's manager, Tiger fires Maggie and cuts off all ties to her, vowing that Roger will ruin her modeling career. Katie has a memory breakthrough, thanks to Pat. She goes right to Dave with the truth.

> **Duncan Gamble:** I really liked the writing on this show. Oftentimes soap opera writers don't write dialogue that is easy to memorize or say because it is not really real. Here, they were very good about writing the way people actually talk. Bad writing for actors is very hard to learn and even harder to say. I still recall they wrote very good dialogue.
>
> My wife, Jane Daly, is an actress and was pregnant when we moved from California to New York after I got the part of Tiger. She had our son and then wanted to resume her career. We were living in Connecticut, so she came into town to talk to agents. She stepped over a couple of bums and some dog shit and had to jump out of the way of a firetruck. She came home and said, "We have to get back to California."
>
> The next thirteen-week cycle of my contract came up, and I went in to talk to Joe Hardy and Felicia Minei Behr. I didn't know if they were going to re-up me or not. We had a very frank discussion about the future of the show. They weren't sure how much longer *Ryan's Hope* was going to be on the air because of that time slot change. If I wanted to leave to go back to California, it was a go because my future may not have been on the show anyway—that was the kind of feeling I was getting. They didn't pick up my next option, and I went back West. I don't recall having any special last episode. I think Tiger was just not heard from again.

In one of the best and well-acted breakup scenes from the soap, Dave, after spending time apart from his scheming wife, goes to the loft to ask her for a divorce. Maggie at first balks and tries to reconcile with him, but seeing it is futile reluctantly agrees. Dave leaves, and then she decides to kill herself to ruin Dave and Katie's lives. She is stopped by Dave when he returns. After hearing her sob story and realizing she only wants to make him feel guilty for leaving her, Dave says, "I just never figured you for a loser. The Maggie I knew wasn't a quitter. She was a fighter, not a coward. You said it yourself. Things change, and you changed, Maggie."

This does the trick, and the feisty, selfish Maggie reveals herself to Dave, to the audience's delight. A riled-up Maggie flushes the pills, packs her bags while calling the loft "a dump," and exits with, "You never could keep your eye on the ball. You just keep your eye on me, Dave. Watch my dust. Oh, for the record, I *hate* pastrami." This, thankfully, puts the nail in the coffin to scenes at Greenberg's Deli.

> **Millee Taggart:** I wish I could say with a great deal of certainty whose idea it was to turn Maggie back into a schemer. I can say we never wrote anything that Joe Hardy did not agree with. He was not a producer you could say that I really need to tell this story when he opposed it. We were a team.

> **Tom King:** Vixens are much more interesting. Good characters are boring. Cali Timmins was so much better playing the bad girl. Joe usually agreed with our ideas. Sometimes he had ideas of his own, and we would develop those.

> **Cali Timmins:** I think scheming Maggie was more fun to play and more the real Maggie. That's who she was. I got to chew the scenery a little more. I remember complaining prior that Maggie lost her drive and fun.

> **Ron Hale:** I don't think happy was the right word for my feelings at the time but more that maybe there is a chance the new head writers were going to do something that was recognizable.

> **Tom King:** We never knew what the actors felt because it is true, they are told not to interact with the writers. Actors tended to want more stories or a bigger story to be in the spotlight. You couldn't please everybody.

> **Millee Taggart:** Tom and I usually agreed on storylines. We would go to the office we had in the studio, but we mostly worked from our homes. At that time, it was the way it was done by soap writers.

Tom King: Millee and I always had an office somewhere. I think we communicated with the staff writers by phone. We'd send the outlines and then call them up to talk them through it. We'd take any questions, suggestions, and so forth. There were never any writers' meetings around a table, which is the way it became later.

Siobhan's mishandling of the Max investigation gets her temporarily suspended from the police force. She and Max continue to grow closer, much to their families' displeasure. Lying to her parents that she is vacationing alone, Siobhan jets off with Max to his childhood chateau in France, where his secret-keeping mother, Chantal (Marisa Pavan), resides. Max was not responsible for the death of his wife, Gabrielle, as he was led to believe. She is alive and (giving that network executive the requested storyline) committed to a padded cell in an asylum. These scenes were actually shot on location in France. Upon their return, Maeve is furious with Siobhan and gives her one of her infamous tongue lashings. She promises that she will not just sit by and let Siobhan put her grandson, Sean, in danger.

Millee Taggart: As far as Tom and I were concerned, this was going to be an obligation story that we were told to write. You get a new job and the network asks for this, so we gave it to them, although we were desperate to get away from what came before.

Joe Hardy got what he wanted with this shoot. He had a budget, and he used it as he saw fit. The network—especially when Jackie Smith was there—was trying desperately to save the show. Up to that point, it had won more Emmy Awards than any other show. Joe was quirky and could mix it up, and so could Jackie. Creatively, they believed in each other. And I am sure he just said, "Do you want to save the show or not?"

Laura Rakowitz: Joe Hardy must have sold his soul to the devil to get the money for us to shoot in France. He told ABC it would boost the ratings because what soap would go to the château country in France? He did a marvelous job, I have to say. He was not kind to me at all, but we worked very closely on location and I learned a lot. This was not what the fans wanted to see, though. They wanted a relevant storyline and didn't care where it was shot. It didn't do anything for the ratings.

Daniel Pilon was part of the storyline that went to France. And

I can tell you the rest of the cast was not happy with that. Marg Helgenberger went too. I think there was some envy, but the cast liked her very much, so it was okay that she got to go. If a Ryan went, it was good.

I had a fabulous time on location. I loved being there and working on the shoot. I hung out with Marisa Pavan and her husband Jean-Pierre Aumont, who was charming and wonderful. I was with old-time real actors, listening to stories about Laurence Olivier and Vivien Leigh.

An interesting story, with lots of potential, developed with Chantal coming to New York and hiring a struggling look-a-like actress named Chessy Blake to impersonate Gabrielle. There is a letter in the family safety deposit box from Max's father that Chantal wants to remain unopened. However, miscasting ruined it, with twenty-seven-year-old Susan Scannell (ex-Kristin Carter, *Search for Tomorrow*, ex-Nicole Simpson, *Dynasty*) hired to play the dual roles of Chessy and Gabrielle, the mother of twenty-five-year-old Gerit Quealy's Jacqueline. It was off-putting and distracting. The cast and crew did not believe it, and the audience certainly did not either. It was an insult to the intelligence of the viewers, thinking that they would not want to watch an age-appropriate actress in the role. However, Scannell gets credit for her lack of vanity. Most actresses try to play younger, so it is a testament to her courage that she played the mother of a someone a bit younger than she.

> **Tom King:** As head writers, sometimes you had to write stories you didn't want to do because of the network. I tend to forget things I didn't like.

> **Millee Taggart:** I never believed the whole padded cell business, but I can believe anything for the right amount of money. I would say her beauty got Sue the role.

> **Tom King:** As I recall, I was against casting Sue Scannell in this role. We never had 100 percent agreement on casting—maybe one or two times. I had an issue with this. Mother and daughter looked the same age. It was silly and the audience really had to suspend disbelief.

> **Gerit Quealy:** Sue was a few years older than me. It was just absurd. Everybody thought it was absurd, and I even think there

was a lot of press about how absurd it was. We all knew that her character would be my mother. We never really gelled.

Tamara Grady: Sue Scannell was easy to work with. You were used to, if anything, casting going toward younger people. It was all about the youth.

Laura Rakowitz: This was ridiculous casting, and the story was so silly. Susan didn't look much older than Gerit Quealy. I sort of zoned out with this. I loved Gerit, though, and loved watching her act. In my opinion, Gerit acted rings around Susan, and sometimes I felt she was the older one.

Malcolm Groome: I thought Sue Scannell was a beautiful woman and good in the part.

Tamara Grady: I loved the story with Marisa Pavan and Susan Scannell. Marisa was the kindest, sweetest person you could ever imagine. One day she invited a bunch of us over to her home because she made spaghetti carbonara. I used to love when she would phone me. She'd say, in a whispery deep voice, "Hello, this is Marisa—Marisa Pavan." She was great—so sociable and never once did you feel she was a Hollywood actor other than that she was professional and always knew her lines.

I was last in touch with her when her husband, Jean-Pierre Aumont, died [in 2002]. I sent her a note, and we corresponded from time to time. She was extremely sweet—I just loved her.

Gerit Quealy: I loved Marisa Pavan, who had this amazing career. I asked if I could call her *grand-mère*. They said no because the audience would not understand the word. I thought it would add some veracity to our—what I called—Euro trash story. I was still grumpy since I was genuinely Irish in real life that I was not on the other side, playing a Ryan. I did think that it would be interesting to develop that side of the family but it was only for this sort of short-lived Jane Eyre–type plot twist.

Unfortunately, the Chessy/Gabrielle story became convoluted and hard to follow, even for the actors, with Chessy pretending to be Gabrielle and then Gabrielle escaping from the asylum and masquerading as Chessy to find out what was going on. Chantal is the puppet master trying to keep Max and Jacqueline in the dark. She succeeds since the characters are as confused as the audience. The upshot is that Anton's letter, which Chantal desperately wants to keep secret, reveals that Max is not his father's biological son. Mysteriously, when the lights go out, someone snatches the letter, and it remains lost. Gabrielle then gives Max a divorce before she and Jacqueline fly off to London to try to build a mother-daughter relationship.

Siobhan, meanwhile, goes rogue. She wants to close the unsolved Sydney Price murder case before she marches down the aisle with Max and to hopefully regain her police job. To that end, she enlists the aid of Laslo, unaware that he is the culprit. The pair began spending a lot of time together.

Gerit Quealy: By this point, everybody's heads were spinning around. There was more laughter and joking during the morning's blocking than anything else. We were just trying to make it work, though I don't remember this time span very well. The story was just so confusing, and I couldn't follow it—a lot of people couldn't follow it, and I still don't really know what happened.

Fred Burstein: When this storyline with Siobhan and Laslo began, the show's hairstylist said to me, "You know I think you would look good with shorter hair." I said okay, and he cut my hair. In a scene I had to go see Siobhan in her apartment. They made her say a line that she hated. It was something like, "Oh, Laslo, I see you got your hair cut." Marg said, "Who the hell cares and who would say anything? He is not my brother that I would kid him about his haircut."

Marg was fine to work with. She is an excellent actress. We never talked other than on the show. I did one scene with her set in a Chinese restaurant. We were eating and talking about something. To me it was just a scene. I learned my lines, and we did it. But afterward, Joe Hardy came to me and said, "That was a wonderful scene you both had. You just went with it. You were in there, and the two of you connected."

Gerit Quealy: I was friendly with Marg, but we didn't pal around together. I threw a party one time at my place, and she and her boyfriend came.

Fred Burstein: Laslo did not purposely push Sydney off the balcony, but she and I were struggling over a tape, I believe. Laslo had flashbacks as Siobhan was investigating it all. I was seeing that she was getting close to finding it out it was me. Then suddenly, the police in the show were asking NASA to look through satellite footage to see if they could zero in from outer space on that balcony on that day to see who pushed her off. They had these blurry shots, and then one day we had a scene where we shot in the middle of Manhattan. We were on this busy street where they set up the cameras. I was to get into a car and drive up the street a little bit to pick up Siobhan. She asked where we are going. I replied, "Don't worry. Just get in. It will be good." She got in. I kidnapped her and took her somewhere upstate. We holed up in a cabin for a while, and she tried to talk me into letting her go. At one point, she tries to leave a note at a store, but I catch her doing that. Finally, her cop partner Bill with Max swoop in with a helicopter and rescue her. That was sort of the end of me on the show.

Gerit Quealy: I disappeared for a bit I think because of the casting and because they didn't know what to do with Jacqueline at that point. I had this thing with Siobhan, Joe was gone, and Laslo was gone. I think the writers ran out of ideas where Jacqueline could go. My contract was up as well. It was mutual on both parts because I really didn't have a storyline.

Fred Burstein: Just before I was let go from the show, Gerit and I went out to Ohio to do a TV show in this big arena. We flew out first class, stayed in a fancy hotel, and were driven around in a limousine. The next day, we did one of those morning news shows. The audience could ask us questions. I thought, "You do not spend all this money if the actor is not doing well on the show." However, shortly after, both our times on the show ended. They do that on soaps. Some people survive and some don't.

I thought I would be on the show for another twenty years or something, so we bought a place up in Kerhonkson, New York. I did not end up working on the show anywhere near twenty years, but Joe Hardy helped us find and get that house. I thought I could still go down into the city for auditions. Nothing was happening, so then I became a waiter. You usually start off as one before you get a big part on a soap. For me it was the other way around. I began writing and sold my first book called *Rebecca's Nap* in 1986.

As the fall begins, Frank and Jill are still at odds. Troublemaking Maggie lets it "accidentally" slip to Frank that she thinks Jill and Max made love. Because Frank is once again thinking of running for political office, he wants his wife to cut all ties to Max and drop him as a client. She refuses. To cool off, she takes a solo vacation right after meeting with an attorney, who had notified Johnny Ryan that he was a beneficiary in the will of a former neighbor named Meg Smith. One day, Nancy Addison's Jill is arguing with Geoff Pierson's Frank about Max, and at the start of the next day's episode, it picks up with a different actor and the announcer saying those dreaded words, "The role of Frank Ryan will now be played by . . ." To say that the audience, as well as the cast and crew, were shocked is an understatement.

Geoff Pierson: It was very odd, and I never understood why I was replaced.

Cali Timmins: I remember after Geoff was told, he came down from the offices literally white-faced. He was devastated for many reasons. There was no lead-up to it, no warning at all. It was obviously political crap going on behind the scenes and another stupid decision from the powers-that-be. I think the cast was like, "Wow, if they could do that to him, nobody is safe." I remember Ron Hale saying, "Anything can happen."

Geoff Pierson: This is my understanding how it went down. They were casting the part of Johnny Ryan's illegitimate son. The cast did not know this was going on. It was a new upcoming storyline. Apparently, they tested numerous actors. It came down to two of them, and somebody believed that they should hire them both: one to replace me and the other to play the character they were originally casting. That is what I was told. I do not know if it was Joe Hardy's decision or Jackie Smith's decision. I never got the explanation. It was peculiar because I just signed a new contract that year for a two-year extension. What went into that decision—I still to this day do not know. They paid off the contract, and it was part of all the new people Joe was bringing in under the new writers at that time.

Cali Timmins: You could imagine how I felt. Everybody was shocked and floored and frightened. It was extremely upsetting. It was not a fun time. Geoff was one of the most solid actors on the show. He was the one everybody felt was the consummate actor and wanted to do scenes with. He received only positive feedback from the directors and producers all of the time. Claire at one time had even said that he was the ultimate Frank Ryan. And he *was* Frank Ryan. I came from an Irish Catholic family myself, and for me he *was* Frank Ryan. Obviously, there were many other wonderful Frank Ryans, but I think he understood the role and played him beautifully. This decision to replace him made no sense at all.

Geoff Pierson: I did *Search for Tomorrow* right after I was let go. I remember they said my character was going to be called Dr. Ryan, but they changed the name to Sullivan. It was quite different doing a P&G soap. I started out on them with *Texas* and *Another World*. I got the impression they stood up and fought for their shows, whereas *Ryan's Hope* was sort of the odd one out on ABC.

Cali Timmins: I talked to Joe Hardy about this, and he said he had nothing to do with it. One story was that Jackie Smith and ABC made the decision. I don't know, but I don't think Joe fought hard enough. I remember hearing the same story as Geoff that they were casting Dakota and they liked both John Sanderford and Christopher Durham for the part. Someone decided to cast one as Dakota and make the other Frank Ryan. John did resemble one of the other Franks [Daniel Hugh Kelly].

Millee Taggart: I remember those auditions. I like to watch them live in case I want to give a note. Chris and John were very good actors. Characters began to emerge. A lot of stuff goes into casting—honesty in performance, clarity, the ability to relate to them, want to root for them—it is a big stew. Maybe the new Frank had a few more chops than the old Frank did? I think they thought John could carry the show. It's a complicated process. Plus, I think Jackie Smith loved watching men that she had the potential to fall in love with.

Tom King: I remember the names of the actors, but I don't recall the drama that went on. I liked this storyline and thought it opened up the show a bit. It gave you a Ryan character a bit dangerous rather than cozy, home-life safe. I thought Christopher Durham was pretty good as Dakota. We looked at a lot of people. Casting is hard. Sometimes people would ask, "Couldn't you get somebody better?" We'd reply, "No! We saw one hundred people."

Christopher Durham (Dakota Smith): I had moved to New York after college in 1982. I was there for six months and doing an off-Broadway show. I got an agent, and it was a time when soaps were at their peak. They were casting bicoastal then, and I got called in for a reading by CBS for *Capitol*. They screen-tested me. I booked the role [of Matt McCandless] and I didn't even know anything about the soap. It was very new and had just started. I didn't even know until I got out to Hollywood that I was a replacement. I think it was only six months into the show. I stayed in Los Angeles for three years until 1985, and it was the only time I ever lived in California.

While I was on the show, I posed for *Playgirl*. They were doing something called the Celebrity Nude. A lot of actors were doing it, but there was no full-frontal nudity because I thought that was the kiss of death. They showed me George Maharis and Lyle Waggoner's pictorials when they approached me. I was hoping when I did it that it would open some doors. I am not ashamed now, but that was one of the biggest regrets of my life because it got you nothing. Who looked at *Playgirl*? Mostly gay men.

I left *Capitol* the month after the pictorial was published. We talked to John Conboy and the other producers to see if I could be released. They were very gracious and agreed. The character was written out and I think came back during the last six months. I felt like I never fit in at *Capitol*. It was so slick and such a cold environment except for Constance Towers and Rory Calhoun. I always gravitate toward older people.

I had to audition for Dakota. I heard of *Ryan's Hope* and knew it was well respected, but that is all I knew. I so wanted to go back East. I tested from Los Angeles and then they flew me out to New York. There were about five or six of us screen-testing for the part. I remember testing so well with Nancy Addison who I still miss. My memory is that she went up to the booth and said to them, "This guy is great." She was talking about me. She and I became the best of friends after I got hired. She was like a sister to me. Nancy was just so warm and lovely. I think it was about a week later when I learned the role was mine. I had left the city to do *Amadeus* in

summer stock. When I arrived at the theater in Milwaukee, they called and told me I had got the role. I was walking on cloud nine because I was so thrilled to live in New York again.

Tamara Grady: Geoff Pierson is a marvelous actor and was great in the role. I didn't care much for John Sanderford. I thought he was the worst Frank.

Christopher Durham: What I heard was that they loved John Sanderford too. They then replaced Frank Ryan with him and hired me as Dakota. I did not know they did this. I was just an actor coming in, trying to get a job. When I started, John was already there, which surprised me. I did not find out about Geoff until later from Cali Timmins, who I adored. She was just too beautiful to look at and was great to work with. She and Geoff were a couple, so I know this affected them, but that is the world of acting on the soaps. What happened to Geoff breaks my heart. I am an actor and know it is tough. Cali, though, handled it quite well.

Malcolm Groome: I do not know what to say about John Sanderford. He was a nice guy, but I did not like his Frank. He was a good actor, but his Frank did not click with me. Although he resembled Danny Kelly, he had a different personality and presentation.

Cali Timmins: I had a very hard time working with John Sanderford. It wasn't his fault, but to me he was not Frank at all. It was very depressing. Our relationship was very different, and it changed the Frank/Maggie dynamic. It was very hard to make it real in any way at all.

Ron Hale: John Sanderford was from what I call the West Coast invasion when they started bringing out people from there. I remember one of his first days on the set as they were camera blocking. He walked over to one of the cameramen and asked, "Is this the close-up on me?" We never did that, and the camera guy, whose name was Richard, was great and with us almost the whole time. He kind of looked Sanderford up and down and asked, "What do you mean?" Sanderford replied, "I just want to know where my shots are." Richard told him not to worry about it, and he would get his shots. Then Richard turned away from him.

We were just a different breed of actors. These guys were concerned about their close-ups. We didn't talk in those terms. It was about the friggin' scene—not how I'm going to look! That was a lot of the attitude that came on the show.

The Dakota Smith drama, with its lasting ramifications, starts when Jill goes off to meet with Meg Smith's lawyer. She is shocked to learn that Meg had an illegitimate son with Johnny. Jill keeps this a secret and tries to dig up more information on Meg and her offspring before letting Johnny know, since it would be so upsetting to the family. Her search takes her first to San Francisco and then back to the East Coast. On the plane, she meets a woman named Sarah Jane. Learning Meg's son is a fisherman living on a boat off the Jersey Shore, Jill decides to meet with him first before telling Johnny. However, she has an accident, hitting her head and awakening with no memory other than her name is Sarah Jane.

Dakota Smith rescues her, and the two are immediately attracted to each other. Jill's brain injury also seems to have affected her sense of style and taste, as she dresses like a Madonna-wannabe and takes a job slinging hash at a local seafood restaurant on the dock. Back in Riverside, Jill's disappearance worries her family for weeks until Jack accidentally runs into her. Keeping this from Frank, he tells Siobhan and Pat, who visit the restaurant, and Pat diagnoses Jill with amnesia. Meddling Maggie gets word what is going on and goes to see for herself what is transpiring. She is wearing a black wig and glasses. Seeing that Jill is quite cozy with Dakota, she gleefully reports to Frank that Jill has taken a lover to try to get him to reignite his passion for her instead. Meanwhile, Roger knows exactly the game Maggie is playing and makes sure to sabotage her.

Millee Taggart: We needed a new Ryan. I named him. I have crazy names for all the characters I created—Trucker and Rocky McKenzie, and Rio Domecq from *Loving*. I just love naming characters. With this storyline, anything is possible. Who knows maybe Johnny did have a one-night stand. I believe if you try to sanctify your characters, it is not real life. Everybody makes a mistake. Not everybody has an affair, but I never thought it was a fake affair or love affair, but it produced a kid. Once Johnny knew that, he would have to bring it to light. The way he handled it when revealed is what mattered.

Malcolm Groome: I thought this was an interesting storyline. However, I know a lot of fans did not like that Johnny had been unfaithful to Maeve. But hey, it is a soap, and sometimes they write things [that are] not right for the character to further the storyline. I thought it worked.

Tamara Grady: I liked working with Christopher Durham. I don't think he at the time was the best actor, but he had a good look, and he brought an interesting side to the story because it gave Nancy Addison [as Jill] something else to play.

At first, I think we were all not impressed with Christopher because we thought he was just another good-looking soap actor. After a while he and Nancy Addison got along well, and she welcomed him into the fold. I remember we hung out a bit together. When somebody new comes in, it is always a little weird at first. You need to let them find their way and let the actors already there do the same with them.

Christopher Durham: I became aware of it [the background story] later and must attribute this to Nancy Addison. She was with the show from the beginning—as were a few other actors, like Bernie Barrow and Helen Gallagher. Nancy embraced me, and we became best friends. I was the newbie and didn't question it because Nancy took me under her wing. We had an important storyline. I felt as if I was enveloped into a totally new family. It was because of Nancy Addison that I felt only love on the show. If the actors were thinking anything bad, I didn't know.

Malcolm Groome: I was more open to Christopher than he was to me. Perhaps coming into an established situation made him a little guarded. However, we worked well together. We were not close back then but are now. We are still in touch and talk on the phone. He is a wonderful guy and sort of a saint with the work he does rehabilitating animals.

Taggart and King continued to concentrate on stories centering on the core families—the Ryans, the Fenellis, and the Coleridges. Two shifted the focus back to Riverside Hospital. In a completely forgettable one with no future bearing on the show, Jack investigates suspected drug trafficking in the hospital's ambulance core. In the other, a trouble-prone DJ is mixed up in a car theft ring and is now an orderly at the hospital where Ryan volunteers as a candy striper. He cannot get her to be more than friends due to his run-ins with the law and her infatuation with Rick Hyde (who rejects her continuously). With Jack and Ryan's help, DJ is able to get it together enough to earn a Dubujak scholarship, and he departs New York City, leaving the path open for Ryan and Rick.

> **Millee Taggart:** We weren't given direction by ABC to bring it back to the Ryan family—you heard the instruction we were given [with the padded cell]—but that was not what Joe wanted to do. And neither did Tom or me. We wanted to return the show to Ryan's Bar, and we did.

> **Laura Rakowitz:** I absolutely think that at this point Joe Hardy gave up and started to refocus the show on the Ryan and Coleridge families. He started to win back the regular cast members, especially Helen Gallagher and Bernie Barrow. They were on the periphery for an exceptionally long time but realized they were the older parents. I remember having conversations with them about this. They were saying that Joe is finally bringing the Ryans back to the fold, and he realizes it is *Ryan's Hope*! It worked for the cast and crew, but I am not sure how it affected the ratings. Those of us on the set certainly had more energy and were happier.

> **Millee Taggart:** Helen Gallagher *was* Maeve, and they just wrote a show for who she was. I also loved Ava's mother on *Loving* when I wrote it because she had that Maeve quality. Maeve was the heart of *Ryan's Hope*.

> **Cali Timmins:** I agree. Helen was the matriarch on the show and off. I was intimidated by her not because she was intimidating—she could not have been more lovely. But in my mind, she had this aura about her, even though she was always very kind to me. We didn't have many scenes together, but we would talk a lot off set.

It is surprising to learn that at this time, Tom and Millee had a personal and professional relationship with Claire Labine. This included the hiring of her children, Eleanor Labine Mancusi and Matthew Labine, as staff writers for a time.

Tom King: We saw Claire Labine fairly regularly on a personal and official basis. She was always very positive about the show, and she never had many suggestions. We would meet for dinner or drinks.

We hired Claire's children, Eleanor and Matthew. I didn't like Matthew after a while. Eleanor was responsive, intelligent, and easy to work with. She was no problem and could hold her own with any writer we would hire.

Millee Taggart: I do agree that Eleanor was a stronger writer . . . Matthew was not the writer I'd hoped for when Claire asked me to give him a shot.

Around the same time, *Ryan's Hope* received some good news when it became the first U.S. soap opera sold to the United Kingdom. Per *Variety*, "Fremantle Intl., through its British Talbot subsid., has made the first American sale . . . which will start in October on Britain's MirrorVision cable network. The sale was for 268 half-hour episodes." The show was the first American soap to be sold to Ireland back in 1980, and, some time after, along with *Loving*, sold to Canada and Italy. Despite the declining ratings, ABC was obviously devising ways to keep the show profitable.

As 1985 wound down, the show saw the departure of hottie Bill Hyde (who had not taken off his shirt in months). With Siobhan married to Max and Bill's brother Rick now the cop du jour, there was no storyline left for him. Also sent off were the newly married Dave Greenberg and Katie Thompson, who headed west to try their luck in Hollywood. Arguably, this was a disappointing move because it would have been fun to watch Maggie interact with the couple and no doubt cause more trouble for them. Instead, the writers thought it better to have her meddle in the affairs of Jill and Frank in the hopes of rekindling Frank's feelings for her.

The shift back to the Ryan and Coleridge families was encouraging news to soap columnist Jon-Michael Reed. He opined, "When a daytime drama veers from its basic concept and core characters, it invariably loses part of its audience. *Ryan's Hope* was conceived as the saga of the Ryan family of New York City. . . When the show's stories strayed from emphasis on members of the Ryan clan, it lost its special luster . . . Now, with intelligent and savvy writers at the helm, *Ryan's Hope* is beginning to make up for lost ground. The Ryans are once again the plot focus."

The year 1985 literally ended with Frank and Jill finally coming face to face despite the roadblocks Maggie put up. However, Jill does not remember him or their marriage. He pushes too hard, trying to get her to recall their life together and sends her back into Dakota's arms. Johnny, meanwhile, confesses his infidelity with Meg to Maeve, who kicks him out of their bedroom. However, being a good Catholic, she forgives him and the two reconcile—before knowing that he has a grown son.

The beginning of 1986 continued with the main focus on Jill, who has regained her memory and moves back in with Frank. Dakota (on the run after being accused of stealing buried treasure at sea) is shot by the police, who try to arrest him in South Carolina. While Jill tells her stunned husband the truth about Dakota and his relationship to Johnny, an injured Dakota shows up at the Coleridge brownstone. He threatens Maggie, telling her to get Jill to come to him or he will reveal that they were in cahoots to keep Frank and Jill apart. A worried Jill arrives and convinces Dakota to see a doctor. After being taken to the hospital, Johnny donates blood to help save Dakota and then tells Maeve why. Conniving Maggie continues making it her business to help Dakota win back Jill so she can step in and comfort Frank.

Ryan, meanwhile, puts the full-court press on Rick, who should have known better. Scenes of jailbait Ryan in her Catholic schoolgirl uniform trying to entice Rick were cringe-worthy to some. The pair grows closer, but Rick still won't marry her until after graduation.

> **Laura Rakowitz:** I thought the pairing of Ryan and Rick was creepy, and it made me uncomfortable. Yasmine Bleeth did a wonderful job in the confines that she had being so young and this being her first acting job. I am not sure that Grant Show did it as well as he could have, and for me, he did not make the pairing work. He also was a bit of a problem on the set.
>
> **Christopher Durham:** Yasmine Bleeth was the most beautiful child actress I had ever seen and was right up there with Brooke Shields. Her mother [who was French] had died of breast cancer. Nancy and I went to her townhouse for her sweet sixteen birthday party. Yasmine was a doll, and I really liked Grant Show too. We used to walk our dogs together on the Upper West Side. He had a Samoyed, and I always had mutts from the Humane Society.
>
> **Millee Taggart:** I thought Grant Show played younger than what he was. Teen romance is not something I am crazy about. To me, Grant gave Yasmine a little more gravitas. Who is she going to

hang out with? I felt Yasmine was mature beyond her years. The pairing did not bother me, and I liked it because I was married to a man fifteen years older than me.

Tom King: It was hard to forget Grant Show. He was so good-looking. But I never felt this pairing worked.

Millee Taggart: When I began writing, I never watched a soap opera unless I was writing it. I love soaps and I love the genre, but I was afraid I would inadvertently steal a storyline. It is the same way when I am writing a novel. I don't read anything because the mind is strange. You can hear an idea and you think it's yours, but it is literally something you just read. With soaps, I never watched anymore. I would always go into a new soap having a fresh eye.

New characters on the scene were Leslie Easterbrook as Devlin Kowalski, a glamorous business colleague of Max's who has a financial interest in Dakota's underwater treasure discovery and a romantic interest in Jack. The district attorney's office begins investigating Devlin for her alleged involvement with an international art scam. Nancy Valen also turned up in the throwaway role of Melinda Weaver, a sisterlike friend of Dakota's from Tennessee. She, at first, is attracted to Rick but then is paired with Pat. The character of Melinda was in the vein of Pru Shepherd from the prior writing regime and, as with Pru, was a major misfire.

Christopher Durham: I had been on the show about a year when I screen-tested as Dakota with about five actresses up for Melinda Weaver. Nancy Valen got the part. I thought that this was a wrong move bringing in Melinda. I had no idea where they were going with her or why she was there. I didn't ask a lot of questions. I was lucky to have a job.

Malcolm Groome: I was confused about Pat's relationship with Melinda. I did not know who she was and why they put us together. I think I was almost fifteen years her senior, and either I was too old or she was too young for that relationship. It was an odd pairing, but Nancy Valen was a doll to work with.

Christopher Durham: Nancy was so sweet and wonderful. We got along great and had a fun time, but I just did not understand this character at all.

Millee Taggart: I have no clue how this story with Melinda came about, especially if someone didn't like it. [Laughing] I don't know. I wasn't there. It must have been Joe's or Tom's idea!

Tom King: I too do not remember the particulars on how Melinda came about, but usually Millee and I agreed. It was probably prodded by Joe Hardy, who then cast the role.

Come Emmy Award time in March 1986, *Ryan's Hope* did not receive recognition in any major category and was honored with only a single nomination for Outstanding Achievement in Music Direction and Composition for a Drama Series. Music director Sybil Weinberger and composer Earl Rose would lose to *Search for Tomorrow*.

Also, during this time, the show suffered a major blow when Marg Helgenberger vacated the role of Siobhan despite a full-court press to convince her to stick around. When she declined, Siobhan, with son, Sean, in tow, jets off for an extended stay in Europe.

Millee Taggart: I loved Marg. But sometimes you can't have what you want. There was nothing we wouldn't have done to get her to stay. But she was on her way.

Maggie and Dakota continue plotting to break up Frank and Jill. To that end, Dakota plays nice with the Ryan family, even accepting Maeve's generous invitation to stay at their home. However, at a party thrown in Jill's honor at the Coleridge townhouse, devious Maggie makes sure that Jill catches Dakota and her in bed together. An upset Jill lashes out at both of them, as a "contrite" Maggie justifies her actions, thinking Jill is over Dakota. While Frank thinks that his wife is making too big a deal over it and that Dakota and Maggie deserve each other, Jill admits that she still loves Dakota.

Maggie's deceitful plan succeeds and an unnerved Jill leaves Frank for his half brother, causing a rift in the Ryan family. Smug Maggie, however, comes out the loser since Frank wants nothing to do with her, much to the delight of Roger Maggie then makes an enemy of Max when she steals an incriminating file from his computer and, with Roger's help, uses it to blackmail him over that and catching him with a former lover named Fantasy. When learning that Roger had a financial windfall in the stock market, a desperate Maggie convinces him to marry her. Roger wants a child so he has a prenup drawn up slipping in a clause that she has to get pregnant and produce a Coleridge heir or she will not receive a dime, that he tricks the gold digger into signing. Their nuptials are almost ruined when Max sabotages their private honeymoon jet and the pair barely escape with their lives. The newly married couple and Max then reach a stalemate.

Millee Taggart: You have to have something to root for. If you have two heroes of equal weight, there has to be a reason to root for one. The idea that Johnny Ryan could have a son who wasn't perfect, wasn't earnest? Think of the life he had. He did not grow up a Ryan. It was intentional to change Dakota. I think we always knew that the reunion would be complicated in a family way, and then it would be something that was upsetting to Johnny and Maeve and the family. I loved Dakota and I loved Nancy Addison as Jill. She was a lovely actress, and I valued her.

Christopher Durham: I did not get to meet Millee and Tom until I was on the show for about six months or so. We moved into ABC's studio at the end of Sixty-Sixth Street. On *Capitol*, John Conboy, who was not a nice man, never wanted the actors to meet or talk to the writers. He kept us very separate. It wasn't the same on *Ryan's Hope*. One day, I got on the elevator, and Millee, says, "Hi, Chris." I said hello and she said, "I'm Millee Taggart. I am surprised you do not know who I am." I knew her name, but I had been taught you do not converse with the writers, but that was not the case here. Then I would see Tom and her come in and out of the studio and I thought, "Oh, wow. Even though you are an actor, you can speak to the writers and say hello."

Rick keeps his promise to marry Ryan after her graduation, and the pair elope to South Carolina, with Jack and Frank in hot pursuit to stop it. There, they had an 1880s fantasy-style wedding in a small village where time is standing still—complete with Ryan's mother, Mary, in attendance. This was Kate Mulgrew's second guest appearance on the show since she left in 1977.

Tom King: I didn't have any interaction with Kate Mulgrew, but I had watched *Ryan's Hope* from the beginning. I liked her as Mary very much and think she was one of the main reasons the show became so popular.

Millee Taggart: Getting Kate back on the show was everybody's first priority since the minute she left. What can I say about her? We broke every rule to get her on. As we moved to the end of the show, it was our dream to bring back all the important people. Delia was in a revolving door—she was on, she was off, she was on, she was off. If you get an actress as a character that is so special—like Kate, like Ilene—you want them on the screen. People tune in.

Everybody says, "I want to watch my stories." That's not what they mean in my experience. They come to watch the people they care about live through their lives and experiences that are on the screen. So, if you have the right characters—a lot of stories are duds, and I have certainly written some myself—people will care about them. To me, to kill off a beloved character is a crime.

Shortly after returning to Riverside, Rick is temporarily suspended from the police force. Working undercover for Frank and the district attorney's office, he gets a job at a trucking company run by a guy named Vinnie to uncover who is controlling a stolen goods fencing operation. More interesting is Frank's rebound romance with African American assistant district attorney Diana Douglas (Tracey Ross), the sophisticated girlfriend of Dr. Evan Cooper (Irving Allen Lee, ex-Calvin Stoner, *The Edge of Night*), Pat's partner in the clinic. Evan was sort of a combination of former characters Bucky Carter and Clem Moultrie, being both friend and colleague to Pat. Diana is immediately attracted to her boss, although she denies it. However, Evan sees through her lie and warns her that Frank will never stop loving Jill.

When Diana learns that Jill filed for divorce and has gone back to Dakota, Diana reveals her true feelings to Frank, who reciprocates. Soon the pair are romping in bed together and giving the middle finger to anyone who is aghast with their interracial romance. At this point, the writers even introduced Diana's parents into the mix, indicating that they would become a major part of the story going forward.

Accompanied by her son, Sean (Danny Tamberelli), Siobhan returns from Europe. She was now played by auburn-haired Carrell Myers, who had the unenviable task of trying to make the audience stop missing Marg Helgenberger. Siobhan rightfully begins to think Max is up to no good. When she confides in her parish priest that she suspects her husband of being an international gunrunner, he mysteriously disappears soon after.

Millee Taggart: I think Carrell did the best she could. It is like if you were going to replace Susan Lucci. What kind of reaction are you going to get? No one could please everybody because it wouldn't be Susan. Carrell tried, but sometimes it is unachievable.

In the late summer, Frank is trying to convince the mob that Rick is truly crooked, and Rick shoots him during a fake assassination attempt that goes awry when someone swaps a real bullet for a blank. This brings Frank's nineteen-year-old son, now going by the name of John Reid Ryan, back to Riverside, complete with his infant son, Owen, in tow, and the mother is nowhere to be found. He refuses to tell anyone about the woman who gave birth to Owen.

Jason "Ash" Adams (John Reid Ryan #2): There was a nation-wide search for this role. They tested actors from San Francisco, Chicago, New York, and LA. I had been working with Bobby Hoffman, who was doing West Coast casting for ABC Daytime. I attended some of his classes. He gave cold readings classes and auditioning technique classes. He really was a terrific guy and one of the last great old-school casting directors. He took an interest in me, which was very flattering and what turned out to be incredibly fortuitous for me.

I had flown to New York a couple of times to screen-test for other ABC soaps. The last one I did before *Ryan's Hope* was for a role on *All My Children*. I found out a lot of this information that I am relaying now well after the fact from either Joe Hardy, who was my boss, or other network people. I didn't get the part on *All My Children*. Evidently what happened was one of the producers of that show had known they were going to bring Johnno Ryan back as a nineteen-year-old single dad. They were already starting to audition actors in New York for the role. This producer, who I wish I knew who it was, sent my tape over to the producers at *Ryan's Hope*, which subsequently led me to fly back to New York to screen-test for Johnno Ryan. There were a few of us who screen-tested. It is kind of brutal how they do it. They fly you out first class, but it is you and the other guys that are also testing all sitting there, staring at each other.

After testing, I thought I did not get it. Most of us don't think we give good auditions. I know very few actors that like auditioning and then sit around waiting to hear if you got the job. Ninety-five percent of the time, you don't get it. John Sanderford was already playing my father, and my resemblance to him had to have helped. That is probably part of the reason I got the part.

When I was cast, I was living in an apartment in Venice Beach. I was only twenty-two at the time, and it was the biggest phone call I had ever gotten when they told me the part was mine. It also facilitated a move to New York, where I wanted to study since I was a kid. I finally got to do that. One of the greatest things about being on *Ryan's Hope* was that I was able to audition for and got accepted as a lifetime member to the Actors Studio. I got to work with all those actors there, on top of getting to act with all the cool people on *Ryan's*.

While drifting in and out of consciousness, Frank cries out for Jill while a worried Diana sits at his bedside. Jill, meanwhile, finally learns how Dakota and Maggie staged their tryst as a ploy to separate her and Frank. That, on top of the money Dakota embezzled from the neighborhood rec center that he runs, makes Jill finally realize what a lowdown jerk he is. She runs to Frank's hospital room. When he recuperates, the two reconcile, leaving Diana as the odd woman out, and hell hath no fury like a woman scorned. She threatens a sexual harassment suit and is then courted by Max to make Frank pay for what he did to her.

This interracial romance rankled the network executives. Taggart and King may have reached too far by pairing Diana with the show's main leading man, whose true love was always Jill. Coupling Diana with Pat Ryan or another lesser character may have sustained the romance and storyline longer.

Tom King: Millee and I would just pitch ideas, and we both liked the idea of doing an interracial storyline. I'm from Alabama, and I grew up with terrible things. It seemed like a good move storywise and sociologically exposing people to something they may have a problem with and try to get them to overcome it. Usually, if you, as a writer, head out on a noble venture like that, it will blow up in your face.

Christopher Durham: Tracey Ross was so sweet and very nice to work with. I was told by Laura Rakowitz that the show was getting hate mail about this storyline. I was like why would they get hate mail? People care about different things, and I just thought it was stupid. Sometimes hate mail, though, is great if they are watching.

Millee Taggart: ABC killed the Frank/Diana romance. It was a controversial story, and when you have a soap that is on the cuff, like *Ryan's Hope* was, you take a risk—but I don't blame them for doing it. They were not quite ready for this, but I felt you don't become successful by refusing to take chances. Look what they did with Luke and Laura on *General Hospital*. I am so tired of hearing about Luke and Laura, but on the other hand they took a risk. They told a story that I always felt was based on characters, but, God, can you imagine being in network meetings about that? You can't have an interracial romance or a gay character, but a rapist? That's okay?

Tom King: I agree; if we paired Diana with someone other than Frank it probably would have played on. ABC went through a kind of convulsion because Jackie Smith, who was the empress of daytime, got sick. We ended up with her second-in-command, who was a lackluster thinker. She was second-rate compared to Jackie. Even though a lot of people disliked Jackie, she was brilliant.

Christopher Durham: Because networks need to make the bucks, they will always stay with the status quo. Television is a fast medium and will do what they think people will accept. It happens, but it is slower than the times—it is always like that. But it should be bigger than the times.

Considering that ABC turned tail and forced the writers to cut short the interracial romance, it is no surprise that *Ryan's Hope* never introduced a homosexual character during the mideighties. While the AIDS epidemic was decimating the gay community, especially in big cities, if there was one soap that could have incorporated this into their story arc realistically and compassionately, it was *Ryan's Hope* because it was set in New York City and had a hospital focus. However, the show, under ABC control, no longer tackled controversial social issues, unlike during its early years when Claire and Paul owned and wrote it.

Millee Taggart: The sad truth is that once the show was out of Claire and Paul's control, many of the features that made it so ground-breaking were curtailed. It was easier to sell a story about

Delia and a gorilla or a woman in a padded cell than a gritty, drawn-from-the-headlines tale. I'm sure it was discussed between us, but to pitch it to ABC would have been futile. "People don't want to see that," was the usual response.

After John Reid's family gets over the initial shock of his being a single dad, they convince him to have Owen christened in the Catholic church. As the ceremony begins, the church doors swing wide open with a bang. Sitting in a pew, Maeve turns to look and then says to Johnny, "Batten down the hatches—Delia's back!" She sure was. This time the producers got it right and brought back Ilene Kristen for her third go-around in the part. Back at Ryan's Bar, Delia is miffed that she was the last to find out that she had a grandson and accuses Frank and Jill of trying to keep him away from her. When Johnny says they could not find her in the phone-book under any of her many last names, the daffy blonde responds, "I didn't want to use Crane. And Coleridge seems obsolete. And Ryan is so complicated. Well, you know—so I thought I would just be Delia. Like Cher. Like Madonna. Like Gandhi." She also plays up her glamorous life on the West Coast, but truth be told, Delia did not get a cent from her divorce settlement with Matthew Crane, and the broke blonde is also back in Riverside to reunite with Roger. John Reid realizes he will forever be in the middle of his warring parents.

Millee Taggart: If we wanted Ilene Kristen back as Delia and Joe agreed, it was done. If he believed in something and you tried, without good cause, to stop it—he wouldn't have it. He would walk out. I fought like crazy for Ilene.

Tom King: Although I liked Jackie, she could be ruthless [after hearing the story of Ilene Kristen's firing in 1983].

Ilene Kristen: I was gone for three years and did a lot of off-Broadway shows. My weight was totally back to normal. But I was broke, and so was my friend Billy Carl, who asked to stay in my extra bedroom. He was one of the most stunning-looking guys I had ever seen. We would eat pasta with jarred spaghetti sauce prac-tically every night. I usually jogged in the park with him, and he would turn the heads of women and men. One day, I am jogging in the park by myself, and I get this feeling that something was coming. I get home around 2:00 p.m., and there is a message on my machine. "Ilene, this is Joe Hardy. I need you to call me immediately." He leaves the number.

I am not calling him right away, that is for fucking sure, and want to make him sweat. I wait until around 6:00 p.m. and get him on the phone. He says, "I need to see you right away. Please come to my office." I went two days later.

He starts by saying, "You know, Ilene, it was not my idea to let you go."

I replied, "Oh really? But you let it happen."

He then goes on to say, "You know nobody can play Delia like you."

"Yes, I know that, but what is it that you want?" I asked.

Finally, Joe says, "We are going to make Delia a grandmother. Though you are too young, we do want you back."

I said, "I'll come back, but I have a really big off-Broadway career going. I need to know if I have to leave the building at four o'clock that I can be out the door. Also, I got my health back, and I do not want to be bothered by this."

He said, "You are in wonderful shape."

I fired back, "I don't know how many times I told you people that the cortisone was causing me problems, and you cannot get that shit out of your system quickly." I started jogging to help me sweat it out of my body.

Joe said, "You can do whatever you want. We want you back."

I returned to the show, and I have to say those were the most fun years I had.

Tom King: I loved Ilene. I had watched her as Delia from the beginning of the show. I just fell in love with her and thought she was the best villainess I had ever seen on a soap. She was fun to watch and made you laugh. When I got to know her off set, she is just as likable in person. Villains are what makes soaps tick. Delia was just a classically good bad girl because she was vulnerable and always on the verge of tears, but at the same time, she was very dangerous. Ilene played her brilliantly.

With the return of Delia, the John Reid story took off. Owen is first kidnapped by a mentally unbalanced neighborhood woman but is quickly found. Shortly after, Owen's picture appears on a missing persons TV show prompting Delia to call in. This tips off a man named Harlan Ransome (Drew Snyder), who learns the boy's grandfather is New York City's district attorney, Frank Ryan. Soon after, Owen's mother, Lizzie Ransome (Catherine Larson), arrives, and it is obvious she is too fragile and indifferent to assume responsibility for her son. She claims she is not there to take him, but John Reid admits that they do not have an official agreement giving him custody. In an ironic twist, Delia helps her son try to keep Owen from Lizzie, even though years prior she found herself fighting Frank for custody of him.

Jason "Ash" Adams: I was hip to what was going on with those characters. It was quite easy to key into. That is good writing—clean, clear storytelling. With the wild energy of Delia and the steely calm of Jill, there was a real contrast between them. There was a strong feminine grace about Nancy Addison and how she played Jill.

Ilene Kristen came off as this frenetic floozy with a heart of gold. Delia wanted to do the right thing and be there for her family, but her problem was her narcissism. That is why Delia was so much fun to watch spin around because she knew if push came to shove, she was out for herself. However, you also knew she was capable of tremendous tenderness and love. Because she constantly flew around in a manic state and felt slighted by everyone who wronged her, she was always defending herself from the judgments of the rest of the family.

Millee Taggart: Sometimes families repeat history, with John Reid fighting for custody of his son. Life mirrors life very often. How many people have divorced parents who divorce themselves? How many single moms raise children who become single moms? I think that is one of the many interesting things about human nature. Although we don't think about it consciously, sometimes we mirror behavior we may or may not have approved of at the time.

Jason "Ash" Adams: Although the parallels were certainly there, when you are playing it, you are not really paying attention to that because you are mired in the character and the storyline itself. You are not sitting back, thinking that this is kind of brilliant that they are threading that story with a past story. You must know your history, but you do not have to know all the threads because you are a fucking young actor trying to remember ten to fifteen pages of dialogue a day. That isn't an easy thing to do, but it also is not easy to write or create these shows. There were some nice, true lines aspiring to where my character came from and the family that I was surrounded with. That is one of the reasons I liked it and one of the reasons I didn't like the whole fucking John Reid thing.

I did not like to be called John Reid. They were trying to keep the connection to Delia Reid Ryan, blah blah blah. She married everybody. How many fucking last names does my mom have? However, I think it took away from the fact that I was a Ryan. I didn't like that. The writers were using my character to blend in the Reids. Hey, man, I'm not a fucking Reid. I'm a Ryan. This is probably one of the reasons I may not have been popular with the writers of the show because I hated that name. I finally won that battle. We were all friends on the show, and the actors wouldn't call me that. Helen Gallagher and Bernie Barrow called me Johnno, which was fine with me. Little John was fine too. Eventually I just became John.

Newlyweds Roger and Maggie hire a butler named Mr. Dowd (Keith Charles) to run the Coleridge household. Extremely devoted to Maggie, the droll Dowd helps her embarrass Delia after she digs up dirt that shows her husband's ex-wife is penniless. At a dinner party thrown at the Coleridge brownstone in Delia's honor, calculating Maggie makes sure all the people Delia owes money to show up—even her dress designer, who literally takes the dress off Delia's back. Trying to save face in front of the Ryans, Delia wraps herself in a curtain and tries to make a graceful exit but trips and sprains her ankle. Maggie's plan backfires when Roger insists that she stay a few nights while she recovers.

Lizzie's sadistic father, Harlan, shows up and demands custody of his grandson. He makes it crystal clear, though, that for a price he will forfeit his rights and bullies Lizzie into going along with his plan. John reveals to Frank that Harlan has abused Lizzie many times in the past. Pressured by her father, Lizzie demands John marry her or else she is leaving town with Owen. He refuses and later sees that Harlan has struck Lizzie once again.

Delia tries to borrow money from Roger to finance a new business but actually it is to pay off Harlan. When he turns her down, she swipes a Coleridge family heirloom necklace, with help from Dakota, and hocks it, replacing it with a fake before going to see Harlan. They also make sure Roger discovers the fake around Maggie's neck, causing a rift in their marriage.

After threatening to kill Harlan, John turns up at his place and finds him barely alive on the floor. The police show up and discover him standing over the now dead Harlan, so John is arrested. Mother and son think the other offed Harlan and try to protect one another. Frank and Jill try to prove it was Delia. However, Lizzie comes forward and confesses that she killed her father in self-defense when he once again assaulted her. Assistant DA Diana Douglas surprisingly decides not to press charges against Lizzie considering she had vindictively (to get back at Frank) denied bail for John on the grounds that he was a flight risk. Now with a change of heart, Diana also breaks ties with Max and drops her sexual harassment suit against Frank. It was at this point that Tracey Ross was unfortunately dropped from the show.

Jason "Ash" Adams: This was an interesting turn and fun to play. My friend Drew Snyder played Harlan. He is a terrific character actor. Harlan basically showed us where Lizzie came from.

I remember testing with about four or five actresses for the role of Lizzie, but the actor has no say. No one person just gets handed these jobs. Every young actor in town wanted a role on a soap, especially during the eighties when they were in their heyday. People were going crazy over these shows.

Ilene Kristen: I loved Ash Adams. He was the right person for the role. The weird thing was that he was only twelve years younger than me, which was freaky. We had good chemistry and were awfully close. He was my best friend there.

Jason "Ash" Adams: Ilene and I were best friends for about ten years. We were inseparable, and I was very fond of her. We had a lot of fun working together. It was an especially important relationship for me.

Millee Taggart: I loved Jason as John and his relationship with Ilene. If I didn't like someone, they would not have continued.

Jason "Ash" Adams: Some of the older cast members took me under their wing and showed me what to do. When I got there, I was the punk from LA. A lot of the cast had been together for a long time, and I was an outsider. I think John Sanderford was too.

He was from LA as well. I don't know what the cast felt about this LA contingent without much soap experience.

Early on I remember going to Bernie Barrow and asking him, "How the fuck do I remember all these lines? I don't know how to do this." Bernie sat me down in his dressing room and showed me what he did. He used to write out all his lines on a separate piece of paper and memorize them that way through his own handwriting. That process was his way for memorization. It worked wonderfully for me. Whenever I had more than a couple of pages of dialogue, I would write it out longhand. That was a big tip.

Ilene Kristen: Bernie was a man of much wisdom. I wrote my scripts, especially with particularly long monologues, out on paper the same way Bernie did. There is something about the brain looking at it in your own handwriting where it becomes yours. To this day, I do the same thing, and I still love to rehearse. I would drive everyone crazy. Ash and I would always run lines. I felt that was part of the job. When you get onto the set, the words should be secondary. I didn't like running lines by myself. I needed that other person. Some people could do it by themselves. Kate Mulgrew was one of those people. I couldn't.

Jason "Ash" Adams: I also like to rehearse, and from what I remember it was never an imposition by Ilene. I liked to get in as much rehearsal as we could as well if the scene facilitated that kind of attention and focus. Some scenes you could get down in the morning with one rehearsal and a couple of dry blockings. If you only have a few lines to say in a scene with six or seven people, you don't necessarily need to rehearse hours and hours other than the basic blocking for camera. It is trial by fire for a newcomer to soaps. Many actors don't make it past their first couple of cycles because they can't do the work.

Millee Taggart and Tom King had other interesting stories going on simultaneously as 1986 came to an end. With his enemies closing in and a bomb discovered in his office that Siobhan almost triggers, Max hires a personal bodyguard named Erik Brenner (Walt Willey). He begins to act overly concerned around Siobhan and her son, Sean. Siobhan finds herself drawn to him but cannot understand why. Turns out Erik is Joe Novak, complete with plastic surgery so his enemies cannot find him, and he is working with Devlin Kowalski for the International Police who are investigating Max.

Although fans were elated to have Joe back on the canvas, strange casting dampened the story. Joe (Walt Willey) had a new face, his hair was now blond, and he had grown almost six inches taller (as compared to Roscoe Born, the definitive Joe in most of the audience's eyes). According to Carrell Myers, when she heard Joe was returning, she hoped they would bring back Roscoe, but since Daniel Pilon was over six feet tall and Carrell was on the tall side, they wanted an actor of equal stature. To be fair to Willey, it was an almost impossible task for any actor to take over this role because of the solid impression Born had made.

Tom King: Millee and I always looked at the audition tapes and voted on who we wanted, but Joe Hardy had the ultimate authority on casting. As I said, his taste was not our taste.

Laura Rakowitz: Walt certainly knew how to hit his marks and say his lines, but I never thought Walt made a believable Joe at all. Joe needs to be sexy and sensuous. You need someone with those qualities, plus being smart. He was not as nuanced as Roscoe Born was in the part. That is what a complicated bad guy should do. Roscoe worked his magic on the audience and worked his magic on me as well.

Tamara Grady: As with Michael Hennessy, Walt Willey wasn't right for Joe either.

Ilene Kristen: Having Walt Willey replace Roscoe Born as Joe was such odd casting.

Jason "Ash" Adams: I became great friends with Walt Willey. He, Ilene Kristen, and Ron Hale really watched out for me and protected me. And I needed that.

9

Claire Labine Regains Control, 1987–88

The year 1987 began with a wedding that most fans were not enthused about—that of Pat and Melinda. It was an odd pairing and arguably did not add anything to the show. The better story was Maggie learning she is pregnant and deciding not to tell Roger, who had since left her for Delia, who is in the midst of opening a store called Déjà Vu that features antique fashions and accessories with an adjacent art gallery. Spiteful Maggie threatens an abortion and then fesses up later that she did not go through with it, after letting her mother and sister think she did. She then vows that Roger will not get custody of her child, and she will keep the baby away from him and Delia. Jill tries to get Maggie to tell Roger that he is going to be a father. When that does not work, she visits Delia at her shop and tells her to back off from ruining Roger and Maggie's marriage without letting it slip that Maggie is pregnant. That scene is unintentionally comical with homewrecker Jill lecturing Delia, whose marriage she was partially responsible for breaking up years earlier. When Roger finally learns the truth, he is torn between his love for Delia and his wanting a family.

> **Millee Taggart:** I loved this storyline. Roger Coleridge was just deliciously low. He was like early JR from *Dallas*. I adored Ron Hale in this role. This story worked so greatly and was one of my favorites. I love a story where there's humor and pathos and acid and profound love and humanity. Each of them showed more than one would expect from them.

Cali Timmins: This storyline was a lot of fun to play. I loved working with Ilene. She is fantastic and the ultimate actress. She just brought life to every scene and just amazed me. She could take anything on the page and make it perky and funny. It could not even be written that way, and she would just do her thing with it. I remember I had scenes fighting with her that were fun to do.

Ron Hale: This was a fun storyline. But I blocked a lot of the storylines out. I remember so much more about the first five years because of the incredible things that were done. Those were wonderful, creative years that made us so special and made my life special because of the quality of work that we were all doing in daytime television. We weren't around sipping coffee or centering around an Erica Kane, like so many of the other shows. We certainly didn't have a Susan Lucci. Once those changes started, it just became blurry to me.

Christopher Durham: Ron Hale was so kind with no attitude. He was hilariously funny as well.

With Joe and Devlin's help, the International Police close in on Max with proof that he is the crime syndicate big-shot with the codename Overlord. Max becomes suspicious of Siobhan and Erik, not knowing he is Joe Novak. One of his minions sees Siobhan on a surveillance tape searching Max's secret room in his office. At this point, the show saw the return of Jacqueline Dubujak and the imprisoned Laslo Novotny. Max allows Jacqueline to come back from London (she disembarks from the plane like a regal princess with loads of luggage, barking orders), and she is immediately intrigued by Erik. She commands him to remove his sunglasses and has a strange feeling that they had met before. Soon after, she and Siobhan separately visit Laslo in prison, for different reasons.

Gerit Quealy: I was in California by this point. My former agent called and told me that they were auditioning actresses in New York to play Jacqueline for a short stint where they were winding up a few storylines. He also told me that they couldn't find anybody that was working out and asked if I would consider coming back from the Coast. Frankly, LA was not for me. I am a cold-weather girl, and I really didn't like it out there, so I said, "Yes, I'll come back!" I signed a new contract, but it was only for a brief period of time.

Fred Burstein: After Laslo was arrested and flew off in the helicopter, I was supposed to be gone for good. I was working in a restaurant upstate in Stoneridge. I was also writing at this point. Joe Hardy called me months after I had left and said, "We need [Siobhan and Jacqueline] to learn a few things and need to bring back Laslo. We have a couple of scenes planned where they visit you in jail." So, off I went to do it.

Gerit Quealy: The original cast members were standoffish when I first joined the show, but when I came back, it was as if I had graduated to the old guard. In the beginning, I had a couple of scenes with Walt Willey where Jacqueline was figuring out what was going on. The writing was very good during this time. It was fun and playful. I remember Bernie Barrow saying to me at one point, "Look at you!" Maybe I needed time away to be not so emotionally involved with what was happening with Jacqueline and not feel so protective of her. I came back crafting the character more separate from myself. I think it is very tough when you are doing a character day in and day out not to over-personalize it maybe? I don't know. Plus being younger too was harder at first.

Fred Burstein: I had a couple of days with scenes with Gerit and Carrell Myers. I had not acted in a while. As I said, prior the directors were always telling me to speak faster. I was only there for a couple of scenes, so I didn't think anyone would care and acted my lines slower, like I wanted to do. Joe Hardy thought these were my best scenes.

Gerit Quealy: Walt Willey had been like an extra: in crowd scenes but always making friends with everybody. In the interim, I guess he made friends with the right people and ended up as Joe. He was good and had a command of that character. However, nobody was Roscoe Born. Yes, he was tall and blond; otherwise, we would have recognized him immediately.

I thought Carrell Myers was too young for Siobhan. Marg set such a standard and not just from an acting standpoint but from a sort of strong presence. Carrell was a gentler person. I don't think the pairing gelled.

Behind the scenes, Millee Taggart and Tom King cut their time short on the show and departed in January 1987. Waiting in the wings to assume head writing control was Claire Labine, and ABC was anxious to have her return to her co-creation.

Millee Taggart: I stayed until I got a job offer to go to California to write *Nothing in Common* for Garry Marshall. It was first a film and then spun off into a television series. At that time, they were ready to cancel *Ryan's Hope*. We knew it was inevitable. They let me out of my contract because Claire Labine really wanted to take her baby home. That worked out perfectly. I later worked with Joe Hardy again on *Loving*.

Tom King: Millee was a friend of producer/director Garry Marshall. We got a chance to work on a sitcom, *Nothing in Common*. When that ended, we came back East to work on another sitcom that Mike Nichols was connected with called *The Thorns* [starring Tony Roberts and Kelly Bishop]. So, there was a while when I wasn't working on soaps.

Millee Taggart: I always had a theory about how long you stay— although I did write *Loving* on and off for six years—which was to try not to sign a contract for longer than one year because after that time your brain is tired. I could go up to two years but then need to go somewhere else. I admired Agnes Nixon and all of these people who wrote shows for, like, ten years. I can never do that. I run out of ideas.

Tom King: I went back into soaps, with Millee, beginning on *Loving*. *Ryan's Hope* had this history of being rather literary, which was Claire. *Loving* was a little more salacious and soapier. I preferred working on *Ryan's Hope* more because I liked that it was like a play. Also, the actors were better. When you launch a new show like *Loving*, you make a lot of compromises in casting because you can't get exactly what you want. There will always be actors not quite good enough. There you are trying to cast thirty parts all at once. It is hard.

Millee Taggart: Tom and I had a great working relationship that was interrupted sadly when we were on *Loving*. For some reason, they fired him but would not let me quit. He was going to be paid off on his contract, but if I quit, he would not get his money. I was so horrified, and that was what broke up our partnership.

Just before Labine came back as head writer, John Kelly Genovese reviewed *Ryan's Hope* for *Soap Opera Digest*. Although Taggart and King were praised for bringing the focus back to the Ryan family by others in the soap press, Genovese found that it was not enough to overcome some of the current storylines, especially when comparing it to the show's early days. He praised Claire Labine and Paul Mayer and described the show's beginnings as "a striking accent color in a graying tapestry of soaps." But then he highlighted some of Labine and Mayer's shortcomings as the seventies turned into the eighties and stated, "Supporting characters appear with a bang and then disappear with a whimper. The plots are either chopped off with little or no payoff or allowed to limp endlessly in the domain of 'enough already.'"

As for the current crop of storylines, Genovese was not a fan of the mob story with Rick undercover or the Jill/Dakota/Frank triangle. He opined that having an illegitimate son "destroyed" the character of Johnny Ryan, and he could not fathom why Frank would dump the elegant Diana Douglas to go back to Jill. On the plus side, he remarked, "the Delia/Roger/Maggie triangle is an amusing relief from the Sturm and Drang that permeates other areas of the show. Best of all, *RH* gave its audience a boffo surprise— the revelation that Erik Brenner (Walt Willey) . . . is presumed dead . . . Joe Novak. Good work."

According to Claire Labine, she did not immediately jump at the offer to head write her show again. She revealed in *On Writing* magazine, "I thought there was not too much chance to save it, and everybody told me not to do it. But if it was going off the air, I wanted it to go off the air looking like itself. And we actually had a wonderful time in the last eighteen months of it. We really had fun."

Insiders were not surprised that Claire Labine came back to write the show, but instead of co-creator Paul Mayer, she brought along her daughter Eleanor Labine Mancusi as her co-head writer. It is unknown if Mayer was invited back or not.

Rachael Mayer: Paul was already in post-graduate school in a whole new life—so no.

Ruth Mayer: Well, we don't know if he was asked.

Rachael Mayer: That's true. He completed NYU and was starting a practice. I know he was done, so it's hard to imagine. He was done after *Santa Barbara*.

Laura Rakowitz: I think they brought Claire Labine back because the show's days were numbered and they wanted her to bring it to a close on a high note. I am not sure if she knew this at the time. The show got a lovely send-off. It was a nice homage that ABC did for Claire. The executives at ABC then were quite different from the ones who were there when *Ryan's Hope* began in the mid-seventies. The idea that they had respect for the show was genuinely nice. However, that is all in retrospect. At the time I thought her coming back was a good sign and the show might survive. I thought the show had sort of lost focus by that point, and Claire tried to bring it back a little bit.

Tamara Grady: I am sure we were all happy about the fact that Claire was back because nobody could write a script like she could. However, I don't know if anybody really thought she could turn the show around.

Returning to head writing *Ryan's Hope*, Labine cut short one of Taggart and King's main storylines, continuing a pattern, as Genovese had pointed out in his review. Erik and Siobhan plan to make an escape but are stopped by Jacqueline, who realizes Erik is Joe and does not believe her father is the head of a criminal network. Distrustful of his wife, Max drugs Siobhan's tea to keep her docile. Ryan accidentally stumbles in on Max's plan to whisk Siobhan away to his mountain lair, so he kidnaps her as well. After learning from Jacqueline who Erik is, Max orders his men to kill him, but Joe evades them. Frank, Jack, and Rick come looking for them, but Jacqueline is unaware of her father's whereabouts. It all comes to a head at the mountain retreat high up on a terrace, overlooking a river far below. Joe has followed Max up there, as has Jack.

There is a revelation, Max pulls a gun, and he shoots Jack in the leg. As he is about to kill Joe, Siobhan rushes Max, who tumbles over the railing into the raging water below. He is presumed dead, although his body is never found. A horrified Jacqueline cannot believe what her father did and, with a released Laslo by her side, announces she will not fight for Joe and will be returning to London. Despite their on-again, off-again feelings about Joe, the Ryan family is thrilled that he is alive. However, at the annual St.

Patrick's Day celebration, the couple announce they are leaving with Sean to start a new life away from New York City.

> **Gerit Quealy:** After I left, I was still auditioning for roles and started to do Shakespeare on stage. I was already in love with Shakespeare from the beginning. I understudied Phoebe Cates at the Goodman in Chicago. It was there that I met Kevin Kline, and he told me that he started out on soaps. We didn't have the Internet, so I never knew so many great actors started out on daytime television. I regret that the pervasive feeling at the time was what it was. I will say that it houses everybody from the very, very good to the very, very mediocre. That can be tough to navigate. You can be in a scene where the better actors are trying to pick up the slack for the people who are barely cutting it. It could be tiring.

> **Fred Burstein:** My family and I are still in our Kerhonkson home [in upstate New York] we got in 1986. Except for doing a *Tales from the Darkside*, I never acted on television again. I went back to college, and I became a teacher while still writing books. And I am still friends with Joe Hardy to this day.

As main characters Siobhan, Joe, and Max exited, Claire introduced two new characters in March. While recuperating in the hospital, Jack befriends rambunctious, rebellious teen runaway Zena Brown (Tichina Arnold), and he goes directly to the Commissioner of Social Services, Emily Hall (Cynthia Dozier), to find her a decent foster home. This entire storyline of the underprivileged Black teenager being taken in by a white family had been done to death and was so beneath *Ryan's Hope*, especially since Taggart and King had introduced and then were forced to discard the intriguing characters of Diana Douglas and her parents. They should have been given prominence instead of being let go. With that said, the show was lucky to have found the talented, spirited Arnold, who made the character more interesting than she deserved to be.

> **Michael Levin:** I tested with Tichina Arnold, and afterward I pushed for her to be hired. Whether that made any difference, I do not know. Tichina was a good actress, and I liked working with her. Nothing much came of the storyline, but it was fun.

Christopher Durham: Tichina Arnold was around seventeen when she was hired. She was so cool and had just done the movie version of *Little Shop of Horrors*. This girl had it together. She was a dynamo and a lovely teenager. I so loved being around her. We had a lot of scenes because Dakota wound up running a rec center that Zena hung out at. Talk about savvy—that kid had it. I thought, "This girl is going somewhere." She has had an incredible career, and I am so proud of her.

Tichina talked about her storyline with me. She said, "They don't hire Black people like me on a soap."

Because I was that stupid, I asked, "What are you talking about?"

Tichina understood something. She replied, "I look like a Black person from the Bronx."

That is where she was from. We would talk, and as a teenager, she was amazingly astute where we were at with race on television.

The other new face was Dr. Concetta D'Angelo (Lois Robbins), the sister of Ryan's college friend Mark (Peter Love). She begins helping her brother, Ryan, and John prove that chemical warfare experiments were being done on campus and were causing sickness among the student body. There is more to this, and the young journalists uncover nefarious goings-on in the lab that put them all in danger. Despite having proposed to Lizzie and seeing a Catholic priest for marital guidance, John is enamored with the beautiful, poised Concetta and cannot get her off his mind.

Lois Robbins (Concetta D'Angelo): I started on soaps with *Another Life* [produced by Pat Robertson's CBN network]. I had an interesting experience there [playing Mandy Bolen]. They did a prayer service every morning, and I was always invited to come. I would decline politely and say, "I would prefer to pray alone." Most of the people working on this were born-again Christians. I am Jewish. The makeup man kept trying to get me to talk about religion. Finally, one day he said, "Do you like to cook?"

I replied, "I love to cook, and I make an amazing lasagna."

He then asked if I was Italian and I told him no. I knew where it was going. He then asked, "What are you?"

And I said, "I'm Jewish American."

The next day I was fired. It was literally in the middle of a storyline, and they just wrote me out of the show. That was quite brutal and eye-opening. I am sure if you asked them, they would have denied that was the reason, but it was quite an abrupt ending.

I had to audition for Concetta. [By then], Suzanne Ringrose was casting. I had met her before. I had done *Loving* [as Christy Connor] after *Another Life*, so they knew me over at ABC. I think my screen test was with Malcolm Groome. The producers and writers were there—not on the stage floor but up in the control booth. They did come down to say hello to me. Joe Hardy was involved much more so than Claire Labine in terms of how the screen test went. I got the part, and I was extremely excited.

The one character that Claire Labine did not like was Dakota Smith. She made it quite clear to everyone regarding her distaste for him and his story that propelled him onto the show. It is a wonder that she did not write him off.

Millee Taggart: I loved Dakota Smith, but Claire had that power. I thought Dakota was a long-term character, but it was Claire's baby. I wouldn't question her out loud about it.

Christopher Durham: When Claire Labine came back during my last year, we had a talk. *Ryan's Hope* was her baby. She told me to my face that she did not like my character and would never have created him. It was because of her that Dakota turned into a bad guy. I was a little shocked by it, but I had a lot of fun with it. Everything changes. Dakota Smith was sort of based on Indiana Jones. He was the hero on a boat. I didn't know he was going to be the illegitimate son of Johnny Ryan. I was just as surprised as the viewers.

Tom King: Claire was probably right to do that with Dakota. I do not recall Claire ever bringing up her hatred of him to us, though. We would have been responsive if she had.

Millee Taggart: The show changed drastically after Tom and I left. It was a bit disappointing because we really believed in what we were doing. We tried hard to base everything in character and family. But I can understand—it was Claire's show, full stop. She felt like she was laying *Ryan's Hope* to rest. I had that feeling all along. She was so happy when I asked to be let out of my contract. She said, "I'll take it home." It was a sad time for many actors in the soap world. It was our favorite.

Christopher Durham: Claire was awfully close with all the original actors so I would see her socially at people's apartments. I knew she liked me, but she did not like Dakota. I knew I wasn't a favorite of hers, but I didn't take it personally. What a turn of character. I got to play a good-guy hero and then a villain.

The show's most interesting spring storyline centered around Concetta. Through John and Ryan, the good doctor meets Melinda and learns that Pat and Evan had found a spot on her lung. She advises Melinda to undergo radiation treatment, but she declines. A brief time later, it looks like Melinda had succumbed to her illness and dies with Pat by her side. However, an autopsy proves it was suicide. After reading Melinda's journal, where her last words were that she knows what she needs to do and that Concetta has made it possible, a devastated Dakota accuses Concetta in abetting Melinda in taking her own life. He requests an investigation into her death.

Besides being accused of mercy killing, Concetta finds herself attracted to John and the two make love. John gets nervous when Concetta asks Pat to help with the campus investigation about the reported illnesses. Although Concetta is attracted to Pat, and John feels guilty that Lizzie is dedicated to becoming a good wife to him, it does not stop Concetta and John from continuing their romantic dalliance.

Malcolm Groome: Melinda's death scene was one of my favorites. We were in the park, and she had her head against my shoulder. That was very emotional for me to play.

Jason "Ash" Adams: Lois Robbins and I had an enjoyable time. It was just an affair. She was about to start a romance with Pat. It was quite a disloyal thing for John to do to his uncle.

Lois Robbins: When my character started to have an affair with Jason Adams's character, John, there was one day where we were rehearsing a scene. We were kissing, and Jason put his tongue in my mouth. Back then, that was just not done. Joe Hardy—this was the only time I ever saw him do this—came out onto the set and yelled at Jason, "Don't you ever do that to any one of my actors ever again!" Oh my God, did Jason get it. Joe was great then. He was not so great when he told me they were writing me off later on.

A major new character appeared on the scene around this time. While helping Delia set up her new art gallery next to Déjà Vu, Lizzie stumbles upon an artist named Ben Shelley. He submitted paintings, and a few were of Maggie Shelby. He turns out to be Maggie's brooding, hotheaded brother, Ben Shelby (James Wlcek). He is using an alias due to trouble he has had with the law. Lizzie tracks him down and convinces him to come to New York. Unaware of who he is, she invites him to a party at the Coleridge townhouse to meet Roger, the benefactor who purchased his paintings. Roger has broken it off with a hurt Delia to be with his wife and baby. He plans to surprise Maggie with the artwork and reunite her with her brother (he figured out who Ben really is), but Maggie is nowhere to be found. While the family frets over the missing Maggie, Roger and Bess go looking for her. Ben then arrives with a chip on his shoulder and gets into it with some of the Ryan family. After insulting Jill, who is now pregnant with Frank's baby, he is punched out by Frank, only to look up and find his mother staring down at him. Ben rehashes family slights and learns what is going on with Maggie. Also at the party, Concetta learns that John and Lizzie are engaged and have a child; Devlin and Ryan warn Jack to stay as far away as possible from troublesome Zena. Concetta lets Pat take her home.

> **James Wlcek (Ben Shelby):** It is an interesting way how I got on *Ryan's Hope*. I auditioned for *All My Children* prior with casting director Suzanne Ringrose. I read for her, and she said something that some people may have been upset with or offended by. I even remember the outfit that I wore and knew exactly what she was talking about. She said, "Your face does not match your body."
>
> At that time, I was never looking to be Arnold Schwarzenegger—maybe Sylvester Stallone in *Rambo II*—and never took steroids or drugs, but I was lifting heavy weights. I had this muscular body with this Howdy Doody face, so I knew she was right. From that moment on in 1986 until yesterday's workout, I have not lifted any heavy weights. *All My Children* loved my test, and Suzanne said I hit the right mark. But I did not get the role because they felt I looked too young for it. I was devastated and went back to my job at Keebler. I thought I would never get this close again.
>
> Later, for Ben, I did not really have to audition. They based it off my *All My Children* screen test. Even though I did not get that part, ABC felt my screen test was so good, they did not want

to lose me and knew *Ryan's Hope* had been looking for quite some time for someone to play Ben. They passed my tape over to Joe Hardy who said, "That's our Ben!" I came in to read for Ben and one of the first things out of Suzanne Ringrose's mouth was, "I'm glad you took my advice."

It was only about seven months since I last seen her, but in that time, I went from lifting heavy weights to only lifting broomsticks. She noticed the difference. The character of Ben was mine to be had. They basically offered it to me right then and there. I went home and my agent called me to officially tell me I was Ben Shelby.

Ryan's Hope was my favorite soap opera when I would be home doing nothing. I worked the graveyard shift at Keebler. I remember being attracted to Cali Timmins, who played Maggie. I was always hot for her. I am not usually into blondes and prefer brunettes more. It was my second or third week on the show and my first time working with Cali. I could not remember my lines for anything. It is a very weird thing to be a fan of someone and then suddenly you are working with them, playing siblings. That was not the only time.

Cali Timmins: I had no idea that Jimmy had a crush on me, and that was cute of him to say. I loved working with Jimmy. He was such a sweet, sweet person and a great guy. I am not sure how much acting experience he had, but to me he was good casting because he was just authentic and salt-of-the-earth. He was the complete opposite of his character in real life. And I liked that Maggie had a brother and working with that relationship.

James Wlcek: The producers knew that Grant Show was leaving to do bigger and better things, so I was kind of there to fill his shoes. And of course, those were tough shoes to fill. He was far more well trained than I was, and better looking. The guy is still like Tom Cruise. We had some scenes together.

Ben was such an amazing character. I only wish I were a better actor at the time to delve into his emotions and not play him so angry. Finding different avenues to take and choices to make as an actor. I am sure I fell into those typical traps. Today, I know I could have made that character so much more interesting, where you would empathize much more with him if I had more sense in building a character better.

The mystery of Maggie's whereabouts leads to Delia. Although Roger had reunited with his pregnant wife, it did not stop Delia from trying to win him back. One of her plans goes completely screwy when she tricks Maggie into thinking Roger is playing secret admirer by sending her romantic gifts. She then whisks Maggie off to a beach house the night of Roger's party. However, a huge rainstorm blows in, flooding the area and trapping Maggie as she goes into labor. Feeling guilty for what she has done, Delia comes to her rescue and in an ironic twist delivers the baby in the back of a van. She then gets Maggie to a hospital, where mother and daughter are fine.

Roger arrives and is stunned to see that the two rivals finally have buried the hatchet. The new parents even ask Delia to be their daughter, Olivia's, godmother. Then to no one's surprise—considering her track record with men with Ryan blood—Delia's friendship with Dakota blossoms into a romance. Jill is angry that Dakota would turn to her long-time nemesis, Delia. Frank tells his wife it is none of her business, but Jill cannot let it go.

Cali Timmins: One of my and Ilene Kristen's most humorous scenes was when she delivered my baby. Comedy is not my thing, but we had fun with it. Bringing Ilene back as Delia was one of the best decisions they made.

Ilene Kristen: My last four years there were the most fun. The Dakota/Delia/Roger/Maggie story was great.

Christopher Durham: I remember Ilene Kristen more than anyone because she is more a comedienne. Our scenes were the best. Ilene is like me, and she can think on her feet. She is terrific and we keep in touch. When they put us together, I mostly remember scheming against Cali's Maggie. Cali was just so sweet, unlike her character. This storyline was totally joyful and fun.

Jason "Ash" Adams: I love Christopher Durham and always loved him. When I got on the show, I thought of him as the brooding, handsome, still-waters-run-deep kind of guy. He didn't say a lot and kept to himself. We really didn't spend any real time together, but we got close on Facebook years later and have had some nice interactions. I always had good memories about him.

Christopher Durham: Jason was great. I think he came on a year after me. We became Facebook friends.

Come awards time, the soap made a bit of a comeback for the 1986–87 season. The show won the Emmy for Outstanding Achievement in Lighting Direction for a Drama Series (with John Connolly and Candice Dunn taking home the award). Grant Show received an Emmy nomination for Outstanding Younger Leading Man in a Drama Series. Despite being snubbed by the Emmy nominating committee, Millee Taggart, Tom King, and their writing team took home the 1986 Writers Guild Award for Best Television Writing in Daytime Serials.

Tom King: I wasn't all that surprised to win because *Ryan's Hope* was such a prestigious show in terms of writing. Claire had set the example. The daytime writing community felt the show was a well-written show. Although we didn't get an Emmy nomination, I had won an Emmy [in 1975] for writing *Another World*.

The ratings were less stellar. *Ryan's Hope* finished 1986 with a yearly ratings average of 3.2, down two points from the year before. It ranked twelfth out of thirteen soaps. Only NBC's *Search for Tomorrow* had a lower rating. Despite losing viewers and ABC's disinterest in promoting the soap any longer, with affiliates continuing to drop the show or not airing it in its noon time slot, morale among the cast remained surprisingly high. The actors seemed to rally around each other and concentrate on the work. However, most were still bitter about the time slot change, Agnes Nixon, and *Loving*.

Ilene Kristen: Agnes Nixon usually got her way with ABC. The cast was concentrating on the acting and creating great scenes. I did not go around thinking about the ratings. I felt it was out of my control. I had to focus so hard on what I was doing.

Jason "Ash" Adams: I really didn't feel any cast discord in the very beginning. I was strictly concentrating on doing my job.

Lois Robbins: I do not remember there ever being a morale problem. I think actors are notoriously optimistic most times. We love to show up for work, and we all did that. Of course, when I came on, they did not tell me that the ratings were lousy and the show could possibly be cancelled. But I remember that *Loving* was not doing well at all in their time slot and that there was talk about cancelling *Ryan's* and not *Loving*. We could not believe this. We were shocked because we thought Claire was so beloved by ABC.

James Wlcek: I was brought on because they were trying to keep the show afloat with some new blood. People tend to forget about the Oliver North hearing that preempted our show for several weeks at a time in certain markets. What could have been boring was not because he was so captivating and enthralling. I remember him being Cool Hand Luke that whole time. That affected our ratings as did that time slot switch to noon to save Agnes Nixon's *Loving*.

Jason "Ash" Adams: I think we all knew we were fighting this losing battle. Agnes Nixon had come in with *Loving*, which was her baby, and everyone knew we couldn't fight her. We had already lost our time slot. *Loving* was the worst show on air. I will scream it from the mountains. *Loving* was a horrible show and a piece of shit! It had a terrible cast except for Luke Perry.

Lois Robbins: I think they stopped doing a lot of promotion with the actors on the show. I did do some things locally on TV, like *Good Morning America*, and I appeared twice on *Live with Regis and Kathie Lee*. It is too bad they pulled back promoting it because it was such an amazing show and so much better than *Loving* was ever going to be.

Although Joe Hardy had been blamed by the veteran cast for many of the wrongs he brought to the show or had foisted on him from network interference, his relationship with them improved and a respect developed. None held him accountable for the situation the show found itself in now. Overwhelmingly, the actors who came on the show after he became executive producer or were hired by him had nothing but praise for him.

Christopher Durham: Joe Hardy came from the theatre and was much more about the storylines and what was going on with the writers. He wanted to tell a story well. He sometimes would come onto the set and say, "Let's try it this way." Joe was the executive producer and much more on the set than I remember John Conboy being (on *Capitol*). John sat up in the production booth, and I am not certain if he ever paid any attention to the actors. He concentrated on the visual aspects. That's okay but a different way of doing it.

Jason "Ash" Adams: I had a lot of interaction with Joe and am almost certain he was the reason that I got the role. I think he was the one who went to bat for me. In fact, he pretty much had me in his office the first few months I was on, either beating me up or praising me. Joe was my mentor. He was the one teaching me how to play the game and to learn what I could get away with and what I couldn't. He was a strict boss but also an incredible friend to me while I was there.

On the set he was very hands-on. He was an incredibly talented man and a successful director on Broadway. He was not a dilettante. This was a guy who spent his life directing and producing and knew of what he spoke. You wanted to listen to him if you took the time to learn where he came from. Some people didn't, but I did. I respected what he said, though at the time I wasn't always happy to have the iron fist come down on the side of my head. However, the other part of the time he always praised me when I earned it.

Lois Robbins: Joe Hardy was an exemplary producer. He really was and had remarkably lofty standards for the show. I think that is why so many people think about *Ryan's Hope* differently than they thought about the other shows. Most of the cast—Helen Gallagher, Bernie Barrow, Ilene Kristen, Malcolm Groome—we were all theatre people. He loved working with actors who had a lot of stage experience.

Ilene Kristen: Joe Hardy was qualified to be a producer despite my little bugaboos with him. By the last four years, I had proven myself so much that I got along wonderfully with all the producers.

In other stories, Ryan and Rick clash over her spending too much time working on the college newspaper. An unexpected pregnancy thrills Rick, but not the mother-to-be, and it shows. Not willing to give up her investigation into the university's possible toxic substance experiments, Ryan is beaten up by two thugs and loses the baby—and her husband, who realizes that they will always have different priorities, leaves town. With Rick gone, Mark thinks he has a clear path to win Ryan's heart, but Emily Hall's handsome, preppy nephew Chaz Saybrook (Brian McGovern), newly arrived in the Big Apple from Iowa, catches her eye.

Brian McGovern (Chaz Saybrook): After graduating from Washington State University, where I was on the rowing team and a theatre major, I moved to New York to study with this acting teacher who had opened her own conservatory. I needed to make money because it was expensive and living in New York was expensive. I did have a modelling agent. I came across a casting house called Three of Us Studios that offered classes in acting on camera. I started working there as a janitor, cleaning toilets and vacuuming studios to pay for some of the classes. One night I was literally vacuuming around students in line to audition for a class being taught by a woman named Sasha von Scherler. They told me she was an esteemed theatre and television actress. Even though I knew I could not afford it, I said, "Screw it." I wrapped the cord around my vacuum, put it toward the side, and got in the line.

I do a scene from *Romeo and Juliet*, and after I finished, they talked to me for a little bit. I am then walking down the hallway to retrieve my vacuum to put it back in the janitor's closet and noticed the man from the audition is following me. He said, "Excuse me, where did you come from?" I told him a bit of my background, and he asked me if I had any interest in doing soaps.

I never thought about it, and I knew nothing about them. I replied, "I just want to get in this class."

He replied, "Oh, you are in this class. The minute you left; we knew you were a candidate." He then said, "I'm Paul Mayer and Sasha's husband. I am helping her out with the casting for this class. I used to be involved with this show called *Ryan's Hope*."

I took the class and Paul would check in with me. I was also acting in small theatre productions around Manhattan. He and Sasha would come to my shows. They were such a wonderful couple. Sasha was such a warm, funny, creative, incredible woman. She was amazing and to learn that Delia was based on her—I had no idea, but she was so much like Delia. I would be working in a shoebox theatre, and they would come, sit in uncomfortable chairs, and watch me perform. They would praise every actor involved in the show and be so specific with their comments. They were just nice people and made everybody feel so good.

Paul was constantly on me to try doing soaps. One day he asked, "Can I just introduce you to a friend of mine?" I agreed and he introduced me to Claire Labine. I had lunch with her and her writers at the studio. It was very nice, and they all seemed like good people. Claire was such a beautiful person—vivacious and warm and *tall*. Her son, Matthew, also rowed in college, and we had a lot of mutual acquaintances.

I left and decided I wanted to do a soap. Claire gave my name to the head of casting at ABC. I read for her and was told there were two shows that they were interested in me for. One was *Ryan's Hope* and the other was *All My Children*. She gave me the choice to audition for both, but since I had this *Ryan's Hope* connection, I decided to keep going for that. I then read for the casting director at *Ryan's Hope* and then for Joe Hardy. I thought that went horribly, but they still wanted to screen-test me. I did it with Yasmine Bleeth, who said to me, "Wow, you must have been impressing people because you are the only one auditioning for the part of Chaz." I thought that must have been a good sign. The screen test went well, and the next thing I know I got an offer. At the time, I only had my modelling print agent and did not have an acting agent, so I had to work out the contract with ABC myself. Claire was helpful and guided me. She did me a really good turn and helped me through it. I got a good deal and a three-year contract.

Meanwhile, after learning that John was engaged to marry Lizzie (who even gets baptized in the Catholic church to please the Ryan family), Concetta breaks it off. The wedding day arrives, and Ben Shelby, who also found out about John and Concetta, crashes it and carries off the bride-to-be to a secluded spot where he delivers the truth to her. Back at Ryan's Bar, in a very tense, well-acted scene, Lizzie returns to confront John, who sheepishly admits to the affair in front of his family. Standing there is Pat, embarrassed and hurt that Concetta and his nephew played him for a fool. Lizzie then tells John off and Concetta as well. Despite John's mea culpas and vows of devotion to her, the devastated almost-bride runs out of the bar. A smug Maggie is the only one smiling because she spurred her brother on to win over Lizzie. Delia notices Maggie gloating, and the gloves come off once again between the two adversaries.

Lizzie later dumps John, kicks him out of their apartment, and turns to Ben. This leads to a jealous John and quick-to-anger Ben getting into fisticuffs a few times on screen over Lizzie. Off-screen, though, it was Catherine Larson whom Adams did not mesh with.

Jason "Ash" Adams: I think it is okay to say thirty-five years later that Catherine and I didn't get along. We were quite different people at that young age. Frankly, there just wasn't any chemistry between us. I think it hurt our storyline and being a soap couple. It was a mistake.

I don't want it to come across that I hated Catherine Larson. I have nothing bad to say about her because I really didn't know her well enough. And it was obvious that she didn't like me very much. We just didn't click and didn't work well together.

James Wlcek: Cathy and I started dating at the tail end of the show. We broke up in April 1989. I adored her. We had a wonderful relationship. I know she and Jason had their differences and whatnot, but I had a good working relationship with Jason. Although at the time I was very much in love with Cathy, if she ever said anything to me about him, I never confronted Jason. I stayed neutral. Cathy was so talented and amazing with me. She was very patient with me as I struggled a lot in the beginning. We had such amazing chemistry. I loved the triangle they wrote for John, Lizzie, and Ben.

Cali Timmins: I can understand why they did not click. I did not know Catherine well, but she was very ladylike. Jason was unique, and his sense of humor was out there. We hung out and he was lovely, but it was a lot. I think he was a young kid trying to come off older and tougher. It sometimes came off as obnoxious. This was not always appreciated by everybody. However, he was well-liked by my good friend Yasmine Bleeth.

Brian McGovern: To be honest, I really didn't click with Jason. I don't know why. There were those actors I felt very warmly about and had respect for, but Jason I never got close with. I am not sure why and felt badly about it. I ran into him about fifteen or twenty years ago and thought, "Okay, fresh start." But after talking with him, I thought, "Nope, we still don't click."

Ilene Kristen: I do know Ash and Catherine were not close at all. Ash had no attachment to her whatsoever. However, I do not recall him ever bitching about that necessarily or them being acrimonious with each other. They were very professional while working.

Catherine Larson was not a very sexy girl, but she had a lovely, very pure, sweet kind of quality. They didn't hire her to play a vixen. I liked her and had no problem working with her at all, though she was not someone I was close to. Of the younger people on the show, I related more with Yasmine Bleeth and Tichina Arnold. Catherine was kind of removed and kept to herself, as I recall.

Jason "Ash" Adams: As an audience member, I would have been extremely disappointed in John and Lizzie's romance because there was no heat in that relationship. There just wasn't. It was all about "my son" and "who is going to take care of this baby?" Then boom! He turns into a toddler within months. Now all of a sudden, we have this two- or three-year-old kid walking around. The relationship between Lizzie and John was always about custody of Owen.

But listen, what are you going to do about that stuff? You're a young actor in your first significant role, and it is wildly important to you. You have no control. Actors have no say in who they cast or anything, for that matter. For the most part, you would fight the trivial things like hair and makeup. You'd fight Saul Bolasni down in wardrobe. Poor fucking Saul. He was the costume designer and had all these punks telling him they don't want to wear this or that. Saul was this sort of grumpy old fashionista. I don't know much about his background, but I would imagine he was an educated, experienced guy from the fashion world. You chose your battles. These were things you could have a say in. Beyond that, the actors did not have much control.

Tamara Grady: I did not notice a lack of chemistry between Jason and Catherine Larson. I thought she was a good actor. As much as I loved Jason, he didn't have the chops that she had. I am sure if they didn't get along it was probably because she didn't want to work with him is my guess.

Lois Robbins: I must say that is the first I have heard of that. They both seemed very congenial with each other, and I never witnessed any bad blood between them.

Brian McGovern: I loved Catherine Larson. As a matter of fact, if I had to say I had a crush on anyone in the show, it was her. We never socialized, but I just thought she was terrific. There was something very sweet about her, and she had a very quiet presence. I think she took things very much to heart, which I think came across in her acting. I can't say I knew of any rift between Cathy and Jason, but maybe that is part of my feelings about Jason? Perhaps, I suspected they were not friendly with each other and, because of my fondness for Cathy, I was taking on her feelings about him to heart? I never thought about it until now.

Jason "Ash" Adams: It is not that I disliked this storyline. It was the backbone of my returning as a single dad with a baby son and a runaway, homeless mate in Lizzie. She never wanted to be with me, and there were times when it was questionable that she really wanted to be with her son. Lizzie was young and very troubled. She had a very horrific abusive background with a crazy father.

Lois Robbins: I thought Jason and Catherine were extremely hard-working and very diligent about making sure they hit their marks and learning their lines. They were very real. I worked more with Jason than with Catherine but never had any issue with their acting ability.

Jason "Ash" Adams: What I did not like, though, was working with the baby. It was just awful and not fun for anybody. Working with kids is different and could be great for the most part. They could be unpredictable and do as they feel. However, they react authentically and organically. Babies are just scared, man. The lights, the noises, and all these people around them, and they don't want to be there. I am all for using a plastic baby over the real thing. Look at the time it took between takes. Then you have to reshoot because the baby's crying over everybody's dialogue. There is a certain time it works, but beyond that it is a fucking nightmare.

Lois Robbins: I remember some scenes with the baby, and it was so difficult. That is where concentration is especially important to an actor.

Delia convinces local political big-shot Malachy Malone (Regis Philbin) to back Dakota for District Leader. Zena purposely causes trouble with her foster family, so Maeve and Johnny take her in as a favor to Jack, who is attracted to Emily after breaking it off with Devlin, another character that was never well-defined. Her portrayer, Leslie Easterbrook, was cut from the show and Gloria DeHaven vacated her role as Bess as well. Despite just reuniting with her son, Bess departs for Australia and has a tearful goodbye with her family. This also cut short her blossoming, comical romance with Keith Charles's Mr. Dowd.

> **James Wlcek:** It was weird about Gloria DeHaven. She was only there for a brief time after I arrived and then was gone. I am not sure if her contract was up or why she left. Bess kind of just went away.

> **Cali Timmins:** I loved working with Keith Charles. I wanted more scenes with him. We became friends off-screen as well, and he would invite me to his home to spend time with him and his lovely family. He had a nice sense of humor like Ron did. He blended right in with that group. Keith just made me laugh.

> **Ron Hale:** Keith Charles is another one I loved. This man's sense of humor was filthy beyond filth. I can't tell you—his jokes made you want to gag. He was one of the funniest guys, and we had so much fun.

Around this time, Emmy winner Louise Shaffer returned to the show. However, she did not reprise her role of Rae Woodard. Instead, she worked behind the scenes as a staff writer.

> **Louise Shaffer:** I loved acting and still do. I loved doing it and the work. However, there were too many times where I was hearing "You are too old for this part." I was never going to get my face lifted. Now I think it is better, and there are more options for older women, but in those days your shelf life was limited.
>
> I always liked writing. I got hold of Claire Labine and said to her, "Would you mind giving me a couple of outlines? I am going to try my hand at writing some dialogue, and if you have a moment to read, could you give me a couple of pointers on what I should be doing?" I wrote a couple of scripts, and she called to offer me a job.

> **James Wlcek:** I loved Claire Labine and Louise Shaffer. They were great writers. Claire was always extremely sweet to me. I was appreciative of her support. It was policy that the writers were told to stay away from the actors. Louise told me that specifically one time

at a Christmas party, but she wanted to let me know how much she enjoyed my performance in an episode she wrote that took place at the Wollman Rink in Central Park. They showcased my ice-skating skills. It was a fun day, and my father even came down from Connecticut to watch me at seven o'clock in the morning. He thought it was the coolest thing that they were letting me do this. *Soap Opera Digest* did a photo shoot with me wearing my hockey stuff in the middle of Wollman Rink all by myself.

Louise Shaffer: One of the very first stories I got to write was about Concetta D'Angelo. I remember my first script had Concetta on the phone with her mother. I decided the mother was speaking to her in Italian. I wrote out the phone call and got a friend of mine to translate it into Italian. I had somebody in the room listening to the Italian and trying to translate for her. It was kind of funny. I also remember writing a love scene for Concetta and Pat Ryan down in a basement somewhere.

Jason "Ash" Adams: I had little interaction with Claire Labine. It doesn't surprise me that we didn't interface much because, from what I understand and learned much later, I evidently wasn't her choice for the part. Whether that is true or not, I don't know, but I heard it from a reliable source a few years after the show had been cancelled. I always wondered why there wasn't any real effort put in. I did not get to know Claire and certainly did not spend any one-on-one time with her.

Lois Robbins: I, too, had no interaction with Claire or any of the writers other than if there was a celebration or an event to promote the show.

Brian McGovern: I got to know Claire and her daughter Eleanor, who is a terrific person. She is wonderful and warm, much like Claire. And she is an excellent writer. She would write scripts occasionally for the show, and I could tell when they were hers because they were really beautifully written. Claire was so in my corner while I was on the show. She and Eleanor really wrote for me, taking so much from my life and who I was.

Louise Shaffer: When Claire started *Ryan's Hope*, she was writing a couple of scripts a week, and Paul Mayer was too. I think by the time I got on the show [as a writer], she and her daughter Eleanor were writing it together. It had all gotten much more stratified by then. The breakdown stage of the shows is where the network has its input. In my experience [here and on *As the World Turns*] the head writer is in the room with the breakdown writers. They all know what the overall arc is, what the month's arc is, and what the week's arc is. Then everybody talks through the breakdown for the five days of the week. Everybody is assigned one, and they go home to write the day's breakdown.

At that point, everybody goes back in the room with the people from the network and that is where they have their say. I think Claire was still available for discussion when you got your final breakdown. But you are talking about somebody who was doing a huge amount of work in writing a show. I tended not to bother her too much. On the other hand, Claire was the one who always did the final edit of the script, which was amazing. On every other show where I worked as a writer, you always had an editor. The head writer never took on that responsibility on top of all the other duties they had. Claire still maintained that. To that extent, you did work more with Claire than you did with anybody else that I ever experienced.

Despite the revolving door of writers during the eighties, the directing team remained stable. Lela Swift and Jerry Evans were still with the show, and Henry Kaplan joined them. His credits included *Dark Shadows*, *The Doctors* and working occasionally on *All My Children* for many years. However, unlike Swift and Evans, who were generally well-liked and respected by the cast, Kaplan was an acquired taste.

Fred Burstein: I worked prior with Henry Kaplan on *The Doctors*. I hated him. He was horrible to the actors, especially if they made a mistake.

James Wlcek: I hated Henry Kaplan at first because he had this weird sick sense of humor that if he put you down it meant he liked you. He would tell you that you were "god-awful" or "terrible," but if he did not do that with you, he did not like you. It took me a little while to get used to that sense of humor. I was so scared of him at the beginning.

Ilene Kristen: Outside of the studio, I really liked Henry Kaplan a lot. But I thought his behavior on set was outlandish and embarrassing sometimes. He would treat the extras and under-fives like they were shit. You are not doing that in front of me. You could do that with somebody else, but I am not going to stand around and not say something. The person is there for one or two days, and you are going to make them nervous so they are going to flub their lines—not on my watch. I would actually take him to the side and say, "Henry, your behavior is very embarrassing. Do you want them to fail?"

He asked, "Do I want *who* to fail?"

"The actor you just treated like a piece of shit—that's who!" I had the confidence and respect to speak out.

Gary Donatelli: By the mideighties I had worked my way up to technical director. I worked on *Ryan's Hope* for two summers [1987 and 1988] to fill in for their technical director, who went on vacation. I would sit in the control room with producer Joe Hardy and whoever was directing the episode. To this day, I remember one of the funniest moments I had on the set. Henry Kaplan was directing. He had just come back from Africa and was carrying around this witch doctor stick. He resembled a lion with that [long white] mane and was a larger-than-life character, who would yell and roar at people to intimidate them, but there was a dark humor to it that you could laugh with. I know Ilene Kristen gave him what-for once or twice for his cruel treatment of the extras.

I am now in the control room with Henry and Joe Hardy, who had just gotten his lunch delivered. It wasn't a bag lunch. It was laid out with a cloth table covering, silverware, napkins, plates, and was a full lunch from soup to appetizer to entree. He sat down, tucked his napkin in his neck, and began eating while the cameras were rolling. Henry is shouting out instructions and using his new stick to point at which camera to tape with. He is doing that. Joe is eating his beautiful lunch, and next to me is a sliding glass door.

It opens and in steps one of two—I guess what I would call—butt-crack-over-the-belt technicians who were instructed to come in and fix a monitor on the wall in front of us. The guy and his friend start walking in and they see Henry pointing his African wand and yelling and Joe eating and smoking. They both quickly jumped back and slid the door shut. When the scene ended, I went outside to see what happened. I asked them if they were going to fix the monitor and one of them asked, "You deal with that every day?"

I said, "Yes, it's okay. It's safe. C'mon in."

They come walking in and don't they walk around the control board to go down to reach the monitor and bend over to show two big butt cracks over the belt. Henry and Joe just exploded with laughter. So, who is laughing at who?

Cali Timmins: Henry Kaplan had this gravitas about him. I remember him coming up to me while I was smoking at the time and he said to me something like "If you stop smoking and focus, you could really go far in this business. You got what it takes." It was very complimentary, although he may have been an anti-smoker. It was his way I think of telling me I had talent. It meant a lot since he was not a man of many words.

Christopher Durham: Henry always carried a baton and wore a caftan. He was bombastic and curt. I think he wanted to be Paul Lynde or something. He was fun, but he could be rude to actors who were guest starring. That upset me sometimes. These were Broadway actors doing two or three days on the show, and he would point his baton at them. I guess he thought he was being funny. He hurt people's feelings, but I do not think he meant to but I did not like that.

Jason "Ash" Adams: Henry Kaplan would walk around with his long white hair and this wand. He would hit us with this magic wand. He was a fabulous character.

Brian McGovern: Henry took getting used to. He was a real character and very theatrical. He carried around this wand and would call you "thing." He never referred to anyone by their name. He would say, "Thing, I want you sitting over here. Other thing, I then want you to move over here." I was so off-put by that for a long while. I did not understand that for what it was. I was insulted but never said anything or had attitude, but I took it personally. Later, watching him with the other actors working on their scenes, [I saw that] he did the same thing to all of us. I realized that I should not take it so personally. That was just him, however, I still didn't enjoy working as much on those days he was directing.

James Wlcek: I never saw Henry mistreat any of the background players, but again I think it was his sarcastic sense of humor. You either get it or you do not. I am surprised I got it because I am a sensitive person and my feelings can get hurt easily, being a Pisces. We would have good sparring matches that I would say to him that I would not say to other people.

Lois Robbins: Henry was always truly kind to me, and I never noticed him being rude to the day players. Some of the actors were there a lot longer than I was, so they may have experienced things that I did not.

James Wlcek: I had an early scene with Ron Hale sitting at a restaurant, and we had to eat steak. Henry Kaplan was the director. Here I was acting with Ron, who I had been watching for so long, and it was so intimidating. Just a few weeks ago I was home, watching him on TV. I was going up on my lines like crazy. I could not eat and talk at the same time. He was so wonderful and supportive. Somehow, we managed to get through it. When you are a new character on a show, a lot of times you have to do what they call "exposition."

Roger's character asked, "Tell me about yourself." And I did in a long monologue. He then made a quick comment, and I had to say basically the same thing again. There were so many lines, and I could not remember them all. I was practically in tears, thinking I do not belong here. I was embarrassed and mortified. I did not think I could do the job learning all these lines every day. It's one thing to do a play, when you go over the same lines and do the show for so long. But to have to let go of twenty pages of dialogue and go onto the next is difficult.

By the time I got to my dressing room, I got a call from Henry. He said, "Hey, you were great. Don't worry about it. Go home and get some rest." I knew he was full of shit, but he sensed something in me and did not give up on me. Nobody was going to be a harsher critic of my performance than me. It was just what I needed at the right time because I do not know if I did not receive that call if I would have lasted much longer on the show. Henry made me feel that he was in my corner and it is okay. I got over it and through it, but it did not happen overnight.

Tamara Grady: Henry Kaplan was totally opposite than Jerry Evans. He was very difficult to work with. I also worked with Henry on *All My Children*. He was a tyrant, and it was always about him. It was funny in a way but not if you were an actor.

Christopher Durham: Jerry Evans was fun to work with and laughed a lot. I was a huge *Dark Shadows* fan as a kid and knew that Lela Swift directed many of them. I would sit there on breaks and ask her about the show. She would say "In those days" (as if it was such a long time ago) "we didn't stop taping for anything. You watch some of those clips, and there are boom lights in the frame and staircases falling, but we kept going." I just adored Lela and thought she was sweet. She totally knew her shots and what she wanted. I am a very precise, on-time guy. She was as professional as they come. So was Jerry.

Jason "Ash" Adams: Jerry Evans was a great guy. We all loved him. One thing that was so impressive to me about Lela Swift was that she was the first female director on *Dark Shadows*. That show scared the fuck out of me when I was a kid. I was so stoked that was her lineage and now I was working with her. Lela accomplished so much before she got *Ryan's Hope*.

Cali Timmins: Everybody loved working with Jerry Evans. He was a great guy and very intelligent. He was easy to work with and didn't bother the actors too much. He was my favorite, and he was very respectful of everybody—no matter who you were.

James Wlcek: Jerry Evans was a sweetheart. After my first week or so, Lela Swift came up to me and said, "The camera loves you." That compliment made me feel supported, which I needed all I could get because I kept thinking I should be back at Keebler.

Cali Timmins: Lela Swift was more of a handful and the opposite of Jerry. She was busier and had lots of ideas. She sometimes would not listen as well to the actors if they had a strong preference in doing a scene a certain way. Jerry would be more trusting and say go ahead. Tamara Grady and Lela were quite the pair. Lela was so high energy. I am sure it was not easy for Tamara.

Brian McGovern: Lela was my favorite. She was so nice, and I felt very comfortable with her. There was something very honest about her. She was very capable and just such a craftsman. She knew what she wanted but was open to ideas.

In the fall of 1987, *Soap Opera Digest* graded *Ryan's Hope* in their biweekly Report Card Column. Its highest grade earned was an A+ in the Families category and the lowest was a D in Adventure—no major surprise there. The publication went on to say, "*Ryan's Hope* has made great efforts to improve stories and characters—and it shows. They put the emphasis back on its core family, the Ryans, and injected a healthy dose of young love ... The show falls short when it tries anything involving adventure, secrets, spies, villains. Some of *RH*'s greatest moments are scenes in Maeve's kitchen."

With Claire Labine back as head writer and picking up where Millee Taggart and Tom King steered the show, the magazine emphasized what made this show popular with its audience. It is too bad that ABC could never quite accept that what was working on *General Hospital* could not be shoehorned into the half hour *Ryan's Hope*. However, when Claire and Paul made compromises and met on middle ground (i.e., the 1980–81 years; the fall of 1983) the show excelled.

This go-around as head writer had Claire Labine following in Taggart's and King's footsteps of traipsing into the office at the studio to start her day. She revealed to Art Chapman of the *Fort Worth Star-Telegraph* that she arrived there at 7:00 a.m. from her home in Brooklyn, to put "finishing touches on final scripts" and then met with her co-head writer, her daughter Eleanor, to discuss new scenes that would be incorporated into outlines for future scripts. By early afternoon, they split the scenes equally and returned to their homes to begin scripting them. Describing the life of a soap writer, Labine remarked, "We work six days a week, and we think about the show on the seventh. You don't really get any time off. It's no decent way for a human being to live. You have to stay sane, balanced, and fit. It's really hard."

The year came to an end with the show close to peak form. Ryan received divorce papers from Rick and, after contesting it for a bit of time, conceded and signed the documents. She is distracted by Mark, who irritates her when he writes a scathing article about Emily Hall and her affair with Richard Rowan (Lewis Arlt) culled from information that he got from her. Mark's action draws an angry Ryan closer to Chaz, who is now working as a stockbroker with a Wall Street firm. Zena kills Lydon, a dangerous man from her past, in self-defense. Jack is able to get a three-month trial run as her foster parent and she then embarks on a singing career. Jack's romance with Emily picks up steam, but Rowan will not let her end their affair. Chaz finds Rowan dead, and Emily is bending over his body, her skeet-shooting rifle on the floor nearby. She is arrested for his murder and hires Jill to defend her. Rowan's death brings his socialite wife, Sherry (played by Diana van der Vlis, ex-Dr. Nell Beulac), back to New York.

Brian McGovern: They were creating Chaz around me. It was weird because they made him a rower from Washington State University. The only thing that was not me was that he was from the farmlands of Iowa. They wanted him to be a fish out of water: this bright-eyed guy who moves to New York and works for a firm in the financial district. The movie *Wall Street* was popular at the time, so they worked in an insider trading plot that was so topical at that time. I believe Claire was using Chaz as the counter to all the corruption and greed on Wall Street. That is why she had him come from the heartland. He was the little guy who wants to do the right thing and stay honest.

John and Lizzie's relationship gets even more toxic when she moves in with Ben at the Coleridge brownstone and refuses to let John see Owen. Besides having John as an adversary, Ben also acquires an enemy in Delia, who vows to reunite her son and his ex-fiancée. To that end, she digs up an old girlfriend of Ben's and brings her to New York. Unfortunately, Delia thought she could control Southern vamp Nancy Don Lewis (Maria Pitillo), who had gotten pregnant by Ben and had an abortion, but the girl proves to be an irrepressible, feisty wildcat.

Nancy Don's schemes to get back with Ben fail and included turning up at his apartment naked but wrapped in a fur coat and even pulling "a Delia" by climbing onto a ledge high up on the hotel she is staying in and threatening to jump. Of course, she is faking but accidentally slips, and Ben saves her. Lizzie sees through Nancy Don and promises that she will never break up her romance with Ben. But when Nancy Don turns up with a black eye, she lets everyone speculate it was Ben that did it. This still does not get Lizzie to go back to John, so Nancy Don gives up on Ben and puts her sights on John instead. To Delia's horror, Nancy Don starts working with John at Dakota's office and is at his side during Christmas Day services with Owen on her lap.

James Wlcek: Ilene was another actress who I was not in her league. I was honored to get to play opposite her. She was great. Our characters hated each other, but we as actors had mutual respect and I thought the world of her. If you do not like the actor you are playing opposite and your characters do not like each other, it makes it more difficult—like art imitating life. When you have mutual respect but the characters have animosity toward each other, you can have more fun with it and be looser with each other.

Brian McGovern: Ilene Kristen was a sweetheart. She was so creative and smart and funny—just a brilliant actress. The audience loved her. She was a force. When she walked into a room during a scene, your eyes immediately went to her. Ilene could always surprise you and she did. Unfortunately, I didn't have many scenes with her, but I loved to watch her work. I wanted to be an actor like her—to surprise people and bring that sort of creativity into my work.

Jason "Ash" Adams: I loved Maria Pitillo. She was a terrific actress, and we had a fun time. I've seen her several times over the years and always love running into her. It is simply great memories. She was not really my love interest, though. Nancy Don came after me for a time, but she was really Ben's love interest. I think that was just to get Ben jealous when he was screwing Lizzie. It was a fuck-you to Ben. On second thought, I guess in soap land Nancy Don does count as my love interest, regardless of the motivation behind it.

Christopher Durham: I liked working with Maria Pitillo, but she was very driven. You knew she wanted to go places, and she did for a brief time.

Brian McGovern: Maria Pitillo was great. Nancy Don was more after Chaz, whose heart still yearned for Ryan. I did not know Maria socially, but I liked working with her.

James Wlcek: I dated Maria Pitillo. She and Catherine Larson were the only two actresses I ever dated. I had met her at a friend's house a couple of years prior to doing *Ryan's Hope*. We had a nice friendship, then dated briefly, then went back to being friends. She was another amazing actress. I also loved the triangle with Nancy Don, Ben, and Lizzie.

Jason "Ash" Adams: Jimmy [Wlcek] was a terrific guy, and I loved him even though he punched me in the mouth three times during fight scenes. The son of a bitch could never *not* fucking hit me! He was a semipro hockey player before he got *Ryan's Hope*. He was a tough mother. Here we were mano-a-mano doing these fights with our stunt coordinator, Danny Aiello Jr., who was the son of the great actor. Danny Jr. was a big part of the show and a terrific guy too.

James Wlcek: Ash and I had great chemistry. We got along well, even though our characters hated each other. We had some fun with that, and I am sorry I actually hit him. They wrote us extremely well together regarding our animosity for each other.

The most powerful story still revolved around Johnny Ryan's rebellious, vengeful son, Dakota Smith. Sticking to her word, Claire Labine made sure the audience hated the character as much as she did. With Delia by his side, Dakota wins the election for district leader by taking full credit for closing down Meredith Drake's testing of toxic gases at Wellman College. Dakota's boastful lie infuriates Jill, who puts the blame for his actions on his devious companion. Frank rightly points out that she is jealous of Delia's relationship with Dakota and that his half brother is a snake in his own right.

Dakota is actually in the pocket of Meredith Drake, so when things go south, he jumps ship. However, knowing of Dakota's dislike of star witness Concetta D'Angelo, whom he still holds responsible for Melinda's death, they pay him to discredit her and ruin her career. To that end, he sends a former patient of hers named Augie Price to the clinic to fake a heart attack, but Pat mistakenly examines the man instead. When he later suffers a fatal heart attack, his wife files a malpractice suit against Pat, who is now in jeopardy of losing his license and practice.

Frank begins to suspect that Dakota is behind this, and when Pat overhears his half brother tell Johnny that Concetta was supposed to be working the night Augie came in, he agrees. With Maeve's blessing, they use Malachy Malone to set up Dakota taking a bribe and get it on videotape. When they blackmail him with it, he professes no involvement with the malpractice suit, but the next day, Pat is anonymously sent an EKG that clears him.

This is all brought out into the open at Mary Ryan's christening party, which Maggie hosts at the Coleridge brownstone. Johnny is upset with Dakota but furious with his other sons and wife. The hostility continues, and a few days before Christmas, Maeve throws down with Dakota in her kitchen with Johnny and Delia in attendance. One of the show's later best-written and best-acted scenes had Dakota calling out Maeve for her phony acceptance of him.

She retorts, "It was hard but never phony." She then points out that he was given every chance to become a member of the family, but his lies and devious actions that almost cost Pat his livelihood went too far. This drives her to the breaking point, and an infuriated Maeve announces to Dakota, "As of this moment, you are no longer welcome in my house. Pack your things!"

Johnny objects and threatens, "Lady, if he goes, I go."

Maeve does not back down, and Johnny walks out. Delia desperately tries to push Maeve to go after him, but she won't. A pleasantly surprised Dakota gloats that Maeve lost and quips, "Face it. He's just tired of you ruling the roost."

After more vicious banter back and forth, an impatient Maeve says, "May I remind you of the reason for the argument in the first place—your imminent departure! I'm still waiting on it."

Dakota retorts, "On my way—with pleasure."

He then packs his bags, thinking he can live with Delia, but she reminds him that she warned him that if he ever did anything to cause a rift between Maeve and Johnny, they were done. With nowhere else to go, he turns up at Nancy Don's apartment. To lighten the melodramatic mood, the writers brilliantly inserted a comedic scene where Delia phones Frank on his work line to tell him what transpired. She tells him to come to the bar. Meanwhile, on his private line, Jill calls about her having to fly off to Australia to help her mother. With a receiver in each ear, a confused Frank does not know what to do and exasperatedly says to both women, "Just hang on. I'll be there. All right?"

Christopher Durham: I knew how reverential fans were to Maeve and Johnny, but they had already turned me into a bad guy, so I just played it. It's a funny thing because I had so much respect for those characters and saw them as people. I knew it would upset a lot of viewers. However, sometimes that is what draws an audience in. I can imagine the die-hard fans didn't like it, but that's okay. If it gets them to keep watching to see what is going to happen—Will they get back together or get rid of Dakota?—that is drama. You don't have to be liked to do an interesting story. You must let that go. Actually, I do not know if this story kept the fans watching or not because at that point the show wasn't doing very well.

Ilene Kristen: I had a wonderful time working with Christopher Durham.

Lois Robbins: I loved working with Christopher too. He is just a great guy and a special person. In fact, we had a scene that was one of my favorite scenes I ever did on the show. I was a little bit sinister in it, and I remember the blocking so well. I cannot recall what I said but we worked so well together. It was on my actor's reel for several years.

Christopher Durham: Lois was amazing. She was a fabulous actress and the sweetest person I ever met. She was very good friends with Nancy Addison and her husband. Lois invited us all to her home.

The show took a big hit when Nancy Addison and Cali Timmins decided not to renew their contracts. Both characters, with their babies in tow, flew off to Australia when word came that Bess was critically injured in a car accident and needed care.

Cali Timmins: I left because I was just ready for more and to do other things. I had done the three-camera videotape shows for a long time, and I wanted to experiment. You get tired of the same character, and I wanted to play varied roles. I also wanted to find out what it is like to work on film. I got work right away and was kind of blown away because I had more respect for the daytime actor. They had to deal with scripts sometimes written at the last minute—it is practically live, and they do it every day. I honestly think some of the best actors are on daytime.

On prime time, you are standing around all day, waiting to do a scene, and it is not about the acting, it is about the lighting, the blocking, the camera position, the editing, etc. I had the opposite problem than what Gloria had and kept thinking, "This is acting?" I am supposed to react to the camera since lead actors would not always be there to read their parts. It was not what I was looking for. Stage acting would have been more fulfilling. It just gave me more respect for the daytime medium. If anybody put it down to me, I would tell them, "You have no idea."

James Wlcek: If Cali did not want to stay with the show, they should have recast Maggie—not so much for Ben but for Roger. Nancy was a beautiful woman and so sweet. I was saddened to hear of her passing. I enjoyed the scenes I had with her. Again, I was out of her league, but she always made me feel good when I worked with her.

The actresses' departure hurt the show immensely since it left their husbands, Frank and Roger, in storyline limbo. They were still married, but their wives were no longer on the show—hindering their characters. Arguably, Maggie should have been recast and Jill killed off. Keeping Maggie on board would have renewed the Delia/Roger/Maggie triangle now that Delia had left Dakota. The audience would have been devastated by losing Jill, but it would have opened romantic possibilities for Frank. It is possible, however, that Claire Labine had an inkling that the show's cancellation notice would be coming in 1988, so she decided to keep a potentially happy ending for Frank and kept Jill alive just in case. She also had an idea to bring back a fan favorite, but unfortunately that did not come to fruition.

Karen Morris-Gowdy: In early 1988, Claire brought me into her home for dinner with Paul. She asked me to come back. I really thought long and hard about saying yes. I did not take it lightly because I loved working with Claire. I was very grateful that she and Paul gave me the opportunity. Claire said, "I promise to give you a good storyline." I said, "I know you will."

However, my time there was so unpleasant toward the end that I didn't trust it would be better. I tried to imagine what my working days would be like and if I could really give it my all, which you have to do on a show like that. I hated to say no to Claire, but I did. We were both crying because she understood. I didn't want to let her down, but I just didn't want to go back. Right after that—my husband and I had a real struggle having children—I learned I was pregnant with twins. It was meant to be that I didn't return.

Around this time, Claire chose her son, Matthew, to be her new co-head writer. Story-wise, things remained heated between Maeve and Johnny, who had moved out of the house and in with Dakota. The family is enraged with

Dakota's behavior, causing the separation of the long-married couple. Meredith Drake's vendetta against Concetta does not subside, and one of their hired thugs locks her and Pat in a closet at the clinic as a warning to scare her. Delia happens to witness this and deduces that Dakota is connected to them and, after breaking into his desk, finds the proof. She convinces Roger to accompany her to Meredith Drake's offices, where they bluff knowing all of Dakota's dirty deeds and want him for their own purposes. Delia's scheme backfires and a hit is put out on Dakota. He is slightly injured, but Johnny is caught in the melee and suffers a heart attack.

As he lay comatose in the hospital, Maeve rushes to his bedside. While the family frets, Delia blurts out that it is all her fault. Tired of her usual pattern of making everything about herself, she is berated until she pulls Frank aside and admits what she and Roger did. Frank now has some leverage to get one of the arrested thugs to give up his bosses. Frank tells Delia not to worry and that the family will hail her as the heroine, which they do. Maeve convinces the family, for Johnny's sake, not to press charges against Dakota. Considering all her past unprosecuted crimes (fleeing after pushing Frank down the stairs and the hit-and-run of Barry and framing Faith for it), Delia has the nerve to be the only one to object to Dakota getting away with his crime so easily. She plots revenge.

Christopher Durham: Helen is amazing and so was Bernie. Between takes, I would pick their brains, and Helen would tell me about working on Broadway. Bernie would tell stories about doing live TV in the fifties on shows like *Kraft Television Theatre*. I was in heaven. I will say it again. It was just like family. Acting-wise, they helped me all the time. They and all the actors on that show were just so professional and giving. The things they taught me and just from watching them—these were pros. If you want to learn, look to the best. And Helen, Bernie, Nancy, and Ilene were the best. I was in heaven. Everybody was always in the moment and totally present. Honestly, I never saw any discord, fighting, or jealousy. It was the best job in the world.

Jason "Ash" Adams: It was a great honor to work with Helen Gallagher. I knew at that time where she had come from and that she was a big Broadway and off-Broadway actress. The great Bernie Barrow had been around forever. They were very patient with my insecurities and at times in the beginning, my unpreparedness.

They kicked my ass a bit, which was beneficial to my development as an actor.

Helen's Maeve was the moral compass of the show. There were several times where I sat there in mortal fear while the Irish wrath of Maeve came upon John. I imagine it had to do with schooling him.

James Wlcek: Bernie was great. He was a true gentleman. I do not think Helen cared for me. She was never friendly to me. In her defense maybe because I was a shitty actor? I do not know. I never gave her a reason not to like me. She was the only one who was not warm and fuzzy, but I did not let it bother me. I thought, "It is what it is, and that is on her." In the few scenes I had with her, her character never liked Ben because he got in the way of her grandson with Lizzie.

Jason "Ash" Adams: Bernie and I used to play tennis. We were both serious competitors. I remember one game where I was beating him at one point. What he would do was go to the line and start coughing like he was out of breath. I had heard that he did this, and I didn't buy it. He tried to manipulate me thinking that I was a young guy and would show some compassion. That is probably why I won.

Brian McGovern: My relationship with Helen was fine. I didn't hang around her very much and never thought she was doing anything on purpose. I feel badly if Jimmy takes that personally. She just wasn't that type of person who would hang out with the younger people. But she was very kind and helpful. I had great respect for Helen. Later, after the show ended, we both studied with Uta Hagen. I thought, "Good for her."

February ended with a shock for Jack. Outraged that his newspaper did not run his column defending Emily Hall, he goes to confront the new publisher and is taken aback to learn it is his former flame, Leigh Kirkland (Felicity LaFortune reprising her role). He threatens to quit until Leigh reminds him their contract states that no one may alter or edit his column without his approval. She schools him that she did not alter or edit a thing but just chose not to print it "to avoid a drastic edit" due to his biased feelings for the accused. An infuriated Jack storms out. Later, he is grateful to

Leigh when, in a surprising twist, a wired Sherry gets Emily to admit that she killed Richard. With Frank and Jack outside the apartment, Emily is arrested, and a contrite Jack submits a new column to Leigh at the newspaper. Jack's love affair with Emily is just another in a lengthy line of romances that petered out. Would he ever find happiness again?

Brian McGovern: Cynthia was short-lived. I think they were just looking for a tie-in to bring my character into the show. I wasn't there very long, and her character was arrested for murder. I cannot say for sure if the outcome played out as originally planned or changed so they could write off Cynthia. Paul Mayer used to tell me that when somebody leaves the show, it sends this ripple of fear through the entire cast. It does not matter who you are or how long you've been on the show. It makes everyone fearful because you suddenly realize that everybody is vulnerable. Your storyline can end so quickly. This was my experience with that. I was new and working with Cynthia, and her storyline ended. It was like my anchor had been cut, and now I was adrift. I was like, "Oh, wow!" You cannot feel very secure in that world.

Michael Levin was unbelievable—such a great guy and a consummate actor. That was one thing about the show, especially with the older actors: everyone was so welcoming and so warm and so smart. They were there to do a good show and put on a good performance. And they gave it their all. Bernie, Helen—they were all theatre people. They were *real* actors. Bernie was a professor and taught acting. These were people who knew what they were doing. Working with them was fantastic.

At the annual St. Patrick's Day celebration in Ryan's Bar (unknown to all, its last), John is celebrated as the new district leader. With Malachy Malone's help, Delia is able to maneuver her son to take over from the deposed Dakota—despite pressure from Frank not to meddle in their son's life. In a comical, well-written exchange, Frank and Delia (the epitome of self-centered, dysfunctional parents) wax poetic with regard to their success in raising their son without giving any credit to Maeve and Johnny, with whom he spent most of his childhood. Trying to convince Delia, who feels John no longer needs her, to cease her meddling, Frank says, "I know it's hard. We look at that boy, and he's not our little boy anymore. He's grown up. He's a man. We've done our job, Dee. All we can do is kind of step back and let him run his own life. All we can do is enjoy it, really." Delia promises to try and lets it slip that she was the one who got John installed as district leader. Frank just rolls his eyes and says exasperatedly, "I didn't hear that."

March also brought some welcome Emmy Award news. Receiving Emmy nominations were Helen Gallagher for Outstanding Lead Actress in a Drama Series, Bernie Barrow for Outstanding Supporting Actor in a Drama Series, Tichina Arnold for Outstanding Ingenue in a Drama Series, Sybil Weinberger and Earl Rose for Outstanding Achievement in Music Direction and Composition for a Drama Series, and Jack Hierl for Outstanding Achievement in Videotape Editing for a Drama Series.

Considering how the characters of Maeve and Johnny were pushed to the background for a few years, it was a triumph that the veterans finally got a meaty story and acted the hell out of it. Only Helen would go on to win. Although the show was robbed of a nomination for outstanding writing, Claire Labine and her team triumphed at the Writers Guild Awards, whose members always seemed to honor and appreciate the show's creativeness when deserved.

While Jack's romance with Emily wilted, Pat decides to take his relationship with Concetta to the next level. Melinda's body is not even cold in the ground when he proposes to Concetta at the airport as she is leaving town to take a new job in California. A shocked Concetta, walking to the gate for her flight, says yes and goes running back to him.

Shortly after, there was another writers strike that lasted until October. As with the one from 1981, it is highly unlikely Claire Labine was writing scripts and unclear if she and her son dictated storylines to follow. Then in June, the cast was stunned when Joe Hardy was let go as executive producer. Jackie Smith, whom Hardy had a great working relationship with, had left her position and was replaced by Jo Ann Emmerich. For some, this was not a good sign for the future of the show.

Joseph Hardy: When Jo Ann Emmerich came on, she fired me. I didn't care for her, and I went away thanking God. I would rather not talk about her. She replaced me with Felicia Minei Behr, who had been working for me [as producer]. I enjoyed my time on *Ryan's Hope* and just loved it. I was incredibly happy they gave me a chance to work on it.

Millee Taggart: Joe Hardy was so good to Tom and me. It was a crime that he was fired. People come in and feel like they have to burn the baby in order to assert control—but they don't. Jo Ann Emmerich was a bit of a harridan.

Jason "Ash" Adams: When Joe Hardy jumped ship, we pretty much knew we were doomed.

James Wlcek: When Joe Hardy left, Felicia Minei Behr took over, and she was wonderful. Joe though was great and would give me some good pep talks and advice. He was extremely good with me. I had the utmost respect for him and always remembered if not for him, I might not have been on the show. His leaving was not a sign to me that the show was sinking by any means. I had a great relationship with Felicia, and she seemed to be on her game. She was passionate about the show and wanted it to succeed. I think she was a great replacement for Joe.

Now divorced, Ryan needs a new place to live. She decides to become platonic roommates with Chaz, despite the attraction between them. Not able to afford her own apartment with her $400 a month budget, Chaz lies to her about the two-bedroom duplex's actual rent of $1,400 and let her think she was paying half, knowing she was too proud to accept his help.

This dose of reality of living in urban New York City was mentioned by *Soap Opera Update* as to why *Ryan's Hope* was so respected and why perhaps it had trouble attracting viewers outside of the big cities. Writer Allison J. Waldman applauded the show for not veering from the Ryan family (except in 1982 and 1984) and for being issue-oriented, unlike *The Young and the Restless*, *All My Children*, and *General Hospital*, who were now loaded with "glamorous, super-personalities." On those soaps, Ryan would have landed a penthouse-style apartment without any explanation of cost or how she could afford it.

On the flip side, Waldman presented a logical explanation as to why *Ryan's Hope*'s ratings were not as high as those other soaps. She opined, "Perhaps the very thing that makes *RH* unique—its urban environment—is one of the things that alienates it from viewers outside urban areas. Maybe they don't care about the cost of renting an apartment in New York City. There can be no definitive reason behind the lack of support the show has engendered, but to the producers' credit, they have not abandoned their realistic storytelling in an effort to find an audience. They've remained true to the Ryans. *Viva verismo* or Erin go bragh—here's hoping the Ryan's can hang in there!"

Christopher Schemering of *Soap Opera Digest* also glowingly reviewed the show during the spring of 1988. His article opened with a strong hint of cancellation due to affiliate erosion. The first half of his review was a complete history of the show, praising its first six years to the hilt and then mentioning issues that arguably hurt the show (i.e., the roundelay of actors playing the Ryan children, the infamous King Kong story, the introduction of the Kirkland and Dubujak families, etc.). He found the current show "greatly improved," mostly due to the pairing and unpairing of Delia and Dakota. He remarked, "Together, in and out of bed, Dakota and Delia were a dynamite duo."

He also heaped praise on the Maeve and Johnny storyline and said, "Most of the acting is a joy . . . special honors go to Bernie Barrow and Helen Gallagher . . . their marital breakup and reunion was heart-wrenching and consummately acted." As for the show's flaws, he began with the absence of Jill and Maggie that left "huge gaps in the story." He added, "It's great to write fascinating characters and vignettes, but sometimes one asks oneself, 'Where's the story?' some of the younger characters have yet to gel."

Perhaps the serial press knew Ryan's Hope's days were numbered and thought that reviewing the show at this pivotal juncture would help it now that, under Claire Labine, it was looking like its old self even more. Both delivered complimentary assessments of the soap and pointed out what was not working. The underlying factor in both reviews, however, was that Ryan's Hope did not deserve cancellation due to its quality and being a bit different than most of the other soaps airing.

During the writers' strike, without the leadership of Claire Labine, the show's storylines suffered and were hit-and-miss. Despite protestations from a returned Sister Mary Joel (now played by Rosemary Prinz, ex-Penny Hughes, As the World Turns), Mark D'Angelo and Ryan begin investigating organized crime figure George Anthony a.k.a. Anthony Donoso. After Ryan's story is published, Mark discovers a bugging device in her apartment. Soon she is being tailed by Silvio Conti (Cesare Danova), a member of the Donai crime family. Ryan unwittingly strikes up a casual friendship with him, unaware of his true motives. Her continued investigation leads to Mark's death, after his story connecting George Anthony to the Donai family is published. His murder is made to look like a drug overdose. Chaz quickly comes to Ryan's side to comfort her. Concetta leaves town with Pat.

Malcolm Groome: I was disappointed in the way they had written my character, and I had done the show long enough. I also wanted to go back to California again, which I ended up doing but not right away.

Lois Robbins: Joe Hardy was the one who gave me my notice. He called me into his office and said that Malcolm was leaving and I would be leaving with him. I begged Malcolm not to leave. He needed a change because he had been on the show for a long time. They kept on him to cut his hair, and he was just irritated by all the restrictions of being on a daytime show. It was unfortunate because he was wonderful—such a good actor and a joy to work with. And it was unfortunate for me because they decided Concetta had to exit with Pat.

Malcolm Groome: I considered myself a character actor before *Ryan's Hope*, and Pat was originally written as somewhat of a heartbreaker, and even a roué. To be clear, the "nice guy" storylines were not the reason I left. I had a lot of fans because of that. Although it would have been fun to have a more multidimensional character to play, I was still appreciative of the storylines I did have. The drug addiction plot was something more to sink my teeth into. And anything with Ilene Kristen was a pleasure. I also loved the scenes with Helen and Bernie when their characters' Irish Catholic values came up against the more modern and secular lives that their children were leading. Pat was always torn between the two polarities.

In a preposterous outcome that rewrote *Ryan's Hope* history, Silvio turns out to be Jack's biological father, Lorenzo, and Sister Mary Joel, who befriended him in the orphanage and who had been a part of his life on and off for years, his biological mother, Angelina! She had to keep Jack's identity hidden from the Donai family due to a family vendetta. Of course, Jack does not take this news very well and forms a strained relationship with his parents. He is distracted from his family issues when his romance with Leigh is rekindled. However, her former paramour, Matthew Strand (Steve Fletcher, ex-Brad Vernon, *One Life to Live*), comes to New York to try to woo her back. He and Jack immediately butt heads over the lovely publisher.

Michael Levin: I particularly did not like this storyline with Jack's parents, and I thought it was rather silly. However, it gave me opportunities to play certain dramatic scenes, so I did not mind it. I was flattered by the attention the story gave me and the change in direction dealing with Jack as a major character, but beyond that I don't know how I felt.

I did like the return of Leigh Kirkland. Felicity LaFortune was a good actress, and I enjoyed working with her.

The bed hopping between John/Lizzie/Ben/Nancy Don continued. Catching Ben in the sheets with Nancy Don sends Lizzie back to the Ryans, much to John's delight, and he proposes marriage to his ex once again. She accepts, and this time the wedding proceeds without a hitch. Ben has a motorcycle accident, and John keeps the truth of his condition a secret from Lizzie until their wedding night. During a bedside vigil, Nancy Don hears an unconscious Ben call out for Lizzie as he comes to. Despite being Mrs. John Ryan, Lizzie hops back into the sack with Ben after he recovers. The busy Nancy Don then begins sleeping with Dakota to get pregnant so she can pass the kid off as Ben's in exchange for keeping mum about Dakota trying to unsuccessfully ruin John's career as district leader. It works, but she miscarries after quarreling with Dakota.

Brian McGovern: During the writers' strike our scripts were coming later and later, to the point where I was thinking that we were going to go on live one day with scripts in our hands. I have no idea who was writing the show then.

James Wlcek: Yasmine Bleeth was a sweetheart. She astonished me. Brian McGovern and I would talk about it. Let's say for the upcoming week we had to work four of the five days. Over the weekend, we would try to have 75 to 80 percent of our dialogue memorized. Come Sunday night, I would try to have 90 percent of Monday's lines ready. Yasmine would come in, not having looked at her pages at all. By the time we were ready to tape, she had memorized, like, twenty pages. It was astounding to me and blew my mind. It is one thing to memorize, but she would also make interesting choices and give her character wonderful nuances.

Brian McGovern: Yasmine was amazing. She could just pick up her script and memorize the lines. She also was on the show longer than Jimmy and me, and I hoped that I would get to that point too. When you are on a show long enough, you begin to understand your character so well that you know what he would do and the writers know what he would do. Nothing surprises you, unlike when you are new and still figuring it out. I think Yasmine knew her character so well that she could pick up the script and just do it. She even did that during my screen test. She was a consummate professional and just had that skill that I still envy.

Jason "Ash" Adams: I was close with Yasmine and adored her. You look at our scenes together, and there is no question that you can just tell we liked each other, unlike with Catherine Larson, who I never spent any time with.

Brian McGovern: Yasmine was such a sweet person too. I truly mean it. Everybody on the show was such good-hearted people and doing their best. Yasmine was one of those.

James Wlcek: The one thing about the show that annoyed me was that they always had me with no shirt on. When I stopped lifting, I lost about fifteen to twenty pounds [and] was muscular. They even would have Ben in his apartment painting shirtless for no reason.

Brian McGovern: Jimmy was a great guy. I absolutely felt exploited. And it is so funny that Jimmy brought this up because we never had this conversation then, and I wished we had since we both felt the same. It made me think that it is how women feel all the time. It felt so gratuitous sometimes, and I would think, "Why do I have to have my shirt off here?" I even joked on set one time because Chaz was in his office at the Wall Street firm and I said, "Oh, good. I get to wear a shirt!" I asked, though, just to make sure. It got silly, and at the time I think I just didn't understand the genre well enough to know that is what you do. It is soap, for God's sake. Of course we are taking our shirts off.

Jason "Ash" Adams: They didn't use me as nor consider me a sex symbol. That was more Brian McGovern, who had that collegiate swimmer's build. Jimmy Wleck was another one always taking his shirt off. I was not doing that so much. I think I was shirtless most only during my affair with Concetta. That was sort of Johnno's only run as sex symbol. I never felt I was the pin-up boy type anyway.

Another entertaining storyline had Roger feeling guilty that he cheated on Maggie, first with Delia and now Sherry Rowan. A jealous Delia hires a private eye to get compromising photos of Roger and Sherry and sends them to Maggie, who immediately cleans out the joint bank account she has with her husband. He goes to visit Maggie in Australia and returns home with his daughter, Olivia, but not his wife. He found Maggie shacked up with a sheepherder living in not-so-nice conditions, so he grabbed his child and hightailed it out of there. He immediately files for divorce. Now a single dad, there are some comical scenes of Roger, Dowd, and Ben trying to figure out how to care for Olivia with no woman in the home.

> **James Wlcek:** This was one of my favorite stories because it was kind of like the movie *Three Men and a Baby* with Roger, Dowd the butler, and Ben left to take care of Roger's daughter. Keith Charles was very sharp-witted. He had a dry sense of humor and was a lot of fun. Ron did too. I liked the way Ben and Roger's characters came around and grew to ultimately like and respect each other.

The storyline that got viewers most excited was the return of Roscoe Born as Joe Novak. Plastic surgery and a late-in-life growth spurt be damned, the fans were thrilled that the extremely popular and handsome actor was back in the role. Joe visits New York because Siobhan has been receiving mysterious threats, and Joe thinks that they are from Max, who may have survived the fall into the river. He begins to do some sleuthing, and wisecracking Federal agent Fenno Moore (Casey Biggs, the last actor signed to a contract by the soap) works with him. Siobhan (now played by Barbara Blackburn) and their son, Sean (Danny Tamberelli reprising his role), eventually join Joe in New York, to everyone's delight.

> **Roscoe Born:** The show did not lure me back. My then wife, Randall Edwards, and I had about two months' rent in the bank. I called my agent and asked him to find out if Joe Novak could possibly still be alive. I saw about five minutes of Walt Willey as Joe and about five minutes of this other guy [Michael Hennessy]. They called my agent back the next day with an offer. They paid me four times what I earned when I first started. Claire Labine was the head writer, and it was clear it was going to be for thirteen weeks.

On the romantic front, Roger and Delia try to get back together, but Roger is still charmed by Sherry, who almost pulls Chaz into an insider trading scheme. Sherry is then distracted when her twenty-something son, Rob Rowan (Michael Palance), returns to New York. Working for the same record label that Zena and her band have signed a deal with, Rob is made their manager. Delia meets the handsome lad and decides to use the smitten Rob to make Roger jealous. However, the spoiled rich boy surprises Delia by being caring and making her feel desirable. She begins to develop feelings for Rob, who is head-over-heels in love with her.

This infuriates Sherry, riles Roger and John, and has the disapproving Ryan family shaking their heads in disbelief. Even Joe tries to convince Delia to stop seeing Rob in a touching scene where they reminisce about their friendship and working together. Considering *Ryan's Hope* had already done the May–December romance with Seneca and Kim and then Rae and Michael, the big to-do about Delia's relationship with a younger man seemed overblown. However, the first-rate acting (especially by Ilene Kristen and Ron Hale) and some truly comical moments and fantasy sequences, with Delia center stage, buoys the story.

> **Ilene Kristen:** I really liked working with Michael Palance. He was such a handsome young man. I had some great stuff the last go-around where I did the tango. For me, I finally made peace with the show because they were giving me a lot of comedy, and I thought, "Okay, I am not doing nighttime comedy, but I am doing it on daytime."

> **Brian McGovern:** Michael Palance and I were asked to ride a float in the Thanksgiving Day Parade in Philadelphia. We were new on the show and got all this publicity, so it was exciting. A fan approached us and said, "Can I get a picture?" I thought, "Wow, I have a fan who wants to take a photo with us!" The guy hands me his camera and goes over and puts his arm around Michael. I thought he wanted one with each of us separately. I took the picture, and the guy takes his camera and leaves. I'm, like, dumbfounded, thinking, "What am I? Chopped liver?!" Michael and I couldn't stop laughing.

In September 1988, ABC's senior vice president for affiliate relations, George Newi, gave a foreboding interview with *Broadcasting* magazine and said, "Nothing is imminent . . . but in daytime the first couple of shows on the air—*Growing Pains*, *Home*, and *Ryan's Hope*—are continuing to lose clearances. In some cases, we are getting down to poor clearances, even by syndication standards."

The following month, the writers' strike came to an end and so did

Dakota, who hightails it out of town. His attempts, including making it look like John accepted bribes, backfire and are finally uncovered. Already told by Johnny he did not want any more to do with him, and before the rest of the Ryan family could chime in, Dakota bids a goodbye to Nancy Don and splits. Now with no place to live, Nancy Don plays up to Chaz, who allows her to crash on the couch at his and Ryan's apartment. Scheming Nancy Don's presence and her lusting for Chaz drives a stake between his and Ryan's budding romance.

Christopher Durham: I was let go. The interesting thing was that the show wasn't doing well. The end of my third year was coming up and Felicia Minei Behr, whom I liked a lot, called me at home. I only lived ten blocks from the studio, and she asked me to come meet her. I am thinking, "What happened? What happened? What happened?" In her office, she said, "I want to let you know that we are not renewing your contract." I said okay and that was it. I never will forget her for that because she could have just called my agent and told him. She wanted to tell me in person because we had a friendly relationship. I thought that was wonderfully sweet and kind of her to do. It made me feel respected. I think I probably would have renewed my contract if they wanted to keep me. Of course, this felt like rejection, and I was saddened, but I knew Claire did not like my character.

I have a photo of my last scene because I think Laura Rakowitz snapped a picture. It was with Maria Pitillo as Nancy Don, with Dakota telling her it is time for him to leave town. I closed the door and that was it. It wasn't any big deal and very nondescript. They just wrote me out. Looking back, I think Claire just had Dakota say goodbye to whomever. I wish Dakota would have had a final scene with Maeve or Johnny to perhaps ask for forgiveness.

When I left, they gave me a big sheet cake, but that was it. It was kind of sad, I guess. When I joined the show, it was owned by ABC, and they used to give us wonderful birthday and Christmas gifts from Tiffany's. During my second year, Capital Cities merged with ABC, and soon after all the gift-giving ended.

After *Ryan's Hope*, I went to *As the World Turns* [as Mark Harrington in 1989] and then to *One Life to Live* [as Dr. Michael Jonas in 1992] but not as a contract player. It just wasn't the same.

Ryan's Hope had the warmest, friendliest environment. We were all like family. I have never forgotten that. I worked with the kindest actors, and it was probably one of the best experiences of my life.

Shortly after Durham's departure, ABC produced a promo highlighting the younger cast in various sexy romantic scenes (featuring many shirtless clips of actors James Wlcek as Ben and Brian McGovern as Chaz, naturally) interspersed with some of the older characters, such as Delia, Joe, Siobhan, and Fenno. The promo ended with the announcer saying, "Romance. It's this much fun on *Ryan's Hope*." It gave hope that ABC was intent on saving the show. Alas, it proved to be false hope, and before the month came to an end, the dreaded cancellation announcement finally came down. ABC was pulling the plug on the show (per *Variety*, clearances had dropped to 75 percent) and stated that it would air the final episode on January 13, 1989. Obviously, George Newi knew more than he had let on to *Broadcasting* the prior month. Although the cast lived with trepidation that this moment would eventually come, they were devastated when it became a reality—as were the fans.

In a statement delivered to the press, Jo Ann Emmerich, ABC's vice president of daytime programming, said, "*Ryan's Hope* has not been rejected by the audience. It has simply been unavailable to the viewers because of the continued diminishing of station clearances. Without sufficient stations to carry it, the program has become a victim of audience erosion." She went on to say that ABC did their best to keep the show on the air and complimented the show's talented cast and crew. This statement simultaneously saddened fans who were going to lose their soap and infuriated them because it was validation that if it was not for Agnes Nixon's masterminding by getting the network to give *Ryan's Hope*'s 12:30 p.m. berth to her *Loving*, the show would still be airing.

Ilene Kristen: It was Halloween day that they cancelled us. I was about to start making real money. I swear to God this is what happened to me on that day. I'm in my dressing room and am on the phone with a friend of mine, who had a lot of unfortunate things happen to her in life. *Ryan's Hope* was a job that I never really wanted, but I'm happy. My friend is talking, and I am feeling sorry for her but all these thoughts like *I have a great job* and *I have finally made peace with the job that I never really wanted* are going through my mind. Then all of a sudden, I have this psychic moment, and it goes "cancelled" in white lettering on a black background. This has happened to me before. I got off the phone and am thinking what does that mean? Then we have an announcement asking everybody to come to the floor. I already knew what was coming, and sure enough they informed us that the show was cancelled.

Brian McGovern: Toward the end of the show, I was getting comfortable, and the writers were picking up on that. They began writing those fantasy scenes for Chaz. One time I was Phil Donahue and another I was Dolph Lundgren from *Rocky*. I think they were doing this because they may have thought, "Oh, there is more to Brian than we know." They were heading more and more in that direction with the show, and just as I started to find my way, we were cancelled.

Louise Shaffer: For me what killed the show was the business model. I think it was never going to be a big, huge show, and I think that is why it still has a loyal following. It was always going to appeal to a special audience. The problem with commercial television is that you are not talking about the audience when you are dealing with ratings. This is something that I find hard even to talk about. On one side of the aisle are the people who love soaps, like the audience, the writers, the producers, the actors, and the crew. And on the other is the network that must watch the bottom line. Egos too get in the way. Did we create this character? Am I being forced to write blah blah blah? There is a huge amount of tension between the two.

The network does not care about the audience because they can't care. What they care about is the marketers and the advertisers. That is who is paying for it. If the advertisers say, "This is the population that we have done our testing, and we know that to sell our product, this is who has to be watching this show," then you are not writing a show for an audience anymore. You are writing a show for the marketing division of an advertiser. You must write for a certain demographic because that is where you are going to make your money. A show like *Ryan's* is not going to appeal to that demographic. It did have a real appeal, but that wasn't the audience the marketers needed.

Jason "Ash" Adams: I had taken a couple of days just driving around Newport, Rhode Island. I called into my answering machine . . . and received calls from my friends on the show. "Hey, man, what's going on? It's Jimmy. Give me a call." Beep. "Hi, its so-and-so. Call me." Beep. "It's your mother [Ilene Kristen] calling. You must call me right away! Call me now. Call me now." Beep. "I told you that you have to call me now! It's important! Call me!" Beep. "Hey, man, it's Renaldo [Ron Hale]. Don't spend any more money. The show's been cancelled." So, I got several messages from cast members who were buddies and then the frantic calls from Ilene, followed by the very staged call from Renaldo.

Ron Hale: I knew it was going to get cancelled. Whoever was left, at that point, knew the writing was on the wall and were making bets. "We might get another thirteen weeks." We just figured it was going to be happening sometime within the next six months. We knew it was over. And again, even then, the main reason that I stayed the last three or four years was because I had three—for lack of a better word—stepchildren that I had to help support. I was able to clothe them, feed them, and put them through college due to *Ryan's Hope*. Even though I may have been totally upset and not happy with what I was doing during those last few years, I had priorities. That was it. Once I got the last kid out, if the show was still running, I would have been out of there in a shot.

James Wlcek: I was devastated when we found out that we were cancelled. It is like being in love with a girl and then she rips the carpet right out from under you, breaking your heart. Working on this show was an amazing experience. I absolutely loved, loved going to work every day.

Brian McGovern: That was such a dreadful day. They called us all to the set. I don't remember who told us, but they let us know that the show was going to end. For me personally, it broke my heart because I am a shy person and it takes me a while to warm up to people. I was finally starting to feel like the cast was family. I went through a period of like abandonment. It kind of worked its way into my performances because I was very sad. I found it harder to remember lines and find my marks because I was just so broken-hearted. That was hard, but I know it was a lot harder for some of the others who had been on the show a lot longer than me.

Roscoe Born: I don't remember how I felt, but everybody was always afraid of cancellation. That is what all soaps are like. Every-body is always on edge. Show business is all about fear. That is what it is all based on—about losing your job or getting blamed for something.

Michael Levin: I didn't feel as shaken as most people did, which was foolish of me. I did not take it as seriously as I should have. Obviously, it was a momentous negative decision in my career. I stayed the entire run mostly because I was never offered anything worthwhile to leave for.

Laura Rakowitz: Feelings were mixed but I think we were all devastated. We walked around for a month in shock. Then it started to set in that it was really happening. We began having schizophrenic days where we were happy one day and then bereft and in mourning the next. It was not easy on anybody, but we all knew we had to do our jobs and put on the best finale we could possibly do. That's what everybody did. We all rallied together, but behind the scenes, we were all crying and miserable. We could not believe how fast the end was coming. Usually, you are on a hiatus when the network cancels your show or they give you two or three weeks' notice. We had months of notice, which was nice of ABC to do that, but we were also focused on getting new jobs.

Tamara Grady: The network had a very superficial view of the show. On our final show that took place in Ryan's Bar, Jackie Smith went up to a prop pay phone to make a telephone call. I said, "That speaks to that these people didn't have any idea what we did for a living." Sometimes the people who are running the show don't really have a clue.

Jason "Ash" Adams: I had been on the show about two and a half years at this point. I remember sitting in the hotel room in Newport with tears in my eyes, with an overwhelming sense of sadness coupled with a sigh of relief at the same time. It was a very strange contradictory feeling because I was done and couldn't wait to move on. I had a three-year contract and would have left anyway.

James Wlcek: What a lot of people do not know was that we were screen-testing a new love for me. I believe Maria Pitillo was leaving the show because there was a lot of interest in her at that time. Eight actresses tested just prior to notification. There were some terrific actresses. It never came to fruition of who was going to get the part.

Jason "Ash" Adams: Our champions for our show were gone. Joe Hardy had already jumped ship. I remember going up to him and calling him a traitor in a half joking way when I learned he was going to *Loving*.

Laura Rakowitz: I had just turned forty, so I was like a baby. People would tell me, "You are so lucky to work on a soap opera. They last forever and never get cancelled." When I worked in LA, I would worry from show to show and think how many years do I have left. Now it was back to the same old drawing board for me to try to find another job. I had to figure out how to translate soap opera work back to film or prime-time television. It was difficult for many people, but we had to find jobs. We had no choice.

Ilene Kristen: I called Claire Labine and told her to use me every day. But it was tough. It was October and we shot through December.

Brian McGovern: Each Christmas ABC would give us a gift. My first year we got a copper pot filled with barbeque sauce, a cookbook that I still use to this day, and other barbeque-related products. It was really neat. The next year, after we were cancelled, our gift was luggage. I thought, "How poignant is that? First, we are cancelled and now we get luggage." *Pack your things! You are outta here!*

The soap press was also disheartened about the news. The eighties saw the coming and going of new serials, *Texas* and *Capitol*, plus the demise of long-running soaps *Love of Life*, *The Doctors*, *The Edge of Night*, and *Search for Tomorrow*. *Ryan's Hope* was now added to this list. Consensus was that the show, during its early years, was "revolutionary" and "beautifully written." It was realistic with real characters with real problems and was superbly acted.

However, during its first five years, it was hampered by too many recasts in the pivotal roles of Frank, Mary, Pat, Faith, and Delia, causing major frustration for the viewers, although the ratings remained impressive, especially in the coveted Women 18–49 Demo. When it was sold to ABC, the network tinkered too much with it, trying to make it like *General Hospital* by including younger characters and fantasy/adventure plots. The introduction of new uber-rich families did not catch the audience's fancy like they should have. Finally, the time slot change to noon was the death knell, no matter how much the show recovered in 1985 from Pat Falken Smith's disastrous head writing reign.

During its last three months on the air, the current storylines began to wrap up. A crazed Max (with Daniel Pilon reprising the role) returns to taunt Siobhan. She agrees to meet with him. He promises to spare Joe and her son's life if she runs away with him. She refuses just as Fenno bursts into the room. A distracted Max shoots him instead of Siobhan and flees. After a few more unsuccessful attempts on Siobhan's life (drowning in a hotel shower stall, anyone?), Joe shoots Max. As Max lay dying, he quotes from "Send in the Clowns."

While paying a visit to Delia at her dress shop, Joe hears a recording of Zena singing that song. That night, Siobhan fumbles with a music box that is stuck, and Joe hears the tune. As he recalls Max's dying words in his head, Joe realizes that Max planted a bomb in it. He pulls Siobhan to the ground. She drops the music box, and Joe shields her body from the explosion. Sadly, he succumbs to his injuries and dies.

Ilene Kristen: Roscoe ran deep as an actor. I loved working with him, and I was probably the closest to him from the cast—other than Randall Edwards, of course. I'm glad they gave us that beautiful scene about our friendship when Joe comes to see Delia. It was just so wonderful.

Roscoe Born: I didn't know they were going to kill Joe until about eight or nine weeks in. They wanted . . . obviously to use Joe as a vehicle to bring back Siobhan. I was set up in this triangle with this other guy [Fenno], who was supposed to take over with Siobhan after Joe dies. Daniel Pilon was a genuinely nice guy, but the character was ridiculous and not realistic in the least.

Johnny and Maeve's dear friend Kevin MacGuinness (Malachy McCourt) returns from Ireland for Joe's funeral and is immediately given his old job back tending bar. Silvio and Fenno discover much skullduggery in Matthew's past and provide it to Jack for leverage against him. Leigh informs a disappointed Matthew that she has accepted Jack's marriage proposal. Delia realizes that the cosmic connection between her and Roger may be too strong to fight. She later gently tries to let Rob down, but the headstrong young man will not let her go so easily. He asks Nancy Don on a date to make Delia jealous, and she accepts, hoping Chaz will miss her.

At a dance club, Rob suggests they go to a quieter jazz bar where he knows Roger and Delia will be. When Delia ignores Rob, the frustrated boy tries to force himself on Nancy Don. She fights him off, and later, at home, Chaz convinces her to press charges. After Sherry bails out Rob, he threatens revenge on Nancy Don. The next night, Delia is to meet Roger and her son at Zena's concert, but she is a no-show, as is Rob. His plan to abduct Delia is foiled by the clever blonde but not before he roughs her up a bit. When John and Roger learn what happened, they go gunning for Rob, as does Chaz. Later, Rob is found beaten to a pulp and remains unconscious.

During the last half of December, past cast members (John Gabriel as Seneca, Earl Hindman as Bob, Dick Briggs as Mendenhall, Karen Morris-Gowdy as Faith, Nancy Addison as Jill, Malcolm Groome as Pat, Lois Robbins as Concetta, and Cali Timmins as Maggie) began to trickle back on screen. Surprisingly, some characters who should have been brought back were not. Glaring omissions were Johnny's renegade son, Dakota Smith; Leigh's sister, Amanda Kirkland; and Bess Shelby. Fans, no doubt, would have also liked to have seen Kelli Maroney as Kim Harris make a spectacular return.

Malachy McCourt: Claire Labine rehired me. It was very strange shooting those last few weeks. I knew that I screwed myself, so it was bittersweet. I heard that the cancellation was all due to Agnes Nixon wanting the show's time slot. She got it, and that was the end of *Ryan's Hope*.

Karen Morris-Gowdy: When Claire called a second time to come back, after the show was cancelled, I said yes right away. I had to figure out childcare, but Claire said she would take as many shows as I could do. She wrote this beautiful storyline for me with Faith's daughter, Grace, and I was grateful. It may have been the story she had in mind earlier, but I don't think we even discussed it then.

Lois Robbins: They brought me back at the end, and I was thrilled to do it. I loved that job. Working on *Ryan's Hope* was probably the fondest memory I have of any of the jobs I had. The thing about this show was its energy and the people who worked on it. I did not even have to think twice about it when they asked me. I was sad, however, because I knew I was coming back for the finale, but I was happy to be working with all those people again.

Christopher Durham: They absolutely did not ask me to come back. Claire Labine detested Dakota, so there was no way in hell I was going to be in the bar when Maeve sang "Danny Boy."

Joseph Hardy: I was not invited back to watch any of the final episodes.

Gerit Quealy: I wasn't invited to the closing party, and that hurt my feelings. I have no idea why I was excluded. I do not know what the criteria were, but a number of people were asked. In a funny way, I wasn't surprised the show was cancelled since it had been going in this downward trajectory. It is always sad when working actors don't exist anymore. From that standpoint and for the longtime cast members I felt badly, but from my personal view at that point, it was what it was.

Rob is in a coma. Roger determines that he will need surgery to relieve the bleeding in his brain and sends for Dr. Seneca Beulac. Meanwhile, Frank and his office consider Chaz, Roger, and John as the main suspects since all had motive to harm Rob. An eyewitness fingers Roger as the attacker, and Delia enlists Fenno, who has quit his job with the Feds to stay close to Siobhan, to help clear his name. A snowstorm delays Seneca's arrival, so Roger has to perform the surgery himself. As a wink and nod to the fans, Seneca meets Sherry and comments that she reminds him of his dead wife, Nell (who was also played by Diana van der Vlis). Rob survives and overhears his mother tell Seneca that Roger is the main suspect. Despite Roger having saved his life, rotten Rob lies and accuses Roger of attacking him. Roger is arrested, but Delia's friend from the shelter, Antoine (Antoine Robinson), was an eyewitness to the beating and refutes Rob's story. Frank threatens to charge Rob for knowingly filing a false police report that could get him six months in jail. When Sherry informs Frank of her offer to set Rob up in Hollywood, he agrees to drop all charges as long as Rob leaves town. Reluctantly, Rob agrees. However, as Sherry and Frank exit his room, Rob says aloud, "Hollywood, here I come. And with a little luck, I will not be going alone."

Ilene Kristen: Starting in 1987, I started volunteering at the Prince George, which was a homeless shelter. I met many children there, and I had a core group of about ten. I was extremely close with Antoine Robinson. I got a lot of the kids involved in acting, and Antoine showed an amazing amount of talent. Claire Labine wrote him into the show playing basically himself. I think he was about thirteen years old at the time. I think he did a wonderful job, and he was on the show for several months. Antoine had a big speaking role and I was so proud of him. These kids had it rough over at the hotel. I got some of the other kids on the show too, in a segment that was part of Zena's storyline.

Bob Reid surprises Delia and the Ryan family when he comes for an unannounced holiday visit. Silvio wants to reunite with his Angelina, but she declines and wishes to remain Sister Mary Joel. Ryan changes her mind about transferring to an out-of-state college but decides to stay clear of Chaz and Nancy Don. However, she agrees to meet with Chaz another day to talk about what went wrong between them. Troublemaking Nancy Don continues down a destructive path and reveals that Lizzie was having an affair with Ben. Outed, Lizzie cops to her indiscretion and John forgives her, determined to make their marriage work. Even so, a delusional Ben still thinks Lizzie loves him more and will eventually leave John.

The night he is cleared of all charges, Roger asks Delia to marry him, and she accepts. Ben wanders in and is stunned by the news, as is Mr. Dowd. The two hope Roger comes to his senses. As the couple are about to make their way up to Roger's bedroom, the doorbell rings. Roger is shocked to see his sister Faith, who has made a surprise pilgrimage home with a six-year-old girl by her side. She reveals it is her daughter, Grace (Caroline Wilde), but she is cagey when asked who the father is. Frank contemplates running for political office once again, and Jill calls from Australia that night. After hearing this news, Jill decides to come home and help with the campaign since Bess is doing well. She, Frank, and their daughter are reunited, and Jill then departs to see Roger and Faith.

The Coleridge siblings have a warm reunion, but Jill and Faith cannot believe that Roger is going to remarry Delia that night in a spur-of-the-moment wedding. After defending his bride-to-be by telling them she is not the Delia of yore and is now a mature, totally independent woman, they both acquiesce and wish him well. Rob does not feel the same way, and on the night of the wedding, he hijacks the limo that Roger sent to pick up Delia. Upset, Delia thinks he is going to kidnap her again, but she is able to get Rob to accept the inevitable. He then escorts her into the Coleridge brownstone.

After the ceremony, a late-arriving Pat Ryan says hello to his former flame, Faith, and introduces her to his wife, Concetta. Faith in turn introduces him to Grace. As Pat picks her up to say hi, Maeve watches from afar and gasps, "Dear God," realizing that the girl could be Pat's. Later, Maeve presses Faith for the truth, but she remains tight-lipped.

This was an interesting plot twist and may have been the story Labine had in mind when she tried to entice Karen Morris-Gowdy to return to the show when Pat was still on the canvas. Having Faith vie for Pat with someone on her own level like Concetta would have been a fairer fight. Previously Faith was in competitions for Pat with unstable women—immature Delia and emotionally disturbed Amanda Kirkland.

> **Lois Robbins:** This would have been a great storyline if they would have done this sooner. It could have been fantastic, and I bet Malcolm would have stayed to play this out. I think there is no doubt that Grace was Pat's daughter, and that is what they wanted to leave us believing. Pat and Faith were the great star-crossed lovers.

> **Malcolm Groome:** I wish they would have done that sooner, and I think I would have stayed for it. The Concetta/Pat/Faith triangle would have been great.

Roger and Delia return from their honeymoon night only to find a delusional Maggie waiting for Roger, thinking they can resume their marriage. After dumping Roger to marry sheepherder Derek, she ignores Delia and has the gall to say to him, "I made a terrible mistake. I'm here to correct it. I want my husband back." She then is shocked when she learns that he has remarried Delia, so she is not welcome in the Coleridge townhouse. Even Dowd sides against her.

A shaken Maggie goes to see her brother, Ben, for comfort, but he too sets her straight and chastises her for leaving their mother alone. He decides then and there to head to Australia. He leaves, and there is a comical catty exchange of putdowns and insults between Maggie and Nancy Don, who has come looking for Ben. After one last meeting with Roger, Maggie vows to get her daughter back and to make sure that he and Delia will not see an ounce of happiness.

> **Cali Timmins:** For the wrap-up, Maggie came off as very mean and bitter. I was just fulfilling a purpose. The show had moved on without Maggie. I didn't complain about it because I was honored to be asked back. But I didn't love Maggie at that time.

10

Last Call!

The last day of filming finally arrived, and the cast and crew were emotional, to say the least. Reportedly, there were laughs, lots of tears, and for some, sighs of relief. Many even had a hard time getting through their scenes due to reality setting in. It was the end of them being together as a group, enacting the wonderful world centered around Ryan's Bar.

Helen Gallagher: I remember that I couldn't sing "Danny Boy" because I was so emotional. I was sitting on the bar at the time. I turned to the cast and said, "Come on, sing." They started to sing, and they saved my life. When I say at the very end, "Have a good life," I meant it. I was very fond of everybody who was in that cast. They were all great to work with, and it was a lovefest in a way. That was the end of the show.

Malcolm Groome: It was poignant. It was a wonderful era for all of us as actors. Like I said, it was a family situation. Even after I left the show, I kept all those relationships with Helen, Bernie, Nancy, Karen, and Ilene. It was an incredibly sad ending, and we all felt it was unjust that the show was cancelled like that. It was a golden era for all of us.

Karen Morris-Gowdy: *Ryan's Hope* was such a rewarding experience that when we came back, it was like an unspoken, "All right guys, this is ours. Let's let it rip!" It was our show and our swan song. Shooting the last episode was very emotional for all of us. For me, I grew up with those people, and I adored them. It was bittersweet for sure and a sad day.

Ilene Kristen: The very last day of shooting was awful. Ash Adams had given up his apartment. He and his brother were staying with me. We slept through the alarm, and there was a snowstorm. We couldn't get a cab and ran the whole way over there. I had to have my hair in this weird, braided hair style. I have never been late. Now I am late and must go through a long hair process. I wasn't feeling well, and we had to sing "Danny Boy." I don't know any of the lyrics. I was so discombobulated, and it was not a happy day.

Jason "Ash" Adams: I loved Ilene. Actually, I stayed at her place a lot. I had given up my apartment because I was going back to LA. One of the show's cameramen sold me his 1970 Cadillac convertible, and I was going to drive it across country with my brother, who was with us also. We classically overslept and were running down West End Avenue in a snowstorm. Late for our last day of work in a very Delia-ish manner.

That last episode was the classic ending party scene where the camera pans around and gives everybody their last fifteen or twenty seconds. It was a big wrap-up, with Helen Gallagher singing at the end while sitting on the bar. It was classic *Ryan's Hope*. Looking back, I think the entire cast was genuinely fond of each other, though we were all very different people. I was the young buck in that crowd amongst the actors playing my family who most had known each other for ten years or so.

Ron Hale: I had mixed emotions. I remember thinking, "Okay, Ron, you knew it was coming and you had time to know this was going to be it. And Helen was going to be there, singing." I sucked it up and we got through it. I remember very well Helen getting emotional and asking us to join in the singing. I got teary-eyed. It was very special.

James Wlcek: I remember crying on this last day. I had made an album with pictures from the time I was on the show. It is in my mother-in-law's attic. I have some wonderful, behind-the-scenes photos. I remember watching Helen sing "Danny Boy," sitting on the bar, but I do not think I was on camera. We had a wonderful wrap party, and a couple of my close friends attended. It was bittersweet. We had a lot of laughs, but there was also a lot of tears. I got everybody to sign my last script, but I do not think Helen signed it. We had the script as if it was a yearbook.

Brian McGovern: I was so rocked that we were ending that I don't even remember what I did in the final weeks. I really don't and felt like I was a walking ghost. I am Irish, so that last scene, with Maeve singing while seated on the bar, broke my heart. What was nice was that so many people had come back from years past for the final episodes. That was neat seeing all those faces.

Lois Robbins: It was brutal for me on many levels because it was also my parents' fiftieth wedding anniversary on the last day of shooting. They were having a big party, and I was trying to catch a flight to get there so I could attend at least part of it. And there was a major snowstorm. So, in addition to being completely bereft that I was missing my parents' celebration and that the show was going off the air, everybody around me was extremely sad too. When Helen Gallagher sang "Danny Boy," there was not a dry eye on the set. It was a sad day in the neighborhood. I knew I would not see a lot of those people ever again. And everybody knew it was such a mistake on ABC's part, so I think we were a tad bit angry as well.

Cali Timmins: I was included for the last scene in the bar where everybody was crying and trying to remember the words to "Danny Boy." That was an incredible moment watching her sing and then her asking us to sing along. A lot of folks didn't even know the words. Between that and everybody being so choked up, it was funny. Helen just carried us through. It was amazing, and I was tearful. It was a sad day. I think I always hoped that *Ryan's Hope* would always be there and I could come back to it. It was my first realization that sometimes things just don't last. Helen ad-libbing, "Have a good life" was just so Helen.

The final televised episode centered around Jack and Leigh's wedding. It opens with Jack getting dressed and gazing at a wedding photo of him and his deceased wife, Mary. In a voiceover, Kate Mulgrew's Mary converses with Jack and begins to question if she really is okay with him remarrying. This gives Jack second thoughts about marrying Leigh, but he then realizes that Mary will always be part of his life, and she agrees. He is then paid a surprise visit by a teary-eyed Maeve, who thanks him for loving her Mary and being a good father to her granddaughter, Ryan. When Maeve returns home, she finds Siobhan fretting over her feelings for Fenno so soon after the death of Joe. She likes the idea of opening a detective agency with him but knows he is in love with her and she with him. Her guilt over her dead husband is preventing her from moving forward. Maeve advises her to not deny her sense of pain and loss but to live also.

Father McShane (Frank Perkins reprising the role) presides over Jack and Leigh's elaborate church wedding. As Jack stands at the altar with Ryan and Zena as bridesmaids, Leigh begins her walk down the aisle alone, when Matthew jumps up to take her arm. Leigh grimaces, thinking he is going to try to stop her, but she is relieved to realize that he only wants to give her away. He then accompanies her the rest of the way. When McShane asks who gives this woman away, Matthew responds, "I do—with reluctance." The couple is then married.

The wedding reception is held at (where else?) Ryan's Bar. Chaz decides to come after all. Ryan professes her love for him, and they reconcile. After Johnny toasts the happy couple, the doors swing open. Making a grand entrance is an ecstatic Rae Woodard (Louise Shaffer) there to congratulate the bride and groom. This is surprising, since she and Leigh despised each other, but fans were able to overlook this.

As the guests, including John, are distracted by Rae, an uninvited Ben crashes the festivities. With John watching from the corner of his eye, Ben pulls Lizzie into the kitchen and plants one last, long smooch on her and says goodbye. As he leaves, John stops him, but he pushes past him as he heads off to start a new life in Australia to be closer to his mother, Bess. He leaves, and Nancy Don enters to say a final goodbye to Chaz and to let him know she is following Ben abroad. She thanks him for his past help. Spotting Ryan glaring at them, Nancy Don quips, "Oh, Ryan. Chill out, will ya?" And then she makes a hasty exit.

While Siobhan says an ambiguous yes to Fenno's plans, Delia confronts party-crasher Maggie, who defiantly states that she is not leaving Ryan's or New York. Rob Rowan walks over and says the same since he has changed his mind about going to Hollywood. Needing to bring in the muscle to handle these two troublemakers, Delia goes to find her brother, Bob, who has just discovered that he won the lottery.

Jack asks a favor of Maeve—would she sing "Danny Boy" before he and Leigh go off on their honeymoon? Not being able to deny him that request, she makes her way over to the bar, just as Pat, feeling he has no choice, asks Faith if Grace is his daughter. She deflects to Maeve, who is about to warble "Danny Boy" for the final time. A portion into the song, a teary-eyed Maeve asks all to join with her in singing. As she finishes, she looks directly into the camera and ad-libs, "Have a good life" to the weeping cast and audience alike. It was a bittersweet moment that still lingers with the show's faithful fans.

As we analyze the demise of *Ryan's Hope*, there was arguably blame on both sides (the creators and ABC) for some misguided decisions that greatly damaged the show. Although Claire Labine and Paul Mayer had very good reasons to keep the show at a half hour, this choice allowed ABC to expand *One Life to Live* and *General Hospital* instead, keeping them in time slots following the network's top-rated *All My Children*. Once ABC bought the show from the creators, as Labine rightfully lamented, she and Mayer should have been more compromising with ABC's suggestions and not at loggerheads with them constantly. They may have been able to keep the integrity of the show yet include some of ABC's ideas to make it glitzier.

The network should never have sacrificed the extremely popular character of Michael Pavel for a quick ratings tick and should have thought through the long-term consequences of killing him off. ABC, however, gets full blame for putting the nail in the coffin with its unfettered determination to make the show like *General Hospital*, beginning with hiring head writer Pat Falken Smith in late 1983. She, undoubtedly, almost destroyed the soap by blowing up Ryan's Bar and focusing on young people at Greenberg's Deli. Then, most egregiously, they gave in to Agnes Nixon's ballsy demand to move *Ryan's Hope* out of its 12:30 p.m. time slot to noon to make room for her low-rated, inferior soap, *Loving*. This was a move *Ryan's Hope* could never recover from, no matter how good the storytelling.

ABC replaced *Ryan's Hope* with reruns of the sitcom *Growing Pains*, which was like a knife in the heart of its fans. However, life goes on after a soap opera is cancelled. And although the cast and crew were devastated and angry that the show was no more, they could not wallow in self-pity and needed new jobs. Many wound up working on other ABC soaps, including the hated *Loving*. The consensus seems to be that all paled in comparison to working on *Ryan's Hope*.

Michael Levin: After the show was cancelled, I realized I missed the money most. I never stayed in contact with anyone other than Helen Gallagher.

Helen Gallagher: I had roles on *All My Children* and *One Life to Live*, and I hated them both. I do not like soap operas, but I felt *Ryan's Hope* was a not a typical soap but more like a play. I was with the show and a lot of the same people for fourteen years on *Ryan's Hope*. You do not establish that overnight with anybody. It takes time.

Ilene Kristen: I jumped to *Loving* and I was supposed to be there, as Norma Gilpin, for only a few episodes, but I stayed a full year. Norma was like a 1940s hatcheck girl, and I used a thick New York accent. Walter Bobbie [as Denny and Wally Anderson] and I ate up the scenery and anything else they would serve us. It was classic. We stood out and the writers, Millee Taggart and Tom King, decided to run with it. I loved what they had me do and loved working with them. It was a lovely and creative year and a lot of fun. I did not want it to end. I eventually got let go, and that was not pretty, but it was a budgetary thing. I had turned down a contract, which was stupid! I didn't like the terms, so I stayed recurring.

Jason "Ash" Adams: The head of daytime casting for ABC called me and asked me where I wanted to go. I said, "Home." They were like, "Whoa, wait a minute," thinking it was because I didn't have a particularly good contract. I told them, "I had a fun time and a good run. The money was fine, but I want to try my hand in pilot season and go for a prime-time series." They told me that happens very rarely and were prepared to offer me three or four times the money I was making on *Ryan's* with a two-year contract. I could go to any ABC soap that I chose. I was young enough that I could have accepted, and it would not have made much of a difference on my career. I could have just done it for the money. However, I thanked them, but I wanted to go home because I missed my family and really wanted to try for a nighttime show.

Interestingly enough, I walked out of there and thought, "You fucking idiot. You just turned down a lot of money and just bit the hand that fed you." I didn't want soaps to be my career. I have several friends that did make that decision, and for them it was the right choice. My friend Walt Willey, for instance, left *Ryan's* and went to *All My Children*. He was there for twenty-some odd years. He did great and loved it. That wasn't what I was after, and I didn't want to do that. It was an extremely hard decision to make since I could have gone to a show of my choosing.

Laura Rakowitz: I hated *Loving*, but I worked there when it was transitioning into *The City*. *Loving* was awful and just a dreadful show. I had a very ugly experience there as a producer. My boss, the executive producer, was abusive and horrible to me. I have blocked from my memory most of what happened there.

Morgan Fairchild had the major lead role in *The City*. She saw herself as this *big star!* She was fine to work with and remembered her lines. I thought she was a mediocre actress but played that part well. Roscoe Born played a singer. We would go out into Central Park with him and do these mini shoots all over New York City. They were so great but weren't incorporated into the story well enough.

With *The City*, we taped it. However, it was put through the Filmlook process that really worked fabulously and made it look like it was filmed rather than videotaped. It was a show that could have gone far had the executive producers and head writers had any love of New York, as those of us who loved being here. It was a fabulous idea that just got burned away by bad writing and bad egos. The creative team were just not the right people to guide this show, and it was a heart breaker. We had a good cast and an interesting, beautiful set. It was multilevel with a working elevator. Unfortunately, despite all this, the show was poorly executed. If the right people were in charge, *The City* still should be on the air now. It had so much potential.

James Wlcek: I already had been working on *One Life to Live* playing Jack Gibson. While there, I tested for a TV show called *True Blue* in 1989. From what I heard, the part I was up for [Officer Casey Pierce] was between Luke Perry, Grant Show, Brad Pitt, and me. I was told I had a good shot for it if I could get out of my *One Life to Live* contract. They let me go so I could screen-test, and then I did not get it. Grant was cast. I was then out of work for a few months before I got [Linc Lafferty on] *As the World Turns*.

After my time ended on *As the World Turns* in 1993, I was seriously thinking of quitting acting to become a cop in Westchester, New York. If it was not for my wife, who had the courage and wherewithal to say, "Jimmy, if you do not at least try LA for a little bit, you will always wonder what if." She sacrificed a lot. We were not married yet, and she got a lot of heat from her dad, who did not want his daughter living in sin three thousand miles away. If it was not for her, I never would have gotten *Walker, Texas Ranger* and *Sons of Thunder*. Working on these shows was the closest feeling I got to being on *Ryan's Hope*.

Louise Shaffer: I tried to write for *Loving*. I got the job, and I was grateful, but God, that was a bad show. It never had anything good going for it. You don't know what it is like trying to write for that thing. Holy mackerel! Writing for *Ryan's Hope* was a breeze because the characters, even up to the end, were well defined. They were interesting and had a lot of levels, unlike on *Loving*. I remember one meeting with [executive producer] Mary Ellis-Bunim, where we were basically being told to write less dialogue and more interaction with the eyes. The reason for that was because we had a couple of actors on there who didn't speak English very well. Could you believe it! You would then get notes like "You mentioned a Bette Davis movie. Our viewers don't want historical references." It was a nightmare. I got fired by Millee Taggart, which was an interesting period in the show, after about a year. I really needed that job, but it was one of those times when, though you need the money, you go, "Thank you, God!" I never would have had the courage to leave it, but thank you because at some point soon I think I will get my soul and sanity back.

Cali Timmins: I was preparing to move to California full time when I was offered to play Paulina on *Another World* [in 1990], and they made the deal too good to refuse. I liked the description of the character that they said it was going to be because she was very different from Maggie. But when I got there, the character was pretending to be somebody who I wasn't—sound familiar? I was in limbo for about a month, not knowing who my character was. I was supposed to be one character's daughter and then wound up being the long-lost daughter of Mac Cory. *Are you kidding me?!*

    It was extremely frustrating. I never would have taken the part if I had known that. I didn't want it to be like Maggie, and then they didn't write it like Maggie. However, if you are going to make me the same character, at least give me some guts. I did not enjoy playing the part, although there were some great people on the set, but it had a very different feel to it. I was thrilled to work with Victoria Wyndham because I watched *Another World* as a child.

There was no comparison between *Another World* and *Ryan's Hope*. There was more backstabbing and competitiveness there. I think that was normal for the soaps, and *Ryan's Hope* was exceptional in that regard. It was just a job and a job that was not a very nice experience. Working on *Ryan's Hope* was one of the best jobs I ever had. Not just because of the character, but for the professionalism and caliber of acting that I was surrounded by. It was wonderful.

Roscoe Born: I did a lot of soaps after *Ryan's Hope*. My favorite character is Mitch Laurence [from *One Life to Live*]. There were some good moments from the latter years, but there was like an eighteen-year gap or so. Those two summers [1985 and 1986] when I played Mitch were the most fun that I ever had with any soap character. Because I had just done *Paper Dolls*, they gave me complete leeway with Mitch. The writers composed a ten-page document on his back history, but instead of using the character's name, they had "Roscoe" all the way through it. When I read it, I thought, "I don't want to use my own name." I didn't know why they did it. But anyway, they treated me incredibly and paid me well. Mitch was just a super fun part. He was funny and just full of life. The audience loved him and he was the most popular character I ever played. Plus, *One Life to Live* got watched more than *Ryan's Hope*. The recognition on Columbus Avenue as Mitch was a hundred times more than the recognition as Joe Novak. Soaps were huge in the mideighties.

I didn't get an Emmy nomination for Mitch, but I was up for best supporting actor for playing Robert Barr on *Santa Barbara*. It was for the year before, when I did the dual role of him and his brother on the show. I think I was nominated because Robert was the most prototypical soap character I ever played. And it was the most prototypical soap triangle I was ever involved in with the show's two leads, Marcy Walker and A. Martinez. I think I did excellent work (I think I did good work on every show I appeared on), but I also think I got nominated because it was high profile, and I did more interviews with the soap press than I ever did. I was sort of like playing ball. I only had a one-year contract, and they really wanted me to continue. I am speculating here, but they may have pushed me for the nomination just so I would want to re-sign. I do not know all the behind-the-scenes machinations of how people get nominated.

While several cast and crew from *Ryan's Hope* moved on to other shows, one actor went back to study and maintained a lifelong friendship with co-creator Paul Mayer.

Brian McGovern: Paul's daughters may not have known this, but he did watch *Ryan's Hope* in the later years to see how I was progressing. I think he had a vested interest in me since he introduced me to Claire and got the ball rolling. I do agree with them, however, that even if they asked him, Paul did not want to go back to the show. He changed his life and was taking classes at NYU to become a psychotherapist. Paul and I became very good friends. We talked once a week until he died. He was my *Tuesdays with Morrie*, just like in the book [by Mitch Albom]. My experience on *Ryan's Hope* was like no other actor, and I can say that quite certainly. It had a profound impact on my life, and I am not saying that career-wise because it did not propel me to huge stardom. For most of us, you just work after soaps and hope for the best.

The relationships I made on that show had the biggest impact on my life more than anything. That was mainly due to Paul. He helped me with a family situation and helped me realize what a gem I had in my then girlfriend, who I had known since college, and to not be afraid to commit to her. I asked Julie to marry me, and we have been married ever since. We had two children, and Paul helped me with my parenting. He was a terrific parent and a loving human being.

He so cared about people. What made him an excellent therapist was that he had such an understanding of the human condition because he had been a writer for so long, then studied human behavior and how we interact. I think it made him terrific in his new vocation and a great friend. He helped me for those few years, and then we just continued on after that, talking, not professionally but as friends. I moved to California, and we talked every week to keep the friendship going. I am a better husband and parent because of him.

Since *Ryan's Hope* was a darling of the Television Academy of Arts & Sciences during its first five years on the air and since the fact that co-creator Claire Labine had returned as co-head writer, it was expected that the nominating committee would honor the show with at least an Emmy Award nod for outstanding writing (especially considering its last few months were perhaps the best written since the show began). Unbelievably, the Academy did not do so, but it did nominate the show for Outstanding Achievement in Lighting Direction for a Drama Series and Outstanding Achievement in Music Direction and Composition for a Drama Series. Claire and her writing team had some revenge when they won the Writers Guild Award for Daytime Serials in 1988 and, quite surprisingly, in 1989 for the handful of episodes that ran in January.

11

Epilogue

After the end credits began to roll on January 13, 1989, fans and viewers of *Ryan's Hope* thought that would be the last episode of the soap they would ever see. It was, until 2000, when the Disney–ABC Television Group (a division of The Walt Disney Company) launched the cable channel SOAPnet. The new network sold itself on same-day night-time repeat viewings of the daytime ABC soaps. As an added attraction, the channel also began broadcasting reruns of prime-time serials such as *Falcon Crest* and *Sisters* plus *Ryan's Hope*. SOAPnet began airing daily back-to-back episodes from Monday through Friday and then would rerun all ten in a row, as a marathon, over the weekend. The broadcast began with the show's premiere episode of July 7, 1975. As the channel began increasing in popularity and was picked up on more cable systems, its audience reach increased tremendously.

Ryan's Hope attracted former fans who were elated that their long-dead story, which they thought would never see the light again, was revived. New fans were also attracted to the midseventies soap opera. The network broadcast the show from its debut episode until the December 1981 episodes (just after the lavish Egyptian costume ball at Delia's Crystal Palace). Viewers tuning in the following broadcast day were dumbstruck to see Kate Mulgrew as Mary Ryan strolling down the streets of New York City again. Without warning, SOAPnet had rewound to the beginning. Loyal viewers were perplexed, while new viewers were happy since many missed the earlier years due to the channel not being available on their cable systems. That is precisely what SOAPnet claimed regarding why they started over— viewer demand. The audience had grown so much since the launch that they wanted recent subscribers to experience *Ryan's Hope* from its beginning.

Though disgruntled and skeptical of the reason for the rewind, the fans were resigned to the matter and were just thrilled to have *Ryan's Hope* on the air, so they sat back and rewatched. But after the show reached the December 1981 episodes a second time, SOAPnet again rewound to the beginning. Now the speculating began and tempers flared. The online forums were deluged with unhappy viewers. Some thought ABC did not have any of the post-1981 episodes on tape, but they did and even ran all twelve years of St. Patrick's Day episodes (from 1976 to 1988) early on. Some thought actor residuals were the problem, while others claimed expensive music licensing was the reason since some of the post-1981 episodes featured pop music. SOAPnet, however, remained mum even when rewound a third time, totally ignoring the show's fans.

As the network grew, it added such popular prime-time soaps as *Dynasty*, *Dallas*, and *Knots Landing* as well as new original programming to the lineup. *Ryan's Hope* became unappreciated, just as it did during its original broadcast run on ABC. The show was moved from its 9:00 a.m. time slot to 5:00 a.m., and the weekend marathons had long ceased. Toward the end, SOAPnet dropped the show to only one episode a day before eventually pulling it off the air completely in 2011—never airing the post-1981 episodes. The network ceased broadcasting on December 31, 2013, and morphed into the Disney Junior channel the following day.

With the renewed interest SOAPnet brought to *Ryan's Hope*, fans were clamoring to see later 1980s episodes. Some longtime viewers began digitizing their old videotapes and releasing episodes from the spring 1983 to the show's end in January 1989 on YouTube. The 1982 episodes remain the lost year, since by February 1983 only 6 percent of the households had VCRs in their homes, according to Eric Zorn from the *Chicago Tribune*. As of this writing, only a handful of episodes from 1982 have surfaced on YouTube or anywhere else.

Historians to this day, when writing about *Ryan's Hope*, praise the show for tackling such topics as infidelity, religious faith, social issues, euthanasia, addiction, etc. credibly and dramatically. Christopher Schemering, writing in *The Soap Opera Encyclopedia*, remarked, "*Ryan's Hope* was shockingly well written, with dialogue that cut to the bone." The show is also lauded for its realistic portrayal of its major heroines, Jill and Mary, who were strong, independent, and career-driven at a time in the 1970s when that was not the norm. Writing in her 2020 book, *Her Stories: Daytime Soap Opera & US Television History*, author Elana Levine remarked, "These women were more overtly feminist than the 1960s characters, albeit still conventionally feminine and embroiled in personal troubles. Jillian suffers greatly but gains strength and security in her work as an attorney . . . Mary's storylines included her efforts to combine her career ambitions with caring for her husband and daughter."

Some of *Ryan's Hope's* former cast and crew were aware of the show's resurgence on SOAPnet and the renewed interest from fans, and some were not. But all agreed that the show deserves to be remembered as one of the best to have ever been offered on daytime television.

Ruth Mayer: I am going to be my father's daughter for a minute, and I am also going to tell what I think the truth is: it was a thousand times better than a regular soap opera. It was written by Paul and Claire, who were playwrights at heart. I think the quality of the writing was just astoundingly good.

I don't mean to be disparaging toward the genre. There are levels. My godfather was on *All My Children*, as was my mother. We grew up with theatre actors, and they kissed the ground every day for those jobs. It saved our lives as a family when my dad became a soap opera writer. He just took such pride in the quality of *Ryan's Hope* in the beginning. It really was his baby, and he loved it. And it was very painful when he was fired and it unraveled. He took a lot of pride in his work.

Rachael Mayer: Ruthie said it so perfectly. It holds up for the script writing and the brilliant cast, who were not typical soap opera actors of the time. My dad was always very protective of the genre because he felt it was an incubator for actors.

Helen Gallagher: I think its popularity then and now has to do with family. It is what we are missing today in our lives—the close bonds between the mother and father with their kids. I think people miss that.

Ilene Kristen: No, it didn't surprise me at all. It was better than everything else on air. I was happy just for it and knew that I was going to get another job from it. On August 13, 2001, I appeared on *Soap Center*—the talk show that was filmed in New York with Mimi Torchin. There was a producer on it named Dane, who passed away. He looked at me and said, "You're going back to work, aren't you?" I told him that I had a lot of disappointments.

While I was filming *Soap Center*, Dane said to me, "I am going to make sure that you are back on some show if it's the last thing I do."

I replied jokingly, "Thanks, but the only show I'd rather do is *One Life to Live* because it shoots practically around the corner from where I live." I told him that they had expressed interest, and he was confident that I was going to be on a show.

I just sat there that day and knew something was going on because everybody was sitting there, staring at me like I was the next new thing. It was unbelievable. I thought, "It's just me, Ilene." The assistants and the writers were all hovering around me, making sure I had everything I needed. And there was Dane, insisting that I was going back to work. I got *One Life to Live* on its own, and they offered me the role of Roxy on September 10, 2001. It was supposed to be a short stint, but as soon as they told me the name of the character, Roxy Balsom, I knew it would be a long run. It was like when I did *Loving*.

I really loved doing *One Life to Live* and playing Roxy. I would have done that show until the day I died for many reasons. It was fantastic. I loved everything about it, from just walking to the studio, to the actors who were all so vibrant. It took me a long time to get that feeling with *Ryan's Hope* because I so wanted to be a comedienne—the next Madeline Kahn or Teri Garr. So, when I finally said, "Well, let me just do that on daytime," I think I did comedy better than anybody. However, comedy doesn't get you the Emmy.

Michael Levin: I did not know that the show is still talked about. If so, I think because it was very good and broke new ground. It tried very hard to be real as they could and honestly dramatic. It succeeded somewhat and was a good attempt. To this day, I know of no other soap opera that was as realistic.

Jadrien Steele: I was surprised to hear that the soap was being rerun but not that there were new fans out there. It was a great show, and I knew a new audience would find it. I only think it was strange that a show from the seventies would be revitalized for an audience in the twenty-first century. However, you see some of that these days more.

Walanne Steele: I think *Ryan's Hope* was more special than a lot of the soaps. It was well-conceived by Claire and Paul and not set in some vague suburban town somewhere. It had more going for it being set in New York and centering around an Irish Catholic family who owned a bar. There was also a bit of a Kennedy connection with a son running for political office. I think that angle made it more interesting than most of the other soaps. I think when they got away from that is when the problems ensued.

I think the premise of the show makes it accessible to audiences in a way that some of the sprawling soap operas are not. It was relatable and not escapist. I think people felt they could connect to the characters. There weren't caricature villainous types on the show. On the other soaps, they are usually upper middle-class people living in the suburbs. They were not down-to-earth the way the Ryans were.

Catherine Hicks: I am surprised because there is so much content now. This makes me happy because I think what it means is that people, no matter what decade, respond to real emotions and real family situations. The writing and the acting on *Ryan's Hope* were good. It wasn't a cheap, sensationalistic soap opera—it was heartfelt and principled. It dealt with some quality topics and the elements of life. That does not become outdated.

Andrew Robinson: I was not aware of SOAPnet rerunning the show, but all of a sudden, I was getting this fan mail for playing Frank. Then people began coming up to me at mostly *Star Trek* conventions with photos of me as Frank Ryan (or with me and Kate Mulgrew) and asking me to autograph them. Somebody told me at that point that the show was being rebroadcast.

Ryan's Hope was a unicorn. It didn't deal with these absurd, unbelievable situations with boring characters in fictional locales. That is one of the reasons why I didn't want to do the show in the first place. The soaps I had seen were all so predictable, with characters in black and white. These characters were like real people. It had an urban, ethnic quality to it. That is why I finally said yes to Paul and Claire because that is how they came across—as real people. They assured me the show was character- and family-driven and it was not ridiculously plot-driven. I think people began to see themselves in a show like this.

Louise Shaffer: I think for some people it was different and I know that has been said a million times. But it wasn't your basic generic Midwestern WASP soap opera. It was set in a real place, New York City, and a real neighborhood. It wasn't based somewhere out in the middle of nowhere. It was extremely specific. I do think for its time the characters were a lot more three-dimensional. The heroines did have a lot of flaws, and the villains were motivated. You at least understood why they were doing what they were doing. You had actors like Ron Hale playing the sort-of bad guy with warmth and charm. They had things the writers wanted to say. It may have not mattered to the young audience, but I think older people appreciated that about it. It delved into religion with the Ryans being Roman Catholic. You had the Abie's Irish Rose storyline with Nana Visitor. You had Ana Alicia on the show. That did a lot.

Gary Donatelli: I really marveled at the beautiful scene work they did on *Ryan's Hope*. The attention span of Americans got shorter as time went on. By the time I was directing on *One Life to Live*, scenes would be two and half to three pages. Sometimes they would be a half a page long and jump to the next set and the next set. It was ADHD soap opera. *Ryan's Hope* had *scenes*! Sometimes a whole act would be an eight-minute scene, and it didn't have to have twenty people in it—it could be just two or three. It was just so well crafted. That is what I really remember most about the show.

Karen Morris-Gowdy: *Ryan's Hope* was such a great show. They could have held on to it if they hadn't tried to change it so drastically. If they had not turned it on its ear so much and integrated storylines, the show still could be running. Actors from other shows would come up to me and say, "I would do anything to be on *Ryan's Hope*."

I think the show is so remembered because of the characters. I think the fact that it was set in New York City. And the relationship between the characters. Everybody was enmeshed. And some were unusual such as Ilene Kristen's Delia. You could not help but to just love her and hate her. You wanted to protect her, but she was maddening. Nancy Addison's Jillian was just so beautiful; you couldn't help but watch her. They had so many different facets to them. I think that was the difference that you could really believe *Ryan's Hope*'s characters were real people.

Kelli Maroney: All the characters were fully fleshed-out human beings that went through things and felt things that the audience could relate to, so we struck a chord. That's what matters to actors, that people are touched in some way by the characters they play. So, all in all, it was one of the best and most important and special times of my life.

Richard Backus: At the time, *Ryan's Hope* was considered sort of the thinking man's soap. It was considered the best-written show with the deepest characters. Even though it was not the most highly rated show, it was very highly regarded in the business. People felt very strongly about it that it was the flagship in writing for soap operas. I think that is why it has held sway after all these years. People still remember it as being a quality product.

Rose Alaio: I wasn't surprised because way back at the affiliate party on Tavern on the Green, Sharon Gabet, who was on *The Edge of Night*, came up to me and said, "I hate you guys on *Ryan's Hope*." I asked why, and she responded, "Because they write real dialogue for real people." I agreed, because they did. It was like they had a microphone in your home. The writers would write the way you talked. After a while, it was just so easy to memorize the scripts. I think that realness resonates to this day.

Harold Apter: I am not surprised by *Ryan's Hope*'s popularity to this day. Working on that show, I am convinced, is the reason I was able to be successful as a writer in LA. The quality of the writing, the casting, and the characterization was high. The Ryans were like a real family to me. It was the way that Claire and Paul framed it. They were regular people—yes, they had the Coleridges and the Kirklands—but it was really about regular people who ran a bar. It never went beyond a half hour, which was also really smart. They did do silly stories too, unfortunately, but they dealt with genuine issues, and the writing had a reality to it that grabs people.

Geoff Pierson: I do not really know all the reasons why *Ryan's Hope* is still so beloved. I do know that many years after I left the show, I could be on a plane or on a set, and a lot of people not in the business would recognize me from *Ryan's Hope*. They would come up to me and talk about watching the show. I do not get it as much anymore because it has been so long—over thirty years. Every once in a blue moon, someone will say to me, "I remember you on *Ryan's Hope*."

I think part of the reason why people do remember it was because it was so different from the other shows at the time. It was focused on a working-class family and was extremely specific, being set in the Washington Heights section of New York City, across from a hospital. It was not the trendy Upper West Side of New York. It had definite location, family, religion, identity—it was not generic at all. I think that is part of the reason.

Cali Timmins: I would love to be more aware of the soap's current following, but I am not surprised. I would be surprised, though, if it was reaching younger audiences. I have siblings in the band The Cowboy Junkies, and they have been around for a long time with an extremely strong, loyal following. When something is special, it just finds its way to survive because it is more than just entertainment. The show had a lot of heart and was unique. It was a wonderful, special time for me, and obviously it is where I met my husband, Geoff, so that made it even more wonderful.

Tom King: I really think Claire Labine was a genius—I really think she was. Claire was maybe the best that ever wrote soaps. I missed the age of Irna Phillips, but I am sure she was really old-fashioned. I loved *All My Children* and thought Agnes Nixon was a genius too, but Claire was literary. Her work had a literary quality and went against the cliches of soap opera. In that respect, I thought she was a game-changer.

Christopher Durham: I think *Ryan's Hope* is almost like *Dark Shadows* but in an unusual way. It was set in a real city, New York, rather than a make-believe city, and the core family were Irish Catholic and ran a bar. It was a blue-collar, grassroots type of show during the beginning years. And I was well aware of the King Kong story with Delia when the show went crazy, but they all do. It is hard to write a show every day and not come up with something over the top. Still, it is one of the most well-respected soaps, and I am very proud to say I was a part of it at some point. Everything about it was just so magical.

Lois Robbins: I think *Ryan's Hope* had a lot of heart and, unlike a lot of the other soap operas, it had a higher quality because of the Ryans being the central family. There was something very real and gritty about the show. It really felt like a slice of life and something very organic about it that I think a lot of the other soaps did not have. And at the center of it were Helen Gallagher and Bernie Barrow, who set the tone for the rest of the show. They weren't rich people but real, working-class people that made them very relatable to the viewers.

Brian McGovern: *Ryan's Hope* was so unique from all other soaps. I may be a bit biased, but I don't think so because I have enough years behind me to look at this clearly. What set that show apart was it had heart. The characters were fleshed-out human beings. It connected with normal people. It was about an Irish immigrant family in New York doing their best. It wasn't flashy or glamorous like all the other shows. It had great actors doing real material. That's what that show was about and made it so distinctive.

The one dissenting comment came from an ABC executive who seems to have looked at the show in terms of what it brought to the network. As Louise Shaffer rightly pointed out, it is a business, and if the show is not making lots of money, with high ratings, it does not matter how good the quality. Prestige does not pay the bills.

Seymour Amlen: In terms of the network, I do not think *Ryan's Hope* has much of a legacy with ABC. It was on the air for several years, and I am sure it still has a devoted fan following. A lot of the viewers thought of these characters as real people.

In 2023, there is still a dream that some streaming service will obtain and run *Ryan's Hope* and other long-gone soap operas. Or that ABC, which owns the rights to the show, will revive more *Ryan's Hope* characters on its sole remaining soap, *General Hospital*, as it did in 2013 with Ilene Kristen reprising her role as Delia. With a bit of rewriting history, viewers are led to believe that a sixteen-year-old Delia was intimate with mobster Victor Jerome and gave birth to baby girl that was put up for adoption. The girl grew up to be Ava Jerome (Maura West), who unexpectedly shows up at Ryan's Bar, now run by the daffy Delia. A pregnant Ava needs her mother's help. She killed the girlfriend of Sonny Corinthos (Maurice Bernard) and is afraid he will murder her in revenge after she gives birth. Delia follows Ava back to Port Charles to try to help sabotage Sonny's plans. When that backfires, Sonny forces Delia back to New York, and Ava is presumed dead. However, she is actually on the run and pops up again at the bar to let Delia know she is still alive. It was hoped that Ilene would become, at least, a recurring character, but it did not come to pass, and she was last seen in 2015. More recently, the Novak crime family has been introduced but, so far, there is no connection to any of *Ryan's Hope*'s characters.

Ilene Kristen: It was bittersweet in that I was certainly willing to play Delia again but felt if they could have gotten the rights to Roxy, I would have actually preferred that. ABC still has the lawsuit with the company that did the *One Life to Live* web series, so they couldn't. They wrote Delia as Roxy, but I muted it because I know how to do Roxy. I lower my voice for Roxy and I change my clothing. I made sure to wear my hair straight like Delia. For the last ten years, I did Roxy, and they didn't know how to write for Delia. I could have written Delia for them. There was some funny stuff, but I still think it would have been better as Roxy.

I thought they would have figured out a way for Ron Hale (ex-Mike, *General Hospital*) to come back. They had a photo of him displayed, and Delia says, "What are you doing with a picture of my husband?"

Sonny says, "That's my father." I then make a quizzical face.

Although I was delighted to play Delia again, it never turned into what I expected it to. My feeling is once you got me, you should keep me. They didn't. The producer must have said, "We don't need Delia there," but Ron Carlivati [the former head writer] wanted her. Shelly Altman was the new head writer, and she wrote Roxy for years. I love working with Frank Valentini. The environment there didn't feel like a home, though I could have made it a home. It just never turned into that.

Although seeing beloved characters on *General Hospital* is a treat and fun for fans if done respectfully and faithfully, what they truly want for *Ryan's Hope* is a new revival soap that mixes cast veterans with newcomers playing the next generation of Ryans, Coleridges, Novaks, and Fanellis.

Here's hoping.

Bibliography

"ABC Hits Key Daytime Group of Women 18–49." *Broadcasting*, April 2, 1982: 69, 70.

"ABC Holding Fast to Daytime." *Broadcasting*, May 16, 1983: 76.

"Actor James Clarke Makes His Presence Known on Asolo Rep Stage." *Sarasota Florida News*, April 12, 2012. http://ryanshopesoapopera.proboards.com/thread/2281#ixzz3P5vnzejq

Bellafante, Gina. "Big City: A Writer Brought 'Ryan's Hope' to Life." *The New York Times*, February 27, 2022: MB 3.

Berman, Bruce. "Patrick James Clarke." *Afternoon TV*, November 1982. http://ryansbaronline.tripod.com/clarkeatvm82.html

"Bill Bell & Claire Labine on Writing Daytime Serials." *On Writing*, December 1997.

"Catching Up with Judith Barcroft, Part 2 of 2." *We Love Soaps*, February 17, 2010. https://www.welovesoaps.net/2010/02/wls-interview-archive-judith-barcroft.html

Chapman, Art. "Lightweight Soaps Can Be Burden for Cast." *Fort Worth Star-Telegram*, November 18, 1987: 1, 6.

Cherwin, Merrill. "Emmys." *Afternoon TV Magazine*, October 1978.

Clines, Francis X. "About New York: 'Ryan's Hope' Is a New Yorker's Fantasy." *New York Times*, November 27, 1976.

Coons, Joanna. "Are Women in Soap Opera Suffering from The Cinderella Complex?" *Soap Opera Digest*, September 28, 1982: 92–99.

___. "Head Writer Claire Labine Celebrates *Ryan's Hope*." *Rona Barrett's Daytimers*, August 1982.

___. "Is It time to Start Watching 'Ryan's Hope'?" *Soap Opera Digest*, August 28, 1984: 101–105.

___. "Joseph Novak: Reflections of a Man Torn Between Two Worlds." *Soap Opera Digest*, February 1, 1983: 14–19, 38, 39.

Copeland, Mary Ann. *Soap Opera History*. Mallard Press; Lincolnwood, IL: Publications International, 1991.

"Daytime Ratings." *Variety*, June 22, 1982: 43, 70.

DeKnock, Jan. "Daytime Soaps Maturing in a Romantic Way." *Chicago Tribune*, July 13, 1986.

"Delia Debuts Her Palace of Pleasure!" *Afternoon TV*, September 1980: 12, 13.

Dennison, Linda T. "Michael Corbett: Is *Ryan's Hope Search*'s Gain?" *Soap Opera Digest*, April 26, 1983: 100, 101.

Dorsey, Tom. "Ex-Louisvillian, Offspring Mourn Loss of 'Hope.'" *The Courier-Journal* (Louisville, KY), January 10, 1989: 1,2.

Doussard, James. "'Ryan's Hope' Is the Hope of Its Kentucky Creator, Too." *Courier-Journal* (Louisville, KY), July 13, 1975.

Eggering, Susan. "King of Suds: Hometown Boy Finds Success as Soap Opera Writer." *The Anniston Star*, October 11, 1986: 6.

Filips, Janet. "Can Rory Metcalf Find Happiness Writing Soaps?" *Journal Herald* (Dayton, OH), December 31, 1980: 20.

"First U.S. Sale of Soap to U.K. Is 'Ryan's Hope.'" *Variety*, September 25, 1985: 66.

Gannett News Service. "There's 'Hope.'" *The Journal-News*, July 9, 1975: 10B.

Genovese, John Kelly. "Critic's Corner: *Ryan's Hope*." *Soap Opera Digest*, January 27, 1987: 102–104.

____. "Critic's Corner: *Ryan's Hope*: Damn Near Perfect, Except. . ." *Afternoon TV*, January 1982.

Golden, Ellen Zoe. "The Lure of Villainy: Why Actors (and Viewers) Love Scoundrels." *Soap Opera Digest*, March 15, 1983.

Goldstein, S. Ezra. "The Soaps: Will Pat Recover? Is Leigh Jack's New Love? Will I Ever Get This Television Out of My Office?" *Dramatics*, Vol. 54, Issue 9, May 1983: 9–11, 31, 32.

Goudas, John N. "Soap Opera Scene." *Daily Record, Northwest, NJ*, March 30, 1980: J4.

Handelman, Jay. "Actor James Clarke Makes His Presence Known on Asolo Rep Stage." *Sarasota Florida News*, April 19, 2021.

Hirsch, Linda. "Soap Operas." *Philadelphia Inquirer*, January 30, 1978: 6-C.

Hyatt, Wesley. *The Encyclopedia of Daytime Television*. New York: Billboard Books, 1997.

Jacobs, Damon L. "Soap's Hope: The Claire Labine Interview, Part Three." *WeLoveSoaps.com*, November 5, 2009: http://www.welovesoaps.net/2009/11/soaps-hope-claire-labine-interview-part.html#uds-search-results

____. "Soap's Hope: The Claire Labine Interview, Part Two." *WeLoveSoaps.com*, November 3, 2009: http://www.welovesoaps.net/2009/11/soaps-hope-claire-labine-interview-part_03.html

Jefferson, Geri. "Jill and Frank? Frank and Jill? Jill and Seneca? Is Anyone Suited for Anyone?" *Soap Opera Digest*, February 1979: 116–118.

Johnson, David. "One Man's Opinion: I Remember Mummy." *Rona Barrett's Daytimers*, February 1982.

Jory, Tom. "Slim and Spicy: ABC Soaps' Success Due to Trimmer, Livelier Plots." *The Austin American Statesman*, September 10, 1980.

Kantrowitz, Barbara. "The Soaps: Three Writers." *The Philadelphia Inquirer*, August 29, 1980: 5-B, 8-B.

Klemesrud, Judith. "Can a Soap Opera Find Happiness in Brooklyn?" *New York Times*, April 11, 1978: 35.

Knopf, Terry Ann. "Daytime TV: ABC Has the Formula for Success: Rx = Jackie Smith + High Adventure, Romance." *Boston Globe*, October 18, 1981.

____. "Daytime TV: Michael Pavel's Midnight Murder." *Boston Globe*, July 19, 1981.

____. "Daytime TV: Soap Writer Quits in a Huff." *Boston Globe*, October 1, 1981.

LaGuardia, Robert. *Soap World*. Arbor House Pub. Co., 1983.

"Lefferts Ankles 'Ryan's Hope'; Costello to Helm ABC Soaper." *Variety*, September 10, 1975: 69.

Levine, Elana. *Her Stories: Daytime Soap Opera & US Television History*. Durham: Duke University Press, 2020.

Loftus, Jack. "ABC Keeps on Packin' Daytime Dynamite: Soap Operas Yield Record Ad Coin." *Variety*, December 30, 1981: 29.

____. "ABC Set to Scuttle 'Love Boat' As Part of Daytime TV Revamp; Reason: CBS Coming on Strong." *Variety*, January 26, 1983: 43, 60.

____. "CBS Can't Get Daytime Payday: Leads in Households, But Not with Women." *Variety*, March 21, 1984: 110, 122.

____. "Network Daytime Shares in a Tailspin." *Variety*, October 27, 1982: 43, 70.

____. "Web Soaps Sour, Daytime Ratings Fall: Viewer Erosion Hurts ABC Most." *Variety*, December 12, 1984: 33, 120.

Longshore, Shirley. "Jacqueline Smith: ABC's Woman of the Hour." *Ladies' Home Journal*, July 1980.

Mayer, Jane. "Soap Operas Search for Their Tomorrow in Bizarre Plot Lines." *The Wall Street Journal*, April 29, 1982.

Mayer, Paul. "Creating 'Ryan's Hope.'" *TV Book: The Ultimate Television Book*. Edited by Judy Fireman. Workman Pub. Co., 1977.

Mulgrew, Kate. *Born with Teeth: A Memoir*. New York: Little, Brown and Company, 2015.

"Nancy's Dream House." *Rona Barrett's Daytimers*, October 1982.

Newhouse News Service. "Collegians Minor in Soaps." *Newsday*, December 18, 1982.

"Nicolette Goulet: Mom Plays Manager for Manhattan-Based Nikki." *The Globe and Mail*, July 7, 1979.

"No Hope for 'Ryan's' Soap." *Broadcasting*, October 31, 1988: 40.

"Nominees for Writers Guild Awards." *Los Angeles Times*, March 11, 1983.

O'Neil, Thomas. *The Emmys*, third ed. New York: *Variety*, a division of The Cahners Publishing Company, 2000.

"Official Report Card: *Ryan's Hope*." *Soap Opera Digest*, October 20, 1987.

Passalacqua, Connie. "Soap Report: No Hope for Ryans." *Santa Cruz Sentinel*, November 20, 1988.

Pellegrini, Neena. "Kristen's Character Stops at Nothing." *The Cincinnati Enquirer*, April 11, 1982: E-10.

Radell, Nerissa. "'Ryan's Hope': Long Awaited Return to Familiar Faces, Familiar Dreams." *Soap Opera Digest*, July 19, 1983: 34–38.

"Readers Poll Results." *Soap Opera Serials*, February 1977.

"Readers Poll Results." *Soap Opera Serials*, June 1977.

Reed, Jon-Michael. "Michael Corbett *Ryan's* Best Hope for Sex Symbol." *Austin American-Statesman*, October 26, 1980.

___. "The New Frank Ryan Gets with It." *New York Daily News*, February 15, 1978: 95.

___. "'Ryan's Hope' Loses 2 Stars." *Austin American-Statesman*, May 25, 1980: 7.

___. "Soap Opera Notes." *NY Sunday News*, November 7, 1976.

___. "Soap Opera Notes." *NY Sunday News*, July 17, 1977.

___. "Soap Opera Notes." *NY Sunday News*, November 6, 1977.

___. "Soap Opera Notes: Kate's Had Enough of 'Hope.'" *New York Daily News*, December 28, 1977: 79.

___. "Soaps, The: Big Ratings Splashdown." *Los Angeles Times*, November 25, 1982.

___. "Soaps, The: CBS' *Capitol* Replaces *Search*." *Los Angeles Times*, January 14, 1983.

___. "Soaps, The: Creators Are Back at *Ryan's Hope*." *Los Angeles Times*, February 11, 1983.

___. "Soaps, The: *Ryan's Hope* Goes Back to Basics." *Los Angeles Times*, December 20, 1985.

___. "Soaps, The: Satirical Look Through the Tube" *Los Angeles Times*, September 11, 1981.

___. "Spring Season Brings New Soap Characters to Life." *The Times and Democrat*, April 29, 1983: 8b.

Reichardt, Nancy M. "Hope Runs Out for 'Ryan's Hope' Soaper." *Los Angeles Times*, November 23, 1988.

"The *Ryan's Hope* Family Speaks Out!" *Soap Opera People*, September 1986.

Schemering, Christopher. "Critic's Opinion: *Ryan's Hope*: Beauty and Blarney." *Soap Opera Digest*, July 14, 1988: 125–127.

___. *The Soap Opera Encyclopedia*. New York: Ballantine Books, 1987.

Scott, Kelly. "Making Soaps: Writers of Daytime TV Serials Put Their Stories

Through the Wringer of Public Tastes and Sponsor Demands." *St. Petersburg Times*, February 20, 1983: 1-E, 9-E.

Silden, Isobel. "Life: Bubble, Bubble, Toil and Trouble: The Story of the Soap Operas." *Los Angeles Times*, July 10, 1980.

"Soap Fans Are Shocked as ABC Fires Star of *Ryan's Hope* Love Triangle." *The Star*, May 19, 1981.

"Stresses and Strains in TV's Network-Affiliate Relationship." *Broadcasting* (Vol. 115, Issue 10), September 5, 1988.

"Substitute Scriptwriters Filling a Creative Void." *The New York Times*, April 21, 1988.

Sullivan, Tom. "'Another World,' an Emmy-Winner." *The Herald News*, July 27, 1976: B7.

____. "Reconciliation and Ireland Trip Add Drama to 'Ryan's Hope.'" *The Sunday Herald News*, December 4, 1977: TV-3, TV-4.

Terry, Carol Burton. "Off Camera." *Newsday*, April 25, 1982.

Terry, Clifford. "The Soaps: Care to Watch Someone's Life Fall Apart?" *Chicago Tribune*, September 18, 1977.

Thesken, Joseph. "Rid Operas of Misery." *Journal-News Hamilton, Ohio*. July 15, 1972: 5.

"Too Much Warmth at This Wedding." *The Miami News*. June 26, 1976: 2.

Tormey, Carol. "Marg Helgenberger: The Old Siobhan Returned." *Afternoon TV*, April 1985.

____. "Peter Haskell: Caught Between Art and Money." *Soap Opera Digest*, October 7, 1982: 22–32.

Townley, Rod. *The Year in Soaps*. New York: Crown Publishers, Inc., 1984.

Trevens, Francine L. "Michael Levin and His Many, Many Wives." *Soap Opera Digest*, October 16, 1979: 43–47.

Von Furstenberg, Betsy and Benita Feurey. "Inside the Soap Opera Bubble. *Good Housekeeping*, January 1984: 8.

Waldman, Allison J. "The Reality of *Ryan's Hope*: Soap Opera *Verismo*." *Soap Opera Update*, May 23, 1988.

Weyn, Suzanne. "Between the Sheets with Joe and Siobhan." Original source unknown. 1982. http://allaboutmarg.com/wordp/index.php/press-archive-interviews/1987-and-earlier/between-the-sheets-with-joe-and-siobhan/

"Where There's *Ryan's*, There's Hope!" *Soap Opera Stars*, January 1984.

White, Cassandra. "Claire Labine and Paul Mayer Write *Ryan's Hope*." *Soap Opera People*, December 1976.

Zorn, Eric. "Age of MeTV Gives Networks That Sinking Sensation." *Chicago Tribune*, February 22, 1983.